AMERITHRAX

The Hunt for the Anthrax Killer

ALSO BY ROBERT GRAYSMITH

Zodiac

The Sleeping Lady

Auto Focus (The Murder of Bob Crane)

Unabomber: A Desire to Kill

The Bell-Tower

Zodiac Unmasked

AMERITHRAX

The Hunt for the Anthrax Killer

ROBERT GRAYSMITH

BERKLEY BOOKS, NEW YORK

B

A Berkley Book
Published by The Berkley Publishing Group
A division of Penguin Group (USA) Inc.
375 Hudson Street
New York, New York 10014

This book is an original publication of The Berkley Publishing Group.

Copyright 2003 by Robert Graysmith
Book design by Julie Rogers

First Edition: November 2003

Library of Congress Cataloging-in-Publication Data

Graysmith, Robert.
    Amerithrax : the hunt for the anthrax killer / Robert Graysmith.
        p.   cm.
    Includes index.
    ISBN 0-425-19190-7
        1. Terrorism—United States—Prevention.   2. Bioterrorism—United States—Prevention.
    3. Anthrax—United States—Prevention.   I. Title.

HV6432.G73   2003
364.15'23—dc21

2003052452

Printed in the United States of America

10   9   8   7   6   5   4   3   2   1

For Inspector David R. Toschi, S.F.P.D

ACKNOWLEDGMENTS

Special thanks to my editor at Berkley Books, Natalee Rosenstein, who asked for this book over lunch one summer day. With editorial skill, she put this one-year story of the testing of America under her electron microscope and made it far better. I am also deeply indebted to the indispensable editorial and production staff who worked to bring this epic tale of the September 12 era into print: Esther Strauss, Sheila Moody, and Julie Rogers.

CONTENTS

CONTENTS

PRLOGUE

*"You cannot spill a drop of American blood
without spilling the blood of the whole world . . .
Our blood is as the flood of the Amazon, made
up of a thousand currents all pouring into one.
We are not a nation, so much as a world."*

—HERMAN MELVILLE

AMERICA WAS THE crime scene. American Flight 11 out of Boston bound for California soared down the Hudson River. At 8:46 A.M. it slammed into the north tower of the World Trade Center. A second plane, United Flight 175, another fuel-laden 767 jet, roared over the Statue of Liberty. At 9:03 A.M. it plowed into the south tower. Until now, on this warm, cloudless Tuesday morning, the city had been unusually hushed. With the Twin Towers in flames, trapped workers leaped from a hundred stories up. Some held hands on the way down. The Towers' unconventional design contributed to their collapse. Single-bolt connections in their frameworks failed to secure the steel floor trusses. Bolts were pulled forward toward the center of the buildings, floor trusses sagged, and millions of three-quarter-inch bolts popped. Thousands of gallons of flaming diesel fuel melted steel girders supporting the spires. Massive floors began to collapse one atop the other all the way down.

The implosion of the south tower came at 9:59 A.M. Almost four hundred thousand pounds of lead inside the thousands of personal computers vaporized when the 110-story tower fell. A thousand tons of asbestos insulation and mercury inside a half-million fluorescent lamps became a deadly pathogen. Dioxins in millions of pounds of plastic chairs and desks and hundreds of miles of soft polyvinyl chloride cable became part of a deadly cloud.

As the building crumbled, mammoth slabs of concrete and car-sized hunks of burning metal rained down upon the rescuers below. The first implosion unleashed an impenetrable fifty-five-mile-an-hour tornado of dark gray dust and white soot. The rising wave of dust roiled up and down West Street and crossed over to cover the American Express office where people huddled for safety. The dust spewed east to Park Row. A black cloud "as dense as toner," according to one witness, descended on people as they ran for their lives. Survivors running in the cloud of dust felt the force tearing at their clothes, a roar in their ears. The dust grew like a balled fist, a fine grayish powder that, with the force of the deadly attack behind it, swept the people along, threw them from their feet, and added new victims to the nearly three thousand already incinerated in the building and on the planes.

The dust turned day into night. The murky forms tossing within its gloom became living shadows. People in the street held hands with others so they would not lose their way. They tried to cover their noses and mouths. The smell was unlike any they had ever smelled. It was not like the smoke of crops burning in a field or that of a flickering fireplace. While there was no beauty to the dark cloud, there was a kind of sweetness to its odor.

The north tower collapsed at 10:28 A.M. Another mountain of powder, ash, and debris packed with hazardous material smashed windows. The swooping dark tidal wave choked everyone it engulfed and howled on through the canyons of New York City. The collapse coated much of lower Manhattan in asbestos-laced dust. New Yorkers, blinded with loss, wore masks just to breathe. Others wore respirators. Entire sections were evacuated as the smoking cloud rose.

No sooner had seven stories of rubble settled than heroes began searching the subterranean passages created by mammoth blocks of concrete. They listened for the faint cries of the trapped and dying, and called out for help themselves only to find their voices silenced by the dust.

In the hours, days, weeks, and even months after the commercial aircraft assaults on New York and Washington, dust hung in the air over Manhattan like a shroud. The fine gray powder that got into the lungs of the rescuers at Ground Zero set about its secret work. Toxic dust collected in the recesses of the fire trucks and lingered there, contaminating firefighters over the next months. It got into the throats of those living miles away. The poisonous cloud stayed where it fell, festering and ulcerating, causing who-knew-what future harm. Even months later the dust could still be smelled as far away as Greenwich Village—an electrical fire odor, like a short in a toaster.

An emotionally stunned America struggled to its feet and tried to stand. No sooner had it staggered a few steps than the next blow fell. The country was still reeling from the twin body blows of the attacks when the first deadly, dust-filled letter was mailed. Only weeks afterward, envelopes filled with a very similar dust and just as deadly as the twin explosions began to sicken the nation's people and to claim lives just as randomly and senselessly as the four jets had that brilliant blue-skied morning.

Dust that appeared very like 9-11 dust trickled from an envelope a thousand miles away in idyllic Boca Raton, Florida.

STRAIN 1

The Satan Bug

THE SQUEAK OF a wayward wheel marked the path of an elderly man. Outside in the Florida sunshine, Americans gathered themselves and reached inward for courage. They prayed there would be a warning next time so they could prepare themselves. Yet a new death already moved among them as silently as the cruising jets in the dazzling blue skies of the eleventh of September. Invisible yet tangible, dead but alive, colorless, odorless, as small as a human cell, the killer hid in a cloud of dust. The dust was eerily similar to that which still choked New York City. It trailed invisibly, a mixture of fine and coarse particles trickling from an envelope, behind the man with his squeaking cart.

The killer within the dust was capable of incredible growth, growth that spawned into billions. It could withstand heat and cold. It did not drink or breathe or eat. In the end it would be a tangled mass of rods and threads, choking out life, yet able to return to inertness outside its victim, to lie sleeping for decades yet be reborn once more as a living microbe. The killer bypassed some—the man at the coffeepot, a visitor from Virginia just leaving, a woman on her cell phone. It briefly touched a mailroom worker and passed on. The airborne cloud of particles was particularly deadly. By the time any symptoms developed, it would already be too late. The old man's envelope leaked invisible death—a killer dispatched by a killer.

Outside the American Media Incorporated building a brisk inshore breeze, humid and smelling of the sea, was blowing. Flags and beach umbrellas strained all over Boca Raton. Sand kicked up on the long golden beach and blew among the palm trees and neat gravel walks. The gumbo-limbo trees swayed—their red peeling bark like blood and bone. Boca sits between Delray Beach and Pompano Beach along Gold Coast Highway A1A, a fifty-mile-long stretch. Wildlife preserves are to its west. Lauderdale-by-the-Sea is to its south as is Miami Beach.

AMI had recently purchased six supermarket tabloids—the *National Examiner*, the *Globe*, the *Sun*, the *Weekly World News*, the *National Enquirer*, and the *Star*. For six million dollars more they'd bought a new sixty-seven-thousand-square-foot headquarters on Broken Sound Boulevard. They had laid down another fourteen million renovating the three-story building near Yamato Road. Since the sea bred dampness, AMI had installed a sophisticated air handling system to protect its yellowed clippings, back issues, reporters' files, business records, and high-tech equipment. A subcontractor, Lasertech International, did the heavy lifting, handling production of all six publications.

Ernesto "Ernie" Blanco, a seventy-three-year-old Miami-Dade resident, was AMI's mailroom supervisor. Since the six tabloids often received packages for celebrities, he was not surprised one morning when a "weird" love letter from a fan ended up in his sorting bin. Though addressed to singer and actor "Jennifer Lopez % the *Sun*," it had been mailed to the *Enquirer*'s previous address in nearby Lantana. But CEO David Pecker had moved AMI to Boca Raton—what had it been?—a year now.

Whoever had written the "J-Lo" letter had been unfamiliar with either the *Sun* or the *Enquirer*. Either that or they had worked from an out-of-date reference. When the odd letter arrived at the Boca Raton Main Substation, which serviced AMI, Blanco collected it in the AMI van. The letter's path had taken it through the West Palm Main Branch, the Green Acres and Lake Worth Post Offices, and finally the substation. No one recalled when that errant letter had been forwarded to the *Sun*. It might have been that day, Friday, September 21, 2001, or a week before or a week after four jets crashed into the WTC, the Pentagon, and a Pennsylvania field.

Blanco began his regular route. Outside the huge tan building, the humid wind gusted and waves crested blocks away. Inside, AMI's new air-conditioning system hummed. "Squeak—squeak—squeak," the wayward wheel complained all the way from the first-floor mailroom where thirty-six-year-old Stephanie Dailey was busy sorting. As Blanco went, his load spilled bluish white powder. Experts with high-tech gear would later be able to read an almost invisible trail of contamination. It marked his meandering path along a series of desks, computers and keyboards, and file cabinets. Hot spots glowed where letters entered mail slots and at each of the thirty-one places where powder and microscopic beads had littered the floor. The Hispanic man paused. He rested a handful of mail atop stacks of copy paper, then moved on. Beads clinging to those reams of paper would infect every copying machine on all three floors.

Delivering mail to AMI's seven hundred employees, Blanco winded his way up to the second floor and finally the third. Along the way, the fan letter with its coarse powder had been surrendered to a *Sun* editor. Because the editorial assistant who was normally there had the day off, the editor perused the mail, discarding some and opening others. The fan letter was opened and a small cheap Star of David dropped out. Inside the envelope was a "childish" one-page, handwritten love letter to Jennifer Lopez. Also enclosed was a tablespoon of "soapy, powdery substance," a bluish dust that resembled dishwashing powder. It might have come from a ruptured detergent packet, a sample, but an inspection revealed no packet inside. The letter was discarded.

Sometime later, a *Sun* staffer retrieved the odd letter from the wastebasket. He had a daughter who was a Lopez fan and thought the fan letter was funny. He passed it around the office for "amusement value." For a moment, staffers on the tabloid ceased writing about alien abductions and Elvis sightings to chuckle over the naive letter. The *Star* had recently written about "J-Lo." The envelope reached the *Sun*'s photo retoucher, Bob Stevens. Coincidentally, the sixty-three-year-old artist lived in Lantana, where the letter had been misaddressed. In a way Stevens's poor eyesight killed him.

Because he was nearsighted, Stevens brought the letter up close to his eyes. "The only difference between Bob and those who watched him open the letter," a staffer said later, "was that Bob held it up to his face." Dust, so like WTC dust, settled over the kind-featured, expressive man. It was a good face and filled with humor. As Stevens held the note near his nose, he automatically breathed in the microscopic killer riding upon the fine dust. Inhaled air flowed through his nostrils and into his nasal cavity. In his nose, hair, cilia, and mucus trapped some of the dust particles, powder, and some invisible ovoid beads about a micron long.

A second breath—Stevens's shoulders lifted and lowered. His chest expanded, then moved downward and in. He drew more tiny beads into his windpipe. Death in the form of those micro-beads rushed past C-shaped cartilage rings along the tube connecting his mouth and nose to his lungs. The tube divided into right and left bronchi as it entered moist lungs, moist to minimize water evaporation. Dry lungs can't exchange gases. Like Ernie Blanco, Stevens was not a smoker. Unfortunately, Stevens's healthy lungs became the efficient entry point for a deadly disease. Someone had designed the beads to gravitate to the wettest membrane in the body and stick like glue.

Inside each lung, bronchi branch off into lesser and lesser limbs. The system is like a brittle, upside-down tree. Beneath Stevens's lungs, a powerful diaphragm muscle contracted and moved down, allowing his ribs to move up and outward. With his chest expanded, his lungs sucked in more air to fill the additional room. The beads were propelled along the fine tree branches into three hundred million grapelike clusters—the fruit of the upside-down tree. Oxygen and carbon dioxide were exchanged in these grapelike air sacs.

Stevens exhaled. His diaphragm relaxed, moved back up, and forced his rib cage down and in. This bellows-type movement increased the pressure inside his lungs, which pulled air up and out of his body. In the exhaled air shimmered the carbon dioxide that red blood cells had deposited, but the shining, glasslike beads had remained behind.

Bob Stevens went back to chatting. Stevens was sunny-faced with neatly combed sandy gray hair. He had an easygoing, almost lackadaisical nature that made him a favorite with the neighborhood children. Yet sunny as he was, his features bore a remarkable resemblance to those of the man in the moon. He had crescent eyes, a wide nose, ruddy cheeks, and large close-set ears. He was not a worrier. He had no wrinkles in his broad forehead.

He put the "J-Lo" letter aside and returned to retouching photos, enhancing them dramatically on his Macintosh computer. He was one of the top retouchers in the nation. Thirty years ago, he had been enticed from his London birthplace to Florida by the *National Enquirer*. Stevens had retouched the famous cover photo of Elvis in his coffin. Stevens was a U.S. citizen now and completely assimilated, some said too assimilated. He was an avid spincaster, fishing for bass and panfish around the region's lakes and canals at every opportunity. As he worked, he manipulated a mousepad decorated with photos of his friends. Affectionately, he touched colored crayon drawings from a colleague's young son. Stevens had taped them to his Mac. All the while, an invisible contagion, stirred by the air-conditioning and disturbed by Stevens's movements, was crawling over his workstation.

For two hours nothing happened within Bob Stevens's lungs. The beads, the airborne spores of a microbe, settled into the grapelike clusters, which were just the right temperature for them. The bacteria infecting Bob Stevens spent whatever time they were not actively infecting men and animals as tough-skinned infectious particles. In that hard-bitten form bacteria could endure great heat, cold, and drying. They could survive in a dormant state for decades. But whenever spores encountered a potential host, they germinated as fast as thought. They became active and started reproducing again.

In no time at all a short, bamboolike rod was floating among the beads. Then a few more little sticks, tiny bacterial rods quivering among blood globules. Who could fathom that such miserably small bacilli—a billion times smaller than a man—could annihilate a human? As Stevens completed his work, the little drifting rods had only begun their task. Continuing to multiply, they hooked together without joints—lining up end to end and ingeniously gluing themselves together. The long threads were a thousand times thinner than the finest silk—twenty-five thousandths of an inch thick.

From a few rods grew myriads, then millions as the bacteria made copies of themselves. Speckled throughout the entire length of each filament were oval glass beads that shone brightly—a string of pearls inside the threads. The tangled skeins of colorless yarn spun until they became hopelessly tangled. One slowly stretched itself out into a long thread, pushing its snaky way toward an extensive network of pulmonary capillaries. The single cell throbbed with energy.

Gases diffuse quickly across the one-cell-thick membranes separating air sacs from blood vessels. A simple exchange from an area of higher concentration to one of lower is made. There is more carbon dioxide than oxygen in the capillaries. Once oxygen is in the capillaries, red blood cells carry it to every part of the body. In Stevens, the oxygenated blood ferried along the tangled threads too.

But the glassy beads and swarming sticks and threads themselves were not the killer. Once activated inside the body, the bacterium secreted a deadly toxin, a poison produced by a living organism. That poison crippled the ability of white blood cells to fight off disease. Rapidly the toxin flooded the lymph system. The constantly circulating lymph is a river of clear liquid derived from blood serum. Flowing out of capillaries, it washes through tissues on a surveillance mission as the body's disease fighter to filter out foreign particles. When experts later speculated that Stevens had been sickened by drinking from a tainted stream they had not been far wrong. It had been a tainted lymph stream.

But the spores multiplied in lymph nodes near the lungs, broke them down, and spread the infection. Unknown to Stevens, a poisonous fluid was building up in his lungs and filling the space between his lungs and chest wall. At first the discharge was watery and bloody. It would soon become a foamy, golden paste streaked with crimson. Patchy areas in his lower right lung hemorrhaged, bled into the middle of his chest, then slowly became solid. The poison moved like a marching army through his organs, causing bleeding and deterioration as it went. Stevens, feeling none of this, returned to his Palm Beach County home, a cozy nest surrounded by the swamps of the Loxahatchee Wildlife Refuge. On Saturday he went fishing, probably at Boynton Beach Inlet. Afterward, he and his wife, Maureen, fine-tuned their vacation plans—a visit to their daughter Casey in Charlotte, North Carolina. As for the "odd," long-delayed J-Lo letter, it was nowhere in sight.

The weekend passed uneventfully. On Monday, September 24, Ernie Blanco, the mailroom supervisor, had a sudden onset of fatigue. Blanco was puzzled. He was in remarkable shape for his age. Over the next three days, he experienced a gradual progression of cough, lethargy, shortness of breath, and fever. He began sweating and experienced mild abdominal pain that he associated with vomiting. But he couldn't vomit. With the exception of a fleeting ischemic attack the previous month, the result of an inadequate blood supply to his heart, he had no underlying chronic illnesses.

On Wednesday Stevens worked very late at AMI. The next day, he and Maureen drove north along the long Atlantic coastline. They flew past islands, reefs, sandbars, and choppy seas, moving relentlessly northward into North Carolina. Along the way to Charlotte they passed neat rows of tobacco plants and fertile farms, crossed swamps, and climbed pleasant hills into cities and towns. On Thursday, September 27, Stevens had an indefinable feeling of oncoming illness. On Friday the family went to Lake Lure and hiked at Chimney Rock about twenty-five miles southeast of Asheville. An elevator inside the granite mountain could have whisked them to the summit, but instead they took an easy trail to a four-hundred-foot-high waterfall. A few days had passed since the bacteria had begun secreting poisons that bound to the protective membranes of target cells inside his body. Stevens was thirsty. He cupped his hands to drink twice from the waterfall.

Stevens was feeling better on Saturday, having undergone a brief recovery. This was the "honeymoon," "eclipse," or "false recovery" period of the disease. It meant that Stevens's immune system was fighting back. The same day, back in Boca Raton, Blanco was suffering from a nonproductive cough. He had intermittent fever and a stuffy nose. The backs of his upper eyelids were inflamed.

On Sunday the Stevenses drove to Duke University in Durham to visit their daughter's boyfriend, and Stevens saw the onset of a mild flu with fever—a cough, then chills and vomiting. Like Blanco, he had felt fatigue and muscle aches at first. But if it was flu, why wasn't he experiencing nasal congestion or a runny nose? He had breathing problems and vague chest pains. His medical history included cardiovascular disease, hypertension, and gout, but none of the symptoms he was now experiencing—headache, muscle aches, and shortness of breath. Stevens wondered if he had picked up some infection in the woods or fishing. He had drunk some water from a stream.

The Stevenses strolled the blue-gray stone walkways of Duke University's West Campus. The 210-foot Duke Chapel tower dominated the fifty-five wooded acres there. The seventy-seven stained-glass windows of the Gothic cathedral shone in the morning light and the air was crisp. They heard the strains of an organ with more than five thousand pipes. A non-denominational hymn wafted over the landscaped acres. Beyond was the stadium, the Medical Chapel Center, and the VA Hospital.

By afternoon, Stevens's cough had worsened. His breathing had become more labored and his head was throbbing. Inside his body, the sticks and tangled threads had multiplied into billions. They teemed venomously, like little snakes, in what had been robust tissues. They choked veins and arteries and with their poison turned healthy red blood a sinister black. Stevens was feeling so poor that he and his wife were forced to return early from North Carolina on Sunday evening. During the ten-hour drive back, Bob's condition worsened. When they got home, he gave Maureen a kiss good night as he always did. "He said, 'I love you,' " she recalled. "And those were his last coherent words to me."

On Monday, October 1, Ernie Blanco experienced intermittent periods of confusion at home and work. He seemed not to know who he was. Blanco was admitted to a local Miami hospital for examination that day. Tests for Legionnaires' disease and hantavirus proved negative and the ER staff could find no blisters or skin lesions. Blanco's white blood count was normal, but his throat was sore. Listening with his stethoscope, the doctor heard the characteristic wheezing sounds of pneumonia. Blanco's inflamed lungs certainly suggested that. The elderly man's chest X ray, taken back to front, revealed diffuse consolidation throughout his left lung and bloody secretions scattered through the lower lobe of his right lung.

Remarkably, Blanco's X-ray findings were dominated by large and progressive pulmonary infiltrations, not by mediastinal widening. Mediastinal widening, an enlarged space under the breastbone and between the lungs, would have suggested another respiratory disease altogether, but one that common sense said had to be out of the question. Doctors decided to use computed tomography, a technique more sensitive and detailed than plain X rays. A series of X rays analyzed by a computer provided several cross-sectional views and a dye injected into the bloodstream clarified abnormalities in Blanco's chest. His CT showed left upper and lower infiltrates consistent with pneumonia. A recurrent left pleural effusion (a fluid buildup in the pleural space) called for placement of a chest tube. Blanco was prescribed an intravenous antibiotic, azithromycin, and hospitalized for pneumonia. His chart read:

> Temperature 38.5°C, heart rate 109/min, respiratory rate 20/min, and blood pressure 108/61 mm Hg. The patient has bilateral conjunctival injection and bilateral pulmonary rhonchi. Examination, including as-

sessment of neurologic function, was otherwise unremarkable. Admission laboratory results included normal WBC [white blood cell] count and serum chemistries, except for hypoalbuminemia, elevated hepatic transaminases, borderline hyponatremia, and increased creatinine. Arterial blood gas values showed hypoxia.

On Tuesday at 2:30 A.M., Bob Stevens awoke suddenly in his Lantana home. The previous day, he had gone to work but had been forced home with a temperature. Like Ernie Blanco he seemed not to know where he was. He was feverish, confused, and overcome with nausea, vomiting, and chills. Stevens had a 102-degree fever and became so disoriented that he tried to get up and go to work. This alarmed his wife, who took him to the emergency room at JFK Medical Center in nearby Atlantis. Though alert and interactive, he spoke nonsensically. He didn't know who he was, where he was, or what day it was. Stevens was admitted for evaluation at 2:20 P.M. The ER staff scrambled to diagnose and treat whatever it was Bob Stevens had. Initial pulmonary, heart, and abdominal examinations were reported as normal:

Temperature was 39.2°C, heart rate 109/min; blood pressure and respiratory rate were normal. No nuchal rigidity was observed. Admission laboratory values included a normal total white blood cell (WBC) count, but the platelet count was low. Serum chemistries were normal, except for borderline hyponatremia and elevated total bilirubin. He had mild metabolic acidosis.

Almost five hours after admission into isolation, Stevens had generalized seizures. He lost consciousness and was intubated for airway protection because of rapid respiratory deterioration. Maureen, who had been sent home at 5:30 P.M., returned at 7:45. At that time a radiologist was studying Stevens's initial chest X ray and comparing it to one he had had taken at JFK a year earlier. The ghostly gray film, also showing the three chest monitors attached to Stevens's chest, revealed an enlarged space under his breastbone. It cast a wide, unsettling shadow. "Prominent superior mediastinum and possible small left pleural effusion" was entered on his chart. The widened area between his lungs signified diseased and enlarged lymph nodes. All of the structures between his lungs—the esophagus, trachea, main bronchi, great vessels, and lymph nodes—were inflamed and bloody. As a whole this was called "hemorrhagic mediastinitis." There was fluid around the patient's lungs, cloudy yellow and tinged with blood.

Stevens was tested for meningitis, an inflammation of the covering of the brain and the spinal cord, which is caused by a bacterial or viral infection. The brain and spinal cord are usually very resistant to infection, so when they do become infected, it is very serious business indeed. Stevens's early symptoms were classic—fever, sore throat, and vomiting following a respiratory illness. Although meningitis is more common in infants than adults, the staff at JFK were very concerned because the disease can lead to death within hours.

After a single dose of cefotaxime, Stevens was started on an alphabet of multiple antibiotics—ceftazidime, gentamicin, metronidazole, doxycycline (a tetracycline), ampicillin, and trimethoprim-sulfamethoxazole. The antibiotic cocktail only made Stevens worse, in fact nearly killed him. When some of the bacteria that had triggered meningitis inside Stevens's spinal cord and brain were slain, they split open, discharging three different poisons into his brain. The sudden toxic influx initiated a grand mal epileptic seizure.

That evening a specialist in infectious diseases at JFK, Dr. Larry M. Bush, continued to fret over a cloudy sample of Stevens's cerebrospinal fluid. Something did not fit. He had incubated the sample for seven hours. While studying the specimen under the microscope, Dr. Bush astutely realized the odd rod-shaped bacteria were not the kind that usually cause meningitis. Three species of bacteria account for more than 80 percent of all cases of meningitis: *Neisseria meningitidis*, *Hemophilus influenzae*, and *Streptococcus pneumoniae*. What was the bacteria that had infected Stevens's brain and its meninges? A gram stain of Stevens's fluid most resembled the topography of a broken country road, but a purple road twisting among blue-violet trees on a red-violet landscape. Bush consulted the notes:

Cerebrospinal fluid (CSF) analysis showed WBC [white blood cell] count 4,750/µL (81% neutrophils), red blood cell count 1,375/ µL, glucose 57 mg/dL (serum glucose 174 mg/dL), and protein 666 mg/ dL. Microscopy examination of the CSF showed many gram-positive bacilli.

Gram-*positive* bacilli? In the bacterial universe, gram-positive bacteria are a minority. A gram stain is a method of staining microorganisms using crystal violet, iodine, and a contrasting dye called gram stain. One of the major characteristics of bacteria is whether they take Dr. Hans Gram's concoction. Microorganisms that retain the violet color are said to be "gram-positive." Those that don't are said to be "gram-negative." Practically the only infections caused by gram-positive bacilli are erysipelothricosis, listeriosis . . . and anthrax.

The specialist believed he was looking at *Bacillus anthracis* in the patient's spinal fluid. But this was an astonishingly rare disease, especially in nature. The bacteria had not been seen clinically in the United States in almost a quarter century.

STRAIN 2

The Cardinal's Cap

ON WEDNESDAY, OCTOBER 3, Stevens began his second day in the hospital. Doctors were still deeply concerned. The photo editor remained feverish and unresponsive to deep stimuli. His fever continued to rise and his lungs were filling with fluid. Dr. Bush called the county Health Department director, Jean Marie Malecki, to tell her of his findings. She in turn notified the Florida Department of Health in Jacksonville of a possible anthrax case in Palm Beach County. It would take twenty-four hours for technician Phillip Lee to know for sure because Stevens's spinal fluid and blood cultures had to incubate. As early as two to three days after onset of symptoms gram-positive bacilli can grow on a blood culture.

As yet, no one had connected the cases of Stevens and Ernie Blanco, one of apparent meningitis and the other pneumonia. The only similarity was that both their X rays had been abnormal. Blood cultures obtained from Ernie Blanco the day before showed no growth of infection after initiation of antibiotics. Cefotaxime and ciprofloxacin had been prescribed.

At the end of the day-long incubation period, *B. anthracis* was isolated from Stevens's spinal fluid and blood cultures. The result provided more confirmation that the rarest form of anthrax had infected someone. Health workers now thought Stevens was an isolated case. Apparently he had contracted some natural form of anthrax. Initially, they had been puzzled to see infection building in Stevens's lungs and enlarged lymph nodes. Immune cells dispatched by Stevens's system to consume microbes in the lungs must have transported microbes back to lymph nodes and infected them. The bacteria had multiplied there, spreading tissue-destroying toxins to other organs via the bloodstream.

Antibiotics can kill or halt bacterial growth. But the unknown bacteria had produced a toxin that rapidly blocked the blood and lymph systems, sending Stevens into shock. Doctors now treated him with the antibiotics levofloxacin, clindamycin, and penicillin G. Penicillin is used to treat most gram-positive bacterial infections, but the doctors were not hopeful. If the infection was systemic, its treatment was problematic.

When the Bacillus of Anthrax went visiting with gold cane and top hat, it carried no calling card. Inhalational anthrax, once it announced its presence, was already a death sentence. By that point it was too late to save victims who had already begun to suffer the distinctive blue or dark swellings along their chest and neck that mark the late onset of inhalation anthrax, also known as pulmonary anthrax.

If high doses of penicillin are injected into the bloodstream at short intervals seven to ten days *before* the first toxins are released, there is a 100 percent rate of survival. Even if detected within the first few days of exposure it is highly treatable. According to David Straus, a Texas Tech University microbiologist, "If you inhaled the spores now and someone gave you antibiotics you would survive because the organisms would not multiply to the density needed to kill you. But the pulmonary form of the disease is almost invariably lethal because it isn't recognized in time." Vaccines exist for anthrax, as they do for smallpox, but are in short supply. Anthrax vaccines are best given eighteen months before exposure, but there is some protection after three doses of the four-dose regimen.

The inhalational variety of anthrax (very rare in nature) is invariably fatal if antibiotic treatment is not given before symptoms begin to show, usually after one to two days. Survival rate at that point is only about 10 to 20 percent. Once symptoms begin: a one- to four-day phase of malaise, frequent fatigue, mild fever and chills, nausea, vomiting, headache, myalgia, grogginess, and nonproductive cough followed by a brief period of improvement; no remedy may be possible.

After the honeymoon phase, the next phase strikes like lightning. The patient suffers respiratory distress, cyanosis, and diaphoresis as microbes multiply in lymph nodes, spreading tissue-destroying toxins to other organs via the bloodstream. A patient infected through the lungs typically suffers distinctive damage to the area between the lungs just below the sternum. That was the case with Stevens.

Phillip Lee called the Centers for Disease Control and Prevention in Atlanta. He spoke with Tanja Popovic, head of the Epidemiologic Investigations Laboratory, and told her of his findings. Stevens's specimens were driven to Atlanta, where CDC lab chief Richard Meyer processed them for anthrax DNA. The specimens tested positive in two quick preliminary tests, but the final confirmation would not be ready until the next morning.

Stevens's condition progressively deteriorated. He had low blood pressure and worsening renal insufficiency. His lips became blue-tinged and his body even more bluish. Anthrax victims often erupted with massive, excruciating blisters, turning the skin black and leathery. Frantic lab work of all isolates at the state lab and at the CDC corroborated inhalational anthrax. One report read:

> Presumptive isolation of *B. anthracis* . . . was confirmed by gamma phage lysis, presence of a capsule, detection of capsule and cell-wall antigens by direct fluorescent antibody, and *B. anthracis*–specific polymerase chain reaction. [PCR is a technique for copying DNA. The DNA from a single cell is sufficient to start a polymerase chain reaction in which a specific segment of DNA can be copied more than two hundred thousand times in a lab.]

On Thursday morning, physicians called an emergency press conference—the first public announcement that a man in Florida had anthrax. "Perhaps he contracted it in the woods," they said. The possibility of an outbreak was dismissed by U.S. Health and Human Services Secretary Tommy G. Thompson, who said, "[It's] an isolated case and it's not contagious . . . We do know that [Stevens] drank water out of a stream when he was traveling to North Carolina last week. But as far as [contamination from] wool or other things, it's entirely possible. We haven't got all of the investigations done and we're doing a tremendous, extensive job of investigating everything. There is no terrorism."

The element of bioterrorism had been the first thought in many peoples' minds since it had only been twenty-three days since the collapse of the Twin Towers. Despite denials, the scare had officially begun.

That afternoon, Florida Lt. Gov. Frank Brogan reported to the media that "a sixty-three-year-old man [had] been hospitalized for pulmonary [inhalational] anthrax." Florida Secretary of Health John Agwunobi elaborated: "The disease is not contagious. While rare, it can be caught naturally." The Palm Beach Health Department said the case was isolated, but was "very likely" to be fatal.

Later the same day, Florida Department of Health and CDC epidemiologists and lab workers arrived in Palm Beach County to assist. That night, Dr. Brad Perkins, chief of meningitis and special pathogens at the Atlanta-based CDC, received an urgent call at his daughter's piano recital. Over his cell phone Dr. Perkins got the bare facts—that Bob Stevens was hospitalized with inhalational anthrax and had been a worker at AMI. Fourteen hours later Dr. Perkins was in Florida leading a CDC unit in an effort to determine how Stevens had been infected with a "remarkably rare" microbe.

The next morning, Friday, October 5, Dr. Perkins was at Stevens's bedside. The critically ill patient remained feverish and was still "intubated," on ventilation support. His condition had progressively deteriorated: abnormally low blood pressure, internal ulceration, bleeding, altered mental state, and massive shock. Severe respiratory distress had continued for almost thirty-five hours. Despite antibiotic therapy, Bob Stevens's clinical condition deteriorated rapidly. The toxin was killing its host by producing secondary shock. Stevens slipped into a coma. He coughed up a yellow, bubbly mess marbled with red.

Around 3:30 P.M., Dr. Perkins took his team to AMI and met with the editors who knew Stevens. He hoped he could get a clue from them since Stevens had been unable to speak. "That was a fairly dramatic meeting," Perkins reported later, "because we were sitting in a room with people who had known him. This was a universally loved guy." Just then Dr. Perkins's cell phone beeped—Bob Stevens had died at 4:00 P.M., dead from inhaling thousands of dangerous spores, the first known anthrax fatality in the United States since 1976.

"Everyone was just in utter disbelief," said Perkins. Death usually follows severe respiratory symptoms within thirty-six hours and that timing indicated he might have been infected earlier than thought, before his trip to North Carolina.

And what of Ernie Blanco, the man who may have delivered a contaminated letter? He may have gotten the powder in his lungs too. In his case nothing yet had been confirmed. Though clinical anthrax was suspected once they learned of Stevens's death, Blanco showed no signs of clinical infection. Why? Doctors took a nasal swab from him and began to incubate it in a petri dish to see if it grew anthrax spores. They believed they would. In the meanwhile, the hospital informed Blanco's family he too might have been exposed to anthrax.

Late that afternoon, the world media, state and federal agencies, even the White House began speculating and wondering if the anthrax was connected in some way with the recent terrorist attacks. The White House had expected a biological attack would be next. Dr. Perkins remained focused on "leading a solid, scientific investigation."

Early the following day, Saturday, October 6, medical examiner Dr. Sherif Zaki and his CDC team arrived by chartered jet and went immediately to the West Palm Beach medical examiner's office to perform the autopsy. Whenever there is the slightest reason to suspect the possibility of a homicide, an autopsy is always done. The Palm Beach County coroner, Dr. Lisa Flannagan, would make the initial incisions. Under the burning lights, the examiner, dressed like the others in biohazard mask, plastic face shield, and three layers of gloves (one pair Kevlar-reinforced), approached a sloped metal table where the bagged body lay. The table's upper half had a grated surface. At the other end was a shallow tub that ran beneath a grating flowing with water. After the bag was unzipped, a careful examination of the victim's skin, scalp, and entire surface of his body would be made. Then the interior of the body would be examined over the next three hours.

Dr. Flannagan made the familiar Y-shaped incision, folded the skin back, then snipped away each of the ribs with a pair of gardening shears. The chest cavity was a lake of blood. They had never seen so much. With a ladle they bailed it out so they could see what they were doing. Because of potential contamination of the morgue, they stoppered the huge quantity of tainted blood inside containers. All of the victim's internal organs were glistening—shot through with signature gram-positive rods of *Bacillus anthracis* from three to eight micrometers in length.

Dr. Zaki and his team examined them to absolutely confirm the type of anthrax that had caused Stevens's death. The surgeon cleared his mind and, like any good detective, began his postmortem examination with no preconceived ideas. They had found no hint of cutaneous anthrax on the exterior of the body. The interior was another story. Dr. Zaki studied the swollen, black lymph nodes—so engorged that they exploded at the slightest touch of his scalpel.

The mechanics of the victim's death were laid out on the tilted table to be read as clearly as a road map or book. Airborne anthrax spores had settled into tiny sacs in Stevens's lungs. Spores are always more deadly when inhaled because they are disseminated more widely within the body. Bacteria from spores germinating in his lungs had produced several toxins that attacked his cells. Beset by a killer like anthrax, the lymph had accelerated its already speedy flow, moving bacteria to lymph nodes to be destroyed. But when the lymph nodes failed to overcome the infection, the multiplying bacteria inflamed the lymph nodes. They became enlarged, bloody, black, and necrotic. The surgeon could see that. It was a horrible way to die. Stuck to the inside of his lungs was more of the thick, gobby paste. Foamy, golden-yellow glue, anthrax sputum exudate, was everywhere.

Rapidly, the rods and threads must have swept through Stevens's body, causing toxic shock, internal ulceration, and bleeding. Once blood poisoning had developed, death had followed the onset of the fulminant phase in one to two days. A secondary pneumonia infection had developed, followed by shock, coma, and instant respiratory collapse. By counting backward the doctor might be able to determine when Stevens had been infected, but not how, nor where the source of that infection was now. His autopsy findings indicated:

> Gangrenous lesions in different parts of the lungs, massive thoracic and gastrointestinal bleeding and inflammatory infiltrates. Hemorrhagic mediastinal lymphadenitis, and immunohistochemical staining showed disseminated *B. anthracis* in multiple organs.

The surgeons examined the patient's cerebrospinal fluid and noted the documented meningitis findings. Meningitis often accompanies inhalational anthrax. Anthrax meningitis, a complication of that form, is characteristically hemorrhagic. Decades earlier, in the world's worst accidental inhalational anthrax release (described in "Anthrax City," chapter 14), 55 percent of the victims had shown evidence of meningeal involvement at autopsy.

In complete medicolegal autopsies the brain is removed and inspected for evidence of disease. A rubber block under the victim's shoulder blades pushes the chest upward and causes the head to fall back so the skull can be sawed open. The surgeon, after carefully avoiding penetration of the brain beneath, gives a twist to a T-shaped bone chisel forced into the cut line. This lifts the skullcap, which is pried off, cranial material still clinging, and allows the victim's brain to be removed for inspection. In this instance, though, after much debate, it was agreed that it was far too dangerous to open the skull with an electric saw. A saw's blade, moving back and forth at high speed, might spread anthrax spores in a cloud of bone dust. Thus, this important step was never accomplished. However, if it had, even the most hardened doctor would have been startled by what lay beneath. After all, who would expect to encounter that rarity of all rarities—the so-called cardinal's cap?

The top of the victim's brain had turned to blood.

STRAIN 3

Inside AMI

INHALATIONAL ANTHRAX PLACES a bloody cap upon its victim's head like the cap a British judge wore when pronouncing a death sentence. As parts of Stevens's body had turned blue from lack of oxygen, the brain tissue had swollen. It had bled horribly, hemorrhaging in the small blood vessels of the brain membrane as badly as the blood had filled Stevens's chest. Though ghastly, the "cardinal's cap" serves a purpose: it gives absolute confirmation of the most fatal kind of anthrax—inhalational anthrax, the most infrequent of the three forms of anthrax.

In the meantime, where had the spores come from? So far the investigation had revealed no obvious exposure to *B. anthracis*. At first Florida and federal health officials believed that Stevens's infection was a fluke, the result of natural or accidental exposure. Federal officials speculated that he had been contaminated by the deadly spores while drinking out of a tainted stream in North Carolina. But tests at specialized labs all confirmed his inhalational anthrax resulted from exposure to dust containing airborne spores. It was possible to distinguish anthrax contracted from airborne spores from the intestinal variety.

Perhaps Stevens, while fishing, breathed in death from some animal that had lain moldering in the soil for a half-century. Just what were the occurrences of natural anthrax in that region? They would have to check. And what about Duke University where Stevens had visited on Sunday?

Spores might have strayed accidentally from bioresearch labs at Duke, though that was unlikely. Frantic tests and lab work spanning the weekend would determine if he had contracted the disease on vacation. "No one has any idea where this came from," said Martin Hugh-Jones of Louisiana State University and head of the World Health Organization's group on anthrax.

While flu kills twenty thousand Americans every year, anthrax had never been reported in the soil or in animals in the U.S. east of the Mississippi River. In fact, there was only one fatal case of inhalational anthrax between 1933 and 1955 in a study of 117 cases. The nation had recorded only 18 cases of inhalation anthrax in the twentieth century and none since 1978. The last Florida case occurred back in 1956. How could Bob Stevens have developed such a remarkable form of a rare disease?

Anthrax cannot be transferred from one person to another, although the bacterium is communicable from animals to humans. Butchers, tanners, farmers—those processing goat hair or goat skins or shearing wool were most at risk. Historically, those who have come into contact with the contaminated wool, hides, leather, and hair products of tainted animals have been those most infected. Spores can enter the human body through the lungs when people inhale spores flecked off an animal hide. Perhaps Stevens's spores had come from imported wool.

Inhalational anthrax was first identified in the nineteenth century when a handful of laborers in a textile mill fell ill. They had been exposed to spores released into the air by the new industrial processes developed to make wool. Mill workers were so frequently exposed to imported animal fibers contaminated with B. anthracis spores that anthrax became known as "wool-sorters' disease" in England and "ragpickers' disease" in Austria and Germany. In the early 1900s, human cases of inhalational anthrax began showing up in the U.S. in conjunction with the flourishing domestic textile and tanning industries.

In the last part of the twentieth century, with improved industrial hygiene practices and restrictions on imported animal products, the number of cases dropped dramatically. In goat hair mills, goat hair was treated at 170 degrees Fahrenheit for fifteen minutes. Moist heat works better than dry heat on the spores. However, even after this treatment, many spores retained their viability. In 1942, a Pennsylvania textile worker and a rug salesman died of inhalational anthrax. In both those cases their lymph nodes, not their lungs, had been the most notably infected.

In 1957, the country's only epidemic of inhalation anthrax occurred. Four woolen-mill workers at the Arms Textile Mill in Manchester, New Hampshire, were killed by inhalational anthrax. Almost all textile mills use air conditioning to control moisture so they can produce uniformly strong fibers and threads. But air conditioning also spreads spores. In the same year, a man and woman living near a Philadelphia tannery died of inhalational anthrax. Shortly afterward, a football player contracted the disease from playing-field soil. In San Francisco, a woman who beat bongo drums made of infected skin, a construction worker who handled contaminated felt, and several gardeners using contaminated bone meal fertilizer also caught the disease.

In rare cases people contract intestinal anthrax from eating undercooked meat, but the GI type of anthrax amounts to less than 1 percent of all cases. The most common anthrax infections are cutaneous, contracted through abrasions and breaks in the skin. Livestock workers are exposed to anthrax every day. Skin anthrax occurs naturally in rural areas around the world, especially around large herds of sheep, goats, and domestic cattle. Cutaneous anthrax accounted for 234 human cases in the nation between 1955 and 1991. A few recent cases in North Dakota, Nevada, and Texas had been cutaneous, contracted while handling animals.

Everything in the autopsy room that had come in contact with Stevens's blackened blood had to be decontaminated or destroyed. The cleanup took nearly three hours.

All day Saturday, October 6, journalists arrived in Florida, attracted by the tragedy of Bob Stevens. Among themselves the reporters speculated that he had been a victim of a deliberate attack. If so, it would be the first documented use of anthrax as a murder weapon in the nation's history.

The following day, the CDC visited AMI again to question employees still on the job five days after Bob Stevens had been diagnosed. By being allowed to remain in the building, employees had received further exposure to anthrax spores. Health workers, protected only by gloves, had done the early environmental sampling with sterile swabs. All were now at risk.

Testers, during this stage of the search, restricted their tests to air vents on the first floor where Blanco and Stevens worked. The air conditioning system controlled moisture so that AMI's workers and mountains of paper and back issues would remain unaffected by the Florida humidity. When the air in a room becomes filled with moisture and odors, it must be removed as conditioned air is blown in. If there were spores the vents might have blown them around. Since they found no spores there, this led environmental officials to report it was unlikely that anthrax had been widely dispersed. Later findings would present a completely different picture of contamination inside the building.

Dr. Malecki painstakingly compiled a dairy of Stevens's travels over the last sixty days so environmental assessments could be made. Perkins dispatched three teams to uncover the source of the anthrax. One group journeyed to Chimney Rock, the second to Stevens's many fishing spots, and the third to his home. All the tests proved negative. After another meticulous sampling of Stevens's home and backyard, the medical detectives were more puzzled than ever. Perkins and his staff decided to make another sweep through AMI. They took away Stevens's office mail slot, mail cubicle, and computer keyboard for examination. They didn't have long to wait for an answer.

Dr. Perkins got word from the CDC's anthrax lab that swabs collected from Stevens's keyboard and the mailroom had tested positive for *Bacillus anthracis*. The entire first-floor workstation was blazing with anthrax. Discovery of anthrax spores inside AMI proved Stevens had not acquired his infection naturally from the soil in the North Carolina wild. And the spores on his keyboard ruled out earlier speculation that he might have inhaled them from imported wool.

The CDC learned that another AMI employee, Ernie Blanco, had developed pneumonia symptoms and was at a local Miami hospital, Cedars Medical Center. They went there immediately. A man in Virginia, who had recently visited the *Star*, had developed pneumonic symptoms like Blanco's. Blanco's nasal swab, obtained on Friday, October 5, had yielded a positive culture for *B. anthracis* on a petri dish.[1] Perkins studied Blanco's results from the CDC:

A left thoracentesis yielded serosanguinous fluid positive for *B. anthracis* DNA by PCR. Bronchoscopy showed bloody secretions in the

---

[1] Subsequent testing revealed a positive PCR test for *B. anthracis* in hemorrhagic pleural fluid and reactive serologic tests. A diagnosis of inhalational anthrax would not be officially confirmed until October 15.

right lower lobe and left lung, with severe mucosal hyperemia, mottling, and inflammation. Bacterial cultures of bronchial washings and pleural fluid did not grow. A transbronchial biopsy showed *B. anthracis* capsule and cell-wall antigens by immunohistochemical staining. The pleural fluid from the second thoracentesis was positive for *B. anthracis* DNA by PCR. A pleural fluid cytology preparation and pleural biopsy showed *B. anthracis* capsule and cell-wall antigens by immunohistochemical staining.

Stevens's and Blanco's symptoms, though, were very different, a fact which further puzzled the medical detectives. Blanco showed no signs of meningitis, yet Stevens did. Blanco had no enlarged space under his breastbone (a symptom unique to the pneumonic form of anthrax), yet Stevens did. And why had the older man survived while Stevens had not? History had shown the elderly were at greater risk from death than the young when exposed to inhalational anthrax and neither was a young man.

Differences in the spore-containing aerosol might have affected the two men differently. Blanco's survival might lie in his lack of susceptibility. In the goat hair mills, where workers were daily exposed to anthrax spores, some developed antibodies and some did not. Why had no other AMI employees become infected? Some of it was luck, some was natural tolerance.

Popular wisdom said that it took the inhalation of hundreds of thousands to millions of anthrax spores to cause the disease. In 1970, the World Health Organization theorized that between 130,000 and 3 million deaths could be caused by aerosolized release of one hundred kilograms of anthrax spores upwind of the Washington, D.C., area. A later study showed that while 100,000 people would die if a nuclear bomb hit a major city and that 10,000 would die in a successful attack on a toxic chemical plant, a million people could die if terrorists launched a biological attack that widely dispersed anthrax. The CDC estimated it would cost the United States nearly $27 billion for every 100,000 persons exposed to pulmonary anthrax.

With Stevens's death scientists determined that only a microscopic quantity, ten to twenty thousand spores, were sufficient to infect a human with pulmonary anthrax. Decades-old Russian tests had determined even fewer might accomplish the same result. In the midst of all the tumult,

Ernie Blanco remained hospitalized on heavy antibiotic therapy, a baffling case to doctors who had become detectives.

At this point, Dr. Perkins urged his boss, CDC director Dr. Jeffrey P. Koplan, to engage the FBI in what he now considered to be a criminal case. Perkins's worst fear was that someone had deliberately released anthrax bacteria, a favorite weapon of modern germ warfare engineers, upon the employees of AMI. Stevens might not only be the nation's first anthrax murder victim, but possibly its first victim of bioterrorism.

"Here you are," Dr. Perkins told *Newsday* later, "you're in Florida, you're down where the terrorists trained, you've just had 9-11. It's easy to conclude it's bioterrorism, but my responsibility was to rule out that it was a sporadic, natural case. That was very much the local focus [in the beginning]."

During the autumn of 1997, the Department of Defense had beat the band to publicize bioterrorism as a national security priority. Drafting a trio of reports, Defense named bioweapons as the new central threat to national security. John Deutch, former director of the CIA, wrote in a 1998 Harvard University study, "If the device that exploded in 1993 under the World Trade Center had [distributed] a deadly pathogen, the chaos and devastation would have gone far beyond our meager ability to describe." Brookings Institute scholars told the Bush Administration they should concentrate homeland security efforts on doomsday terrorist scenarios that have the potential for causing the greatest number of deaths. Since developing defensive biological strategies presupposes the need for testing material, the United States should quickly gear up to produce an offensive biological capacity. Through congressional hearings they laid the groundwork for a whole new series of defensive programs against the threat of anthrax, but most were never implemented.

"Terrorists will use weapons of mass destruction as soon as they perfect the means of delivering them," said former FBI deputy director Oliver Revell. "Both nuclear and chemical are difficult [to deliver], but biological are much less so. They are readily available and can be delivered through many means. Where you have groups that have state support, then I think biological pose a serious risk and that genie is already out of the bottle. Would they be able to wipe out the population of the United States? No. But could they cause thousands, perhaps even hundreds of thousands, of casualties? I think the answer is absolutely yes. With the Internet, with

Global Positioning Satellites, and with mobile communications, a small terrorist group has more command, control, communications and intelligence capability than nation-states had, except for great powers, years ago."

The FBI had already established a tiny presence in Dade County, Florida, because the skyjackers of the jets crashed into the WTC and in a Pennsylvania field had spent time in the area. Since Stevens had been stricken, the number of agents in Dade had doubled and would soon triple. Newsmen in choppers hovering above AMI televised the covered portico and terraced front of the tan and white building below. A number of cars were parked in the employees' lot in back. Along a windbreak of palms, an American flag fluttered in front. The words "American Media," in black upper- and lowercase, were set off by black-trimmed windows. From above, the complex's extensive air-conditioning system on the roof was visible as two huge rectangles.

After Koplan called FBI Director Robert S. Mueller III, an army of federal investigators inundated the region looking for a possible connection to 9-11. But the government agents and Dr. Perkins perceived the outbreak and its aftermath differently. The FBI saw the AMI building as a crime scene jam-packed with clues that would lead them to a killer. Perkins visualized the site as a means of identifying the source of a contagion and saving lives.

A few years earlier, Dr. Perkins had been part of a New York City bioterrorism exercise. On Sunday, November 9, 1997, city emergency workers evacuated "victims" of a mock bioweapons attack a few blocks from City Hall. Perkins's experience with law enforcement there had been eye-opening. The mock scenario concerned a Manhattan office building deliberately contaminated with "anthrax" by terrorists. One NYPD officer was asked what he would do in the event of such a situation. "Bring in the tank," he said. "The tank?" asked Dr. Perkins. "It's a show of force," the cop replied. "So I had been educated about this," Perkins said later, "but investigation was easier before the FBI was really involved. Before Public Health was in charge. Now it was a criminal investigation. At that point I decided to chemoprophylax [treat with antibiotics] people who had worked in the building."

The risk, according to other experts, was minimal. An official statement was issued to remind citizens that anthrax was not contagious. In

Boca Raton, anyone even remotely connected with AMI's supermarket tabloid the *Sun* was implored to come in and be tested. Spores can take up to sixty days before beginning to germinate and the CDC might still be in time to save lives. At seven o'clock that Sunday evening, Dr. Malecki ordered the evacuation and sealing of the tabloid building.

On Monday, October 8, television cameras captured long lines stretching in front of a white annex building—the county Health Department in Delray Beach. Seven hundred plus AMI employees and a horde of recent visitors to the contaminated building had answered Perkins's call. Physicians swabbed the nostrils of anyone who had been exposed to the work site for even one hour since August 1. At least two weeks passed between the time officials believe anthrax entered AMI and the office was shut down. During that span 350 employees continued to work in a hot building. Janitorial crews vacuumed and cleaned each of those days. After the building had been closed, the air conditioner had kept running to prevent heat and humidity from damaging AMI property. All this activity might have disturbed the spores and spread them.

One thousand seventy-five nasal swabs were taken from employees and cultured in dark red agar, sheep's blood in jelly. Anthrax spores thrive in any type of blood nutrient. The swabs were expected to pick up any spores trapped in nose hairs and mucus. Sometimes an exposed person might have a negative nasal swab, but there was no test to tell who might develop anthrax in the near future.

A preliminary test would show results within twelve to twenty-four hours. In the "quick test" antibodies bind to anthrax antigens on the spore surface. The lab would confirm evidence of *B. anthracis* DNA in pleural fluid and blood by polymerase chain reaction (PCR). The most definitive test, the gold standard, was to let the spores germinate over time and form a characteristic glassy, gray colony, on which technicians could perform a genetic test. They used the definitive test on Ernie Blanco.

As a preventive measure Dr. Perkins put all of the over one thousand employees and visitors on ciprofloxacin antibiotics, giving each patient two weeks' worth of Cipro pills and refills for prescriptions. Ciprofloxacin, a whitish, lozenge-shaped pill, was considered an effective and powerful antibiotic cure for all known forms of anthrax. Cipro sometimes causes serious diarrhea and other side effects. It also kills normal bacteria in the gut, leaving only resistant germs. To be really effective, Perkins's patients would have to take the antibiotic for the next two months.

In the meanwhile, public anxiety escalated as fast as the tension between Dr. Perkins and the FBI. "I felt lives were on the line," Dr. Perkins told the press. "The FBI believed some criminal was killing people and their only objective was to nab him." The FBI took the lead, assuming control over the AMI building in the Arvida Park of Commerce, their crime scene, and making it a command center. What the feds really wanted to learn was if the bacterium was part of a second attack by the now-dead terrorists. However, so far they'd been unable to find any traces of anthrax where the terrorists had been. Gradually, they were concluding that the AMI case was an isolated case of "foul play."

Since the FBI and Palm Beach County Health Department had ordered the AMI building sealed, the suites of offices had remained virtually untouched. Only federal agents and an air-conditioning repair crew had been allowed back inside. The FBI even excluded the CDC. Now that it was very much a criminal investigation, communication between the FBI and CDC broke down. To defuse tension between the two agencies, Dr. Perkins invited an FBI agent into his inner staff, then dispatched a CDC epidemiologist to work alongside the FBI chief at the AMI site.

Dr. Perkins called his boss, Koplan. Within two hours, he had "immediate, clear support from the highest levels of government [Attorney General John Ashcroft and HHS Secretary Thompson] that saving lives was the higher priority." Ashcroft made the message forcefully clear to the FBI director. In the meantime, Dr. James Hughes, director of the National Center for Infectious Diseases, asked Dr. Mitch Cohen, a senior scientist and director of the Division of Bacterial and Mycotic Diseases, to pack a bag and get to D.C.

On Tuesday afternoon, October 9, Cohen flew to Washington, D.C., "to act as an interagency liaison" inside the Bureau. He would live out of his suitcase for the next three months. The press was now spreading the word: "A man who died of the rare pneumonic form of anthrax on Friday now appears to be the victim of a deliberate attack. If confirmed, the case will be the first documented and fatal attack with anthrax, long feared as a biological weapon." Since 9-11, the nation had feared a chemical or biological attack might be next. President Bush reassured the country, saying that the Florida case seemed to be "a very isolated incident." Then the

New York City Department of Health notified the CDC of a person with a skin lesion consistent with cutaneous anthrax. The CDC sent a team to New York City to provide epidemiologic and lab support to local health officials.

Back in Florida, Perkins's team looked for ways to catch future outbreaks early. To do this, they looked to the examples of the first two victims. During the course of illness, both men had shown markedly increased white blood cell counts. Even in the first stage of the illness, their blood cultures grew *B. anthracis.* Doctors could also identify the bacteria by pleural or transbronchial biopsy specimens by immunohistochemical staining with *B. anthracis*–specific cell-wall and capsular antibodies. They did have a less complicated tool. Chest X rays had been a sensitive indicator in both patients. Neither Stevens nor Blanco had a normal chest X ray. A more sensitive indicator in spotting multiple abnormalities in the lungs and middle sternum would prove to be a CT.

Meanwhile, Florida Senator Bob Graham reported that, according to his briefings by the U.S. Health Department, the chance that two people in the same office would inhale anthrax spores "by anything other than human intervention was nil to none." Surveillance systems were initiated in Palm Beach and surrounding counties. The bioterror plot was fiendish beyond belief. Stevens was a victim of a deliberate attack by anthrax. Worst of all it was a type of anthrax that had been man-made.

An Anthrax Task Force was formed, comprising members of the FBI, U.S. Postal Inspectors, CDC, and local police. They wanted to know why someone with a high degree of technical skill and an array of special equipment had gone to great effort to render anthrax spores into an aerosol. In order for anthrax to be inhaled and enter the lungs it had to be "aerosolized" into particles between 0.4 and 0.0002 inches. That was smaller than a red blood cell. The first question the Task Force asked themselves was: How had the poison been delivered?

As of Wednesday, October 10, state and federal specialists were still speculating on how the spores had been introduced into AMI. Environmental Protection Agency hazardous materials teams examined the sealed plant. A fence had been built around it.

Each member of the Hazmat team donned a second skin of specially blended materials to help seal out harmful contaminants, followed by a yolk-colored biological safety spacesuit (a pressurized airtight jumper that zips or buttons diagonally across the chest), oxygen mask, and a clear, soft plastic bubble for a helmet. Some headgear was square, some bullet-headed, and they were different colors. Racal hoods, for instance, were the familiar transparent head bubbles. Each self-contained air supply was connected to an oxygen tank slung over the shoulder and held in place with black straps. Air pressure supplied by an electric motor sucked air from the outside and passed it through virus filters before injecting it into the suit.

This arrangement surrounds the body with superfiltered air and keeps the suit under positive pressure to seal out any hot agents. Any airborne virus particles would have a tough time flowing into it. Each man pulled on thick black Army-issue butyl-rubber gloves and attached them to the suit with locked rings. The one-piece suit slipped into the boots and splash guards were pulled outside to protect the boots. The boots were taped to the legs of the yellow suit in an airtight seal and the gloves taped to the sleeves. No matter the color of the suit, everything was tucked and taped.

Now that they were ready, the team picked up their portable chemical detector, the APD 2000, which recognizes chemical warfare agents. Silently, they entered the locked tomb. Palms were blowing outside. There were warm winds off the ocean between the sudden rains that were prevalent until October. Inside the deserted building everything was as it had been left. Under their soft helmets, the hum of their blowers filled their ears.

Reverently, the specialists wandered the eerie, dust-covered rooms. Dust shrouded coffee cups. Family photos were scattered on employees' desks and workstations. The water level in the fish tanks was sinking. A smiling, broad-faced photo of Bob Stevens in a blue-gray shirt still beamed from his desk. He had combed his thin chestnut-colored hair neatly for the picture. The collection of colored crayon drawings on his computer moved slightly in a draft from somewhere or from the furtive movements of the searchers.

As the Hazmat team canvassed the ghostly and shuttered offices, they were understandably wary. If there had been enough anthrax in the office to kill one worker and infect another, then there must be incalculable millions of invisible spores all around them. Spores could have been on the employees' clothes, shoes, hair, on the desks, floors, and in the outdoor air. Had any escaped into the neighborhood? And for all intents and purposes the bacteria were immortal.

That afternoon, a third AMI employee tested positive for anthrax spores in her nose. Like Ernie Blanco, Stephanie Dailey worked in the AMI mailroom. The CDC's theory that the deadly spores had been sent through the mail now seemed to be bearing fruit. Spores were also discovered at the post offices and routes leading directly into AMI headquarters. Samples taken at the West Palm Main Branch, the Green Acres and Lake Worth Post Offices, and the Boca Raton Main Substation all tested hot for environmental contamination. Inexplicably, there was a hot spot at the Blue Lake Post Office away from the path the letter had apparently taken. That made no sense unless cross-contamination was possible.

The FBI scanned some tabloid articles: BIN LADEN TERRORIST TELLS ALL; TERRORIST STILL IN AMERICA—WHERE THEY ARE, WHAT THEY'RE DOING, HOW YOU CAN SPOT THEM; and INSIDE JENNIFER LOPEZ FAIRYTALE WEDDING—LIFE MUST GO ON. They wanted to know all about the mail sent to the six tabloids. "I'm not sure the FBI is ready for the amount of weird mail we get," Grant Balfour, a *Sun* writer, told *Newsweek*.

On Thursday, the team ferreted out additional spores in a receptacle in the AMI mailroom. Blanco had placed his letters on a stack of copy paper and that paper in turn had contaminated every copier in the building. The spores trailed Blanco's route as he made his regular rounds from the first-floor mailroom up stairs and elevators to dozens upon dozens of desks and cabinets. The path was densely contaminated. Spores presumably were stirred up and transported as mail was sorted and delivered and in the daily movements of the staff. The EPA eventually took 462 samples from inside AMI.[2] A total of eighty-four places were found to be contaminated. Seventy-eight percent of the contaminated samples were from the first-floor mailroom. Sixty-six anthrax-laden samples were found on the first floor, including thirty-five from desks, computers, keyboards, file cabinets, and mail slots of cubicles. Spores were found in air filters and vacuum-cleaner bags. An additional thirty-one samples were vacuumed from the first floor.

On Saturday, October 13, Dr. Perkins learned five more of Stevens's coworkers had been exposed to *B. anthracis*. He was glad he had already

---

[2] The EPA teams took their samples from October 20 to November 8, 2001.

put them all on the powerful antibiotic Cipro. He did not expect the five to develop the disease. Apparently, there was no explanation why, unless one considered them simply lucky. They probably did not die because few spores do not cause illness and the immune system stands ready to defend against them. Seven days later, their blood tests would show anti-anthrax antibodies. But how had they been infected? Several of the infected worked in offices for the *National Enquirer*. The *Sun*'s Carla Chadick pointed out that those offices "are way the heck down the hall and around the corner."

The business of America, even if it was gossip, had to go on. The AMI operation moved to another Boca Raton building after their headquarters was closed. The CEO discussed returning to their space off Yamato Road within a year if enough AMI employees agreed. It was doubtful they would. Stephanie Dailey was at home resting, taking antibiotics and on the road to complete recovery. Dailey, a young woman with delicate features and big eyes, had shown up on the news dressed in a black shirt and faded jeans. She was flanked by her supportive parents. Her father's face, as long and worried as a bulldog's, showed the family's deep concern. Blanco's condition gradually improved and (on oral ciprofloxacin) he would be discharged from the hospital "miraculously cured of the usually fatal disease after twenty-three days at death's door."

No anthrax-tainted letter was found in Stevens's office though they tore the place apart. "We still don't have a letter," one fed said bitterly. "We still have a death, and a lot of anthrax that was there." Spores should have been found at points leading out of the building. AMI burned its own trash and stockpiled paper for burning. No trail of spores led to the disposal bin. Had more than one "weird" letter been sent to AMI? The mystery of the misaddressed J-Lo letter had to be solved. Since the letter was not recovered and since no trail showed it leaving the building, it might still be somewhere inside the AMI plant.

The EPA's first findings had suggested a less-dangerous anthrax preparation: one with spores that fell where they were released, not airy spores that hung in the air waiting for victims. No one appreciated that anthrax powder could act like an aerosol, floating long distances or being carried on a person to infect others hundreds of feet away. After testing, they were surprised by how far the material had spread throughout the three-story AMI building.

Spores fell not just in the mailroom, but also in such remote places as atop a room divider, in a nook between banks of shelves, and on computer monitors. Even as HHS Secretary Thompson was assuring Americans that Stevens probably caught anthrax while traveling in the North Carolina countryside, some in the CDC were arguing that it was possible that U.S. mail facilities might be contaminated. Few at first believed that lethal anthrax spores could leak from sealed envelopes.

Some CDC investigators urged their bosses to close the local Boca Raton post offices that would have processed the anthrax letter. But CDC officials decided not to act. This decision was not made without a great deal of debate. "My immediate instinct was to close the Boca Raton post office," said one. "If we had closed the post office in Florida, it would have set a precedent to immediately close post offices elsewhere if anthrax-laced letters began turning up later."

As yet the public knew nothing of the vastness of the conspiracy. Anthrax had become an active agent of biological terrorism. New York was still reeling and licking its wounds, America's wounds. "Frankly, when I heard the news [of 9-11]," said Stan Bedlington, a retired CIA counterterrorism analyst, "I thought, 'It's got to be biochemical.' This is frightening enough and yet, you could take a small plane and sprinkle anthrax over New York City and wipe out half the population." In the nation's capital, the new president was anxious to nail the anthrax killer.

Was there a connection between the now-dead terrorists and the anthrax mailing? Following leads, the FBI began checking where the 9-11 terrorists had lived. During the summer the skyjackers had been sighted all around the Boca Raton area. Reports that the hijackers had inquired about renting crop dusters resulted in one hundred panicked calls about suspicious powders. They had even had dealings with AMI.

STRAIN 4

The First Suspect

"WE KNOW MOHAMMAD Atta was within three miles of the building," American Media Inc.'s Steve Coz said later. And it was true that Atta, suspected mastermind of the 9-11 atrocities, and two other sky-jackers had attended the same flight school near AMI's Boca Raton head-quarters. In fact he had trained all over Florida.

Atta had first gotten flying lessons on the Sun Coast at Jones Aviation in Sarasota, but had been asked to leave after three weeks. Atta and Mar-wan al-Shehhi, saying they were cousins who wanted to be pilots, then trained at Huffman Aviation in Venice, south of Sarasota. The pair paid ten thousand dollars in cash for four months' instruction. Their flight teacher, Rudi Dekkers, remembered that the two men "spoke quite good English." They took another six months of lessons from another Venice school, the Florida Flight Training Center. During that time they lived in a pink house just to the north.

In December 2000, Atta and al-Shehhi trained on a jet airline simu-lator at SimCenter Aviation in Opa-Locka, near North Miami Beach on the Gold Coast. On December 27, they abandoned their broken private plane on a taxiway at Miami International Airport. In spite of this the pair earned a certification for single-engine planes in July 2001. On August 16, 17, and 19, Atta and three other hijackers rented a single-engine, four-seat Piper Archer at eighty-eight dollars an hour from the Palm Beach

County Park Airport in Lantana. Not only did fifteen of the nineteen hijackers have Florida connections, but five of the terrorists who crashed United Airlines Flight 175 into the WTC had spent considerable time in Florida. Four days before 9-11, Atta was living at 3389 Sheridan Street in Hollywood, Florida, just south of Boca Raton and Fort Lauderdale. Atta and al-Shehhi frequented Bud's Lounge in Delray Beach and had drinks at Shuckums Oyster Pub and Seafood Grill that night.

"We know [Atta] was within a mile of Bob Stevens's house," Coz said. "We know that the FBI is now going to local pharmacies to see if he did in fact get Cipro. We know he showed up at a pharmacy with red hands."

After Stevens's death from anthrax, the White House had been ringing the FBI every two hours. They too had heard the rumors that Atta had visited Huber Drugs, a Delray Beach pharmacy north of Boca Raton, a few miles from the AMI building, asking for an antibiotic to fight anthrax. In truth Atta had asked for medication to soothe an inflammation of his hands, a redness that stretched from the wrists down. "My hands burn," he said. "They are itchy." The pharmacist, Gregg Chatterton, sold him acid mantle, a cream. The irritation appeared to have been caused by bleach or detergent. Detergent effectively breaks up clumps of anthrax spores into smaller, more lethal particles. Atta's irritated hands raised fears that Atta had been using caustic chemicals in a bioterror experiment.

"There are people in this area who have very direct recollection of seeing [Atta]," Coz continued. "He worked out in a gym [the Delray Beach gym] where some of our employees were." Other terrorists trained in Boynton Beach, which adjoins Boca Raton, a few miles north of AMI and even closer to Bob Stevens's home.

AMI chief executive David Pecker speculated that AMI had been targeted because of its name. American was also the name of American Airlines. United Airlines may have been a symbol for the United States. "I think this is an attack against America. The World Trade Center was attacked, the Pentagon was attacked, and American Media was attacked and I think this was the first bioterrorism attack in the United States. If you just look at the incredible coincidences, you cannot arrive at any other conclusion in my mind other than this is a bioterrorist attack." A photo of Osama bin Laden had been emblazoned on the front page of the *Globe* with the headline WANTED DEAD OR ALIVE. The word ALIVE had been crossed out. Two weeks later Bob Stevens was dead.

The wife of *Sun* editor Mike Irish was a Florida real estate agent. Gloria Irish had helped two of the 9-11 terrorists, al-Shehhi and Hamza Alghamdi, find apartments in the Hamlet Country Club. She recalled al-Shehhi as friendly and smiling. He told Mrs. Irish that he was doing pilot training and wanted only a three-month lease.

Ziad al-Jarrah, twenty-six, and Ahmed Ilbrahim Alhaznawi, twenty, had entered the U.S. on June 8, 2001. A week later Alhaznawi and Jarrah moved into a two-hundred-dollar-a-week flat attached to a private home on Bougainvillea Drive in Lauderdale-by-the-Sea, twenty miles south of Boca Raton and the AMI office. In July, Jarrah extended his membership in the U.S.-1 Fitness Club in Dania, Florida. The clean-shaven, horse-faced young man passed his pilot's certification test at the end of the month. Jarrah had been born in 1975 in the Bekaa Valley of eastern Lebanon. His father was a government official and his mother a schoolteacher.

Both men spoke little English so it was their neighbor and landlord, Charles Lisa, they sought out on June 25 to ask advice about a "gash" on Alhaznawi's left calf. Lisa applied peroxide, wrapped the leg, and directed his two tenants to Holy Cross Hospital in Fort Lauderdale. Alhaznawi and Jarrah came into the hospital emergency room that evening. Using their own names, not aliases, the pair identified themselves as pilots. Alhaznawi wore a wide black mustache and had large staring eyes.

"I got it from bumping into a suitcase two months ago," Alhaznawi explained of his wound to emergency room physician Dr. Christos Tsonas.

"That's a curious injury," Dr. Tsonas replied.

He studied the inch-long blackish lesion on Alhaznawi's lower left leg. It had red, raised edges and was a little less than an inch wide. Dr. Tsonas recalled that the man appeared to be in good health, and that he denied having an illness like diabetes that might predispose him to such lesions. "They were well-dressed foreigners," he said. "I assumed they were tourists." One of Jarrah's neighbors, Nancy Adams, recalled the young man with close-cropped hair always carried a briefcase.

Dr. Tsonas concluded the man had a minor infection, an encrusted boil or infected scrape. He removed the dry scab over the wound, cleansed it, and prescribed Keflex, an antibiotic that is widely used to combat bacterial infections. Keflex is ineffective against cutaneous anthrax. Dr.

Tsonas took no cultures and had no thoughts of anthrax. At that time it was an unheard-of disease in the United States and unfamiliar to most doctors. Anthrax was "regarded as an obscure, rarely seen disease that had caused only a few deaths." Cutaneous anthrax has a low fatality rate. Without treatment victims might heal on their own.

Dr. Tsonas's encounter with the two men had lasted perhaps ten minutes. By October, he had entirely forgotten about them until federal agents showed up after Bob Stevens died. They showed the physician pictures of Alhaznawi and Jarrah. The FBI had discovered Dr. Tsonas's prescription among possessions Alhaznawi left behind when he moved out in late August. The agents gave Dr. Tsonas a copy of his own notes from the emergency room visit on June 25 and he read them over. Amid news reports about the first anthrax victims, Dr. Tsonas, like other doctors, had thrown himself into learning more about the disease. He wanted to be prepared. His hospital was relatively near AMI, so victims there might come to Holy Cross for treatment.

As he examined his notes, he said, "Oh, my God, my written description is consistent with cutaneous anthrax." He was astonished and discussed the disease and its symptoms with the agents, explaining that it could possibly explain the leg wound. A spider bite was unlikely, he said. As for the hijacker's explanation, a suitcase bump: "That's a little unusual for a healthy guy, but not impossible," he said.

Both men were suspected of participating in the hijacking of United Airlines Flight 93 on 9-11. Jarrah died along with Alhaznawi on the Boeing 757, which crashed into a Somerset County, Pennsylvania, field after passengers on the plane fought back. Jarrah was thought to have taken the controls. When the wreckage was fine-combed no anthrax spores were found. Nor were any ferreted out in the two terrorists' condominium.

Upon closer scrutiny, another question arose. Alhaznawi was examined only days after he entered the U.S., an indication that the infection developed before his arrival. And Lisa recalled it as a "gash." There was simply not enough intelligence to draw a specific conclusion. Thomas W. McGovern, the leading authority on anthrax for the American Academy of Dermatology's bioterrorism task force, said it was "highly unlikely" for someone to contract cutaneous anthrax on his lower leg.

"So there's just no there there," said one investigator. "But it sure is intriguing." After his meetings with the FBI, Dr. Tsonas was contacted again by a senior federal medical expert, who asked him detailed questions about his tentative diagnosis. Experts at Johns Hopkins also called Dr. Tsonas, saying they, too, were studying the evidence. Much later, the FBI asked Tara O'Toole and Thomas V. Inglesby, who head the Johns Hopkins Center for Civilian Biodefense Strategies, to evaluate Tsonas's diagnosis. They prepared a two-page memo, which was circulated among senior government officials. They concluded that Tsonas's diagnosis of cutaneous anthrax was "the most probable and coherent interpretation of the data available." After the memo became public later that conclusion was endorsed by D. A. Henderson, the top bioterrorism official at the Department of Health and Human Services, and plain-speaking Richard Spertzel, former head of the UN's biological weapons inspections in Iraq.

Dr. O'Toole said that after consulting with other medical experts on the Alhaznawi case, she was "more persuaded than ever" that the diagnosis of cutaneous anthrax was correct. "This is a unique investigation that has many highly technical aspects," she said. "There's legitimate concern that the FBI may not have access to the kinds of expertise that could be essential in putting all these pieces together." John E. Collingwood, an FBI spokesman, said the possibility of a connection between the hijackers and the anthrax attacks had been deeply explored. "This was fully investigated and widely vetted among multiple agencies several months ago," he said in March 2002. "Exhaustive testing did not support that anthrax was present anywhere the hijackers had been. While we always welcome new information, nothing new has in fact developed."

SOMEWHERE BETWEEN THE end of April and the third week of May 2001, Mohammad Atta showed up at the U.S. Department of Agriculture in Homestead, Florida. A clerk ushered him into the office of Johnelle Bryant, new manager for the farm service agency. Hers was an important job—arranging or granting government-financed loans for agriculture, real estate, and farming-type operations.

"He had very scary-looking eyes," she told ABC News much later. "His eyes were black—so black that his iris was almost the same color as his pupil, which in itself gave him the appearance of being very, very scary. Very intense. And then—with his accent—he came across as very intimidating. How could somebody be that evil, be that close to me and I didn't recognize it?"

At first Atta declined to speak with Bryant, saying with repugnance she was "but a female." Though Bryant explained she was the manager, he still balked at conducting business with her. Finally she said, "If you're interested in getting a farm-service agency loan in my servicing area, then you would need to deal with me." Her servicing area included Dade, Broward, Palm Beach, and Monroe Counties. Atta reluctantly agreed. Bryant wrote his name down, spelling it "A-T-T-A-H." He leaned forward and said, "No, A-T-T-A, as in 'Atta boy!' I'm originally from Egypt, but I've just moved here from Afghanistan. I left all my belongings at home to move to the U.S. to start my dream, which was to go to flight school, and get my pilot's license and work both as a charter pilot and a crop duster." Slow-moving, low-flying fixed-wing agricultural crop dusters were a common sight over Florida fields, delivering their spray of liquid fertilizer or insecticide. The fixed-wing aircraft were built to carry large tanks of liquid chemicals.

"It wasn't actually a crop duster in itself that he was wanting to finance," Bryant recalled. "He wanted [to modify] a twin-engine, six-passenger aircraft that he could use both for charter flights and crop-dusting." Atta intended to pull the back seats out and construct a huge chemical tank that would fit inside the rear of the aircraft. He intended to run the spray nozzles along the wing span. "I could use it to stay up in the air longer while spraying sugarcane out in the Broward County area," he said, ". . . wouldn't have to land and reload, just continue spraying."

Bryant explained that a tank of that size wouldn't fit through the door and, although the aircraft would have a greater chemical capacity than a regular crop duster, his modifications would take up every available square inch of the interior except for where the pilot would be sitting. "You wouldn't be able to use the same aircraft for both crop-dusting and as a charter plane," she said. "That wouldn't work, but it's very creative."

"It most certainly would work!" said Atta. "I'm an engineer and I know how to solve those problems. I have an engineering degree and have studied in Germany." Atta had lived and worked in Hamburg.

The entire time Atta was in her office, his emotions kept going up and down. Bryant found him "persistent and frightening." He had an unusual habit—when listening to her responses to his questions, he'd press his lips together so tightly they became a straight line. When she told him the agency couldn't finance the type of operation he was interested in, Atta jumped back in his chair. He accused her of discriminating against him because he was not a citizen. She tried to "speak nicely to him," to calm him down.

Atta had learned of her agency from a forty-dollar book he had purchased off cable TV. The book advertised how to obtain free grants or loans from the government. "Actually," said Bryant later, "we have a loan limit of $750,000 and he was asking for $650,000. He also thought that all he had to do to obtain the money was to actually just come in to my office, tell what he wanted the loan for, and obtain the cash without any kind of application processing."

As she explained the application process to him, he became very agitated. He said the book said, "Come to your agency and get up to $750,000." He was also under the impression the loan was going to be in cash.

"He actually believed that he could walk into the office and say that he needed $650,000 to purchase an aircraft with," said Bryant, "and that I would give him $650,000 in cash."

Atta was obviously disappointed. When he noticed a huge, black, older model safe in her office, he asked what would prevent him from stealing all the cash inside.

"For one thing," Bryant told him, "there's no cash in that safe."

"And what's the second thing," Atta asked, "that would prevent me from coming behind your desk, cutting your throat and making off with all the cash in the safe because you don't have audio or visual security in your office?"

"Number one, there's no cash in the safe. Number two, my training would prevent you from coming behind the desk and cutting my throat."

Atta kind of stepped back and said, "So you've had military training?"

Bryant explained she had had about six months of karate training, in a martial art called *Koname Ru*. Atta was very surprised that a woman would have such training.

He pointed to a picture over her desk, a going-away gift to her from her former coworkers in the national office, and tried to buy it. He started throwing money on her desk. Bryant recalled, "He wanted that picture really bad—said it was a really beautiful picture of Washington, D.C., capturing all the buildings and monuments in one panoramic photograph."

"It's one of the prettiest, the best I've ever seen of Washington," he said. As he looked at the aerial view, he asked about the Pentagon, the Capitol, and the White House." He picked the Pentagon out himself. He said he wanted to go to New York and visit the World Trade Center.

"It's not for sale."

At that he put more money from a huge wad down on her desk.

"You don't understand," she said. "It's a gift. It's not for sale for anything."

His face became very bitter at that point. "How would America like it," he said, "if another country destroyed Washington, D.C., and some of the monuments in it, like the cities in my country that have been destroyed?"

At the end of their one-hour interview, Bryant turned him down for the loan because the program was intended for actual farming purposes and as a non–U.S. citizen he did not meet the basic eligibility requirements. She referred him to other government agencies and to a bank downstairs.

"Would my plans to be out of the country for a few weeks interfere with my eligibility for a loan?" Atta said, mentioning Madrid, Germany, and a third place, a country that Bryant could not remember.

Atta traveled widely. He went to Switzerland on January 4, 2000, and Germany in March. On May 30, 2000, after failing to enter the Czech Republic through Prague's Ruzyne Airport due to inadequate documentation, Atta journeyed to the Czech Republic under his own name. He entered by bus on June 2, this time with correct papers. There he met with an Iraqi agent in a Prague transit lounge. Ahmad Khalil Ibrahim Samir al-Ani was a veteran spy and a crackerjack used-car dealer who operated under diplomatic cover. Atta and al-Ani did not leave the cafe and Atta took the next flight out.

In June 2000 and March 2001 Atta visited Spain and the Czech Republic. Atta's last departure point for the U.S. before 9-11 was once again Prague. On his trip to the Czech Republic on April 8, 2001, Atta stayed at the Prague Hilton and at Kutna Hora. In June 2001, the Czechs expelled al-Ani, and, after 9-11, Czech authorities denied any meetings between Atta and any Iraqi intelligence officials who may or may not have given him anthrax bacteria. Twenty days after Bob Stevens's death, Berlin detectives began trying to find out for certain if Atta had received anthrax spores from Iraqi agents.

In April or May 2001, Atta opened a bank account at a branch of Sun Trust. On several occasions in August, he led several Mideastern men to inquire about crop-dusting at the Belle Glade State Municipal Airport, about an hour northwest of Fort Lauderdale. Atta and Zacarias Moussaoui (suspected to have been slated to be the twentieth highjacker) collected all the information about crop-dusting aircraft they could. "How much fuel and chemicals could the plane carry?" Atta asked of an Air Tractor AT-503. Were the terrorists researching a means to deliver biological or chemical weapons over Florida by air?

On July 18, 2001, he left Miami for a third visit to Spain. During his ten days there Atta rented a car and spent four days in Madrid, probably waiting for a final go-ahead.

Five years earlier, the Office of Technology Assessment had theorized that a small private plane, loaded with 220 pounds of spores, could fly over Washington, D.C., and leave an invisible mist that might kill a million unsuspecting people. They estimated release of a single warhead of anthrax spores could kill thirty thousand to one hundred thousand.

Atta was only the first of four 9-11 hijackers to apply for a federal loan to finance the acquisition and modification of crop dusters. The others were Marwan al-Shehhi, Ahmed Alghamdi, and Fayez Rashid Ahmed Hassan al Qadi Banihammad.[3]

Atta later returned to Bryant's office, slightly disguised with glasses. He claimed he was an accountant for al-Shehhi, who was with him. He said he wanted five hundred thousand dollars to buy land for a sugarcane farm. Alghamdi and Fayez Rashid Ahmed Hassan al Qadi Banihammad came separately seeking loans. They were not as successful at dealing with people as Atta, and he had failed miserably.

The rejection of their loan requests altered the hijackers' plan, a plan they had kicked around for the last five years. The terrorists had intended to pack a twin-engine plane with explosive chemicals and convert it to a flying bomb. When Atta reported to his group he could not get funding,

---

[3] Abu Zabaydah, a top lieutenant of Osama bin Laden, told this to his American interrogators after his capture.

they switched to hijacking passenger jets. In the fall of 2000, hijackers who had been learning to fly small planes switched to simulator training in the large jets they would fly into the World Trade Center and Pentagon. But even a few days before 9-11 Atta was still asking about crop dusters.

Had the strain of anthrax that killed Bob Stevens originated in some Afghan cave? Since early summer 1998, Islamist terrorists under the command of Osama bin Laden had been actively testing chemical and bacteriological weapons in a well-equipped, fortified compound hidden near Qandahar. In September 1999, Ahmad Ibrahim al-Naggar, a member of Egyptian Islamic Jihad, confessed to Egyptian security that Egyptian Islamic Jihad, an ally of bin Laden's Qaeda network, had purchased anthrax spores from an East Asian country. The same Southeast Asian factory had already supplied anthrax spores to the Indonesian-based Islamic Moro Front, a terror group closely associated with bin Laden. Al Qaeda was supplied the deadly bacteria by mail and without identification for $3,685, and that included shipping costs.

After paying $7,500 up front, Al Qaeda also bought anthrax spores from factories in the Czech Republic and from East European and Southeast Asian labs for as little as $10,000, again without identification. They purchased *E. coli* and *Salmonella* for $5,000 in the Czech Republic. Additional samples of deadly anthrax may have been obtained from North Korea for a smaller amount of cash.

Special chemical- and biological-agent production labs had been purchased in the former Yugoslavia in early May 1998, and shipped via Pakistan to Afghanistan, where anthrax was a common veterinary disease. "It's in Afghanistan," molecular biologist Paul S. Keim of Northern Arizona University said. "If a cow dies of anthrax it will bleed out its nose. All you have to do is scrape up a little blood, put it in a petri dish, and you have anthrax." You can get spores from either the soil or a carcass.

Training in the use of chemical agents for Al Qaeda took place in Afghanistan. An instruction manual was recovered from the home of a Libyan Al Qaeda member in Manchester, England. Rabbit and dog test animals were later found near bin Laden's Jalalabad training camps. Convicted terrorist Ahmed Ressam testified that he spent six months in 1998 at one of bin Laden's Afghan training camps learning to release cyanide into the ventilation systems of office buildings. Bin Laden was also interested in the use of "low-flying aircraft for the distribution of toxic materials."

They may have had the supervision of a few Ukrainian expert chemists and biologists. Al Qaeda training included "kits" with toxins and chemical agents. Some terrorists were being trained to grow "lethal biological cultures" using substances easily available on the commercial market.

The CIA had predicted that a bioweapon attack by bin Laden was "highly likely." Once the FBI learned that the 9-11 terrorists had a host of connections with the Boca Raton area and with AMI, they began searching for anthrax residue among the terrorists' corpses. The FBI searched the charred remains of Flight 93, which terrorists had crashed into a Pennsylvania field when the passengers rose up against them. Was there any trace of anthrax in the body of Alhaznawi, which was recovered from that crash site? They analyzed the remains of American Airlines Flight 77, which had crashed into the Pentagon. They conducted exhaustive testing for the presence of anthrax spores anywhere the hijackers had lived or worked or trained or died. They found none.

The anthrax was probably not mailed by Al Qaeda. It did not fit their style. "Sources," said the FBI, "suggest Al Qaeda may favor spectacular attacks that meet several criteria: High symbolic value, mass casualties, severe damage to the U.S. economy and maximum psychological trauma."

The strain of mailed anthrax had been sensitive to every oral antibiotic—penicillins, tetracyclines, and quinolones such as Cipro. A terrorist set to do the maximum damage would have employed a more advanced strain, a virulent, engineered anthrax that would be impervious to antibiotics and cause greater casualties. It was rumored that the Russians had such a strain at their secret Siberian bio-installation—Vector.

But the anthrax letters had been mailed after the terrorists died in the plane crashes. Were they sent by a confederate? Law enforcement emphasized that the anthrax cases had not been linked to bin Laden. "These diseases are a punishment from God," bin Laden said later of the anthrax attacks, "and a response to oppressed mothers' prayers in Lebanon, Iraq, Palestine, and everywhere." Within a few weeks, the White House would begin discounting the 9-11 terrorists as the originators of the anthrax letter.

The FBI pursued the 9-11 terrorist-anthrax connection doggedly, but Atta and his terrorists weren't the only ones toying with the idea of buying up crop dusters and sprayers that could be outfitted to spray invisible clouds of anthrax over U.S. cities. The investigators had no shortage of suspects in the bio-attack against America. One of America's greatest foreign enemies had a biological warfare stockpile, much of it kept in secret, and had actually modified crop dusters to spray liquid anthrax.

One week after the terrorists died and more than two weeks before Bob Stevens's death, someone mailed a handful of anthrax letters to some of the most famous and trusted names in America.

STRAIN 5

The Postman Always Rings Twice

"A lunatic. With the killer of all times. It gives me the creeps. This whole operation gives me the creeps."

— A CHARACTER IN *THE SATAN BUG*

IT WAS ONE envelope, then two, a handful inserted very carefully into a mail slot. The letters all fluttered into the belly of the same mailbox, but their paths would soon separate. The plastic bin used to catch the mail deposited into the box barely registered the weight of the letters that would shake a nation. A gloved hand posted them into the center box of three blue mailboxes sometime on Tuesday, September 18, 2001. This day was a one-week anniversary of sorts. Only a week earlier jets had crashed into the World Trade Center, the Pentagon, and a Pennsylvania field. Dust still howled around Ground Zero. Firemen and volunteers, digging for the bodies of thousands, unknowingly inhaled powder as lethal as the bacterial dust mailed to AMI.

It was quieter here on Nassau Street, except for the busy hum of traffic in the business district around the trio of corner boxes. The envelopes lay atop others, alike, yet unalike. These letters were the most unique ever mailed in America. The envelopes, though, were plain and white and of the thirty-four-cent prestamped metered variety. By using metered envelopes, the mailer avoided any possibility of being traced back through the stamps. Saliva might give away the identity of the mailer through DNA, the molecular code upon which so much modern biotechnology research depends. They can be bought directly from post office vending machines (without creating much notice) in sets of five. The killer's first mailing probably used all five. The main Princeton post office stood only a couple of blocks away, one of four New Jersey post offices that would be contaminated by anthrax spores.

The envelopes, of an extraordinarily cheap, porous paper, were a smaller size than traditional business-size envelopes—measuring approximately 6¼ inches by 3½ inches. The hand-printing on the envelope slanted down to the right. The writer had trouble keeping words in a straight line on unlined paper. He clumped them together as if he were afraid he would run out of room by the time he got to the right edge of the small envelope. He almost did.

Were the letters neatly taped? It was hard to tell in the darkness of the box. A ray of light as another letter fell. Yes, taped, but not as securely as later letters. It was as if the killer came to have second thoughts about hurting anyone except the addressee. The anthrax mailer had not yet realized how porous the envelopes were. Their wide pores allowed even the crude, less-refined anthrax spores he was mailing to slip through the paper. If the microscopic particles inside, no bigger than a human cell, had had a voice it would have been the whispering hiss of a cobra.

Amerithrax's own name had a harsh sound, like that of a James Bond villain like Drax or a real-life killer like Zodiac. Though Amerithrax was just as fantastic and as much a supercriminal as they, he had not named himself. The FBI had christened him. Their code name for the anthrax mailer was a combination of "America" and "anthrax."

The latex-gloved hand of Amerithrax was crawling with bacteria. He would have to dispose of the glove as soon as possible. He took one last look at the center mailbox of three stout curbside boxes on the corner in the business district of Princeton, New Jersey. The boxes were lined up on Nassau Street near the intersection of Bank Street across from the Princeton University campus. Nassau Street was New Jersey Route 27, which stretched northeastward through the town of Franklin Park (which would later appear in the return address on more anthrax letters). Wills,

O'Neill & Mellk, a law firm, lay directly behind the mailboxes. On Nassau Street was a gift store, Go for Baroque, and around the corner was a fabric store, Pins and Needles. If the slots of the boxes had faced toward the traffic, he could have mailed them from a vehicle. Was it raining in the Ivy League town when the letters were mailed? Some of the letters would arrive wet.

Later, the FBI would create a model of the letters' route. From mailboxes to entry post offices to regional sorting centers to destination post offices and final destinations, anthrax flowed like a river, a twisting trail of spores spreading death as they went and branching off into lethal tributaries. When officials said Stevens became infected from a stream, it had never in their wildest dreams occurred to them this might have been a mail stream.

Mail drop boxes in New Jersey were later tested based on postal coding that designates when items enter the mail system. Utilizing processing codes imprinted on some envelopes and packages, inspectors later traced the paths of three letters known to have contained anthrax spores, pinpointing how their passages through the system contaminated numerous machines, allowing other mail to pick up spores from tainted equipment. Using the codes, the Postal Service was able to locate the box where the anthrax mail originated. But in this early day, cross-contamination by a sealed envelope was considered impossible.

The mailbox that was used to send the poison letters into the system was technically not a storage box. However, on occasion it was used as such by carriers who walk the route carrying mail in a shoulder bag. This saved them a backbreaking second trip to the post office.

Collection time varied, depending on the amount of mail and traffic. The time listed on the collection box suggested that somewhere between 10:00 and 11:00 A.M. the mail would be picked up. But these boxes were normally picked up later in the day, closer to 3:00 P.M. The mail dropped in the box was collected by mail carrier Cleveland Stevenson, 45. Amerithrax's envelopes joined the others in one of the plastic tubs that were shuttled around to the central processing center and other post offices. Amerithrax's letters went into a sack, and into a system that went to the Route 130 post office and five other local post offices such as Palmer Square in Princeton Borough two blocks from the contaminated box.

The thousands of drop boxes and forty-eight post offices all fed into the Hamilton Processing Center, the main postal distribution center. The sorting station lay in Hamilton Township near Trenton and about fifteen miles from Princeton. Trenton, which lies along the wide Delaware River, had been the national capital for little over a month at the end of 1784.

At Hamilton that evening, Amerithrax's letters were collected with other mail in trays. The trays were emptied onto moving conveyor belts that brought them to an edger-feeder, which separates envelopes by size. The edger-feeder advanced the deadly letters to a facer-canceler, a sensing device that processes thirty-five thousand pieces per hour. The facer-canceler located the stamps in the upper right-hand corners, arranged the envelopes so they all faced in the same direction, then canceled and postmarked each. Within three hours of each other, two of the terrorist letters were postmarked by the same machine. Richard Morgano, thirty-nine, did routine maintenance on postmarking machines out of the New Jersey post office at a Kuser Road business. He was on duty when the media letters were postmarked. Two of his machines later tested positive for anthrax spores. Morgano had a cut, providing an entry point for bacteria, and so was unknowingly infected by the invisible spores.

Next an optical character reader read the addresses on the letters and sprayed a bar code across the bottoms of the envelopes. A computerized zip (zoning improvement plan) code translator sorted the letters according to their destination. High-speed sorting machines handling hundreds of letters per minute propelled the letters on a conveyor belt into one of hundreds of bins, each designated for a different post office. Parcels going in both directions may have been contaminated by the tainted letters. Amerithrax's letters raced outbound to NBC News anchor Tom Brokaw, the editor of the *New York Post*, and others.

On their way, the media letters sickened Teresa Heller, thirty-two, a mail carrier in the West Trenton Post Office. Heller was a prompt, friendly, ponytailed woman that West Trenton residents knew as "Terry." How she came into contact with "hot mail" has never been fully explained. She might have become infected by mail that had picked up spores at Hamilton before being sent to the West Trenton Post Office. Heller picked up the letters and packages for her route there.

Amerithrax's onslaught against the media left behind a traceable path of poison as it moved through the system. At one point the letters separated. Traces were later found at the Morgan Central Postal Facility in Manhattan, where spore samples on five sorting machines tested positive. The government later responded with a statement that the facility was safe and should remain open. Morgan fed Radio City Post Office and a letter from Amerithrax to CBS passed through. When it arrived at CBS it would infect another victim and a create a hot spot that was later traceable by field testing.

Along the way from Morgan, the letters to NBC and the *New York Post* went through Rockefeller Center Post Office, but left it unscathed. Subsequently, at the *Post* there would be a confirmed case, two suspected cases, and a positive sample. At NBC–New York there would be a confirmed case, a hot spot, and another suspected case. From Morgan out, a letter from Amerithrax to ABC traveled through the Ansonia Post Office, which was not contaminated. However, at ABC searchers would later discover a positive sample and a confirmed case of anthrax. From Morgan outward, not one bit of cross-contamination occurred, unless the mysterious source that killed a woman in the Bronx was in fact a cross-contaminated letter (investigation would not reveal how she became infected).

Before the mailings, Amerithrax surely had had anthrax in his possession for some weeks. And he already had equipment available to refine airborne spores and make them tiny enough to reach the depths of the lungs. However, only a group with access to advanced biotechnology seemed capable of manufacturing such a lethal anthrax aerosol. Had Amerithrax cultivated and weaponized the powder or stolen it from somewhere else? Weaponization, in the case of anthrax, meant genetic modification of the spores to alter their incubation period, milling to refine their particle size, and the addition of stabilizing agents. Finally, it meant the loading of a biological weapon into a delivery system, in this instance an envelope. If he already had anthrax, he must have had a motive before that. Were the mailings his way of striking back? Was he a discharged scientist who took weaponized anthrax on a last day of work? Or was his intention something altogether different? Media communications were the killer's first choice and maybe his true target. Amerithrax either wanted publicity or wanted to sway public or official opinion.

On Friday, September 21, Ernie Blanco was just delivering a lethal letter to the *Sun* in Boca Raton. Elsewhere in the nation, it was a typical, horrible day after 9-11. In New York dozens of fires as high as a thousand degrees Fahrenheit raged under the twisted rubble of the mammoth Trade Center. They were still burning and would smolder for another four months. Almost two hundred thousand gallons of transformer oils and diesel fuel had escaped beneath the twisted landscape. The day before, EPA monitoring had discovered high levels of dioxins and heavy metals in runoff water and air around Ground Zero. USGS scientists' chemical leach tests of the corrosive dust and airfall debris samples found them "quite alkaline," due to high levels of concrete, gypsum, and glass fiber particles. Like Amerithrax's anthrax, any fibers in settled dust would eventually become airborne by rainfall, changes in wind direction, or such simple human activity as walking.

Emergency workers and volunteers at the scene were still wheezing and suffering from upper and lower respiratory distress. Asbestos, heavy metals, and dioxins drifted through the dusty downtown air. As New York tried to catch its breath, the White House struggled to guess the terrorists' next move. They speculated loudly that an airborne biological terrorist attack might be next. The public reacted in a burst of panic buying. Over the last two days there had been a run on fifty-dollar gas masks, one-hundred-dollar water-purification kits, and thirty-eight-dollar chemical body suits. Into this atmosphere of dread, flew Amerithrax's latest letter. It arrived without fanfare in New York, between 48th and 51st Streets and Fifth and Sixth Avenues, and was addressed to the anchor of the *NBC Nightly News*:

TOM BROKAW
NBC TV
30 ROCKEFELLER PLAZA
NEW YORK NY 10112

Erin O'Connor, Brokaw's thirty-eight-year-old assistant, noticed there was no return address, but the transmittal envelope was postmarked "Trenton, New Jersey, 09/18/2001 (Tues.)." The metered numbers read: "10112+0002." She opened the envelope slitting it right to left. The letter inside, a Xerox copy, read:

09-11-01

THIS IS NEXT
TAKE PENACILIN NOW
DEATH TO AMERICA
DEATH TO ISRAEL
ALLAH IS GREAT

The killer was either anti-Semitic or wanted people to think he was. He had misspelled penicillin, possibly on purpose. The note was in capital letters. Every maniac from Zodiac to the Unabomber favored uppercase printing. It was harder to match to an individual and gave a more terrifying aspect to messages, as did purposeful misspellings. A zero in front of a single-digit month suggested someone who worked with computers. The poor block printing suggested someone inexperienced with writing by hand. The writer was definitely unused to printing in both upper- and lowercase. He had made the first character of each sentence larger in an attempt to capitalize uppercase letters. The initial character of the first two sentences and the last line were also boldfaced: "T-T-A." As in the terrorist "A-T-T-A"?

The one-page letter itself was odd-sized. Because of the irregular edges it was easy to see it had been cut by scissors. The NBC letter measured 225 millimeters long by 215 millimeters wide. It had been cut from standard copy paper 279 millimeters long and 215 millimeters wide. Amerithrax had trimmed 54 millimeters from its length to create an almost square letter.

Why? He might have wanted the letter to appear as if someone European had composed the letter since European letters had a height-to-width ratio of 1.41. to 1. Yet Amerithrax had cropped it so clumsily. Why did he trim the letter? He had another reason.

The threatening letter was slightly damp along one side as if it had been in water. The writer promised, "THIS IS NEXT." What was next? O'Connor found out as she stapled the letter to the envelope, a common practice to keep the two pieces together and easy to access. As she shot a staple into the porous paper, a "relatively crude" substance spilled onto her. The envelope had contained some kind of "dark, sand-like powder."

When anthrax bacteria are dried and form tiny protective spores, anthrax turns into a white or beige powder. NBC had gotten an earlier letter filled with powder, but that was not unusual. For the three years preceding 9-11, the threat of bioterrorism had received widespread publicity in the United States. Dozens of offices had received envelopes containing white powders alleged to be anthrax. So far not one had actually contained anthrax.

On Tuesday, September 25, the phone rang at the New York FBI Field Office. Since 9-11, agents had been working out of a makeshift, but secure, bunker. The phone lines had been constantly busy. Most of the agents were out on cases. NBC-TV security was on the line about a letter to Tom Brokaw postmarked September 20 from St. Petersburg, Florida. The letter contained powder resembling talcum and a "threatening" note which read, "The unthinkable. See what happens next." Like the Trenton letter O'Connor had opened, this one carried no return address.

The next day two FBI agents normally assigned to investigate drugs dropped by NBC to pick up the letter. They entered by the main entrance on Fifth Avenue between 49th and 50th Streets. Flags of a hundred nations blew in the wind. A sunken space, Tower Plaza, was topped by the gold-leafed statue of Prometheus. Behind Tower Plaza loomed a seventy-story tower, the GE Building.

As it turned out O'Connor had no time for an interview, so the agents stuck the St. Petersburg letter in an evidence vault until she did. As a result they did not test the powder until at least two weeks later. Nor did they immediately notify City Hall. Their delay in identifying the white powder later confirmed fears that the FBI wouldn't recognize bioterrorism when they saw it.

Over at the New Jersey Post Office, postal repairman Richard Morgano was studying his hand. What once had been a minor cut was now a small lump—like an insect bite. By day's end that bite had developed into a rash. Amerithrax's media letters had been sealed and taped when they passed through the postmarking machines Morgano had been repairing. Had the hardened spores been microscopic enough to pass through the porous envelope? Experts said that was not possible. But it was true that paper has tiny invisible pores and merely handling the unopened letter could have given a postal worker anthrax.

At NBC–New York, another assistant, Casey Chamberlain, twenty-three, remembered a St. Petersburg letter that contained talcum powder.

By Friday she too saw the beginning of a small, localized lesion on the surface of her skin, then a rash just like Richard Morgano's.

On Saturday, September 29, the seven-month-old infant son of a producer to Peter Jennings at ABC–New York fell ill, apparently bitten "by a spider." As far as his mother could tell, the baby got the bite while visiting the ABC headquarters with his baby-sitter. That was the only time she had ever taken the infant to work. The baby spent almost an hour and a half in her office, the cafeteria, and at a birthday party on an upper floor. The following day, the boy developed a non-tender, abnormal accumulation of serous fluid in the connective tissue of his left arm. The back of his arm swelled to frightening proportions. His mother was frantic. Doctors treated the two circular skin lesions, which had begun weeping, with intravenous antibiotics.

Over the weekend, O'Connor felt like she was coming down with an illness. Her low-grade fever was accompanied by a throbbing headache. Within days she had a bad rash below her left collarbone. The rash had started with a small painless lump that resembled a bug bite. Within a few hours, the bite became a reddish brown irritation that started to swell until it was a solid bump. The papule enlarged and ulcerated. The rash became more irritated and necrotic (filled with dead tissue). She saw her doctor, Richard Fried, who was concerned enough to take a biopsy, a sliver of the tissue, and send her to a specialist.

On Monday, October 1, the same day Ernesto Blanco was hospitalized with pneumonia in Florida, postal worker Teresa Heller and Claire Fletcher, Dan Rather's assistant at CBS, developed inflammations with purplish brown or black centers. That afternoon, Erin O'Connor went in to see her doctor to get some relief.

The physician studied the wound and described it as: "an approximately five-centimeter-long, oval-shaped lesion with a raised border, small satellite fluid-filled spots." The outbreak was less than 0.2 inches in diameter, but he noted a profound swelling filled with fluid. He associated the strongly defined injury with a swollen gland in her neck—lymph nodes fighting back against infection. Serous fluid from the injury tested negative by gram stain and culture in preliminary tests. Doctors had not seen anthrax in decades and so, until Bob Stevens's death, that disease seemed out of the question, especially in the big city.

Over several days O'Connor's inflammation developed a purplish black center, depressed and surrounded by an area of swelling. Encircling it were one- to three-millimeter vesicles, pouches filled with yellow fluid. As is classic with skin anthrax, there was little pain. The malignant pustule, a blister containing pus from a collection of white blood cells, progressed from a fluid-filled blister to a painless ulcer one- to three-centimeters in diameter in two days. The "feverish blister" split the skin and the painless welt developed a black, ulcerous scab that soon loosened and fell off. The doctor prescribed the heavy-duty oral antibiotic Cipro. Since that cleared the injury, O'Connor was given two weeks' worth.

On Tuesday the infant's "spider bite" had become ulcerlike and developed a black scab like O'Connor's. Anthrax was so rare that no one realized the well-defined injury was not from a spider. Spider bites often have black spot at the center. The baby required intensive care, his clinical course of treatment "complicated by hemollytic anemia and thrombocytopenia."

O'Connor's serum specimen was collected for PCR testing. On Saturday, October 6, her doctor alerted the New York City Health Department that "We've got a possible anthrax case." In turn Dr. Marcie Layton rang up Stephen Ostroff of the CDC. Only after the Health Department called Barry Mawn did the fifty-six-year-old head of the New York FBI Field Office discover the delay in investigating the St. Petersburg letter to Brokaw. Mawn and his eleven hundred agents had been working eighteen-hour days since 9-11. The call from NBC about the first letter was "one of maybe about eight thousand leads we had received," Mawn told FBI expert Ronald Kessler. "The letter should have been sent to headquarters for immediate testing. The agents who normally pursue drug cases handled it like a drug case." Mawn made sure the powder was tested as soon as possible at the CDC. There was crucial urgency because it might be the first salvo in another terrorist attack on New York City. The St. Petersburg letter was delivered to lab chief Richard Meyer in Atlanta. Surprisingly, it turned out not to contain anthrax. That afternoon, three technicians began processing a variety of objects from O'Connor's workstation. They found no spores either.

By jet that afternoon Dr. Zaki's pathology lab at the CDC received O'Connor's tissue sample encased in an inch-square paraffin block. The sample was sliced into hundreds of wafer-thin sheets, each mounted on a glass slide. Zaki and research assistants Jeannette Guarner and Wun-Ju Sheih ran each slide, working frantically to locate any magenta-colored anthrax rods on the landscape of tissue. By 1:00 A.M., Zaki had found only two, both on one of the last slides, at opposite ends. But that was enough. O'Connor's tissue sample had tested positive by immunohistochemical staining for the cell-wall antigen of *B. anthracis*. An hour later, Mayor Rudolph Giuliani was on the phone with the CDC. He wanted to make a public announcement, but was getting conflicting information. Army analysts, studying some of the same tissue as Zaki, had found no rods. Since the St. Petersburg letter was a hoax, the question was: "How and where had O'Connor gotten infected with anthrax?"

The cutaneous variety she had contracted was the most common type. When treated with penicillin it was rarely lethal. With treatment virtually all cutaneous patients survive; without treatment some 80 percent survive. The fatality rate is approximately 20 percent and death occurs only if generalized blood poisoning ensues. With antibiotic treatment the rate of fatality is only 1 percent. Antibiotics often are effective, as in the case of Brokaw's assistant, even after the skin lesion turns black.

Cutaneous anthrax is contracted when spores breach the skin through minor cuts and abrasions. Underneath the surface, they flourish into toxin-producing bacteria that assault surrounding tissue. The body responds by sending immune cells to consume the invading microbes. However, as in the case of inhalational anthrax, the poison spreads as immune cells carry microbes back to lymph nodes and infect them too. After an incubation stage of one to twelve days, a painless, depressed, black scar (usually with surrounding water-filled swelling) develops. It is the black scablike crust that gives the disease its name—*anthracis*—the Latin translation of the Greek word for coal, *anthrakis*.

On Friday, October 12, O'Connor was at home recovering. When the FBI reinterviewed her by phone, she suddenly remembered a second envelope addressed to Brokaw. It had been received within a week of the St. Petersburg letter and filed in an interoffice folder reserved for questionable mail. At the time she hadn't thought much of it, but now recalled that a "dark, sand-like powder" had spilled out. Following her directions, an NBC security guard took the elevator down to her third-floor office. He quickly found the folder in her drawer. Inside was the missing letter. He decided to open it for further examination in a second-floor mailroom, then returned to the sixteenth-floor security office. Now the elevator and the second, third, and sixteenth floors were contaminated.

It was still very early Friday morning when NYPD officers, with the Brokaw letter in a plastic bag, raced up to the city health department lab. "They took it to our lab," said the city deputy health commissioner, Dr. Isaac Weisfuse, "and the handling of it caused a contamination event at our lab later that day. The police didn't know how to handle samples." As anthrax powder puffed out of the envelope in clouds, two of the three lab workers inhaled it. Unlike their counterparts at the CDC, the technicians had never been offered anthrax vaccines. The two men took Cipro then conducted nose swab tests on themselves. After both technicians tested positive, they were too traumatized to continue work. The lab was sealed until cleanup could be accomplished and this delayed analysis of the second Brokaw letter.

However, so few spores remained in the envelope after the sandy powder was spilled that the FBI asked the Army to delay any analysis. What remained was heavily adulterated with "vegetative cells," which in dry anthrax powder are generally dead and therefore harmless. Vegetative cells are anthrax bacteria before processing in the lab converts them into hardened spores. What the FBI and the Army needed was one of the anthrax letters unopened. They could not imagine how that could happen.

Once they had their sample, Army specialists still had to grow the suspected anthrax spores in a nutrient medium until they germinated into live, rod-shaped bacterial cells. Unidentified gram-positive bacilli growing on agar may be considered as contaminant. The lab would attempt to characterize the organism by further biochemical testing—motility testing, inhibition by penicillin, and absence of hemollysis on sheep blood agar. If *B. anthracis* was present, antibodies in a test kit would bind to antigens on its surface and the antibodies fluoresce. An antigen is any molecule capable of simulating an immune response. An antibody is a protein made by B lymphocytes that react with a specific antigen.

Reporter Judith Miller had not yet heard about O'Connor's anthrax infection. At 9:15 A.M., Friday, October 12, she was busy at her desk at the *New York Times*'s 43rd Street headquarters between 8th Avenue and Broadway. As the author of a new bestseller—*Germs: Biological Weapons and America's Secret War* (with coauthors Stephen Engelberg and William Broad Miller), Miller had her share of odd mail. As she completed a phone call, she distractedly slit open a stamped business-type envelope, failing to notice it had no return address. The plain letter was postmarked St. Petersburg, Florida, a retirement town about two hundred miles from AMI, on the Gulf of Mexico. A cloud of talcumlike powder puffed over her.

"It looked like baby powder," Miller wrote later. "A cloud of hospital white, sweet-smelling powder rose from the letter—dusting my face, sweater and hands. The heavier particles dropped to the floor, falling on my pants and shoes. 'An anthrax hoax,' I thought." Had Miller left some touchy bioweapons expert out of her comprehensive book? Was it professional jealousy? She and her coauthors had spoken to most of the experts.

Bioweapons expert William C. Patrick III was the former chief of product development in the Army's offensive biological weapons program at the U.S. Army Medical Research Institute of Infectious Diseases (USAMRIID) at Fort Detrick, Maryland. Those in the know called it the Institute. When the nation abandoned germ weapons in the early 1970s, Bill Patrick became a private consultant on biological defense. He had also been a knowledgeable source for Miller's book. He had told her spores were sometimes cut with baby powder to mask them with a smell that was reassuringly familiar. "Anthrax has no smell," he said, "and is hardly ever white."

And so, because the unsigned note threatened President Bush and the Sears Tower in Chicago, Miller asked a nearby reporter to ring security. Just then her phone rang with news that Tom Brokaw's assistant had contracted anthrax from powder in a letter she had opened in late September. The FBI thought it had had a Florida postmark. Security guards in gloves arrived, placed Miller's letter and envelope in a plastic garbage bag, tossed their gloves in after it, and sealed the bag. Miller washed her hands in the rest room and tried as best she could to rub the powder from her pants and shoes. When she returned, a senior editor put his arm around her and walked her to the medical department on another floor. When Miller got back, other editors rushed to her side and brought her tea.

Within twenty minutes, investigators, police ambulance service, and police officers wearing gas masks and light brown head-to-toe biohazard suits rushed into the office to check out the suspicious letter. Miller stayed with them, pointing where the powder had fallen and answering questions about anyone she might know in Florida. The men took photos, performed tests, and evacuated two newsroom floors, leaving Miller's floor silent except for continually ringing phones. Outside the street was cordoned off. Miller would have to wait to learn whether the powder contained anthrax. An antigen test supplied to federal and local authorities could be performed in fifteen minutes to determine if anthrax spores were present; however, it was often unreliable.

Newsweek reporter Jonathan Alter was a lot closer to the crime scene than he wanted. His desk was about fifty feet from where the exposure took place. As part of his part-time job as contributing correspondent for NBC News, he kept an office on the third floor of 30 Rockefeller Center. That floor was now sealed off by men in Hazmat moon suits. Only a short time before, employees had been eating pizza near where the powder had fallen. Alter wondered if they were safe.

The cast of *Saturday Night Live* was rehearsing floors above in Studio 8-H. They had been on hiatus from June through August and recently returned. Will Ferrell, Tina Fey, Ana Gasteyer, Darrell Hammond, Rachel Dratch, Jimmy Fallon, and the rest of the comedy stars were evacuated from the building. Marci Klein, the show's talent coordinator, who lived downtown near the World Trade Center, was not at work the day they discovered anthrax at 30 Rock. "I was at home," she reported, "and when I called my office after hearing the news, a lot of people there were obviously hysterical. Drew Barrymore was the guest host for that week's show, and she said, 'I am going to leave, calm myself down, and go back to my hotel.' I completely understood. Then I made sure to tell everyone that if they didn't feel comfortable staying in the building, they should go home. Some people did say, 'I am getting out of here, and I will come back when it is fine.' It was a very scary situation, just horrible. I calmed Drew down, but I felt bad for her. Everyone thought she had left town and she didn't. She stayed and she did the show. And this show is really scary to do under the best of circumstances."

Steve Higgins, also of *Saturday Night Live*, said, "Marci was in control on the anthrax crisis, and so it's one of those things where you go, 'Too many cooks spoil the broth. If they need me they will call me.' I did talk to Drew about it after she talked to the doctor. She was freaked out in the beginning, but then in the end she put on that game face and went ahead with it."

At midday, O'Connor sent word she was more concerned about her coworkers at NBC than about herself. "Anthrax is not contagious," Alter wrote, "but fear is." At 30 Rock the line of people waiting to be tested "looked like a soup kitchen at Thanksgiving. Two hours, minimum," Alter said. People were given an option to come back later or wait. Most waited. People even cut in line to be tested. Inside, they filled out several forms and were asked about symptoms: "Where and when were you in the building in respect to the hot spot?" "What about vents in offices?" After questioning by agents, they had their nostrils swabbed, but that is not a reliable test for anthrax.

The NYC Department of Health had little data on inhalation anthrax. Once pulmonary symptoms appear, the spores have already germinated and begun to release toxins like a deadly flowering garden. Thirty "Rockers" were given Cipro starting immediately after exposure. Since the mortality rate for inhalational anthrax was so high—90 percent—a patient must take the antibiotic for two months to be effective.

"I had been on the third floor," said an MSNBC staffer. "I remember the date because it was my boyfriend's birthday—October 8, 2001. And they didn't take away the letter until the twelfth of October. I came over from New Jersey when it was announced that Tom Brokaw's assistant had cutaneous anthrax. At MSNBC we had a lot of military, terrorism, and former FBI people all sitting around. I told them, 'Oh, my God, I was in the building.' 'You better go in,' they said. 'You don't know if it was weaponized.' I went in Friday and the line was so incredibly long that I couldn't get in. I went back two days later and went right in and they tested me. I was given enough Cipro for a month. I took it for a week and then I got an e-mail that my test had come back negative and I could stop taking the medication. I had people calling me up and saying, 'I heard you had to go on Cipro!' 'It's OK,' I said, 'I'm all right.' It was just a horrible time in New York coming so soon after 9-11."

NBC Nightly News was moved across the street to the *Today* set. "This is outrageous and maddening beyond my ability to express in socially acceptable terms," an exhausted Brokaw told his viewers. Later, he choked up over his assistant suffering for an attack probably intended for him.

Environmental sampling revealed anthrax contamination of the NBC third-floor Rockefeller Center work site, specifically implicating mail and package delivery. The *Virginian-Pilot* later reported that "protective gear, office equipment, papers, carpets" were to be incinerated at Norfolk.

After the announcement of O'Connor's anthrax, doctors at the NYU Medical Center attending the ABC producer's infant son considered a possible diagnosis of cutaneous anthrax. A skin biopsy from the hospitalized infant was hurried to the CDC for testing. The child was bleeding internally. On October 15, the sample would test positive by staining for the cell-wall antigen of anthrax. A serum specimen collected ten days earlier would test positive for *B. anthracis*. No suspicious letter was identified at his mother's workplace; like the AMI letter, it had vanished into limbo. Mother and child, treated with Cipro, clinically improved.

B. anthracis grew from swabs (two nasal and one facial skin swab) from three other workers, suggesting exposure to anthrax. One of the exposures was in a law enforcement officer who brought the letter containing anthrax from NBC to the receiving laboratory. The other two exposures were in the technicians who had processed the letter in the laboratory. Environmental sampling in both workplaces was ongoing. Investigations of other exposed persons continued. Some of the adults were placed on ciprofloxacin or doxycycline, and the treatment was to continue until sixty days after final opportunity for exposure.

The first reports of anthrax letters to the media appeared in the press. As word of O'Connor's infection spread, New Yorkers rushed to have themselves tested. The proper procedure was a very sensitive first test, then more specific follow-up tests—such as PCR. If PCR is positive, then aggressive environmental samples, nasal swabs, sputum, and blood, as well as cerebrospinal fluid in suspected meningitis cases, should be obtained. Dr. Meryl Nass, a biological warfare epidemiologist, thought patients should be treated prior to any signs of illness. "I would propose consideration of bronchoalveolar lavage in highly exposed patients," she said. This is a technique in which a doctor instills salt water through a bronchoscope. When the saline is suctioned back it carries any cells and bacteria with it.

President Bush asked all Americans to live their lives as normally as possible. "Our government is doing everything we can to make our country as safe as possible," the President said. Vice President Cheney said there may be links between the domestic anthrax incidents and September 11 and Osama bin Laden. "I think the only responsible thing for us to do," Cheney told PBS's Jim Lehrer, "is proceed on the basis it could be linked." But Cheney knew at this point he could not prove it. An earlier Pentagon briefing had revealed that bin Laden's global network had the ability to produce biological weapons of mass destruction.

Officials also assured the nation that anthrax spores could not leak out of a sealed envelope, and certainly not in quantities enough to cause the most dangerous form of the disease, inhalational anthrax. Should a spore or two escape, they said, they would at worst cause a case or two of very treatable cutaneous anthrax. But how had the Hamilton mail workers been infected? None of the envelopes had been opened in their presence.

In Columbus, Ohio, three employees of the *Columbus Dispatch* remained in quarantine after one of them opened a Halloween card and found a powdery substance. The card had a Dayton postmark, but no return address. A preliminary report on the powder was expected late Friday, October 12, from the Ohio Department of Health.

On that day, CNN, the *Los Angeles Times,* and the *San Jose Mercury News* stopped accepting outside mail. The *Miami Herald* continued to provide latex gloves to concerned employees just as it had since Bob Stevens had died seven days earlier. The New York offices of *Newsweek,* the AP, ABC, and CBS stopped mail deliveries to staffers as a precaution. The Fox News Channel received a questionable envelope filled with a powdery substance. All of their mailroom workers were tested. The woman who got the envelope tested negative for anthrax exposure.

Senator John McCain gave an interview to *USA Today* columnist Walter Shapiro on the subject of fear. "The way you live with fear is that you suppress it," McCain said. "Anyone who is faced with a life-threatening situation will have fear. Anyone who says they don't is either crazy or a liar. The trick is to channel it into productive missions and activities. That's the way I've handled it in the past." He might have been commenting on the events that came later that morning.

At noon on that Friday, McCain was already en route to Arizona when it was announced that Brokaw's assistant had contracted anthrax from a letter addressed to Brokaw. She had developed skin anthrax on September 25, but was diagnosed several days after opening a letter that contained white powder. Until then only AMI had been hit. Now a second news outlet had been attacked. It was an attack designed to rivet attention of the public and guarantee coverage and widespread panic.

That night from Phoenix, McCain spoke on Chris Matthews's show, *Hardball*, on CNBC. "I think you have to realize there is reason to fear," he said, "but you have to suppress it. You have to channel it, and it can be beneficial in a way because it will make you more alert. It will make you more efficient. And it will make you more aware of everything that's going on around you. You know, Ernest Hemingway's famous definition of courage was 'grace under pressure.' And basically that's what he was saying. You've got to show grace under pressure and that grace is to go on with your life, not let it rule you, not let it overcome you."

It had been one month since the tragedy at the WTC. As the first reports of anthrax letters made their way into the media, the FBI was speaking of multiple mailed envelopes from St. Petersburg. Later on Friday, police closed in on First Avenue N where the main post office in St. Petersburg was. Shortly after 5:00 P.M. St. Petersburg police chief Mack Vines's intelligence officers came to his office to inform him of what was going on. The FBI was investigating multiple mailed letters from there. Vines's detectives were working with them, the U.S. Postal Service, and the Manhattan homicide squad of the NYPD.

"We're on top of the issue," he told the press. "We're working with the Bureau to determine if we can identify any type of situation relating to the postmark. We're just trying to develop any kind of information that would tie in to something like that. We'll see if we can trace some of these things back."

At 10:00 P.M. paramedics rushed to the mail processing center in St. Petersburg to check some workers who were complaining of headaches and other symptoms. They thought they had been exposed to something a couple of days earlier.

In New York, Mayor Rudolph Giuliani, flanked by Police Commissioner Bernard Kerik and FBI agent Barry Mawn, conducted a press conference. All they knew was an assistant to Tom Brokaw had opened a "threatening" letter to her boss and come down with the skin form of anthrax. Giuliani said two suspicious letters postmarked from St. Petersburg had been sent to NBC and the *New York Times*. He criticized the FBI for being slow to react. There were "some similarities," said Mawn, between the NBC and *Times* handwriting on the letters. The *New York*

Times assured its readers that no copies of the newspaper had been printed in their Manhattan headquarters.

Doctors would confirm Richard Morgano's cutaneous anthrax on October 17 and Claire Fletcher's and mail carrier Teresa Heller's cases the following day. At first the CDC thought Heller might have handled one or more terrorist letters before they reached the Hamilton Mail Processing Center, but when the FBI began an investigation for possible suspects along her route, they found none. And if she had delivered contaminated mail then why weren't any illnesses reported along her route? Now authorities suspected she might have become infected by mail that had picked up spores at Hamilton before being sent to the West Trenton Post Office where Heller picked up mail for her route.

There had been so many recent hoaxes (such as the bogus St. Petersburg envelope), that an actual anthrax letter might have been discarded after infecting some unknowing person. Since Amerithrax had used pre-metered envelopes, sold at post office vending machines in sets of five, the total number of letters mailed might be that number. If his mailing to the media was five letters, and NBC, CBS, ABC, and possibly AMI amounted to four lethal letters—where was the fifth anthrax letter? A deadly, unsuspected fifth time bomb might be ticking away somewhere in New York.

People in the city, still gasping amongst the deadly unbreathable residue of 9-11, had discovered that they might also be breathing an invisible pathogen. Mid-October testing had shown significant asbestos contamination in the indoor air of buildings within a radius of a quarter-mile of Ground Zero. After the collapse of the Twin Towers, Kevin Mount, a heavy-equipment operator, and many other sanitation workers had been driving dump trucks filled with debris away from Ground Zero. His only safety equipment was a paper dust mask. As time went by, he became sicker. "His breathing is deteriorating each day," his wife said. "He can't walk up a flight of stairs without being out of breath." The nation felt that way too.

STRAIN 6

The Lost Letter

ON SATURDAY, OCTOBER 13, 2001, the day after Erin O'Connor tested positive for cutaneous anthrax, the NBC bioattack was reported in depth. If, somewhere in New York, an unsuspected anthrax letter was leaking invisible death, the coverage might bring it to light. As for where it could be, the detectives realized that Amerithrax had targeted all three major networks based in New York. They ticked them off: an NBC letter addressed to Tom Brokaw, an ABC letter addressed to Peter Jennings, and a CBS letter to Dan Rather. When Rather's twenty-seven-year-old assistant Claire Fletcher contracted cutaneous anthrax, he was heartbreakingly distraught on the *David Letterman Show*. He collapsed in Letterman's arms, the stress of 9-11 and the recent attack at his office weighing heavily on his shoulders. One bad break for the investigators was that all the anthrax-laced letters and envelopes but Brokaw's had been destroyed before anyone became aware how deadly they were and how many clues they might offer. As for other targets, a suspicious letter addressed to the Fox News Channel's Bill O'Reilly had shown up sometime after October 8. The phony return address listed the name of Sean Hannity, another of FNC's top personalities. Shortly before October 13, CBS News in Washington, D.C., had received an envelope with powder visible on the outside. A total of fifteen letters to the media had been mailed from Indianapolis, Indiana. These were apparently part of that mailing.

One had been mailed to the Indianapolis FBI. Another had gone to the Defense Security Service, part of the Department of Defense located in Indianapolis. The last was posted to the Community Oriented Policing Services in Washington, D.C. All said, "You die now." Police arrested an Indianapolis man for sending three hoax letters doused with white powder. Released on bond, the suspect promptly vanished.

On October 9, an envelope had arrived addressed to: MR HOWARD TROXLER, ST. PETERSBURG TIMES, ST. PETERSBURG-FL. 33701+ 4204. It had no return address, though the postmark indicated the letter had been collected south of St. Petersburg at the beginning of October. That covered a lot of ground—Seminole, Largo, Gulfport, Bay Pines—in mid-Pineullas County. The "337" meant it had been processed at the main post office on First Avenue N. As the columnist opened the enveloped a white salt- or sugarlike substance had spilled onto his desk.

"HOWARD TOXLER [*sic*]," ran the wavering blockprinting,

1ST CASE OF DISEASE NOW BLOW AWAY THIS DUST SO YOU SEE HOW THE REAL THING FLYS. OKALHOMA-RYDER TRUCK! SKYWAY BRIDGE—18 WHEELS.

This letter, like the others, was filled with misspellings. The writer was not familiar printing all capital letters. He had dotted the uppercase "I."

At least the crank knew Chicago geography. Judith Miller's letter (mailed from St. Petersburg on the same day) had mentioned the Sears Tower in Chicago. However, by day's end Troxler and his desk had tested negative for presence of anthrax and other pathogens, and so had Miller, whose letter was found to contain only talcum.

Could the hoax letters to Miller and Troxler have been perpetrated by Amerithrax? They were different from the Brokaw letter, though. The writer had affixed them with thirty-four-cent stamps. The envelopes were different sizes. If Amerithrax had sent them too, then he had been in New Jersey on September 18 and in Florida two days later.

The fact that the St. Petersburg mailing contained fake anthrax might mean only that Amerithrax kept his supply in New Jersey. The choice of St. Petersburg as a return address also had a double meaning, at least to those involved in engineering bioweapons. St. Petersburg, Russia, was the site of a facility represented as a civilian pharmaceutical and medical complex. Actually, it was a secret lab where four hundred scientists had toiled developing anaerobic bacteria for antidote-resistant bioweapons. That bacteria, dried and ground into powder, had once been packed into munitions shells aimed at the West.

Bob Stevens or others at AMI had probably received similar hoax letters before, but since they were so used to seeing them, an authentic terrorist letter had probably been dismissed as a hoax. The missing J-Lo letter may have been mailed from St. Petersburg, not so far from Boca Raton. But if Amerithrax had sent hoax letters as dry runs, they still might contain a clue to his identity. The postmark on the September 20 letter to NBC led postal officials and the FBI to converge at the main post office in St. Petersburg. They were frustrated when they learned that the Postal Service had no way of tracking a single letter to its source. Investigators were impeded on another front. They had still not found a link between the 9-11 terrorist attacks and the letters.

That afternoon, a check to a vendor in Malaysia was returned intact to a Microsoft office in Reno, Nevada. The envelope not only contained the uncashed check, but pornographic pictures snipped from a magazine and dusted with "anthrax spores." Though reported as testing positive for anthrax, the powder turned out to be another hoax.

THE TERRORISM PRESIDENT Bill Clinton had witnessed during his presidency[4] had included a growing number of hoaxes in which people claimed to have dispersed deadly biological agents like anthrax. Of the 128 such fakes reported in the twentieth century, 57 had occurred since 1984. All but 10 took place in the 1990s. "The radical right may or may not possess the expertise necessary to launch effective biological attacks here in America," author Daniel Levitas writes, "but in the wake of 9-11, there is no shortage of highly charged racial issues for hate groups to inflame and exploit." Right-wing activists had already stockpiled a number of bio-agents.

When the FBI raided the Arkansas compound of the Covenant, the

---

[4] Thirty-five days after Bill Clinton took office in January 1993, Islamic radicals detonated a bomb under New York City's largest building complex, the World Trade Center. Collapsing walls, smoke, and fires claimed the lives of six people and injured almost a thousand.

Sword, and the Arm of the Lord in 1985 they unearthed thirty-three gallons of cyanide. Four members of the Minnesota Patriots Council were arrested and convicted for possessing ricin, the potent toxin derived from the beans of the castor plant. Ricin acts swiftly and irreversibly and is thousands of times deadlier than cyanide and twice as deadly as VX nerve agent. The Patriots intended to smear this favorite tool of assassins onto auto steering wheels and doorknobs to kill law enforcement authorities. In 1993 Arkansas survivalist Thomas Lewis Lavy also smuggled ricin in from Canada.

In 1995 in Ohio, a right-wing Army veteran, white supremacist, survivalist, and Aryan Nations member named Larry Wayne Harris placed an order with the nonprofit American Type Culture Collection in Rockville, Maryland, a nonprofit biological supply house for academic and government researchers. Using the state lab license number of the water treatment plant where he worked as a microbiologist, Harris ordered three vials of freeze-dried bubonic plague for $240. Since requests for such dangerous pathogens were required to be made on the letterhead of a university or laboratory, Harris manufactured his own stationery. The order was still being processed when he phoned ATCC less than two weeks later to ask why his order was taking so long. Company officials grew suspicious (legitimate medical researchers knew it normally takes a month to fill an order) and turned him in. Harris eventually pleaded guilty to one count of mail fraud and operating a lab without a license—the most serious charges under existing law at the time. He was sentenced to eighteen months probation.

In 1998, Harris was rearrested in Las Vegas and his car quarantined after he bragged of possessing "weapons-grade anthrax . . . enough to wipe out a city." His "anthrax" turned out to be a harmless veterinary medicine, an innocuous vaccine strain that didn't give people the disease, but triggered an immunity to it. The charge was dropped. Harris then self-published *Biological Warfare: A Major Threat to North America*, a do-it-yourself manual for "mass destruction."

A discussion of Harris dominated a March 6, 1996, Senate Judiciary Committee hearing. "It is apparent," said the committee's chairman, Orrin G. Hatch of Utah, "that there has been kind of an ignoring of the potentials for harm." Partly as a result of this incident, Congress passed a law in April 1996 requiring germ banks and biotech firms in the U.S. to check the identity of all prospective buyers. Weeks later, Congress passed a law that imposed tough requirements on the domestic disbursement of pathogens and made it a crime to threaten a biological attack. The two hundred U.S. labs that kept germ collections would now have to register and submit to federal inspections. By the time the law was passed, it was already too late. Lethal anthrax was already in the hands of terrorists.

In late 1997 and continuing into the next year, anthrax hoaxes became a fad. In 1998, the FBI arrested two would-be terrorists in Las Vegas. The two had planned to release anthrax bacilli into the atmosphere. In this case their anthrax turned out to really be anthrax, but of a nonpathogenic vaccine strain. In California alone, over the last two weeks of December there had been a baker's dozen of anthrax hoaxes. On December 27, 1998, in Pomona, California, police received a call claiming that anthrax had been released in the Glass House nightclub. Seven hundred and fifty guests were quarantined inside the club for four hours.

By the spring of 1999, reports of anthrax hoaxes to the FBI reached two to three per day. Approximately 180 of them were anthrax threats. Over the last two years white powders had been mailed to courthouses, schools, various Florida magazine publishers, churches, and abortion clinics. Phony anthrax was dispersed among shoppers in California. Those threatened showered vigorously and took antibiotics. In Mill Valley, California, a powder was left in a teacher's mailbox at Tamalpais High along with a threatening note. Toxicology tests came back negative for anthrax. However, these false alarms triggered civil defense responses involving the police, paramedics, emergency care physicians, and firefighters. Anthrax hoaxes shut down post offices and stores and sent Hazmat teams scrambling. They created such widespread panic that one expert remarked, "There is no reason that the hoaxes may not be the strategy of a terrorist."

In January 2001, twenty-five anthrax threats were received across the U.S. and Canada. A typical case occurred at a Wal-Mart in Victoria, British Columbia, where a letter was received that was claimed to contain anthrax. The clerk who opened it was given a precautionary dose of Cipro, but testing determined the powder was not anthrax.

Also that year two office buildings in Trenton, New Jersey, were evacuated after workers opened packages containing a white powder—another false alarm. There were no traces of any actual pathogens. An Internal Revenue office in Covington, Kentucky, was sealed off and two hundred employees quarantined because of a harmless powder. Brown powder in an envelope was sent to a state agency in Ohio. A Halloween card filled with yellow powder arrived at the *Columbus Dispatch*. Yellow powder in an envelope opened by an Ohio couple in October 2001 was accompanied by a note that read: "You are now infected with anthrax."

In the midst of a national anthrax panic, Kamal Dawood, a Palestinian construction worker, tossed fistfuls of yellowish-brownish powder into a Brooklyn mailbox outside an elementary school. Although tests proved the powder was not anthrax, the charge against him was threatening to use a weapon of mass destruction—the anthrax that people thought he had tossed on the mail. If convicted, he could face life in prison.

On the same day, a Maine woman mailed a taped envelope addressed in block letters to her friend Janice at the post office in Somersworth, New Hampshire, as a joke. "I specifically chose [table] salt," she said later, "because it was granular, and I thought it would be impossible to mistake it for anything else, certainly nothing that would hang in the air and get into someone's lungs. It was very spur of the moment." The envelope (which was alleged to have leaked onto a postal worker) contained no threatening communication. Thus, the first trial of a person charged with committing an anthrax hoax would end in acquittal.

A Los Angeles fire captain mailed a letter containing a check impregnated with powder to his ex-wife's divorce lawyer. The draft was inscribed with the words "choke on it." He had allegedly mailed similar envelopes before 9-11, but those acts went unnoticed and unpunished. But now the nation was in a panic. He struck a deal with the government that reduced his crime from a felony to a misdemeanor.

Also in October 2001, while AMI employees were still being inoculated, a first wave of anthrax hoax letters were sent to almost 280 Midwestern abortion clinics and women's reproductive health clinics. They were delivered through the U.S. Postal Service on October 15, with the return addresses of "US Marshall Service" and "US Secret Service." A second wave the following month traveled by Federal Express. All were from a common source and signed "the Army of God." According to the letter writer, a father of nine, God had told him to kill abortion doctors. The envelopes for the October letters were marked TIME SENSITIVE and URGENT SECURITY NOTICE ENCLOSED. The text read: "You have chosen a profession which profits from the senseless murder of millions of innocent children each year . . . we are going to kill you. This is your notice. Stop now or die."

The FBI lab analyzed all but seventy-four of the letters and determined the envelopes had been prepared using four-color ink-jet printing. Chemistry Unit personnel examined the powders—flour and chalk dust. They tested negative for anthrax. However, fingerprints recovered from a Federal Express receipt from the second wave of letters sent three weeks later turned out to belong to a self-described "anti-abortion warrior" already on the FBI's Ten Most Wanted Fugitives List. The previous February, while awaiting sentencing for a 1999 federal firearms violation, Clayton Lee Waagner had escaped from an Illinois jail. During a ten-month crime spree of carjacking and robbing banks, the forty-five-year-old fugitive took a break. He visited a onetime friend, Neal Horsley, in Georgia the day after Thanksgiving. Waagner told him he had mailed the threatening letters, targeting forty-two abortion clinics.

Waagner was rearrested in December near Cincinnati, Ohio, after being recognized by a sharp-eyed Kinko's clerk. Waagner now claimed responsibility for mailing more than 550 letters filled with powder. U.S. District Judge Susan Dlott would sentence Waagner to nineteen years and seven months in prison on firearms and theft charges. She ordered him to serve the term after completing a thirty-year sentence in Illinois on escape and other charges. Waagner said he would appeal. "I'm not remorseful," Waagner told Dlott. "I'm not begging for forgiveness for what I did, because I thought it was right." On the same day, Attorney General John Ashcroft ordered Justice Department lawyers to get tough and prosecute all alleged anthrax hoaxers.

"The anthrax killings are exactly the kind of crime that screams 'copycats,' " former FBI profiler Candice DeLong said. "I worked the Tylenol murders back in the eighties. In thirty days there were one hundred verified copycats and some of them serious enough to kill people. This is the same kind of crime. You've got a whole lot of weirdos in this country that don't know how to handle their anger and they're in their basements and they see something like this and say, 'That's a good idea.' They've been thinking about it all along anyway and then they just come out of the woodwork pretty much riding on the coattails of the first person who did it."

Most perpetrators of copycat threats have been Americans: individual scientists or physicians with grudges against colleagues, former spouses, or employers; or white supremacists acting alone or in small groups. One case even involved a Massachusetts grandmother who had mailed eighteen threatening letters to the Massachusetts state attorney general. Six of them held white powder. The Postal Service aggressively investigated more than eighty such hoaxes a year. Fifty-seven people had been charged with state and federal crimes for allegedly committing bioterrorism hoaxes—but not one had ever sent actual anthrax through the mail—until now.

But what of the missing New York letter? Perhaps, since there is a Division of Dead Letters, there should be a division of deadly letters, of anthrax letters not yet found.

ON FRIDAY, OCTOBER 19, 2001, a *New York Post* entertainment writer, Joanna Huden, thirty-one, was confirmed with cutaneous anthrax. At the beginning of the month she had gone to NYU Medical Center with a blister on the knuckle above her right middle finger. She thought it might be a spider bite. However, photos of O'Connor's anthrax wound, shown on the news, alerted her. The FBI rushed to the *Post* to see if they could learn where she had contracted the disease. On the same day, a male coworker of Huden's began showing visible signs of cutaneous anthrax. Now investigators, certain they had narrowed the site of the contagion, launched an intensive search of the *Post*'s mailroom and offices. They already had a good idea of the timeline. Huden had shown her first symptoms on September 22, shortly after Amerithrax had mailed the Brokaw letter. The male coworker had been infected much later. His cutaneous anthrax infection would be positively confirmed three days later, proof that the letter might still be on the premises. A *Post* memo a week earlier had asked employees to hunt through their work areas for any suspicious mail and place it in a bin for later testing. Huden's coworker might have been infected during one of those searches.

A *Post* employee also recalled opening an envelope filled with powder, but believed that letter had been thrown out sometime earlier. The search for the lethal envelope trailed into the afternoon. Police found the envelope Friday evening in the *Post* mailroom. It was another of those prestamped post office envelopes, postmarked "Trenton, NJ 09/18/2001 (Tues.)" and processed at the mail processing center in Hamilton Township. It was addressed in the same style of blockprinting as the Brokaw envelope, but said:

EDITOR, NEW YORK POST
1211 AVE. OF THE AMERICAS
NEW YORK NY 10036 + 6701

The letter was still unopened after its delivery. This was because people had been warned not to open letters without return addresses. In any case, anthrax spores had gotten out of the sealed envelope. While hunting down the discarded anthrax letter, another employee at the *Post* contracted anthrax. The active search may have disturbed spores from their resting place and spread them throughout the office. They may have leaked from a split in the office mailbag. Mark Cunningham, thirty-eight, another of the newspaper's employees, would see the onset of cutaneous anthrax symptoms on October 23, and have that confirmed five days later.

Yet the FBI conducted no interviews with people who cleaned the mailrooms where loose anthrax had been tossed into trash baskets or spoke with people who had handled that trash. Before being discovered, the letter had gotten damp or wet somehow. The envelope showed a water stain in the upper left-hand corner. Had it rained the day it was mailed or had it been kept inside a plastic bag where water droplets might have sweated against the plastic? It might have been kept in a refrigerator or packed with dry ice during transit. Whatever the reason, the "relatively crude" powder inside had turned to mush. Dampness caused the anthrax to clump together. Another one-page letter inside, stained with water along the right side, read exactly like the anthrax letter O'Connor received:

09-11-01

THIS IS NEXT
TAKE PENACILIN NOW
DEATH TO AMERICA
DEATH TO ISRAEL
ALLAH IS GREAT

It was a Xerox copy of the Brokaw letter, which had been a copy of an original that had probably been destroyed by now. The *Post* letter had not been flat when copied. Amerithrax had held it at a slightly different angle. And the Xeroxes differed in one other aspect. The *Post* letter had been trimmed with scissors to a slightly different size. The investigators could tell from the irregular edges. This letter measured 165 millimeters wide and 230 millimeters long. The one-page handprinted Brokaw letter had been cut practically square. This letter had 50 millimeters cut from the side and bottom.

Both letters had been trimmed from standard copy paper 215 millimeters wide by 279 millimeters long. Why? And what was the purpose of the four odd folds on each page?

And why the *New York Post*? Wouldn't the *New York Times*, a venerable, respected institution, be a more fitting symbol of America as a terrorist target? Why was a hoax letter sent to Miller and not one laced with anthrax? Did Amerithrax read the *Post*, a workingman's paper with a big circulation? It seemed Amerithrax was after a larger audience. He wanted his actions reported, but his letters had been too subtle. He had neglected to mention anthrax by name. He would remedy that.

"We are in the middle of a war," the *New York Post* editorialized. But who was waging it against America? Agents drove the *Post* letter, containing a small damp amount of a powdery substance, to the U.S. Army Medical Research Institute at Fort Detrick, Maryland.

STRAIN 7

A Place of Interest

THEY CALLED IT the Institute. Like anthrax itself, the Institute had begun life in a cow pasture. For a decade the National Guard had used the field as an airport and training camp for pilots. But in 1942, the Army selected old Detrick Field, with its rocks and open fields of buttercups and red clover, to become the home of its offensive biological weapons program. Overnight, the pasture mushroomed into "Camp" Detrick. Like multiplying bacteria, 250 buildings and quarters for five thousand swarmed over this stretch of rustic farmland. Nestled in the foothills of the Catoctin Mountains of western Maryland, the camp occupied fifteen hundred acres in Frederick County some forty miles northwest of Washington, D.C. To the north of the facility stood Woodsboro and the Monocacy River. To the east lay Ceresville and to the south, Buckeystown and Frederick.

By April 1943, that rural field, a distant memory, was crawling with more than seventeen hundred officers and enlisted personnel from every branch of the armed services. The pasture had been transformed into the top secret Institute—the brain center of the nation's bioweapons program. From the beginning there were constant security fears. Every scientist endured a six-month-long background check. A top secret clearance was a prerequisite to work at the prestigious hub of the U.S. germ warfare research. The Army issued a .45-caliber side arm to each of its scientists and ordered them to keep the weapons within easy reach on their workbenches.

Every page of lab research, all testing and reports, each phase of small-scale production, technical papers, and intercourse with industry and universities were initiated and integrated through the maximum-security encampment. During World War II, the technicians who toiled at the Institute were surrounded by barbed-wire fences, floodlit towers, and guards with machine guns. German shepherds strained at their leashes as sentries patrolled the wooden, tarpapered margin of "Black Maria," the Institute's first offensive biological weapons lab. The Army charged the technicians of "Black Maria" with developing an efficient biological delivery system. "Get the germs to the enemy forces as intact and deadly as when they began," they ordered. Inspired by British tests at Porton Down, the scientists briefly considered using flies as anthrax carriers.

Institute scientists regularly investigated dysentery, glanders, typhus, and brucellosis. Brucellosis, like anthrax, was a disease found in cattle. Like anthrax it was not transmittable by humans, but contracted by direct contact with secretions and excretions of infected animals such as contaminated milk products. The symptoms were remarkably like those of anthrax, including enlarged lymph nodes, joint pain, chills, fatigue, and long-lasting high fever. And like anthrax, brucellosis could be spread by aerosol. Unlike anthrax, brucellosis, with only a 5 percent fatality rate, was antibiotic resistant. The Institute cultivated botulism, smallpox, plague, paralytic shellfish poison, and cholera. Cholera bacteria thrived in water, while other pathogens did not. Cholera's stability in water made it perfect for contaminating reservoirs. But anthrax, called a "professional pathogen" because of its hardiness, was the hands-down choice of most bioweapons engineers. It remained the Institute's biggest and most successful project.

During the prewar years, the Soviet Union and Britain had already added anthrax to their arsenals. The Institute's pilot plant produced anthrax in ten-thousand-gallon tanks. The U.S. plant was so successful that, in September 1944, Britain ordered five hundred thousand bomblets that would each emit an ounce of anthrax mist that, if left untreated, would kill nearly every infected person. None of the weapons developed were ever used.

Between 1945 and 1950, the United States, along with Britain and the

Soviet Union, continued postwar bioweapons research, evaluating agents that had shown the most promise. The Institute would travel anywhere on earth to collect a sample of any deadly disease. In 1956, they developed agriculture agents to attack the Soviet wheat crop and Communist China rice paddies. They stored the pathogens at Rocky Mountain Arsenal near Denver (which also manufactured plutonium for nuclear weapons) and at Edgewood Arsenal in Maryland.

The Institute's eight-story Building 470, a windowless skyscraper among the flat buildings, dominated the landscape. From its beginnings in 1952, Building 470 was a prototype factory for making anthrax—from seed stock to dry, lethal spore powder to be loaded into bombs or rockets. A single "run" within one of the forty-foot-high fermenters inside produced an eighteen-hundred-gallon batch of anthrax mixture, about seven thousand grams of anthrax each week. Only the "Eight Ball," the facility's enormous one-million-liter aerosol test chamber, was more striking. Inside the hollow, four-story metal sphere the Institute's scientists exploded germs to create infectious aerosols for testing, until 1973 when the "Eight Ball" burned to the ground. To weaponize anthrax, to make it stable and durable enough to survive delivery, was difficult. The Institute produced five thousand anthrax bombs, but even the most capable dispensed only 3 percent of its spores. The rest were destroyed by the vast temperatures of detonation.

Throughout the 1950s and 1960s, scientists working in Building 1412 continued perfecting germ weapons. In secret large-scale experiments, the Army's Institute standardized a value of eight thousand inhaled anthrax spores as the lethal dosage for 50 percent of the exposed human population receiving it—the so-called LD50. This stood for a dose fatal to half the population, the "log-normal" model used to calculate risk factors and anthrax munitions requirements. The model took into account that some people were more susceptible to infection than others. In more intimate tests, scientists discovered they needed only four thousand spores to achieve LD50.

Theoretically, one hundred grams of dried anthrax could wipe out a small city. The eight billion lethal doses contained in a single gallon of anthrax was enough to kill every man, woman, and child on earth. At the Institute, as in Russia, they cultured anthrax in huge quantities. A few grains of freeze-dried anthrax bacteria inside a stoppered triangular vial were taken from a refrigerated vault. A nutrient medium was added and the mixture was transferred into larger containers to incubate forty-eight hours in thermostatic oven boxes. The correct temperature was crucial— too much heat could destroy the anthrax bacteria.

Over two days, the scientists nurtured death, coaxing it into growth until the meager seed stock had grown to billions. When the liquid mixture was withdrawn from the ovens, technicians siphoned it off into large flasks connected to air-bubbling machines. The machines distributed oxygen evenly, encouraging more bacteria growth.

Each new generation of bacteria was shifted to progressively larger vessels until the resulting translucent cola-colored froth was piped under vacuum pressure into giant fermenters to incubate. After another two days the bacteria mix was passed through a centrifuge, then concentrated thirty times further through a separator. When it reached its maximum concentration, the anthrax resembled coffee swirling with cream.

Separated from its liquid base, the anthrax bacteria had to be dried to powdered form. It was difficult to do without destroying them. Then the tiny protective spores they formed had to be milled, also without killing the bacteria. The result was a fine, odorless powder usually colored white or beige. Weaponizing anthrax meant making the organisms a smaller, standard size for use in aerosol form. To enter the lungs and trigger inhalational anthrax, bacterial spore-particles had to be smaller than five microns wide. Spores between one and five microns wide jetted right by nose hairs and cilia along the windpipe, breaching the respiratory system's natural defense system. A single microscopic invader under five microns wide could penetrate deep into the lungs, multiply in the moist respiratory mucosa, and produce millions of deadly offspring.

But since an ordinary human cell is about ten microns wide (a human hair is ten times wider), grains larger than ten microns rarely reach the lungs. It would take two hundred spores to span the thickness of a hair. The mechanical milling required to make fine dust artificially also creates an electrostatic charge sufficient to bind anthrax spores into large clumps. Those lumps are harmless because they cannot reach the lungs. To keep the spores separate and deadly, the fermented anthrax culture had to be mixed with additives to stabilize it.

The Institute's bioweapons specialists had settled on a chemical additive, silica, to remove the static between the particles and prevent them from clinging together. The Iraq and Soviet biowarfare programs used a substance called bentonite, a mixture of pharmaceutical-grade silica and aluminum, instead of silica. Bentonite, a clay additive, is the generic term for a class of natural or processed clays derived from volcanic ash useful in reducing the static charge of spores. Spores milled to the right size and purged of electrostatic charge are still hard to separate.

Weaponizing was also about keeping the individual particles light enough to hang effortlessly in midair like gossamer so they could be inhaled before settling to the ground. The Institute's wispy spores could be sprayed widely in the ragged skies to float for miles. But what sprayer could dispense such a fine mist to infect substantial numbers of people?

Over the years, a high number of Detrick scientists had become victims of their own pathogens. Two women workers gave birth to babies with severe birth defects and both children perished. Four men working at the Institute died from exposure to pathogens, two from anthrax infection. In 1951, William A. Boyles, a forty-six-year-old microbiologist, inhaled anthrax spores on the job just before Thanksgiving and died on November 25. In 1958, fifty-three-year-old Joel E. Willard, an electrician who worked in the "hot" areas of Building 470, succumbed to inhalational anthrax in July. He had been changing lightbulbs in a test building where animals were exposed to anthrax. A sampling taken after Willard's death showed the building was so "grossly" contaminated that Willard had to be buried in a lead casket. The Institute named Boyles Street and Willard Place in their honor.

Boyles and Willard, like every worker at the Institute, had signed a waiver that gave the government rights to their bodies if they died from a disease contracted at the Institute. "Dr. [Ralph E.] Lincoln had me pull a sample of Willard's dried blood," said W. Irving Jones Jr., an Institute biochemist. "We were able to grow [the anthrax bacteria] right up. And it was deadly." Willard's substrain of anthrax, successfully tested on animals, was used for a new and more powerful weapons strain.

Like the Soviets, the Institute had no qualms about using human accident victims to boost the killing power of their anthrax arsenal. Ken Alibek, a former deputy chief of the Soviet bioweapons program and now president of Advanced Biosystems, a consulting company in Manassas, Virginia, told the tale of an unfortunate scientist, Nikolai Ustinov, and his encounter with the Marburg virus. In 1967, in Marburg, Germany, twenty-five lab workers were infected with an agent, previously unidentified, but now called the Marburg virus. Seven of them died. Ustinov accidentally pricked himself while injecting a guinea pig with Marburg virus. Two weeks later he died an agonizing death. "No one needed to debate the next step," Alibek recalled. "Orders went out immediately to replace the old strain with the new, which was called, in a move the wry Ustinov might have appreciated, 'Variant U.' " Alibek, with his bowl-shaped haircut, appeared amiable for someone who had worked hand in hand with death for so many years.

The original weapons strain of anthrax used at the Institute had been a variety called Vollum after the British scientist who isolated it from an Oxford cow just before World War II. British bioweapons engineers made the first alterations. They replaced the Vollum strain with a substrain, "M36," by passing the original strain through a series of infected monkeys to increase its virulence.

In 1951, the Institute perfected the Vollum microbes to create Strain 11966. After Boyles's death, references to the M36 variant of Vollum were replaced by references to the highly deadly "Vollum 1B strain" of anthrax for use in anthrax warheads. In the Vollum 1B strain, particles of aerosol mist measured only one micron, a highly desirable quality in a lethal aerosol.

The virulent, heightened bacteria collected from Willard's and Boyles's bodies enabled the scientists to isolate and upgrade the Vollum strain a second and possibly third time. The Vollum weapons strain was changed by passage through Boyles's body into Vollum 1B. "That's where Vollum 1B came from," said Bill Patrick, a tireless problem solver and manager who formerly headed Detrick's product development division. "It's 1-Boyles." Patrick was born July 24, 1926, in Furman, South Carolina, and earned a bachelor's degree in biology from the University of South Carolina and a master's degree in microbiology from the University of Tennessee in Knoxville. He joined the bioweapons program at Fort Detrick as a production manager in April 1951 while simultaneously working toward a doctorate in microbiology at the University of Maryland.

After the Institute's bioweapons program was shut down, he became a private consultant. His business card showed a skull and crossbones. Atop his stationery was a drawing of the Grim Reaper, his black scythe labeled BIOLOGICAL WARFARE, his boney outstretched arm sowing a rain of germs. Patrick had been an Iraqi weapons inspector in 1994 and was probably the only man in America who knew how to make weaponized anthrax. Patrick also knew how easy it was for a terrorist to launch a germ attack against America.

"Anthrax gets stronger as it goes through a human host," said Bill Walter, who joined the Institute in 1951 as a "principal investigator." "So we got pulmonary spores from Bill Boyles and Joel Willard. And finally we got it from Lefty Kreh's finger."

Bernard "Lefty" Kreh worked rotating nightshifts at the Institute as a plant operator. Wearing a bio-suit and sucking air from a tube on the wall, Kreh's job was to scrape anthrax "mud" off the inside of a centrifuge with a kitchen spatula. One day his finger swelled up "like a sausage" with a skin anthrax infection. For the next month, the Institute isolated him behind a glass wall inside its hospital.

Kreh's finger became the source of a new substrain of anthrax isolated and designated "BVK-1," for "Bernard Victor Kreh." On log sheets the designation became "LK" for "Lefty Kreh." "Lefty's strain was rather easy to detect," Walter said later. When technicians grew a colony of bacteria on a growth medium "it came out like a little comma, perfectly spherical." Lefty Kreh's finger provided another step forward in the Institute's search for the deadliest anthrax ever.

Though considerable expertise was needed to culture, mill, and weaponize the spores, U.S. biologists eventually ceased relying on mechanical milling machines to transpose desiccated paste colonies of anthrax bacteria into refined dust. "The new U.S. process concentrated the organisms into right-sized particles, while maintaining their virulence, without milling them," said Patrick of his patented processes. The optimal U.S. process instead employed a refined spray-drying technique that produced microscopic, dry particles of biowarfare agents in a single step, safeguarding them in special coatings, making them tough and durable enough for wide spreading by aerosol sprayers. The spores had become floating gossamer, deadly dancing butterflies.

During the Cold War, germ and chemical weapons in the hands of a foreign enemy were a long-standing concern of U.S. intelligence officers. Bioweapons were as dangerous as nuclear missiles. Several nations, including the U.S. and the USSR, had formally reserved the right to use biological weapons in reprisal if first used against themselves, implicitly maintaining the right to develop and stockpile the increasingly deadly pathogens.

President Richard Nixon officially put the Institute out of the offensive germ business, declaring U.S. support for an international treaty banning bioweapons.[5] On November 25, 1969, he signed an executive order renouncing use of lethal biological agents and weapons and ordered the unilateral dismantling of the U.S.'s offensive bioweapons program. The President promised to confine U.S. biological research to "defensive measures," and affirmed, "Mankind already carries in its own hands too many seeds of its own destruction." The time allotted for the destruction of global germ arsenals was three years, the time it took the U.S. to scrap its own biological weapons. The Preamble to the 1972 Biological and Toxic Weapons Convention reads:

> [We are] determined for the sake of all mankind, to exclude completely the possibility of bacteriological agents and toxins being used as weapons; [We are] convinced that such use would be repugnant to the conscience of mankind and that no effort should be spared to minimize this risk.

It prohibited development, production, stockpiling, or otherwise retaining biological agents or toxins "of types or in quantities that have no justification for prophylactic, protective or other peaceful purposes." The treaty also forbade "weapons, equipment or means of delivery designed to use such agents or toxins for hostile purposes or in armed conflict."

By March 1975, when the BTWC came into force, the Institute had decimated its aggressive germ arsenal. However, the treaty was shot through with holes, setting no limit on the quantities of germs kept on hand for research and allowing any kind of research as long as its purpose was defensive. But, as Dr. Patrick observed, defensive work could look a lot like offensive work. With an eye to the future, the CIA stored 100 grams of *Bacillus anthracis* at the Institute, the same amount they had previously calculated was enough to level a small city. It defied logic that

---

[5] Chemical weapons such as mustard gas had been put to devastating use. The blistering gas was lethal when inhaled. Phosgene, the most dangerous of the group called choking agents, accounted for 80 percent of all chemical deaths during World War I. The 1925 Geneva Protocol prohibited wartime use of both chemical and biological weapons.

the Institute was not producing offensive biological weapons clandestinely. The Russians were.

The Soviet Union, first to sign and ratify the BTWC, began secretly inflating its collection of viral and bacterial warfare agents. It ordered sixty-five thousand technicians and researchers at fifty remote labs and testing sites to cook up twenty tons of smallpox virus a year and develop two hundred strains of anthrax. Some strains would end up in the hands of terrorists. Over the next twenty years, the Soviets steathily constructed the greatest arsenal of bioweapons in the history of the world. They lived in constant fear of Western inspectors who would show them as having breached the international accord prohibiting such research. Their folly would result in the greatest anthrax calamity in history, a "biological Chernobyl." The Soviet Union continued to develop biological weapons well into the 1990s. In September 1998, Presidents Bill Clinton and Boris Yeltsin agreed in Moscow on a program of "accelerated negotiations" to strengthen the Convention. The United States has taken the lead in efforts to update the treaty.

LATE FRIDAY NIGHT, October 19, 2001, two breathless FBI agents arrived at the Institute with the sealed *Post* anthrax sample in hand. It had been sandwiched in layers of aluminum foil and placed inside a plastic Ziploc bag. The lethal nature of the envelopes and letters had curtailed normal USPS forensic examinations at its ultramodern National Forensic Lab just outside D.C. Until the evidence underwent special processing, a search for latent or identifiable fingerprints, indented writing, or an analysis of ink, paper, and saliva DNA could not be made. In the meantime inspectors were scanning post office videotapes from the forty-six branches that feed the Trenton mail stream. Concurrently, the Justice Department was sifting through sales records from the major U.S. glove box manufacturers. Its agents had already spent two days quizzing pharmacists in the Trenton area about anyone who had bought Cipro—two to three months' worth. No prescriptions had been issued in those quantities for either Cipro or Penicillin. The plastic bag was sealed with red tape inside a white plastic container marked with a biohazard label. The agents halted at a gate like that of any military base except that an Abrams tank was parked nearby. There was a white sign saying USAMRIID and other signs cautioning

10 MPH and CAMERAS ARE UNAUTHORIZED. They observed guards in camouflage with armbands and M16s at the entrances and walking a concrete island, a guardhouse, and around a yellow-, white-, and straw-colored building. Clusters of brick and concrete buildings, light-colored, modernistic, blocky, and forbidding, crowded a two-hundred-acre site. Some were guarded by concrete barriers, a defense against truck bombs. Large pipes running beside the buildings and a tower that could have been a heating station gave the facility the appearance of a pharmaceutical production plant.

The windowless headquarters building at the heart of the complex employed 450 military and civilian scientists and had its own guards on twenty-four-hour alert. Fort Detrick was an obvious terrorist target. The Institute's deadly weapons and secrets in any enemy's hands would be a disaster. When terrorists plowed a fuel-laden jetliner into the Pentagon, the Army swiftly locked down the Institute, evacuated four thousand civilian and military personnel, and filled the skies around the Institute with military helicopters.

An animal hospital faced the complex on the other side of the road. One lab was dedicated specifically to developing vaccines against biological agents such as anthrax. The Institute's modern mission was to "develop strategies, products, information procedures and training programs for medical defense against biological warfare threats and naturally occurring infectious diseases that require special containment." Within the CIA's arsenal of pathogens powerful enough to kill millions were large amounts of the anthrax bacillus. At Fort Detrick, they stored about one hundred grams.

With so much anthrax at the top secret Institute, the agents, with their anthrax sample, felt as if they were bringing coals to Newcastle. The mailbox where Amerithrax had posted his poisoned letters was roughly 180 miles away from Frederick, Maryland, little more than a single evening's roundtrip. About the same number of miles separated Boca Raton from St. Petersburg where hoax letters had been mailed. Distributing anthrax had always been a difficult problem for the Institute's scientists because it dissipates so easily in the wind. Amerithrax had conquered that problem. He used the U.S. mails.

The Institute had numerous safety measures to counteract infections. All their biowarriors were given a series of vaccinations before being allowed into "hot zones." They gobbled antibiotics and constantly washed their hands. They were covered in sweltering head-to-toe body suits with hoods, masks, two pairs of rubber gloves, and two pairs of boots. They breathed purified and overheated air as they worked at their "hot boxes" or "glove boxes" under germ-destroying ultraviolet light. Hot boxes are glass housings with fume hoods, a removable rear panel, and attached rubber gloves. Reaching inside through the clamping rings and gloves, technicians could manipulate beakers of microbes, assemble fragile biological bomblets, or pack an envelope with powdered anthrax as Amerithrax must have done.

The Army facility's modern labs, filled with unearthly light, were equipped with electron microscopes, chromatography devices, high-grade centrifuges, and laser equipment. Anthrax experiments utilized dryers, granulators, jet mills, pulverizers, vibrating sieves, mixers, feeders, and classifiers. The *Post* anthrax sample the Institute's scientists were attempting to analyze presented problems from the beginning. The dampness that had caused the anthrax to clump together also made analysis difficult. But it did seem to be purer than the Brokaw sample. What experts needed was a dry, unopened envelope with enough anthrax for them to identify the exact strain it came from. Learning the strain might lead them to the source and possibly to Amerithrax. Amerithrax, whoever he was, had a motive for what he had done. It was possible he had been laid off from a facility and was striking back.

In February 2001, labs had exchanged microbe samples, including anthrax, without reporting the transfers to the CDC as required by law. No one was apparently harmed but the lapses could have placed the public at risk. The department's activities lacked sufficient federal oversight. At one Department of Energy facility, scientists experimented with anthrax bacteria for years without anyone being notified.

The visiting FBI agents were very familiar with the Institute. Only twenty-four days earlier, someone had fingered one of their former researchers as a potential bioterrorist. This "person of interest" had allegedly once worked with tasteless, odorless, invisible, deadly anthrax at the Institute. The odd thing was the tip-off had come at the same time or just before someone had mailed real anthrax letters to the media.

STRAIN 8

Experiment in Terror

ON WEDNESDAY, OCTOBER 3, 2001 (just as Bob Stevens was beginning his second day in the hospital), FBI agents asked the subject of the anonymous tip-off letter to drop by their Washington, D.C., Field Office. Eight days earlier (as NBC security was phoning the FBI about a suspicious letter from St. Petersburg), some unknown person had mailed a letter to the military police at the Quantico Marine Base in Virginia. Neatly typed and single-spaced, the letter alleged that Dr. Ayaad Assaad, a fifty-three-year-old Egyptian American senior scientist with the EPA, was a potential biological terrorist.

Assaad, a well-respected U.S. citizen with a top-security clearance, had worked as a researcher at Fort Detrick for almost a decade. The anonymous writer knew details of Dr. Assaad's work at the top secret bioweapons lab. The writer displayed a detailed knowledge of Assaad's personal life and about his family. He even knew which commuter train he took. "Dr. Assaad is a potential bioterrorist," warned the lengthy letter in excellent English. "I have worked with Dr. Assaad, and I heard him say that he has a vendetta against the U.S. government and that if anything happens to him, he told his sons to carry on." Dr. Assaad's coworker accused him of "planning to mount a possible biological attack" in the wake of 9-11 and claimed he "had the motive and means to succeed."

The letter was sent on to the Federal Bureau of Investigation for further action. The FBI knew the U.S. Army conducted top secret biological warfare research at the Institute. In 1997, when cutbacks during the previous administration slashed funding, Col. David Franz, commander at the Institute, had to fire some staff. At first he laid off technicians, then began firing scientists. Older scientists like Dr. Assaad were allegedly chosen for the job cuts. After losing his job, Dr. Assaad filed a still-pending age discrimination lawsuit against the government. His suit told of "a bizarre and vicious atmosphere" at the Institute in which he and other Arab scientists (all U.S. citizens with top-security clearances) were ridiculed, denigrated, and subjected to racial slurs and harassment. A self-styled "Camel Club" awarded a rubber camel as a prize for the worst performance of the week. Assaad's lawyer, Rosemary McDermott, stated that there were people at Fort Detrick who harbored an "intense dislike" of Dr. Assaad, particularly a rival, a ricin research colleague. Studying the vicious letter, the agents agreed: somebody sure didn't like him.

On Wednesday morning, Dr. Assaad arrived at the FBI's field office in downtown Washington to answer a few questions. He ended the day sitting in a windowless cell being interrogated. Of course he had a motive. He had been laid off from USAMRIID, but then so had many others who had lost their security clearances at facilities where anthrax was handled or stored. When agents showed him the poison pen letter, Assaad burst into tears.

Later, after O'Connor was stricken with cutaneous anthrax and talk of the anthrax letters was on everyone's lips, Assaad said he believed the person who composed the anonymous letter to the FBI and the person who sent the anthrax-laced envelopes, with messages praising Allah and denouncing Americans, to NBC and the *New York Post*, was one and the same. "My theory is," he told the press, "whoever this person is knew in advance what was going to happen [and named me as a] scapegoat for this action. You do not need to be a Nobel laureate to put two and two together." The anonymous letter was sent eight or nine days before the first anthrax case was announced.

The FBI believed Assaad was the victim of a false accusation. After clearing him of any involvement in the letter attacks, they began looking into a link between the anonymous letter writer and Amerithrax, the FBI's code name for the anthrax killer of Bob Stevens.

Ms. McDermott said that Dr. Assaad believed the letter to the FBI "was a deliberate attempt to frame him" by a former colleague. In history scientists have been notoriously jealous of each other. The first American crime to attract national attention was committed by a scientist. Dr. John White Webster, professor of Chemistry and Mineralogy at Harvard, murdered Dr. George Parkman in 1849, dissected him, burned the corpse in his lab furnace, and put the leftovers in the dissection vault.

Had Amerithrax been the author? Had he written the Assaad letter to settle a personal score? The wording was vague, but suggested that the writer of the letter had knowledge of the anthrax letters mailed September 18. Assaad was falsely accused of "planning to mount a possible biological attack" at a time when only the culprit knew that a biological crime had already been committed. Amerithrax must have waited impatiently for a week for a reaction before sending the Assaad letter. Stevens had not yet taken ill. One letter had gone missing. The first wave of death had apparently failed to generate the panic Amerithrax had hoped for. The nation's anthrax scare only began on October 4, the day after Assaad's interrogation.

AS YET NO one knew what Amerithrax's secret lab looked like, but logic and speculation suggested its essential makeup. Investigators theorized this layout: He kept his inner bacteriological lab dark to screen out ultraviolet rays harmful to anthrax bacteria. And surely, if he was culturing his own anthrax, his lair smelled of meat from broth in a fermenter tank. In any case the overriding smell of household bleach to decontaminate working surfaces would be present.

But first of all Amerithrax had needed a virulent strain of anthrax to weaponize. Where he had obtained the bacteria was the unanswered question. Amerithrax would need a secure staging area, a Biosafety Level 2 area that might only be a kitchen, bathroom, or hallway. Inside this entry chamber, lit by a blue ultraviolet light, would be a decon shower—possibly only a tub of bleach detergent and water. To protect himself he might don a Hazmat suit with a respirator or an Army surplus gas mask (though the FBI believed Amerithrax was inoculated against anthrax). In either case he would pull on a pair or two of disposable gloves made of lightweight nitrile, latex, or vinyl and wear some sort of plastic head covering.

Amerithrax's working lab, Level 3, would be kept under active negative air pressure—a ventilation system as simple as a window fan that sucked air out of the room through a HEPA filter into the outdoors. Air drawn into the lab entered through another vent. All other windows were sealed with duct tape. Possibly Amerithrax bought his equipment over the counter—pipes, glassware filters, a fermenter to breed colonies of anthrax, and the nutrients to propel rapid growth and spore formation. Harvested anthrax slurry could be processed by a pharmaceutical sprayer into cakes. A secondhand horizontal or vertical milling machine would be needed to grind down dried spores to the most infectious size. Or he might have jury-rigged a makeshift pulverizer filled with steel ball bearings for small quantity processing. On the most rudimentary level, his equipment might consist of a heat lamp and thermostat, a pressure cooker, boxes of Q-tips, and bouillon cubes to brew, dry, and convert his spores into microscopic "lung-friendly" particles.

Several years earlier, government agents involved in a top secret Pentagon project had fanned out across the country to see if they could secretly construct a biowarfare lab. The agents had found it remarkably easy to buy all necessary equipment on the commercial market. Ten months before the first anthrax letter was mailed, the Pentagon's well-equipped mini-bioweapons plant had produced pounds of powdered anthrax simulant. That simulant could be weaponized by the addition of anthrax spores.

SOMEWHERE IN AMERICA a glove box threw its illuminated light onto intent features shielded by transparent plastic and framed in the center of a square hood. The rasp of an oxygen tank could be heard. Amerithrax adjusted his bulky containment suit. It might even have been homemade.

Amerithrax moved deliberately. The spores he used were so light and so refined that it was hard to get them onto a slide. The airy spores kept floating off, flying off the spatula he used to fill the envelope. Getting his gossamer anthrax into envelopes was a ticklish endeavor. He inserted his arms through the long attached gloves and reached midway into the sealed airtight chamber. This allowed him to manipulate a vial taken from the processing lab. He slowly poured some anthrax onto a letter—anthrax more potent and more easily disbursed than that on the NBC and *Post* letters. The spores were a different size, smaller and more deadly. He had refined them to get rid of impurities such as dead anthrax germs that had been in his first mailing. Fine powdered anthrax made spores more deadly. The spores would not stick to tape, but they would anchor inside human lungs. Amerithrax may have become angry when the media panic he had envisioned did not ensue. Perhaps he said to himself, "I'll show them. I'll make the spores more deadly, the letters more obvious and shoot for a higher profile target." Now he would attempt to assassinate two senators. Along the way a lot of innocent people got murdered.

He had laid out the first of two unfolded letters and two preaddressed and prestamped envelopes inside the glove box. This time his targets were not the media, but political targets—two U.S. senators. Both were Democrats. He had made two very specific choices. He knew what committees they sat on and what speeches they had recently given. He had written a very interesting letter and made very interesting choices of victims.

"What they do, rather than what they say, betrays who they are," writes FBI expert Ronald Kessler of serial killers. "By reading those signs, profilers can often determine from the crime scene the kind of person who committed the crime and the fantasies that propelled him—in effect, the criminal's signature."

Amerithrax's other tools lay inside the glove box: one or two stoppered vials, a large sealable Baggie, a roll of cellophane tape, a wet sponge, and Clorox for disinfecting. He laid out the first letter and put spores from one vial into the center of the letter. In slow motion (quick movements stirred the stagnant air) he folded the letter with two horizontal folds. This was followed by two vertical folds on each side—a "pharmaceutical fold," the way small portions of medicinal powders had been dispensed for centuries. This interior packaging was to keep the anthrax from escaping through the flap or corners of the envelope.

There were easier ways to fill an envelope with weaponized anthrax. Anthrax expert Martin Hugh-Jones suggested one. "You could go out early in the morning, with a few plastic bags," he said, "and pour it into the letters in the open air. As long as you did it with the wind blowing left to right, say, across you, then you'd be pretty safe. What you don't want is to have it blowing to your back—that creates turbulence and you'd inhale it." Some in the FBI believed Amerithrax's lab was outdoors; however, he probably filled his envelopes in the following manner:[6]

As was his practice, he had scissored off the bottom portion of the two one-page threats. First, a more square letter made for a neater pharmaceutical fold. Second, the copy machine may have made gripper marks that could be traced back to the photocopier he had used. "The original," theorized case expert Ed Lake, "may have been written lower on the paper and when the copies were made the writing was moved higher, the copies had to be cropped because they showed identifying marks on the underside of the lid of the copier."

Amerithrax slowly placed the folded letter into its envelope and used the sponge to wet the glue on the flap. He was sweating under his hood. The roar of an oxygen tank filled his ears. Now the spores were doubly sealed against escape. When he had finished the second letter, Amerithrax used cellophane tape from a roll around the edges of both letters. Was this to prevent cross-contamination with the other mail or to keep the deadly germs inside so they would be at their deadliest when the envelope was opened? But the microscopic spores did leak out, giving anthrax to those who touched the unopened letter. Spores escaped through the very large, fifty-micron pores of the envelope. Whether by design or not, they contaminated the mail system and postal environments—and no one would know in time. All paper has invisible tiny openings (pores) and merely handling the unopened letter could give a person anthrax. Amerithrax put the sealed envelopes into the Baggie and used standard procedures to disinfect the outside of the Baggie and everything else still inside the glove box. Of course, he was inoculated with an anthrax vaccine.

When his work was done, Amerithrax removed the sealed, letter-filled Baggie from the glove box. Upon leaving his lab, Amerithrax underwent a final disinfecting procedure by showering with bleach. He shut off the compressed air. Unfastening his Hazmat suit, he slipped out of it and hung it up to dry.

Amerithrax's second mailing was ready by Columbus Day, October

---

[6] Cyber-sleuth Ed Lake theorized that this was the sequence in which the anthrax mailings were prepared.

8. Postal deliveries to homes and businesses over the Monday holiday had been curtailed, but the post office was still pulling mail from neighborhood collection boxes. Typically a single employee at each office was assigned to do a run on this not widely observed holiday. Mail processing facilities were operating with a skeleton crew.

All day television cameras had been running footage of nearly a thousand AMI employees and visitors to the six tabloids. They had lined up in Delray Beach in front of the county Health Department. President Bush was on the air too, reassuring the country that the Florida anthrax case was apparently "a very isolated incident." It was the same day that the New York City Department of Health notified the CDC of a person with a skin lesion consistent with cutaneous anthrax. Next morning, October 9, the CDC's investigators arrived in New York. They provided epidemiologic and lab support to city health officials all day Tuesday.

All of Amerithrax's letters were mailed on Tuesdays, the same day of the week as the 9-11 attack. Amerithrax probably made a broad daylight drop on a crowded corner at a major entrance to Princeton University. His secret means to deposit the letters and remain uncontaminated was evidently not a noticeable maneuver. Perhaps he dumped them inside from a larger Baggie. He pocketed the Baggie into a pocket filled with bleach and left the area. Death was on the wing now. Amerithrax could be anywhere in the nation, secure behind a false return address. He let the boundless facilities of the post office unwittingly act as his executioner by proxy. He had made the Postal Service his accomplice as it forwarded and delivered his deadly mail to his unsuspecting victims "like a missile," according to the Postmaster General.

Letters inside a collection box have a tendency to stay together. Through bar codes and magnetic strips and an invisible trail of spores and infections postal inspectors later traced their path. And so a clumping of mail definitely developed around both letters. They would sail along with each other, at least for a while.

It takes letters about two and a half hours to get from postbox to bar code machine. Bar codes on Amerithrax's new letters indicated a processing time that suggested Amerithrax's letters had been collected from their mailbox around 3:00 P.M.

The first transmittal envelope (prestamped with a thirty-four-cent eagle stamp) was postmarked "Trenton, NJ 10/09/01 (Tues.)." The envelope, handprinted by a right-handed adult, was addressed[7] to:

SENATOR DASCHLE
509 HART SENATE OFFICE
BUILDING
WASHINGTON D.C. 20510+4103

Sen. Thomas A. Daschle of South Dakota was the Senate majority leader, the nation's top Democrat. Sharp-featured with a lynx-eyed, intelligent look, he is a lean and fit man with a strong thrust to his chin and a determined set to his mouth. Though not yet well-known nationally, he was about to be propelled into the spotlight. This morning he is dressed in a dark suit with a red power tie and powder blue shirt.

At some point water damaged the Daschle letter. There had been water damage to the Brokaw and *Post* letters too. Was it raining the day it was prepared? Had the envelope fluttered out of the box and into a puddle as the postman placed it in his plastic bin? Though mailed almost a month apart, three of Amerithrax's letters had gotten damp. Had the damage occurred in Amerithrax's lab or was something in his anthrax process causing the letters to be wet? Could the dampness be involved in his method of transit to the mailbox? The spores might have been refrigerated to preserve them and prevent germination or hidden in some wet container.

The blurring of the address was significant. It made the nine-digit zip code written very close to the bottom of the Daschle envelope partially illegible. It delayed the letter, a letter that would arrive too late to influence the USA Patriot Act (as in Provide Appropriate Tools Required to Intercept and Obstruct Terrorism) Daschle was debating. The zip code might now have to be read by hand by a human being who could direct it to the right slot. The return address read:

---

[7] Lake theorized that Amerithrax copied the address from a computer printout because the word "building" was on a line by itself. "Computer formats have two address lines because only twenty-five to thirty characters are allowed per line. There is no comma between city and state on all the letters. This is very unusual, but computers don't put down commas."

4TH GRADE
GREENDALE SCHOOL
FRANKLIN PARK NJ 08852

Greendale was a nonexistent grade school in New Jersey. Did the address have some symbolic meaning? More than likely the return address was to make the letters more acceptable to politically savvy senators who might see some value in answering a child's letter. Besides, the Postal Service had been cautioning Americans against opening any letters without return addresses. Judith Miller had chastised herself for not remembering that when she opened hers at the *New York Times*.

The second letter, sailing along with its companion, was addressed to Senator Patrick J. Leahy of Vermont, Democrat and chairman of the Senate Judiciary Committee, another major player in the Patriot Act debate. It read:

SENATOR LEAHY
433 RUSSELL SENATE OFFICE
BUILDING
WASHINGTON D.C. 20510-4502

Both Leahy and Daschle were Democrats and important figures in the debate over "the Antiterror Bill." On Friday the Senate and House would be arguing whether to pass the 342-page law, which would amend fifteen different federal statutes. Whatever Amerithrax's intentions, his letters would arrive too late to influence the October 12 vote.

Later, postal inspectors were able to determine the route the two letters from Princeton, New Jersey, traveled. They were identified using masses of computer data recorded as each letter entered the highly automated sorting centers. Upon entry, each letter is scanned for an address, given identifying bar codes recording its time and place of posting, and rushed on its way. Available data included digital images of almost every hand-addressed envelope, which optical scanners cannot easily read. Letter codes sprayed on the back of some letters during processing later enabled postal inspectors to get a more precise idea of which letters were touched with anthrax.

Data stored on magnetic tapes in the thousands of sorting machines in the 362 regional sorting centers around the nation are a way for postal inspectors to check on a lost letter. This time the data could be used to identify the tens of thousands of other letters that passed through the central processing station within an hour or so of each other about fifteen miles from the Princeton mailbox. The same sorting center had processed the anthrax-contaminated mail sent in September to NBC and the *New York Post*.

Amerithrax's two letters were still in close proximity to each other when they arrived at the Hamilton Processing Facility in Hamilton Township. At 5:27 P.M., amid tons of bills, credit offers, birthday greetings, and chatty letters, an anthrax-laced letter to Sen. Patrick J. Leahy zipped into the humming, high-speed machinery at the postal sorting center. Powder from the Leahy letter coated the lens of the electric eye that scans bar codes on envelopes.

Exactly twenty seconds and 283 items later, an envelope addressed to the John Farkas household on Great Hill Road in Seymour, Connecticut, followed the Leahy letter through the machinery. As the machine pounded the mail, the Farkas letter picked up highly refined anthrax forced through pores in the cheap envelopes. Later, a post office facility in Wallingford, Connecticut, would report a cluster of three million anthrax spores in the dust under a sorting machine.

Norma Wallace, fifty-seven, of Willingboro, New Jersey, worked as a repairperson for the Hamilton Processing Facility. When the facility's automated mail-sorting machine jammed, she went in to fix it. Wallace found powder on the electric eye. Taking a deep breath, she leaned down to rub it away.

A forty-three-year-old South Asian woman, Jyotsna Patel of Princeton Junction, New Jersey, was working at a different mail-sorting machine. Though Patel was not near the broken machine, she still fell victim to an invisible cloud created as the envelope was squeezed and unsqueezed by mail-sorting equipment and by personnel touching it and placing it in stacks and in mail bags. Tiny spores floated through the large coarse envelope as far as an outside loading dock at the regional distribution facility. A Hamilton employee from Levittown, Pennsylvania, thirty-five-old Patrick O'Donnell, was working there at that moment. A Hamilton bookkeeper later got skin anthrax from mail that was delivered to his office.

The sorting machines later tested positive for anthrax spores and were responsible for transmitting spores to inbound mail as it was segregated at Hamilton for distribution in the Trenton area. The cross-contamination (which many experts believed to be impossible) touched some of the 464 postal centers in central New Jersey. Mail from boxes in Princeton was routed through three centers before it went to Edison or Eatontown, New Jersey, for further processing.

Anthrax spores were left at Edison and Eatontown, parts of the Carnegie Center in West Windsor, and at a smaller post office on Palmer Square in downtown Princeton. Moving against the flow, cross-contaminates moved through distribution plants processing bulk mail in Hackensack, Central New Jersey, and Newark Main all the way to the Bellmawr Distribution Plant. Later, the Stamp Fulfillment Center in Kansas City would receive letters from the D.C. mail center that had processed Sen. Tom Daschle's letter and would test positive for anthrax.

Letters for the greater D.C. area, including Daschle's and Leahy's, were next funneled through the Carteret Hub and Spoke Facility in New Jersey. On Wednesday, October 10, they headed on to a brick-walled mail hub on Brentwood Avenue northeast of the Capitol, the Brentwood Mail Facility. The U.S. Post Office Main Branch on Brentwood Road NE, the sorting center that served all of Washington, hummed with activity round the clock. Its more than two thousand workers seemingly never rested. They managed four million pieces of mail a day. Amerithrax's letters were among them. All of the considerable mail for lawmakers' offices passed through Brentwood before being routed to either the House or the Senate. At one end of the vast facility was a loading dock. At the other was the express mailroom. In between was an ocean of air, its flow impeded by few barriers throughout the huge barn. Bagged letters were sorted into bar-coded trays and conveyed by belt to large-tray sorting machines.

At 7:10 P.M., the Daschle letter was manually fed through Sorter No. 17, one of the huge high-speed machines that channeled up to 550 letters per minute. A series of belts on the machine seized each letter and pinched it, compressing the envelope. No. 17 pounded and punched the mail like an old prizefighter. The conveyor belt fed an endlessly hungry mouth that filled with powdered paper. The giant was huffing and puffing by 8:00 A.M., Thursday, October 11, wheezing until it was shut down by a worker in mask and gloves. He unclogged it with a few powerful blasts of compressed air from a hose. Dislodged anthrax spores floated into the air, "self-crumbling" as they had been designed to do. They broke into smaller and smaller particles, each microscopic bit sweating a "splatty white goop" around its border. It was some sort of additive.

Sometime during this period, Bill Paliscak, a criminal investigator for the U.S. Postal Inspectors, removed a filter above No. 17. Dust showered down on him from the sorting machine. He breathed some into his lungs. His face and body became swollen, the membrane around his lungs became inflamed, and he grew unsteady on his feet. Within days he could only speak haltingly and had lost his short-term memory. He was in horrible pain and there seemed to be no cure.

Four workers at thirty machines inhaled a snowstorm of fibers into their lungs as they toiled. The paper fibers were sweet, warm, and deadly. Was there a finer fragrance? The odor of all their variations—cotton, hemp, pulp, even sugarcane and rice papers—filled the vast sorting room. That most permanent of erections, an Egyptian tomb, was permeated with similar smells. Astonishingly, its papyrus scrolls and papier-mâché sculptures, seemingly fragile, have lasted thousands of years. The paper of the tomb was as eternal as anthrax. Each letter in the endless stream had a personality and a mission. The letters wore their watermarks and postmarks like tattoos.

On Thursday the Daschle letter and the Leahy letter took separate routes in the automated system as electronic eyes translated addresses in the bar codes. The two letters were diverted through different sets of sorters, bins, sacks, and ultimately trucks. But anthrax spores that had puffed out of the Daschle envelope during the sorting process evidently settled on the Leahy letter, which had taken a sudden detour from Brentwood.

The Leahy letter was misrouted and made an unexpected side trip to the State Department. The sorting machine's optical reader had misconstrued the blurred handwritten zip code on the Leahy letter and translated it into a digital bar code, turning 20510-4502 into 20520-4502. Afterward the Leahy letter was trucked to a separate sorter at the U.S. State Department, Facility Annex 32 in Winchester, Virginia. Meanwhile the Daschle letter continued on straight to Capitol Hill. The accidental detour, experts later said, might also explain the extra level of potency in the smaller size of spores in the Leahy anthrax in that envelope.

"An additional process of milling, like a mortar and pestle," suggested Ken Alibek, a former Soviet germ-warfare official. "The high-powered sorters could have acted like a mill," said an investigator months later, "crumbling the microscopic clumps of deadly spores into smaller and more floatable bits with each pass." He added that the overall grade contrasts were probably caused by "different batches of the product, one more sophisticated than the other." The Leahy letter at this point simply vanished near the State Department mailroom. Potentially, it was the most dangerous of all Amerithrax's letters.

Also on Thursday the USPS wrote its employees that "The U.S. Postal Service has had no confirmed incidents involving the use of the mail to transmit any harmful biological or chemical weapons," and asked its workers "how likely was it that someone would receive a harmful biological or chemical substance in the mail?" The USPS answered its own question: "Presently, we have not seen any real incidents—including anthrax—only threats or hoaxes."

In the meantime, the contaminated Daschle letter was routed through a *second* postal facility on Friday, October 12, long after it should have been delivered. Water damage to the address on its envelope (the blurred zip code) had delayed it just as a misread at the Trenton post office had misrouted the Leahy letter to the State Department.

On Saturday, October 13, the Daschle letter was processed yet again at Brentwood. The facility's three giant machines, each canceling, coding, and sorting some thirty thousand pieces of mail an hour, whipped letters by so swiftly that enormous lines of employees functioned in a white blizzard generated as the paper crumbles slightly while flying on its way. Workers should have been shivering in the snowstorm swirling about the seventeen-and-a-half-million cubic feet of Brentwood's interior. Not one of them knew the danger they were in.

The postal workers trusted the air, never guessing it could kill them. And why shouldn't they? Amerithrax's poison had no smell, no taste, and there was no way to know if one were inside the invisible cloud or not. It floated and settled by like a biblical plague, striking down the unfortunate and sparing others for no reason at all as it passed.

Mailworker Thomas Morris Jr., a fifty-five-year-old Brentwood distribution clerk, handled mail destined for federal offices. The thirty-two-year Postal Service veteran lived in Suitland with his wife, Mary, and son, Thomas Morris III. Saturday morning, he came into contact with anthrax spores.

"A woman found an envelope, and I was in the vicinity [ten feet away]," Morris said later. "It had powder in it. They never let us know whether the thing was anthrax or not. They never treated the people who were around this particular individual and the supervisor who handled the envelope." Helen Lewis, fifty-one, a clerk in the government mail sections, had handled an envelope leaking a suspicious powder. Lewis tried to get medical attention according to Postal Service policy for possible anthrax exposure. However, she was denied treatment by the Washington Hospital Center. She later received Cipro at Providence Hospital. She later told UPI, "They said they could not treat [for anthrax] because they did not want a panic. My question is, Why didn't they give the rest of my colleagues Cipro? Why didn't they treat them on the sixteenth? Why didn't they treat them on the seventeenth? The eighteenth? The nineteenth? They could be living today if they received it." The Postal Service said later this letter tested negative for anthrax.

The Daschle letter finally broke free of the whirlpool and traveled on to Capitol Hill through a mail sorting facility that serviced the House and Senate and 177 federal agencies. Cross-contamination traces later turned up at offsite mail centers serving the White House, the State Department, the CIA, Walter Reed Army Medical Center, Landover (Justice), the BATF, the Anacostia mailroom adjacent to the BATF, and the U.S. Supreme Court Warehouse. Fifty-six USPS facilities serviced by Brentwood later tested positive for environmental samples of anthrax. These spread to two post office stations, Southwest and Friendship, and to two branches, Dulles and Pentagon.

The Daschle letter reached the Capitol police mail intake around noon. Senate-bound mail was hauled to the P Street NW mail-sorting room, the Dirksen Senate Office Building's mailroom for distribution. From there the anthrax-laced letter was sent down a hallway to Daschle's offices in the Hart Building. The Capitol rests at the center of the Russell, Dirksen, and Hart Senate Office Buildings (all to the north); the Supreme Court Building, the Library of Congress, the Longworth and Rayburn House Office Buildings (to the south); the Humphrey and Ford Office Buildings, the National Air and Space Museum, and the U.S. District Court. On the way the letter infected sorting trays, trucks, and even mailbags.

Cross-contamination from the Daschle letter carried from the P Street sorter to a mail-bundling machine at the Gerald R. Ford House Annex.

The annex housed the Congressional Budget Office and a child care center, but no anthrax spores got beyond the mailroom. However, the Ford annex handled mail for the Longworth House Office Building, where more than one hundred lawmakers had their offices, and spores were later found in three sites there.

On Sunday, Norma Wallace, the Hamilton mail sorter, became ill with vomiting and diarrhea. She found a scab on the back of her neck that did not respond to antibiotics. She continued work anyway. By the next day, she had a mild fever and chills. Aspirin didn't help. The vomiting and diarrhea improved, but over the next two days she had fevers to 38.4 degrees Celcius with shaking chills, headache, and fatigue. A nonproductive cough developed, along with mild shortness of breath and anterior chest pain. Then her coworker Patrick O'Donnell became ill with the same symptoms.

In lower Manhattan, amid the whirling vapors, people still struggled for breath. When two of the Con Edison substations providing electrical power for them were destroyed by the collapse of Seven World Trade Center, more than 130,000 gallons of oil and insulating fluid had been released from high-power voltage lines and transformers. The smoldering underground fires choking rescue workers contained fiberglass. All over the nation, as mail was handled gingerly, people washed their hands religiously, brushed invisible particles from their clothes. They choked, loosened their collars, and wondered if America would ever catch its breath again.

STRAIN 9

Outbreak

BRIGHT AND EARLY Monday morning, October 15, 2001, Amerithrax's long-delayed letter to the Senate Majority Leader reached its destination.[8] Forty of Senator Daschle's aides were already at work in his sixth-floor Capitol Hill offices in the Hart Building. Jet fighters still patrolled the skies above them. The day was unusually hot and humid and for that reason the powerful air-conditioning system was functioning at full blast. A storm threatened. During the Senate and House votes on the USA Patriot Act on Friday, the Senate had passed a version that favored Attorney General John Ashcroft's views. Daschle had argued for a firm money-laundering provision in the bill, but was averse to the rapid timetable of the legislation. Senator Leahy had abandoned the modifications guarding against an infringement of constitutional liberties his people had told the ACLU he would fight for. On October 4, he had been attacked by several conservative talk show hosts. The House had voted 337–79 to pass the bill. Though Daschle's letter had arrived, there was no sign of Leahy's letter.

At 9:45 A.M. coffee was brewing in the suites and there was the pleasant murmur of voices in the background. The envelope in the basket bore

---

[8] This was the same day the first wave of anti-abortion hoax letters mailed by Clayton Lee Waagner arrived at over 270 Midwestern abortion and family planning clinics.

the same Trenton, New Jersey, postmark as envelopes NBC and the *Post* had received weeks earlier. Amerithrax had neatly sealed the seams of his tainted envelope with Scotch tape. Inside the bright airy room, a female intern turned the envelope in her hands. She felt a small bulge at one end, but slit open the flap anyway. A puff of choking gray powder disgorged itself onto the desktop. Motes of dust shimmered in a bright shaft of light.

Robin Cook's 1999 novel, *Vector*, opened with anthrax mailed in an envelope:

> With his thumb and index finger, Jason tried to determine the source of the bulge . . . he picked up his letter opener and sliced through the envelope's top flap . . . at the same time a coiled spring mechanism propelled a puff of dust along with a handful of tiny glittering stars into the air . . . he sneezed several times from the dust.

Similarly, the Daschle letter had exploded in a puff of powder.

A message inside, photocopied from an original, written in the same childlike printing as previous letters, read:

09-11-01

YOU CAN NOT STOP US.
WE HAVE THIS ANTHRAX.
YOU DIE NOW.
ARE YOU AFRAID?
DEATH TO AMERICA.
DEATH TO ISRAEL.
ALLAH IS GREAT.

Amerithrax's letter to Tom Brokaw had failed to drive home the fact that the powder inside was anthrax. This time the killer warned specifically of it, but failed to recommend an antibiotic. His earlier advisement, in any case, had been false. Penicillin was not the best antibiotic for anthrax; Cipro was. But suggesting Cipro might have revealed a degree of medical knowledge on the part of the anonymous mailer he wished to conceal. He did use the phrase "You die now," just as fifteen letters posted from

Indianapolis to the media had. For the first time Amerithrax used closing punctuation and threatened not just individuals, but a nation.

Amerithrax had done a more orderly job of printing sentences composed of capital letters this go-round. And the eight printed lines were closer together than on the six-line Brokaw letter. The first character of each sentence was larger, as were the words "America" and "Israel." The FBI had been openly skeptical that foreign terrorists had mailed the anthrax letters. "Handwriting and linguistic analysis," they said, "forensic data and other evidence" had led them to believe at this point in their investigation that Osama bin Laden's Al Qaeda network was not the force behind the anthrax attacks.

Daschle's aide hurled the letter into a wastebasket and called the police, who notified health officials and sealed off the office. Some of the floating particles were sucked into the high-powered air-conditioning system and blown throughout the Hart Building for over half an hour. A specialized bioterrorism team from Quantico, clad in Hazmat suits, rushed to the office of the South Dakota Democrat. The Hazardous Materials Response Unit tested the air, and at 10:30 A.M. shut down the air conditioners. They swabbed the noses of staffers and lobbyists for anthrax spores and did a preliminary field test with handheld "Smart Tickets." First responder and law enforcement agencies often used these commercially sold, hand-held immunoassays for the swift detection of *Bacillus anthracis*. The instant screening devices were intended only for the sorting out of environmental specimens, not for treatment of patients. The rapid field tests were intended to be used in tandem with more sensitive antibody tests and microbiological cultures. When a polymerase chain reaction for the detection of anthrax spores in the Daschle letter tested positive, the entire office building was evacuated and sealed off.

The anthrax sent to Brokaw and the *Post* had been relatively crude—the *Post* sample less so—and contaminated with harmless cells. Many of the spore clumps had been too large to penetrate deep into the lungs where they could inflict the most harm. There was something different about the half-teaspoonful of anthrax mailed to Senator Daschle. It was more refined, light and airy. It had spread speedily once the envelope was opened.

By car, FBI special agent Darrin Steele and his partner rushed two rapid assays (a fragment of office carpet in a sealed white plastic container, and the Daschle letter and envelope in double Ziploc bags) to the Institute.

At Fort Detrick, they handed the specimens over to the Special Pathogens Laboratory for expert analysis. First, the letter and envelope were brought to Biological Safety Level 2 (BSL-2). Whenever a clinical sample was potentially infectious the lab personnel used BSL-2 or Level 3 (BSL-3) facilities to handle clinical samples. The highest and hottest containment level was Level 4 (BSL-4)—decon showers, air locks, air hoses coiled from the ceiling, and bright blue full-body spacesuits.

Masked technicians in closed-front lab coats with cuffed sleeves and several pairs of latex gloves stretched over the sleeves studied the sample in BSL-2 conditions. Visual inspection of residue inside the bags suggested that they were dealing with an extraordinarily high concentration of *Bacillus anthracis* spores that had been processed to a surprisingly fine grade. Everyone began to wonder about the level of expertise Amerithrax had brought to bear in the powder's production.

"In the four years that the special pathogens sample test lab has existed," said Col. Erik Henchal, chief of the Institute's diagnostics systems division, "this was the first time we had ever received a real impression that this is something to be very concerned about."

From BSL-2, the Daschle letter and its pair of surrounding bags were placed inside a third plastic bag and taken to a more secure BSL-3 lab behind entry door AA3. That night, in a specially sealed room, something strange occurred when John Ezzell, a civilian microbiologist, and his colleagues expectantly gathered around a huge electron microscope. It had fallen to him, as the Army's consummate anthrax scientist, to examine the spores. Though he had been immunized against the disease, Ezzell wore a respirator over his nose and mouth as he made his analysis. He removed the aluminum foil from the first sample and attempted to put the two grams of uniformly light tan powder under the microscope.

The microscopic spores magically leaped from the microscope slide. They wafted away weightlessly, climbing up into the laminar-flow hood. The glass safety cabinet was open in front, but under negative air pressure. Whenever the lanky Ezzell tried to weigh a sample, the spores refused to rest on the scale. They would not adhere to sticky tape. The slightest breath of air, arm movement, or tabletop vibration propelled them into the air. As spores flitted about under the hood like gas, Ezzell began to worry about the number of escapees clinging to the top. Soon there would not be enough to analyze. Ezzell was seeing weaponized anthrax for the first time in his life.

He and his team transferred a few spores from the envelope to a microbial culture dish where they could germinate and grow into thriving colonies for genetic analysis. Then they sequestered the bulk of the powder and confined further inspections to the dish samples. To quell the stream of floating spores, they immersed some in special chemical fluid. They embedded others in thin slices of paraffin. Now they could examine and test them without further airborne escapes. Even then, the scientific detectives ran short of spores long before they had completed every test they had hoped to do. A battery of biological assays followed.

First, electron microscope studies of the paraffin-lodged powder showed that the particles were remarkably small and had finer anthrax particles than the previous letters. They were only 1.5 to 3 microns (0.0015 to 0.003 millimeters) in diameter. Amerithrax had taped the envelope seams and flap shut, presumably to keep spores from leaking out.

Yet investigators found that the porous paper of all the premetered envelopes had extraordinarily large pores. "It had to be one of the most porous materials," an official said, comparing the cheap paper of the attack envelopes with standard ones. "Whether that was by chance or design, I have no idea." The pores in the envelopes, up to 50 microns wide, were bigger than the largest Daschle anthrax clusters and could have allowed anthrax to effortlessly escape into the general mails.

Apparently, a very large refining had taken place between mailings. Initial analysis demonstrated the Daschle sample to be remarkably pure—one trillion spores per gram. Unmilled anthrax spores contain debris and these under the microscope were almost entirely purified spores. Purity and small size were a perfect recipe for inhalational anthrax, the dream of every bioterrorist. The unadulterated Daschle anthrax was characteristic of material made by the optimal U.S. process patented by Bill Patrick, which did not use milling.

Amerithrax had refined his anthrax into a fine aerosol weapon between September 18 and October 9. Some experts thought the smaller size was only the result of milling by the mail sorters. And the spores sent in September might not be smaller at all, just lesser in quantity and hastily refined. They might have been made less effective by contact with moisture, which caused clumping. Others conjectured that Amerithrax had simply used material of different grades.

A biologist assisting in the investigation said the increasing potency of anthrax in the letters suggested Amerithrax might be a thief who had stolen several anthrax samples. "Maybe he didn't pocket one vial but two or three," he said, "if we're assuming this was an opportunist." Between mailings he may have cultured live anthrax germs in some makeshift lab and improved his product. Anthrax spores were notoriously fast growing.

The Institute's tests for antibiotic sensitivity indicated the anthrax bugs were not resistant to standard antibiotics. Cipro, doxycycline, and amoxicillin (a form of penicillin) were effective against them. Presently, the FDA indicated that Cipro, penicillin G procaine, and doxycycline were effective against inhalational anthrax. They had also approved tetracycline, minocycline, oxytetracycline, demeclocycline, and penicillin G potassium for clinically ill patients with anthrax infection.

Tests confirmed the Daschle anthrax belonged to the Ames strain, the most common strain, but then so did all of the terrorism-related specimens they had been able to retrieve. The anthrax letters contained 7 to 10 grams of material, of which 2 to 3 grams were pure weaponized spores. Seventy-five percent was noninfectious material and contained particles used for weaponization.

But the Institute's experts uncovered a new additive in the Daschle sample, a chemical coating to increase shelf life and potency and prevent clumping. Another lab with a special device could tell them what that substance was. The Armed Forces Institute of Pathology in Northwest Washington's energy-dispersive X-ray spectroscope could detect the presence of extremely tiny quantities of chemicals. The results might tell them who was involved in the anthrax mailings.

The FBI also decided to helicopter a sample of the Daschle anthrax for additional testing to the Hazardous Material Research Center at the Battelle Memorial Institute in West Jefferson, Ohio. Battelle, a military contractor, was near Columbus, the site of an avalanche of anthrax hoax letters. Battelle did bioweapons research with the Ames strain of anthrax for the CIA and the military. They also did secret work for the Pentagon and other government agencies. Their analysis of the purity and size of the Daschle sample would differ dramatically from that of the Institute, causing great consternation at an FBI that was unused to dealing with scientists.

Meanwhile, mailworker Norma Wallace's coworker, Jyotsna Patel, became ill. She suffered from intermittent fever with chills, dry cough with chest discomfort, shortness of breath, muscle ache, and fatigue. Later on Monday, she developed "head stuffiness," nausea, and vomiting. She became mildly confused and no one had any idea why.

The next day, Tuesday, October 16, Peter Jahrling, senior Institute scientist, was up before dawn to study the Daschle sample. After him, Tom Geisber began analyzing "a heap of dry particles," a corner of the envelope, and the two test tubes delivered by the FBI. Elsewhere, the nation was buzzing about anthrax discovered in the Hart Senate Office Building and in a House office mailroom. Rumors spread that Daschle's letter had also contained a little Star of David like the one sent to AMI in Florida. Anyone who had been in and around the Hart Building or on the fifth or sixth floor of the southeast corridor when the Daschle letter was opened was considered exposed. Exposed meant they had come into contact with spores, the dormant bacteria with capsules around them, but did not yet have the disease.

Biologically, the spores sent to NBC, AMI, and Daschle were indistinguishable from each other. "Physically, the spores sent to Daschle," said Dr. Richard Spertzel, "are in very small particles and readily dispersible into the air," allowing the twenty-two Senate staffers and Capitol police to inhale them. It didn't help that the woman who opened the anthrax letter panicked, tossing it into a trash can and releasing spores into the air.

Tuesday morning when 625 staffers arrived at the Hart Building, they discovered the entrance to the southeast corridor blocked by a police barricade. Twelve Senate offices had been closed. Workers were lined up for nasal swabs and three-day supplies of Cipro. Dr. John Eisold, the Capitol's attending doctor, and his technicians, culled from the D.C. Department of Health, New York, and the CDC, conducted the swabbing and analysis. Anyone who tested positive would have their antibiotic regimen increased to sixty days. Initially, there were twenty-two positive results. As the morning waned, the limited supplies of Cipro and even cotton swabs ran out four times, but were replenished. Capitol Hill workers received Cipro, but the Hamilton postal workers didn't. Cross-contamination of the mail, according to experts, was impossible.

That afternoon Senator John McCain called his staff into his office to calm them. Standing behind the leather chair in front of his desk, he began by joking. "Because of everything that's happened," he said, "I've decided to put Joe Donohue in charge of any disaster. We're going to call him Commander Joe. Joe, you can go over to my place and pick up a uniform." There was laughter all around since the youthful Donohue was an office favorite. Then McCain became more serious.

"If anyone sees anything suspicious in the mail, report it to an authority, call the Capitol police," he said. "It's OK to be afraid, but we need to channel that fear and be aware of our surroundings." The senators had been briefed and a separate emergency response team in the Capitol was on top of the anthrax, so they were in a safer place than others. "These are strange times," he said. "I appreciate the hard work everyone's doing."

Senator McCain made his way to the Dirksen Building, where his Commerce Committee staff kept their offices, having been moved there after control of the Senate passed to the Democrats. McCain was unaware that the Dirksen Building was exposed to anthrax too.

"Stop snoring. Get up!" McCain said as he entered the staff's offices, joking along the same lines he had with his other staff members to keep spirits up. He gestured toward a tiny, dark-haired woman, Pia Pialorsi, press secretary for the committee's minority. "I just want everyone to know Pia's going to be in charge," said McCain.

FBI Director Mueller spoke to the press at the National Press Office in Washington, D.C. "This afternoon," he said, "I want to spend a few moments at the outset talking about the anthrax issue. As most of you know, the FBI is investigating anthrax exposures and suspected anthrax exposures in Florida, in New York, here in Washington, D.C., and elsewhere around the country where such exposures have been reported. Every threat is taken seriously. Every threat receives a full response. We have no choice but to assume that each reported instance is an actual biothreat. And while organized terrorism has not been ruled out, so far we have found no direct link to organized terrorism." And this was true. Al Qaeda and Iraq headed the list of suspects in these early days, but no one could link them to the anthrax mailings.

"There are, however, certain similarities between letters sent to NBC in New York and to Senator Daschle's office here in Washington," Mueller continued. "We're now testing, analyzing, and comparing powders from these letters to each other and to what we know from Florida. And I should point out that the tests are being done under the auspices of the CDC. Since October 1, the FBI has responded to more than 2,300 incidents or suspected incidents involving anthrax or other dangerous agents. And as all of you know, an overwhelming majority of these incidents have been false alarms or practical jokes . . .

"However, I want to reiterate the comments of the Attorney General. Hoaxes, pranks, and threats involving chemical or biological agents are serious crimes and warrant a serious response. They will be investigated thoroughly and vigorously by special agents of the FBI, by the postal authorities, by local authorities, and by other law enforcement. As the indictment discussed today makes clear, individuals who attempt to prey on people's fears or even to pull a prank will pay a price. In addition to the price that they are paying, they should know that they are squandering millions of dollars in public health and law enforcement resources, resources that could be better spent in responding to actual terrorist acts. More importantly, they are taking manpower and time away from individuals who could be ensuring that there are no future terrorist acts.

"As incidents arise, we are working closely with . . . city and state public health officials, and with a host of federal, state, and local law enforcement authorities. FBI investigators and specially trained scientists, public safety officers, and hazardous materials response experts are being called upon as needed, whether they be at the federal government level or the state or the local level. We are making a concerted and coordinated effort to keep state and local law enforcement authorities informed and involved. Quite obviously, their skills and expertise are top notch, and we need their help."

More than ten thousand Hill staffers were put on antibiotics after the Daschle letter tested positive, a move that almost certainly saved many lives. "Everybody in that room [the Daschle office] would have died without treatment," said one CDC official. Sixty people in the Hart Office Building were within breathing distance of the powder. Thirty-one Senate staff members initially tested positive for anthrax exposure, but no one had contracted the disease. The cleanup went on as government offices were shuttered and workers sent for testing. Furnishings, drywall, and carpets were ripped out. Computers were carted away from the large Daschle suites.

In New York, Gov. George Pataki's Manhattan office was evacuated after an anthrax field test gave a false positive. Pataki's mail had passed through Morgan Central, which had processed the Brokaw, *Post*, and other media letters. Authorities assured the nation that should an anthrax letter pass through a postal center there could be no cross-contamination with other pieces of mail.

Health experts continued to insist that anthrax-tainted envelopes posed little danger as long as they were sealed, that there was no way other mail could become dangerously contaminated. The government advised that postal workers at centers that had handled the tainted letters did not have to take prophylactic antibiotics. Patel's temperature was 38°C when her husband took her to her primary-care physician. The doctor started her on levofloxacin for bronchitis. Because she worked in New Jersey and the anthrax was in Washington no one suspected anthrax and therefore no laboratory studies were performed at this time.

Postal officials were begging for testing of their employees and buildings, but "didn't get a lot of cooperation" from health authorities, who were focused on Capitol Hill. Tim Haney, Brentwood's sorting center manager, made the first use of digital records to trace a tainted letter. He and Patrick Donahue, the Postal Service's chief operating officer, sought to determine on their own which machine the letter had passed through. They tracked down the codes imprinted on the Daschle letter, and those codes identified the machine. Then they got descriptions of the powder mailed to Tom Brokaw and examined the machine for that kind of material. "We were thinking sugar, salt, thinking something might be lying on the floor," Donahue said.

On Wednesday morning, twenty-eight workers who worked in or near Daschle's office had tested positive for anthrax exposure and were on antibiotics. This was less than thought at first. Field detectors are notoriously inaccurate. What the government needed was a quicker, more accurate and precise test. An antibody-based anthrax detector was in use, but antibodies are difficult to make and variable in quality.

The first tests at the Senate bulk mail–handling facility were negative. Despite growing evidence that the anthrax was "aerosolizable," investigators assumed the heavily taped letter sent to Daschle could not have contaminated "upstream" mail-handling sites. Still the investigators didn't seek advice from the U.S. Postal Service.

None of their leaders were on the crisis management team that began meeting regularly in the secretary of the Senate's office. Leader of that team was Republican Senator Bill Frist of Tennessee, the only doctor in the Senate. His experience as one of the nation's foremost heart-and-lung transplant surgeons put him in the front ranks of any battle against bioterrorism.

As a member of the Subcommittee on Public Health and Safety, he and Sen. Ted Kennedy had helped draft and pass the Public Health Threats and Emergencies Act of 2000. On the Monday morning the Daschle letter arrived, Frist was in Nashville acting as host to a bioterrorism roundtable. Asked about the Daschle letter as he entered a press briefing, Frist made no comment, only recalling a hoax letter labeled ANTHRAX he had received three years earlier. Frist prayed the Daschle letter was a similar kind of beast. He went on to the Nashville Rotary Club to deliver a speech about bioterrorism, ironically written a day or so earlier on the subject of anthrax. Frist was concerned. His Public Health Subcommittee staff worked a few doors down the hall from Daschle's suite. Frist immediately flew back to Washington where Senate Republican leader Trent Lott requested he act as liaison for the Republican senators in the investigation of the attack on Daschle.

That same afternoon, Frist held two press conferences in a public health command center Daschle had quickly set up on the third floor of the Capitol. Later, to answer detailed queries about anthrax, Frist set up a website. Privately, he considered the nation's hospital system woefully unprepared for such a biological attack. Meanwhile, in the Hart Building, staff members were still working in their fifth- and sixth-floor offices. Because the Quantico hazmat response team had shut down the air-conditioning system everyone there was hot and tempers were frayed. By Wednesday, all of Frist's staff had tested negative, though one individual's test results had been lost and he would have to be re-swabbed. Dr. Eisold's team had taken more than six thousand nasal swabs during the first three days of the outbreak and thousands more environmental swabs.

Panic and near hysteria reigned under bright skies as top officials passed on misinformation masquerading as fact. Rumors spread that anthrax spores had gotten into the ventilating systems and the tunnels of the Senate office buildings and that the tunnels and subway leading from the Hart Building had been sealed off. When the leaders of both chambers met at the White House early Wednesday morning to see the President off to China, they discussed whether to close down Congress (whether both agreed to do so remains in dispute).

Shortly before 10:00 A.M., the House leadership announced that they would go out of session that afternoon and stay out until the following Tuesday, October 23. Speaker Dennis Hastert, an Illinois Republican, flanked by the Democratic leader Dick Gephardt, ordered the House adjourned, its offices closed for sweeping by an environmental crew, and most of the staff went home at 10:30 A.M.

However, at a briefing on the anthrax situation held later that morning in the Senate Dining Room, most of the senators bridled at closing up shop. "That would send the wrong message," they said. Furious House Republicans, who had expected the Senate to do as they had done, accused the Senate of acting symbolically. The Senate vowed to remain in session until Thursday afternoon, though its offices were closed. Rep. Peter T. King, a New York Republican, told CNN that the Senate's action was "pompous, posturing windbagging."

The House's failure to keep going, or appear to keep going, as the Senate had done while its offices were swept, did some harm to the national spirit. After traces of anthrax were unearthed in a House annex where mail is collected, in two House members' offices, and in the Ford building, the widespread criticism of the House for fleeing proved unjustified. At 1:00 P.M. Frist conducted a "tense" briefing of all the Senate chiefs of staff in the Capitol basement. "The high-level staffers in the room," wrote Frist, "were angry, frustrated, and resentful." Two hundred Capitol Hill staffers were told to start taking Cipro.

House and Senate office buildings were closed the rest of the day to allow for environmental testing, work that was to continue through the weekend. It was hard to trap an invisible killer—2,500 to 50,000 spores (enough to kill half of most test animals) didn't even cover the point of a pin. At this point it remained unclear whether Congress would go back into session next Tuesday as planned. Capitol police parked cars across all roads to the Capitol Plaza to bar traffic. They moved huge cement planters in front of the Russell Building stairs to block any bomb-laden trucks from being driven up the stairs. Trucks had already been banned from all major roads on Capitol Hill. On television screens all over America, citizens saw their leaders evacuating the seat of government.

After his staff left that afternoon, McCain was asked if he thought the House leaders had panicked in deciding to shut the House down. "I think Americans understand and feel very concerned about the situation," he said. "That was clearly the intent of the people who've done these things. Our job as leaders is to calm people down and not have people panic, or the terrorists succeed. Some people say we should shut down and go home. I say that would be raising the white flag. If we tell people to get on with their business and we go home, that sets a *fine* example."

Asked about the FBI's warning on October 11 that there would be another terrorist attack over the "next several days," McCain replied, "I don't think that was the best way to present it, nor was the statement by the Attorney General that endorsed the leak that there was a hundred percent chance of retaliation if we used military force."

In Hamilton Township, Linda Burch, a fifty-one-year-old maintenance employee working on the facility's mail-sorting machines, sought treatment for an outbreak on her forehead. A doctor drained liquid from the sore and prescribed oral antibiotics. However, as she awaited test results, the lesion "progressed and ulcerated."

The CDC was mystified. Cross-contamination could not have provided enough spores to cause such a serious form of the disease. The developments raised the possibility that another letter contaminated with anthrax had been sent to Congress by Amerithrax. This hypothetical letter may have passed through the Ford Annex before finding its way to a House office. Officials, however, admitted one letter could have contaminated others while passing through mail-handling equipment. Dr. Eisold said employees in the Ford mailroom were being tested and would be treated if necessary.

Federal and New York officials had given the go-ahead to tens of thousands to go back to their jobs near Ground Zero. But there were hot spots on rooftops a half-mile away. Eye, throat, and nose irritations and persistent wheezing and coughing were the high order of the day. The downtown dust was highly caustic. High "alkalinity levels" made it as potent as household drain cleaner. Oppressive dust left those with allergies gasping.

In California, almost four hundred emergency responders who had worked at Ground Zero in the three weeks after 9-11 were sick. No good turn goes unpunished. They would file workers' compensation claims because of illnesses they had contracted from the air. America was gasping from coast to coast, choking from grief.

STRAIN 10

Kiss Tomorrow Good-bye

ON WEDNESDAY, OCTOBER 17, 2001, hazardous materials specialists from the Fairfax County Fire Department in Virginia arrived at the Brentwood plant. They had come in advance of the CDC at the request of postal officials to test for anthrax bacteria. By seven o'clock that evening, Hazmat workers in protective gear were moving among unprotected postal employees working nearby. "How come you aren't testing the people?" one mailworker asked a tester. He got no answer. However, the preliminary results of the tests were negative.

Two nightshift mail sorters at the Brentwood complex, express mailroom worker Leroy Richmond, fifty-seven, and an unnamed worker a year younger, were ill. They had seen the onset of low-grade fevers, chills, sore throats, and stiff necks. Their mild headaches were not associated with visual changes or other neurologic symptoms. Both soon had minimal dry coughs, a heaviness in their chests, shortness of breath, night sweats, nausea, and spates of vomiting.

On Thursday, *Business Week Online* complained in an article titled "Postal Security Is Hardly First Class": "Not only is the USPS not testing everyone who could have conceivably touched these letters, but it isn't communicating with employees what its plan is . . . and where one-hundred-percent security can't be ensured, at least have a plan."

Also on Thursday, Postmaster General John Potter conducted a televised press conference on the main floor of Brentwood to assure everyone the mail was safe. He took the opportunity to offer a million-dollar reward for the apprehension of Amerithrax. On the same day a Brentwood plant manager reportedly made a series of entries in a diary or log: "The mail was leaking and a postal machine tested hot for anthrax."

A second anthrax spore test confirmed that the swabs "tested hot." A batch of mail from the Brentwood facility was received at Howard University and left traces of anthrax in the university mailroom. The traces provided the first concrete evidence that cross-contamination of the mail was possible. But the Brentwood facility wasn't evacuated. Its postal workers, predominantly African Americans, were not put on antibiotics, though the chiefly white Capitol Hill staffers had gotten antibiotics immediately.

Thomas L. Morris Jr., a Brentwood distribution clerk, was feeling ill too. He had felt the first symptoms on Tuesday while bowling in his league. He had been so fatigued that he had halted his play and returned home to Suitland where he lived with his wife and son. Unknowingly, Morris had come into contact with anthrax spores on October 13. Because he was having trouble breathing and was suffering anthrax-exposure symptoms, Morris, whose past medical history included diabetes mellitus, visited his primary-care provider. He arrived at Kaiser Permanente Marlow Heights Medical Center for a throat culture.

Morris had a fever and a cough productive of green sputum, but none of the shortness of breath, chest discomfort, or gastrointestinal symptoms that his coworkers were experiencing. His white blood count was slightly elevated and he had a temperature of 38.9°C. He had normal heart rate and blood pressure, and a respiratory rate of 24/min. Morris was infected, though he didn't know it, which meant spores were multiplying in his body. A few days had to pass before the anthrax bacteria, those strange subvisible beings, could produce the toxins that bind to the protective membranes of target cells.

The time between exposure and infection was anywhere from two days to six weeks for inhalational anthrax. Spores could hide in lungs for days or weeks before multiplying. It takes time to hamstring the ability of white blood cells to fight off disease and allow the bacterium's toxin to freely ravage the body.

Morris had a remote history of sarcoidosis, a mild disease in which abnormal collections of inflammatory cells commonly form in organs of the body, most frequently the lungs. It struck mostly African American men, like Morris, causing aching joints, a slight fever, shortness of breath, and enlarged lymph nodes. Unfortunately these were also symptoms of inhalational anthrax. Morris had been free of sarcoidosis for the past twenty-five years.

Morris told a nurse practitioner he thought he had anthrax, but the nurse and physician supervisors reportedly told Morris he only had a virus, the flu. They told him to take Tylenol for his aches and pains and sent him home. No chest X ray was performed nor were antibiotics prescribed. (All of this was according to Morris later.) A hospital spokeswoman later said the nurse called Maryland health authorities about Morris and followed their recommendations, and Morris was sent home with a diagnosis of a viral syndrome.

A fourth nightshift Brentwood employee, forty-seven-year-old Joseph Curseen, worked in the same sorting area as Morris, but in another section. Curseen had a wonderful mustache. It lifted like the wings of an eagle. While not as magnificent as a handlebar or military mustache, it was wonderful all the same. He had a slight goatee that underscored a full lower lip and set off his high forehead and heavy-lidded eyes. Like his three compatriots, Curseen developed a mild nonproductive cough, nausea, vomiting, and stomach cramps.

In New Jersey, Patel appeared at her local emergency room. She labored to breathe. A chest X ray revealed a moderate mass to the right and minimal left pleural effusions. Her antibiotics were altered to azithromycin and ciprofloxacin, but Cipro was discontinued twenty-four hours later. On Friday, her chest X ray showed increased soft tissue in the mediastinum. Her doctor added clindamycin and ceftriaxone to her medication. Patrick O'Donnell, Patel's coworker, was in stable condition and responding well to antibiotic treatment. He was found to have skin anthrax. Norma Wallace, like Patel, went to a local ER because of persistent fever and worsening chest pain. Wallace, the first New Jersey postal worker to contract anthrax, was confirmed with inhalational anthrax and was put on levofloxacin. Her chart read:

Temperature 38.4°C, heart rate 120/min, blood pressure 159/95 mm Hg, and respiratory rate 18/min. She appeared ill with increased respiratory effort, had decreased breath sounds at both bases, and had a 0.5- to 1.0-cm healing scab on the anterior neck. Initial WBC was normal except for elevation in neutrophil band forms. Blood for *B. anthracis* DNA by PCR was positive, as were immunohistochemistry studies for *B. anthracis* cell-wall and capsule antigens from pleural fluid cytology preparations. Her chest X-ray showed bibasilar infiltrates and a small right pleural effusion but no mediastinal widening. Initial differential diagnosis included atypical pneumonia versus inhalational anthrax.

On October 18, the USPS dispatched a *NEWS Talk Special Edition* to its Postal Supervisors and Postmasters. The three-page letter cautioned against "overreaction," and stated:

The following is a mandatory stand-up talk that must be read to your employees. Three decision trees are attached . . . 1. Possible room or area contamination by airborne gas. 2. Open mailpiece with suspicious powder spilling onto surface. 3. Discovery of suspicious unopened/sealed envelope or parcel. Managers are required to discuss the three decision trees in the context of local emergency action plans and resources. Make copies of the scenarios and distribute them before the talk so that employees can make notes. The decision trees provide guidance on immediate actions to take in the event of three scenarios involving the potential release of anthrax spores. They have been coordinated with the Inspection Service.

Please also make it clear to employees that overreaction to deposits of various powders and dusts not associated with suspicious mail are overwhelming emergency response resources. Employees who come upon a powderlike deposit that is not from an envelope or package should not assume the worst. Spills of make-up, powdered sugar, soap powder, talcum, and many other powders occur every day at work, in public places and at home. At work, these spills occur in locker rooms, bathrooms, breakrooms, offices and even on the workroom floor. So be alert for suspicious mail, but let's not overreact to spills of products we all use everyday . . . The current problem with anthrax hoaxes and actual terrorists activities has created a difficult situation for first responders to incidental spills and leaks of hazard-ous materials.

The Postal Service's previous policy, issued in 1999, called for evac-uating any postal facility upon discovery of a suspicious letter. New USPS guidelines, issued on October 19, stated that discovery of a "suspicious unopened/sealed envelope" should trigger postal supervisors to shut down equipment, evacuate and cordon off the area." The CDC said it left Brent-wood open (in violation of its own written emergency regulations) because it was confident that tiny anthrax spores couldn't pass through a sealed envelope. CDC spokesman Llelwyn Grant told UPI the agency's response "was based on the science that we knew at that time. There was nothing to suggest that anthrax could be a threat as far as anyone coming into contact with a closed letter."

Later, according to Judicial Watch (a conservative watchdog public interest law firm), a log thought to be from a Brentwood supervisor sug-gested the Postal Service more than suspected the facility was contami-nated—they knew it was—and had identified a specific machine that had sorted the Daschle letter, No. 17. An entry dated October 18 allegedly said the Postal Service had arranged for a company called URS to test the facility for anthrax. CDC officials were informed of this and a positive reading for anthrax when they arrived at Brentwood the next day.

The CDC wrote that, "most, if not all, bags, envelopes, and the like are not acceptable outer shipping containers." They mandated that sam-ples like anthrax mailed to researchers had to be wrapped in three-layered packaging, consisting of sturdy, watertight containers to prevent leakage. Barbara Hatch Rosenberg, chairman of the Federation of American Sci-entists Working Group on Biological Weapons, later said, "The CDC had given some thought to the prospect anthrax could leak during mailing and certainly they knew [the Daschle letter] was not packaged according to prescription. I don't think there was any question there was anthrax in the letters and it was getting around. For the CDC to say it did not know it could leak out of a sealed envelope is not a good argument."

By Friday, October 19, after considerable debate and a brief shutdown of the regional processing center in Hamilton Township (so the FBI could take samples), employees there and in Ewing Township, twenty miles

ROBERT GRAYSMITH

away, began a weeklong regimen of antibiotics. The thirteen hundred nasal swabs taken so far had tested negative. But those results were not definitive. Spores could be lost during the simple act of nose blowing. Officials increased the regimen to thirty days, then sixty.

Members of the letter carrier's union received this letter:

Dear Brothers and Sisters: Brother Al Ferranto, NALC Director of Safety and Health, has been meeting with the Postal Service at the Headquarters level on a daily basis dealing with the concerns over possible anthrax in the U.S. mail system. He has tirelessly worked to maintain up-to-date communication and to express NALC concerns . . . Letter carriers upon request will be provided with a filtering face piece and/or [hypoallergenic] gloves to protect them from possible contact with mail that has been contaminated with anthrax spores . . .

If it is determined that the mail in question is a viable threat, Letter Carriers should request . . . to be medically tested. If local management does not agree to allow Letter Carriers to be tested, please call my office immediately so myself or my staff can get involved. Please encourage Letter Carriers to remain calm and deliver the mail in as normal a manner as possible and do nothing which unnecessarily alarms the public or other Postal Employees, while we do the utmost to protect the men and women that deliver our nation's mail . . .

Sincerely and Fraternally, Dale P. Hart, National Business Agent, NALC.

At Brentwood, the unidentified postal worker's mild headache had not abated, but worsened. It was now constant and global. The postman could see no reason for the accompanying muscle aches, nausea, feeling of oncoming illness, drenching sweats, and discomfort from bright light. He had a mild, dry cough, a feeling of fullness in his chest upon exertion, and pain on the surface of his lungs. Meanwhile, his coworker Leroy Richmond, a Stafford, Virginia, resident, was experiencing the same familiar symptoms—including fever and chills. He was hot and achy, short of breath, and stoically taking aspirin to endure the discomfort. The thirty-two-year USPS veteran worked in a cubicle near No. 17, Joseph Curseen's machine, the same machine that had processed the Daschle letter and had been spray-cleaned in Richmond's presence. All day Friday, Richmond's

122

headache weighed him down. Finally, he went to see the Brentwood office nurse.

The nurse, suspecting flu or a severe chest cold, directed Richmond to Kaiser Permanente in Woodbridge, Virginia, for further examination. He arrived there in no acute distress, but with decreased breathing sounds. Dr. Michael Nguyen, Richmond's primary-care physician, ordered him to Inova Fairfax Hospital in Falls Church. Because of the recent Capitol Hill evacuation he also alerted county health officials. By the time Richmond's wife, Susan, had driven him to the ER, his chest had tightened to a painful degree. His cough was mild and dry, like his coworker's. His white blood count was normal. Though, Dr. Thom Mayer, head of the emergency room, observed no skin lesions, he had a hunch Richmond's illness might be inhalational anthrax.

Upon Richmond's arrival, attending ER physician Dr. Cecele Murphy observed that the patient was:

> afebrile and normotensive. Heart rate was 110/min, and he was not tachypneic. Serum albumin was decreased, but serum chemistries and renal function were normal. Arterial blood gas values showed adequate oxygenation.

Richmond's physical examination appeared unremarkable. His admission laboratory results were normal, except for elevated bilirubin and hepatic enzymes, low albumin, and hypoxia. Dr. Murphy listened to his decreased breath sounds at both bases. Then she scanned his X ray, which showed a widened mediastinum (especially in the right paratracheal region). A small air space showed opaquely in his right lower lobe. Suspicious, Murphy asked her patient, "Where do you work?" "I handle mail at Brentwood," Richmond said. Murphy ordered a more detailed CT scan. After the computer had analyzed the series of new X rays, the cross-sectional view revealed a widened area in the middle of the patient's chest. A forest of enlarged, diseased lymph nodes (the largest node measuring 4.2 centimeters) had created a shadowy mass between Richmond's lungs. There was bleeding and fluid within both lungs. Inhalational anthrax! She immediately put Richmond on Cipro, rifampin, and clindamycin.

At midnight she rang local health officials, who in turn notified the Senate Crisis Center and Senator Frist. Frist got the news around nine o'clock on Saturday morning and thus was the first top-ranking official to learn that anthrax in the city had probably "jumped" from the Hill. Frist was attending a short briefing when he learned that the CDC team had been contacted by a local physician. A mailworker not connected with Capitol Hill had exhibited "shortness of breath, an abnormal chest X ray with enlarged lymph nodes, but clear lung fields."

The X rays prompted a gut reaction in Frist, causing him to be "truly alarmed." "I believed the information could portend a national catastrophe," he wrote later. "Were postal workers safe? Would our mail system be shut down locally—or possibly nationally—just as the air transportation system had been paralyzed a month previously by the terrorist attacks on Washington and New York? What was next?" A potential anthrax epidemic could cripple the Postal Service and gridlock the two billion pieces of mail it moved annually. Definitive blood tests on the patient wouldn't be available for twenty-four hours, but Frist wasn't going to wait. An unprecedented and unexpected war at home had put postal workers on the front lines.

He leaped up from the meeting and phoned former Pennsylvania governor Tom Ridge, President Bush's new Director of Homeland Security, informing him they had a potential national emergency, "with disease appearing and behaving like we had never seen before." Within an hour Frist had set up a conference call with his command staff, HHS Secretary Thompson, Ridge, and other key leaders. He cautioned everyone to brace themselves and the country for "a national nightmare." Each member of Frist's public health team spoke for five minutes. Thompson listened gravely, then told Frist's team to make a list of everything they would need. "You will have it," he promised. He ordered emergency antibiotic stocks broken out and delivered to health workers for distribution the next day. Within eleven hours Dr. Murphy's patient's admission blood cultures grew *B. anthracis.*

At 5:00 P.M. Saturday, Brentwood workers routinely cleaned the three gigantic mail-handling machines with blowers, unknowingly spreading invisible contamination. Sorter No. 17, through which the Daschle letter had passed, was one of the machines cleaned by compressed air. The powerful blasts created air currents that created whirlwinds within the barnlike Brentwood facility, turning it into a death trap. Silently, there came a parade of illnesses in people who had been nowhere near the three sorting machines in Brentwood. On Saturday Joseph Curseen had a syncopal episode at church, but did not seek medical attention.

After five days of fever and headache, the unidentified Brentwood postal employee rang the Kaiser medical advice line. While Leroy Richmond's illness had manifested itself in breathing problems, his coworker's sickness exhibited itself through visual disturbances. He was suffering from photophobia and his vision was intermittently blurred. Like Richmond, he rushed to the emergency room at Inova Fairfax. When he arrived his pulse was 127/min, and respiratory rate 20/min. Admission laboratory results were normal and no organisms were seen on a gram stain of his cerebrospinal fluid. However, a front-to-back chest X ray showed widening between his lungs, especially on the right side. Next a noncontrasted CT scan of his chest displayed vast amounts of fluid in the pleural space on both sides. Admission blood cultures grew *B. anthracis* within fifteen hours. Ciprofloxacin, rifampin, and clindamycin were begun as treatment.

Washington Health Commissioner Ivan Walks refused to identify the postal worker hospitalized at Inova Fairfax. He reported to the press only that his symptoms were "suspicious" and that he was being tested for anthrax while under treatment. Officials said it was too early to draw any links between the letter that arrived at Daschle's office, the anthrax finding at the Ford building, and the sick postal worker.

At 4:39 A.M., Sunday, October 21, Thomas Morris made an emergency call to 911. He was short of breath and sounded frightened. He had rung for an ambulance a few minutes after he began vomiting. It was obvious that he already suspected an anthrax infection was the cause of his difficulties. He remembered a colleague handling a letter containing a suspicious powder the week before.

"Um, my name is Thomas L. Morris Jr.," he began. "My breathing is very, very labored."

"How old are you?" the operator asked.

"Um, fifty-five . . . Ah, I, I don't know if I have been, but I suspect that I might have been exposed to anthrax."

"Do you know when?"

"It was last, what, last Saturday a week ago . . . at work. I work for the Postal Service. I've been to the doctor. Ah, I went to the doctor Thursday, he took a culture, but he never got back to me with the results."

Morris explained that "there was some hang-up over the weekend . . .

Now I'm having difficulty breathing and just to move any distance, I feel like I'm going to pass out. . . . My breathing is labored and my chest feels constricted. I am getting air, but I—to get up and walk and what have you—it just feels like I'm going to pass out if I stay up too long."

"O.K., which post office do you work at?" asked the operator.

"This is the post office downtown, um, Brentwood Road, Washington, D.C., post office," Morris said, then paused. "A woman found an envelope [on October 13, 2001], and I was in the vicinity. It had powder in it. They never let us know whether the thing [had/was] anthrax or not. They never, ah, treated the people who were around this particular individual and the supervisor who handled the envelope. Ah, so I don't know if it is or not. I'm just, I haven't been able to find out, I've been calling. But the symptoms that I've had are what was described to me in a letter they put out, almost to a T . . ." The dispatcher had given him a letter by the Postal Service describing the symptoms of anthrax. "The doctor thought that it was just a virus or something, so we went with that, and I was taking Tylenol for the achiness. Except for the shortness of breath now, I don't know, that's consistent with the, with the anthrax."

"O.K.," said the operator, "you weren't the one that handled the envelope—it was somebody else?"

"No, I didn't handle it, but I was in the vicinity. . . . I don't know anything . . . I couldn't even find out if the stuff was or wasn't. I was told that it wasn't, but I have a tendency not to believe these people."

"And did you tell your doctor that this is what happened?"

"Yes, I did," said Morris. "But he said that he didn't think it was that. He thought that it was probably a virus or something."

"I'm going to get the call in to the ambulance."

There was a long pause. Morris was breathing with great effort now.

"Did the doctor give you any kind of medication or anything?" said the operator.

"No," said Morris, "he just told me to take Tylenol for the achiness."

"Hold on a second. I have an ambulance dispatched so it should be there shortly."

"O.K."

"If there's anything, if your condition starts to worsen, have your wife give us a call back, O.K.?"

"All right."

"All right then."

"Thank you," said Morris, ending the call at 4:50 A.M.

Early Sunday morning, Joseph Curseen arrived at an emergency room at Southern Maryland Hospital Center. He'd been vomiting and sweating profusely. His white blood count was slightly elevated, but he had normal serum chemistries and coagulation values. His past medical history included asthma. His chest X ray was initially read as normal, but later review noted an ill-defined area of increased density due to a mass in the right suprahilar region. He was discharged after receiving intravenous hydration.

An ambulance rushed Morris to the Greater Southeast Community Hospital. Morris reached the emergency department with worsening symptoms, including chest tightness, fatigue, chills, myalgia, nausea, vomiting, and shortness of breath. His temperature was "38.9°C, pulse 93 to 150/min and irregular, respiratory rate 20/min, and blood pressure 119/73 mm Hg." The doctor observed signs of respiratory distress. Examination findings included:

> rales at the right base with diffuse wheezing and tachycardia. WBC count was 18,800/mm3 with a differential of 73% segmented neutrophils, 6% bands, 11% lymphocytes, and 8% monocytes. Hematocrit was 55%.

A chest X ray showed soft tissue fullness around his trachea and the condition of the middle and lower lobe of his right lung seemed compatible with pneumonia. Fluid was steadily building up in the space between his lungs. An electrocardiogram disclosed atrial fibrillation. The patient was intubated, ventilated, and administered levofloxacin, diltiazem, and insulin.

Soon after admission, Morris became hemodynamically unstable. He went into cardiac arrest and died just before 9:00 A.M., only hours after his eleven-minute call for help. Like Stevens, his blood cultures would grow *B. anthracis*. Autopsy findings would include hemorrhagic mediastinal lymphadenitis, and immunohistochemical staining that would show evidence of disseminated *B. anthracis*.

At what time government officials informed the Postal Service of what they knew about the Brentwood employee and the implications of his infection isn't known. A USPS spokesman said the service learned on Saturday night. Senior vice president Deborah Wilhite said it was earlier, in the afternoon, before the three sorting machines were cleaned with compressed air.

At 10:00 A.M., just before he was about to appear on a news talk show, Frist learned that a patient's test results had come back with a diagnosis of inhalational anthrax. The local public health office fully mobilized and within hours began testing Brentwood employees at a site made available by Washington Mayor Anthony Williams. By afternoon, groups of twenty at a time were being frantically shuttled from station to station for testing.

As the number of known cases of exposure to anthrax grew, the press began speculating that the anthrax could have come from foreign terrorists—but which group and which country? However, the authorities were unable to even identify the quality of the Daschle sample. Was it weapons grade or not? Were the spores nearly pure or adulterated? As federal experts investigated the residual Daschle sample, the picture became fuzzier, not clearer. Everyone said it was unprecedented and unthinkable that a sealed letter could produce inhalation anthrax. There were no hard and fast rules in these days after 9-11.

The Hart Building contamination proved that key government buildings could be totally immobilized for several months. The Daschle letter showed how mail processing in sorting centers could produce cross-contamination. But based on their limited experience, they again made a decision not to close the Brentwood postal sorting office, a sprawling building that handles most of the mail in the nation's capital. And when workers there started getting sick, some were told they had the flu and sent home.

Leroy Richmond was suffering respiratory distress from the fluid buildup. He was treated with diuretics and systemic corticosteroids, which limit platelet function much as aspirin does. Finally, his doctor performed a therapeutic thoracentesis by inserting a needle between two ribs and withdrawing fluid with a syringe and later through tubes. As Richmond recuperated, the chest fluid reaccumulated and the painful procedure had to be repeated twice more. All three pleural fluid specimens disclosed yellow fluid streaked with blood.

The doctors had barely suspected mail handlers were at risk for getting inhaled anthrax infections. Then the CDC reported that it appeared the spores used in the Daschle letter might be much more deadly than in earlier mailings. This was contradicted by high officials in the government soon after.

Morris's inhalational anthrax was confirmed postmortem on October 23 at the Prince George's County facility. He was the first postal worker to die from anthrax. And no one had believed him.

"He died needlessly because of the negligence," said Johnnie Cochran, the lawyer his family later retained. Tara Underwood, Morris's stepdaughter, said the family heard the 911 tape, but she would not say whether the family was upset with the Postal Service or was considering any action against the agency.[9] "We're not making any statement at this time," she said. A Kaiser statement said Morris died "because someone put anthrax into an envelope and sent it through the mail." Five months later, (March 26, 2002) his family would file a multimillion-dollar lawsuit accusing a Maryland medical center of misdiagnosing Morris's symptoms three days before his death. The case would be settled out of court for an undisclosed sum.

Late on Sunday, after Morris's frightening and haunting 911 call for help and his terrible death, as sudden as a bolt of lighting, the Brentwood plant was closed. Bags of mail were trapped inside. Traces of anthrax were discovered at several offsite mail facilities that served government offices—the space agency NASA, the White House, and the Supreme Court. Scores of technicians moved through those buildings. Testing surfaces did little to establish where spores might have drifted. Many were too fine to have settled on any surface and could be anywhere.

Norma Wallace's fever persisted. Fluid was now escaping on both sides of her rib cage through small apertures. Doctors changed her antibiotics to ciprofloxacin, rifampin, and vancomycin. Sometimes two or three antibiotics proved more effective than one at eliminating a pesky bacteria. Meanwhile, Jyotsna Patel's cell pathology was about to test positive for *B. anthracis* cell-wall and capsule antigens by immunohistochemical staining.

On Monday, Brentwood postal worker Joseph Curseen made his way falteringly to a Maryland hospital. He complained of flulike symptoms,

---

[9] When Morris's 911 tape aired on television on November 8, 2001, he was called a "victim of terrorism."

but was sent home. That evening he visited the emergency room again. This time he reported muscle aches, chills, indigestion, another spate of vomiting, and a second fainting episode. Curseen looked ill, his skin was mottled, and it felt cool to the touch. His abdomen was mildly distended and he was in respiratory distress and wheezing on both sides. His signs:

Temperature 35.6°C, blood pressure 76/48 mm Hg, heart rate 152/min, and respiratory rate 32/min. Curseen's white blood cell count was 31,200/mm3.

Doctors administered penicillin and ceftriaxone. Ceftriaxone should not have been used for treatment of anthrax. *B. anthracis* isolates produce a wide-range antibiotic that inhibits the antibacterial activity of ceftriaxone. By now Curseen was suffering from respiratory distress. Tubes were placed in his trachea and mechanical ventilation was begun. Soon after, the doctor observed signs of abdominal cavity inflammation.

Chest and abdominal CT scans showed that, like in Wallace, fluid was escaping on both sides of Curseen's rib cage, but through larger apertures. A CT of his head was normal. With growth of *B. anthracis* from clinical specimens, a treatment of rifampin and levofloxacin was begun. Within eighteen hours gram-positive bacilli would be visible on the buffy coat blood smear, and blood cultures would grow *B. anthracis*.

Joseph Curseen died in the early afternoon the day after Morris and within six hours of admission to the hospital. Postmortem findings included prominent hemorrhagic mediastinal lymphadenitis and evidence of systemic *B. anthracis* infection by histopathologic and immunohistochemical tests. Again, confirmation was on October 23. Two other postal workers remained hospitalized. Nine others were ill with symptoms. Officials were still testing twenty-two hundred postal employees.

On October 22, just as the House and Senate reopened a day early, the unnamed Brentwood worker showed signs of worsening respiratory distress. Inhalational anthrax was confirmed. The next day, like Leroy Richmond, he had bloody pleural fluid drawn from his chest to relieve his worsening respiratory distress. With the fluid removal, his condition improved, but later he required a second thoracentesis.

Linda Burch, the postal maintenance employee, saw her eyelid and half her face swell up. The doctors performed a biopsy, diagnosed anthrax, and gave her the prescribed cure. She began to recover. On October 25, 2001, the *Washington Post* reported that Brentwood employees, working out of a tent in the parking lot, had discontinued mail delivery to residential area codes in D.C. because those codes were contaminated. Fourteen of twenty-nine mail-sorting areas at Brentwood were "quarantined" for high exposure to anthrax.

On October 28, Leroy Richmond was still struggling. He had anemia from the serious destruction of red blood cells by infection and a deficiency of platelets involved in clotting. Physicians drained the poison from his system and replaced it with clean blood in a plasma exchange. Plasma is the liquid part of the blood that remains after all the cells are removed. This effectively halted the destruction of red blood cells. His blood values swiftly improved. Richmond, a deeply religious man, remained hospitalized in stable condition and wondering what sort of monster had inflicted such agony on him.

Meanwhile a tireless search for the source of the anthrax continued in the hunt for Amerithrax. FBI Director Mueller allowed the Washington field office to direct the anthrax investigation under agent Van Harp, who would lead the investigation. As the inquest into the airplane attacks wound down, Harp had practically the entire office of 659 agents working on the letters. In Washington, Van Harp pursued three theories:

1. Amerithrax was from Al Qaeda. That first possibility was becoming more remote by the day. On Thursday, October 18, President Bush, while vowing to uncover the person behind the mailings, reported that there was no evidence that the anthrax letters were linked to the terrorist attacks on the World Trade Center and Pentagon.

2. Amerithrax was not one person, but a domestic extremist terrorist group.

3. Amerithrax was a lone domestic suspect like the Unabomber. Informal policies and lax security at U.S. biological labs could have provided an opening for someone with a grudge or a desire to make money on the black market to steal bacteria.

A fourth possibility arose—a foreign country waging war by mail. There were a number of suspect countries that had squirreled samples away in universities and private collections. Six countries had been able to produce anthrax in an easily inhaled aerosol make it hardy enough to survive bomb blasts. The Soviet Union had continued to develop biological weapons into the 1990s, "seeding" Cold War allies such as North Korea with bioweapons know-how.

Scientists in Pyongyang, Korea, had placed an order with a Japanese firm for large quantities of plague bacteria, cholera, and anthrax in 1970 and traveled to Soviet facilities several times in 1992 and by 2001 reportedly had all three types available for use. Syria and Algeria might still be conducting bioweapons research. China was suspected of maintaining an offensive-bioweapons program and Egypt had developed biological warfare agents. Even the U.S. had numerous biological agents to be used to develop defense strategies for biological attacks.

Some experts thought they knew not only what country had been behind the anthrax mailing, but where they had gotten their anthrax spores. Dr. Richard Spertzel said that while it was not known whether Iraq had obtained the common Ames strain of anthrax, Iraqi weapons scientists had repeatedly tried to acquire it.

Spertzel also said a top Iraqi scientist had directed his team to evaluate mobile laboratories, facilities in which germ stocks could quickly be moved and hidden from inspectors. And while Soviet weapons scientists had used milling to make smaller particles, Iraq did not; Dr. Ken Alibek testified that the anthrax from the letters that he had seen had shown no signs of milling. Milling created a static charge that made the small particles clump together.

And what of the coating that circumvents the material's tendency to clump together? Shortly after the first anthrax victim died in October, the Bush administration began an intense effort to explore any possible link between Iraq and the attacks. The focus on Iraq was based on its record of developing a germ arsenal and also on what some officials said was a desire on the part of the administration to find a reason to attack Iraq in the war on terrorism. "I know there are a number of people who would love an excuse to get after Iraq" said a top federal scientist involved in the investigation. The President was among them.

The CIA had long assumed Iraq's agent of choice to be anthrax. In Mideast history anthrax had always been a presence. The Bible called it the "fifth plague" of nine terrible plagues that afflicted the hapless Egyptians after the Pharaoh refused to free the Israelites. Anthrax was the curse of blight which fell upon the Egyptians in the Book of Exodus, the sooty "morain" that killed livestock and affected people with black spots.

But biological terrorism has been around since ancient times. Persian and Roman warriors stuffed rotting animal carcasses into the drinking wells of their enemies. Marauding Tartars ended a long siege of the port of Kaffa on the Black Sea by catapulting bodies of bubonic plague victims over the city walls in 1346. The ensuing disease victims' flight may have carried the plague to Western Europe.

The modern history of anthrax contains accounts of anthrax feasts or "wedding banquet" scenarios in Iran, Iraq, Kazakhstan, Siberia, and various African countries. In these cases, contaminated meat not cooked enough to kill anthrax bacteria was shared by a large group. For millennia hide workers in the Middle East used dog feces in tanning hides. This practice made tanners and shoemakers prey to echinococcosis, a helminthic disease often passed from dogs to humans.

Research on anthrax as a bioweapon began more than eighty years ago during World War I. Anthrax bacteria were used by the German army to contaminate animal feed, poison horses of the opposing cavalries, and infect livestock. An infected sugar cube laced with anthrax by a German spy is still teeming with deadly spores. The Soviet biowarfare program, launched before World War II, geared up during the Cold War. By the 1980s the Soviets could manufacture thousands of tons of weaponized anthrax in twenty- and fifty-ton reactors annually.

Russia pretended to halt bioweapons work in the 1980s—just as Iraq started. Iraq acquired anthrax technology from "rogue" former Soviet Union scientists. "These were people I knew very well who were in Iraq or Iran and other Muslim countries," former Soviet bioweapons scientist Sergei Popov told *Newsweek*.

Wrongly, the U.S. believed that Iraq had not yet weaponized its virulent biological materials. Iraq, though a signatory to the 1972 treaty banning biological weapons like the Soviets, had conducted drying studies for anthrax so that it could be spread by air. As early as 1974, Iraq began to develop drying technologies to extend the shelf life of bioweapons like anthrax. Elisa D. Harris, who was not a weapons expert, but had served for eight years on the National Security Council, said that if a foreign state was involved, Iraq was a likely candidate.

Iraq not only had anthrax, but the U.S. had provided it with samples of the Institute's Vollum strain for thirty dollars. One couldn't help but think of thirty pieces of silver.

At a 2002 Senate Armed Services Committee hearing, Sen. Robert Byrd, a Democrat from West Virginia, asked Defense Secretary Donald Rumsfeld about the germ transfers to Iraq. Government invoices "read like shopping lists for biological weapons."

"Are we, in fact," said Byrd, "now facing the possibility of reaping what we have sown?"

STRAIN 11

The Second Suspect

MOHAMMAD ATTA AND his fellow terrorists basking in the Florida sunshine hadn't been the only ones interested in acquiring and adapting crop dusters. Atta had met with Iraqi intelligence before 9-11. He knew Saddam Hussein considered crop dusters essential for the airborne spread of anthrax germs. In August 1988, Saddam's biowarfare program had successfully tested and sprayed an anthrax simulant, field-testing it in simple aerosol sprayers attached to slow-moving fixed-wing crop dusters. A converted crop sprayer, normally used for dry chemical pesticides, could be used with Iraq's new Zubaidy sprayers.

Zubaidy sprayers (named after their developer, Dr. Tariq Saleh Mohammed Zubaidy) were actually just converted crop sprayers. Dr. Zubaidy had adapted this type of sprayer, used for laying down dry chemical pesticides, and linked it to a low-volume tank to take small-particle aerosols. In spring 1990, Iraq purchased forty top-of-the-line agricultural aerosol generators from an Italian company. The Italian generators were each capable of dispersing eight hundred gallons per hour. They were compact enough to fit on the back of a small boat, pickup truck, or single-engine aircraft and could spread either liquid or dry anthrax.

In early August 1990, the Iraqi germ team modified aerial pesticide sprayers with special two-thousand-liter tanks filled with bacterial agents. Anthrax could be dispersed from a canister strapped to the wing of an

Iraqi warplane, from aerial bombs, or from smaller unmanned "death drones." Later, Iraq modified the Zubaidy spraying device to fit a drone aircraft.

"I'll tell you that RPVs [Remotely Piloted Vehicles] carrying biological warfare drop-tanks filled with anthrax, now that's an effective weapon," said Hamish Killip, a United Kingdom inspector. "Incredibly simple and incredibly awful. Once you have a drone up and running, it would be the most ghastly weapon, like the Nazis' V1 buzz bombs."

In October 1989, Vladimir Pasechnik, a top Soviet biologist and former director of the Institute for Ultra-Pure Biological Preparations in Leningrad, had four hundred scientists doing research on modifying cruise missiles and sleek, low-flying robotic craft. Because a light, short-range drone was unstable, a spraying device attached to the bottom of the fuselage had to be compact and vibration free, capable of withstanding buffeting in high desert winds. Iraq located the perfect device in 1988 from Niro Atomizer in Denmark for ten thousand dollars each. However, Iraq was blocked from importing those special spray dryers.

Iraq's most effective anthrax platform was a helicopter-borne aerosol generator that worked like an insecticide disseminator. Any commercial helicopter fitted with a standard hook device to its belly could take up to ten of these sprayers to lay down a huge amount of "line source" biological agent, dry or wet, over a vast area. The Zubaidy device was tested from helicopters at Khan Bani Sa'ad, an airplane engine testing facility north of Baghdad. An anthrax simulant, successfully field-tested in crop-dusting sprayers, helicopters, and fighter aircraft, was now adapted to speedboats.

The Iraqis could slip aerosol-generator-equipped speedboats into the Gulf at night and unfurl a path of lethal aerosol. According to experts, such a cloud "could kill ninety percent of the U.S. troops there." During fall nights in the Persian Gulf region an oppressive layer of overheated air crouches atop cool air near the ground, trapping and suspending dust and any stray particles. Depending on prevailing winds and the pressure of the inversion layer, the consequences of an anthrax cloud would be "horrendous."

It was easier to buy anthrax than large experimental animals, as Iraq found out when they attempted and failed to purchase rhesus monkeys from the United Kingdom in 1978. When they tried to buy chimps from

Britain's Chipperfield's Circus, they were turned away. During the 1980s lethal strains of anthrax were available from more than fifteen hundred microbe banks around the world.

Most prominent was the U.S. germ bank, the American Type Culture Collection in Maryland near the Institute. The ATCC was the largest lending library of microorganisms on the globe. In 1985, Saddam initiated a crash five-year bioweapons production program, "the Double-Edged Sword of the Cousin of the Project." Iraqi scientists began concentrated, targeted research on anthrax and botulinum toxin. Since the U.S. Department of Commerce had authorized sales of anthrax to Iraq, the rogue country purchased starter germs from the ATCC, which housed "particularly virulent variants of anthrax."

In April 1986, the Iraqi Minister of Trade's Technical and Scientific Materials Import Division (TSMID) legally bought thirty-six strains of ten different pathogens from ATCC for thirty-five dollars. They included tularemia, Venezuelan equine encephalitis once targeted for weaponization at Fort Detrick, and seven strains of anthrax. Those seven included three types of deadly anthrax strains isolated at the Institute, including a Lederle Labs strain and the so-called Vollum 1B strain. Vollum 1B was then still being perfected from the dried blood of microbiologist William A. Boyles, an anthrax casualty. None of the strains were of the Ames variety.

The pathogens, in glass vials, were expressed to the University of Baghdad, ostensibly for vaccine research. Instead they wound up at the Muthanna State Establishment, eighty miles northwest of Baghdad. Al-Muthanna was the huge chemical and biological weapons complex where the Iraqi bioweapons program had first begun in earnest. In March, May, and September 1986, the ATCC mailed the University of Baghdad six strains of botulinum, the single most poisonous substance on earth. Botulinum can cause dizziness, blurred vision, muscle weakening, and finally respiratory failure and death.

The May shipment also included three strains of gas gangrene, which kills tissue, causes internal bleeding and liver damage, and creates toxic gases inside the body. In the same year, the CDC shipped germs to the Iraqi Atomic Energy Commission and samples of botulinum toxin and botulinum toxoid (used to make vaccines against botulinum toxin) to al-Muthanna. From this and the botulinum from the ATCC, the Iraqis made 5,300 gallons of botulinum toxin. They gave the various poisons designations based on color and appearance: botulinum—"tea"; anthrax—"coffee"; and clostridium—"sugar." Thus, the U.S. helped stock Iraq's bioweapons arsenal from the onset.

In 1987, TSMID began buying tons of yeast extract, bacterial growth media (which looked like powdered milk) for anthrax. They started production deep in the desert thirty-five miles southwest of Baghdad at Al Hakam, Iraq's extensive new biological warfare production facility in Jur Al Shakar near the Euphrates. Two years earlier, Al Hakam (code-named Project 324/subunit 900) had received fermenters and two anthrax cultures from France's Pasteur Institute. As they continued with their quest to weaponize anthrax, they filled seventy-five Scud warheads with the brown liquid concentrate. They readied twenty-five anthrax-filled bombs at a small airfield in western Iraq opposite the Israeli border. Work continued throughout the year under a government organization—the Technical Research Centre, which housed Biosafety Level 3 buildings and a forensic research lab and animal test centers.

Carefully disguised Iraqi-built fermenters were stored at Al Hakam. The top secret facility masqueraded as a chicken feed factory that produced only animal feed and "natural biopesticides." In 1988, they also manufactured aerial bombs and 122-mm rockets. Saddam was able to purchase anthrax growth medium by the ton from the United Kingdom. However, when Saddam attempted to order high-powered ventilation drivers from another British company, he was rebuffed.

In March, Iraqi warplanes dropped chemical weapons on the Kurdish town of Halabja and surrounding villages in northeastern Iraq. During the Iraq-Iran war Saddam killed at least five thousand of his own people instantly with hydrogen cyanide, a blood agent. In June Iraq refined its bacteriological arsenal and field-tested artillery shells and battlefield rockets filled with anthrax simulant. On September 29, eleven strains of germs, including four types of anthrax, were mailed from ATCC to TSMID—which the CIA already knew was a front for Baghdad's purchases of germ weapons materials.

Lethal glass vials filled with anthrax ended up in Al Hakam (one of the microbes, Strain 11966, had been developed for germ warfare by the Institute in 1951). Saddam's scientists turned the shipment into 2,200 gallons of anthrax spores. The numbers were staggering. Al Hakam alone concocted 18,000 gallons of anthrax culture and 1,300 gallons of concentrated botulinum. The facility set as its goal 11,000 gallons of anthrax and botulinum a year. Its scientists agglomerated the crude anthrax spores into a finer, longer-living form of dry, small particles perfect for aerosolizing. To reduce particle size to the respirable ideal, Iraq used "sequential filters" in devices about the size of coffins and bentonite as an additive. The production setup was virtually identical to that used at the Institute during the 1950s.

Over at Al Fadhaliya scientists worked with fungi and at Khamisiyah Weapons Depot they stored nerve gases and wheat smut for destroying crops. At Al Walid Air Base in western Iraq they maintained a huge biological arsenal of R-400 bombs and buried another 157 bombs near Airfield 37 and Aziziyah. Other storage bunkers contained 1,850 gallons of wet anthrax.

It wasn't until February 23, 1989, that the U.S. Commerce Department got around to banning sales of anthrax to Iran, Libya, Syria, and Iraq. At least seventy-two shipments to Iraq had already been made. By 1990, al-Muthanna's scientists were busily cooking up plague in twenty-gallon fermenters, freeze-drying the bacteria, and storing them in glass vials. They produced several hundred gallons of the germs that cause gas gangrene and conducted inhalation and blast experiments on large animals—rhesus monkeys, sheep, and beagle dogs.

Al-Muthanna's glass vials of anthrax ended up at Salman Pak, Iraq's latest chemical weapons plant. The key biological facility stood twenty-five miles southeast of Baghdad on a bend on the Tigris River where there was also a terrorist training camp. At Salman Pak blind fences crisscrossed in the desert surrounding five large labs spaced two miles apart. They had built two Biosafety Level 3 lab complexes on a peninsula as early as 1974. In vast, hangerlike spaces only ordinary ceiling fans served for ventilation. Sliding metal doors concealed 1,400-liter fermentation tanks where they manufactured dry and liquid anthrax.

Thursday, August 2, 1990, at 2:00 A.M., Saddam sent his tanks rumbling across the Kuwait border. Within a day, Iraq had seized control of Kuwait. Six days later, Iraq had annexed it as Iraq's nineteenth province and moved its troops to Kuwait's border with Saudi Arabia. Possession of Kuwaiti oil fields increased Iraq's power within the Organization of Petroleum Exporting Countries (OPEC) and threatened not only the world's oil supplies, but the Mideast balance of power.

Immediately after the invasion, Saddam's biowarfare teams at eighteen biological war sites all over Iraq begin loading warheads into cluster bombs and 122-mm rockets. Of the 157 bombs, 50 were filled with anthrax. Of the sixteen missile warheads, five were packed with anthrax. The bombs and warheads were shipped to Iraqi Air Force commanders at four bases near Saudi Arabia and in western Iraq near Israel. They were to be used in case of nuclear attack. Spray tanks and drop tanks were readied for fitting to fighters, helicopters, and drones. At the ideal attack altitude of 275 feet, they could spray two thousand liters of anthrax into the prevailing winds sweeping northwest to southeast. Any displaced anthrax germs could drift toward Iran and Saudi Arabia where U.S. bases were.

On August 6, the U.S. Navy flashed its commanders an urgent warning. According to a CIA report, Iraq's bioweapons program, the most extensive and aggressive in the Arab world, was in advanced stages of development. *Bacillus anthracis* might be available for weaponization. By year's end the Iraqis could deploy numerous biologically filled aerial bombs and artillery rockets effective against ships at distances of up to twenty-five miles.

CIA experts cautioned: "Botulinum toxin and . . . anthrax bacteria lend themselves to covert dissemination because even small amounts placed in the food supplies are sufficiently toxic to kill large numbers of people. Iraq also could covertly use spray tanks or aerosol generators purchased for its chemical warfare program to create large toxic clouds of bacterial agents upwind of a target area."

On August 7, 1990, American forces began moving into Saudi Arabia. Few soldiers were inoculated against anthrax. CIA analysts were apprehensive that if Saddam felt his personal position was hopeless he might use anthrax against a military installation or major Saudi oil facility. The following day the Army surgeon general's office recommended immediate inoculations against anthrax and botulinum. One hundred and fifty companies had been approved to manufacture anthrax vaccine, but only fifteen possessed the equipment to do it.

The first effective vaccine, developed in 1955 at the Institute, had its shortcomings. Anthrax's deadly nature precluded testing on people and the immune systems of monkeys, mice, and guinea pigs, while resembling those of human beings, were not really reliable animal models (anthrax vaccines intended for animals should not be used in humans). Researchers continued working toward a more precise correlation. The vaccine effectiveness, though efficacious in monkeys, had not been tested on humans. A handful of patients, after taking the series of shots, suffered serious reactions including brain damage and death. The existing formulation was "highly reactogenic" and trials never actually resolved whether the vaccine protected against all strains of the anthrax bacillus, much less inhaled spores.

The FDA had only licensed the vaccine in 1970. On Christmas Eve 1984, David Huxsoll, head of the Institute, and Dr. Richard Spertzel, a top germ specialist there, dictated a crash paper calling for stockpiling enough anthrax vaccine to inoculate two million soldiers. Soon after, Gen. Maxwell "Mad Max" R. Thurman admonished that the military was seriously underprepared if American forces were ever attacked by weaponized anthrax. Army Major Robert Eng also pleaded to build a stockpile, arranging for the purchase of 500,000 doses of anthrax vaccine—at least enough to provide 160,000 soldiers with the first three shots of a six-shot series. Thurman's and Eng's cries went unheeded. By the mid-1980s shortages of the vaccine were emerging.

In 1988, the Army contracted to buy large quantities of anthrax vaccine—three thousand doses. A cell-free protective vaccine had been produced for use in humans, a sterile filtrate from a culture of B. anthracis. A cell-free filtrate vaccine meant it contained no dead or living bacteria in the preparation. There was only one licensed manufacturer of anthrax vaccine in the nation, an antiquated lab operated by the Michigan Department of Public Health in Lansing. The government allowed the contractor five years to meet the order.

The primary component of the Michigan vaccine, protective antigen, prevents the disease by blocking the anthrax toxins from penetrating its host's cells. But Michigan could not meet the demand. On the day Iraq invaded Kuwait, the lab had only produced enough vaccine to shield 150,000 of the 500,000 U.S. troops in the region. The antibiotics had to be administered within twenty-four hours of contracting anthrax, a disease that showed symptoms only after it was too late. The only answer was to inoculate the soldiers before they set foot in the Persian Gulf region, but there was not enough time for the long series of shots. Soldiers would not have even partial immunity until after the war started.

On January, 17, 1991, at 2:38 A.M. local time, the first Allied air strikes against Iraq began. "Operation Desert Storm" first crippled Iraq's ability to launch attacks. The Allies bombed Baghdad, leveled Salman Pak, flattened Taji, site of Iraq's long-range missile program and a mustard gas facility, and obliterated Fallujah II, a chlorine and phenol plant for nerve agents and mustard gas.

By January 21, Allies saw no outbreak of disease in Baghdad, though balky, inaccurate detectors continued to signal signs of anthrax. Chemical alarms kept ringing. After five weeks of high-precision bombing, the coalition began a military ground assault on February 24. Within one hundred hours the U.S. had driven the Iraqis out of Kuwait and back across its border. The elite Republican Guard fled at top speed, only pausing to loot and torch numerous Kuwaiti oil wells. Under President George H. W. Bush's orders, the U.S. stopped short of continuing to Baghdad to oust Saddam, a decision that would cause America great grief a decade later. One hundred and forty-seven U.S. troops were killed in combat, including thirty-five lost during errant bombing and friendly fire artillery strikes.

In March, Iraq accepted the terms of the cease-fire. As a condition of surrender they agreed to halt future nuclear, chemical, or biological weapons of mass destruction and to allow UN inspectors from thirty member nations to locate and destroy any surviving Iraqi biowarfare facilities. On April 6, Iraq accepted UN Resolution 687 requiring it to end its program of weapons of mass destruction, to declare all locations and all related research, development, and production, and to allow for monitoring and verification of compliance.

U.S. troops exploded Iraqi weapons depots without adequate precautions against fallout. Their full-body chemical protective gear, activated-charcoal outer garments, proved cumbersome. Nearly half the GIs' gas masks fitted improperly. Biodetectors meant to find airborne spores were inefficient and any fallout and exposure might go undetected. Some of the captured Iraqi soldiers could have been carrying anthrax antibodies. The Institute's suggestion was this—if any Allied troops died from anthrax in the Gulf region, their bodies were to be saturated with Clorox and sealed in special body bags. One hundred new bags were already in preparation.

In the fall, veterans who had been on duty in the Gulf began getting sick. By 1998, ninety thousand Gulf War vets reported physical distress from something they had contracted while serving on active duty. They suffered periodic blurred vision, low-grade fever, rashes, stomach and intestinal distress, chest pain, increase in urination, diarrhea, nausea, constant chills, sores, running noses, heart problems, chronic flulike symptoms, and memory loss. The government claimed it was only "psychological stress."

Dr. Meryl Nass, with the Department of Internal Medicine at the University of Massachusetts, suspected that 10 to 35 percent of anthrax vaccine recipients had developed illnesses resembling chronic fatigue syndrome, multiple chemical sensitivity, autoimmune illnesses, and/or neuropathies, also known as "Gulf War syndrome."

"This is the trade-off you are making when receiving this vaccine," said Dr. Nass. "The vaccine presently available has caused long-lasting medical illness in a significant proportion of those who receive it. All existing doses are currently under quarantine by FDA for manufacturing lapses. Even if FDA releases the quarantined vaccine for military or civilian use, the manufacturing lapses and risk of chronic illness 'remain.' The side effects of an unproven vaccine could cause more death and illness if widely administered." The GIs had been given an antidote to Soman nerve gas— pyridostigmine bromide, atropine, and another chemical. Had the experimental drug PB sickened them? Or some unknown pathogen Saddam had been perfecting?

Before the Gulf War, the threat from weapons of mass destruction wasn't very real. After the war it was a "very real threat." The U.S. discovered Iraq had concealed a grim arsenal bigger and far more deadly than imagined. Dr. David R. Franz, a former colonel and senior scientist at the Institute, headed three UN inspection teams in Iraq. He believed Iraq had used dummy anthrax during testing. Inspectors unearthed powderized *Bacillus thuringiensis* (BT) at the Al Hakam plant. The particles were as small as one to five microns in size, the same size of the spores later mailed to Senator Daschle.

"A relative of anthrax is *Bacillus thuringiensis* (BT)," Dr. Franz said, "which produces a toxin that kills the common bollworm. Formulated as powder, pesticide BT has larger particles than anthrax because pesticides have to fall through the air to coat leaves. Military bioweapons experts use BT and similar nonlethal bacilli as a stand-in for anthrax when ironing out production." Franz added that the Iraqi "BT was missing the glue [a gene] for the toxin that kills bugs, rendering it totally useless as an insecticide."

Iraq produced thousands of gallons of anthrax, but in a wet form slightly more viscous than whole milk. Bio-agents grown only in liquids and produced in a liquid paste form are called "slurry." Stephen D. Bryen, who headed the Pentagon's Defense Technology Security Administration, reported that United Nations inspectors in Iraq found no "dusty" anthrax. He also observed that the Iraqis, like the Soviets, tended to mix together various germs (or strains) and chemicals in their weapons, presumably to defeat countermeasures. The mailed powdered anthrax was all of a single strain, the so-called Ames strain that had been developed in the U.S.

Dr. Khidhir Hamza, a former top official in Iraq's weapons program, believed he knew who had mailed anthrax to Brokaw and Daschle. "This is Iraq," he later told CNBC. "This is Iraq's work. Nobody has this expertise outside the U.S. and outside the major powers who work on germ warfare. Nobody has the expertise and has any motive to attack the U.S. except Saddam to do this. This is Iraq. This is Saddam."

He said Iraq had developed the capability to weaponize anthrax even before he defected to the U.S. seven years ago and continues to maintain that capability. "I have absolutely no doubt. Iraq worked actually even before the Gulf War on perfecting the process of getting anthrax in the particle size needed in powder form and disseminate the way it is being disseminated now. Probably this is the first wave. I'm not trying to frighten everybody in this, but probably this is the first wave."

STRAIN 12

Cry of the City

ON OCTOBER 17, 2001, the FBI had sent a sample of the Daschle anthrax to Battelle for further testing and confirmation of the Institute's analysis. Battelle was an Ohio military contractor that did secret work for the Pentagon. As officials accused Institute scientists of processing samples too slowly, the CDC was castigating the FBI for sealing off access to the Daschle letter and its contents. The FBI was awaiting another series of test results from the Armed Forces Institute of Pathology in Northwest Washington. With their energy-dispersive X-ray spectroscope they were to attempt to identify the additive in the new anthrax. Some investigators thought it might be the clay bentonite, used by Saddam Hussein's bioterror cooks in Iraq.

Since BT (*Bacillus thuringiensis*) had been found at Iraqi anthrax plants after the war, the FBI was also investigating that angle. Amerithrax might have used BT as dummy anthrax to perfect his strains between mailings. Agents secretly monitored an equipment auction at one of the nation's largest BT insecticide producers. At gun shows they found a bioterrorism cookbook sold by antigovernment militia groups. The anthrax recipes inside contained sufficient instructions to make the deadly powder, as did sites on the Internet.

Maj. Gen. John Parker, commanding general of the Institute, told a caucus of senators at 10:30 A.M. that the Daschle anthrax was "essentially

145

pure spores." Parker had studied it himself through an electron microscope. Working from photographs, Dr. Ken Alibek thought the Daschle anthrax had not been done with a regular industrial process and might even be "homemade." A Defense Department official characterized the latest anthrax as "run of the mill." Bill Patrick, now a private consultant on biological defense, rated the Daschle anthrax as a seven on a scale of ten. "It's relatively high grade," he said, "but not weapons grade." Expertise was needed for that. "Weaponizing germs," said Sergei Popov, a 1992 Soviet defector and biowarfare scientist, "is not a basement production."

"If I have a small amount of anthrax," Leonard Cole of Rutgers wrote later, "it would take a few days to develop a huge arsenal of anthrax. In ten hours, one bacterium can yield a billion. A knowledgeable high school graduate could do it." At the same time General Parker was speaking to the Senate, the FBI dispatched a helicopter to the Institute to pick up a sample for a second opinion.

When Homeland Security Director Tom Ridge went to the White House briefing room to announce the latest news of the anthrax investigation, he was asked: Was the Daschle anthrax weapons grade, as Hill leaders had been told? Ridge insisted the anthrax was not "weaponized." However, he later had to reverse his opinion of the amateurish quality of the Daschle anthrax and concede that terrorists "intended to use this anthrax as a weapon."

When Tommy Thompson saw the Institute's test results on the Daschle letter spores—"treated to hang suspended in midair," "pure," and "finely milled"—he needed to see the President "right away." He rushed to the Oval Office to meet with the President and Ridge. The spores, according to the FBI, were "much more refined, more potent, and more easily dispersed" than the New York media anthrax. The Institute found that the Daschle anthrax contained as much as one trillion spores per gram—much, much more than had been detected by Battelle from the sample shipped to them in a single test tube. The Daschle powder was nearly pure spores and "highly aerogenic." It behaved like gas. Ridge reported the concentration of the anthrax powder was extraordinarily made "to be more easily absorbed." On October 22, the Battelle laboratories delivered a completely opposite opinion to the FBI.

The Battelle experts said the particles had a large-size range and told the FBI it looked like "puppy chow." While single spores predominated, some clusters ranged up to forty microns wide—far too big to penetrate human lungs. The big clusters suggested the powder was far less than American weapons grade and as much as fifty times less powerful than the Institute had determined.

Ridge and Bush adviser Karen Hughes interrupted a National Security Council meeting to tell the President of the conflicting analyses. Bush told them to "get everyone together and work it out." Ridge picked up the phone and said, "I need scientists!" Tom Ridge's ruddy face was not quite as square as a concrete block. He was a tall man, cut from Rushmore granite in a dark blue suit and blue tie with white polka dots. Clean-cut, with big hands, he had the intense look of a fullback who could do some real damage. His first press conference would be an anthrax press conference and he would be so unknown that people would say, "Tom who?"

The disagreement between the two scientific teams initially puzzled the FBI. However, the scientists quickly recognized the flaw. The tests had been conducted differently. When the FBI had transported a sample of the anthrax for additional testing to Battelle it had been altered. The Institute's scientists had irradiated part of the anthrax powder. This was "a safety technique that leaves the spores aerodynamic and other characteristics undisturbed."

Unaware that the Army laboratory had irradiated the material, Battelle used a different safety technique. They placed the anthrax in an autoclave, a sterilizer that used superheated steam under intense pressure, to kill the spores. This produced a far lower estimate of the concentration level and induced Battelle scientists to conclude that the material was more liable to bunch together in lumps, and thus less likely to become airborne than the Army scientists had estimated. Now the FBI commenced flying up to two hundred forensic samples a day by helicopter from Brentwood, New York, and New Jersey postal facilities and the New York Post to the Institute. Treated as criminal evidence, the specimens were analyzed (ten tests per environmental sample) inside Suite AA3. Col. Erik Henchal, an Army biologist, and his team ultimately analyzed more than thirty thousand samples. The Post sample turned out to be nearly pure spores.

NALC President, Vince Sombrotto, met with Bush and Ridge at the White House. "The proud members of the NALC do not walk with fear," Sombrotto said after meeting with Bush. "We will rise to the occasion because, as the president just said a few minutes ago, we're all soldiers in this war and tomorrow when I visit Trenton, I will pass his message along to all the letter carriers . . . that they're in the front lines of our war against these terrorists." The union leader told his letter carriers that the nation was depending on them as an anchor of "normality" in a difficult time.

"We cannot function in this country if fear is going to be our constant companion," Sombrotto said. "So long as we continue to deliver the mail, we'll be standing up for America in the war against terrorism. As I have said on numerous occasions, it is the familiar sight of a letter carrier walking down the street, shouldering a mail satchel, firmly holding the mail, that is reassuring to the citizens of this country . . . the Postal Service soldiers on—as it must—because the nation's commercial, social and even emotional health depends on it. If we let them make us cower, the terrorists will have won. So long as we continue to stand tall and deliver the mail, we'll be standing up for America," Sombrotto concluded. "God bless America, and God bless all of you." A toll-free hot line was set up to help carriers deal with trauma.

On October 24, a tense nighttime meeting presided over by Tom Ridge was held in the Roosevelt Room of the White House. Attorney General Ashcroft, the FBI's Robert Mueller, and Allyson Simons, Tommy Thompson, and sixteen other top officials and experts were in attendance. Ridge addressed the lack of communication between the CDC, FBI, and the Army. He told them to share information with each other—and take orders from him. Ashcroft, worried that another anthrax release might be imminent, was furious and took the Army, HHS, and FBI to task. Not a few there feared Amerithrax might be "a state actor," possibly dispatched by Iraq.

On October 25, another shipment from the rapidly dwindling supply of Daschle anthrax was sent to Battelle. The contractor subsequently produced estimates divergent from those of the Army scientists. The Daschle anthrax might be weaponized, pure and deadly, but there was barely enough left to test. The next day the USPS put new safety measures into place.

"Headquarters is purchasing nitrile gloves and N-95 filtering face pieces for all the processing and distribution centers in the country," USPS Chief Operating Officer Pat Donahoe wrote mail plant managers on Friday, October 26:

These items will be shipped directly from the manufacturers to your plants. Each box of N-95 face pieces provides instructions for its use. Attached is a mandatory safety talk on hand protection. Please ensure that your employees who desire these added precautions be given this personal protective equipment to use, as needed . . . wear your gloves, and wash your hands with soap water every two hours during your tour, and other times as appropriate.

J. Gerard Bohan, manager of Maintenance Policies & Programs wrote (noting that this was an interim policy to be updated as more information became available):

Implement the following procedures immediately:

1. Do not use compressed air for custodial cleaning.

2. Avoid dry sweeping of the floor and dusting other surfaces. Use a vacuum cleaner equipped with a HEPA filter or wet methods to clean the floors and other surfaces.

3. Wet mop using a ten-percent bleach solution (one and a half cups of household chlorine bleach in one gallon of water) to clean areas that cannot be using the HEPA-filtered vacuum.

4. Employees may wear a filtering face piece respirator (N-95) and nitrile or vinyl gloves for comfort. These tools are to offer comfort and an additional measure of security during the current crisis.

5. Dispose of worn out or damaged gloves and respirators by placing them in the trash.

6. Minimize the generation of dust when changing the bags in the vacuums. Place the full vacuum bag in a plastic bag and seal the plastic bag. Place the plastic bag in the trash. It is a good work practice to wear the filtering face piece respirator and nitrile or vinyl gloves while changing the bags in the vacuums.

7. Wash your hands with soap and water thoroughly when the gloves are removed and before eating.

The USPS temporarily closed the Princeton Post Office, while in New York, Morgan Post Office employees were given the option of working on another floor or at the Farley Building across the street. That afternoon, the USPS awarded a $40 million contract to the Titan Corp. of San Diego to provide eight systems of electron beam equipment to sanitize mail. By this point, 5,477 suspicious incidents had been reported. Scares averaged 608 a day.

Meanwhile, the FBI awaited an analysis from the Institute of Pathology to learn what additive their energy-dispersive X-ray spectroscope had identified. Both the U.S. and Iraq used a chemical additive in processed anthrax. These additives removed the electrostatic charge between spores created by the mechanical milling process that made fine dust. For their process American scientists had settled on a special form of silica to keep the particles from binding together. Silica was a common industrial drying agent.

Soviet and Iraqi biowarfare programs used bentonite instead. Bentonite, a clay additive, with aluminum helps reduce the static charge of spores so they float freely and stay as small as possible. The sophistication of the Daschle anthrax suggested that Iraq was behind the attacks.

Federal scientists tracked down records of Iraq's biological arms program and biological samples. They analyzed them in laboratories run by biologists Paul S. Keim of Northern Arizona University and Paul J. Jackson of the Los Alamos National Laboratory in New Mexico. They reexamined seven anthrax strains that Iraq bought from ATCC in the 1980s.

None of the strains were identified as the suspected strain, Ames, and none of the seven matched the mailed anthrax. Instead they resembled a strain labs across the world used in research. The CIA knew Iraq had unsuccessfully tried to buy that Ames strain from British researchers in 1988 and 1989. Raymond H. Cypess, president of the germ bank, put to rest the theory that mislabeling might have accidentally put the lethal Ames germ in Iraq's possession. "We never had [the Ames strain]," he said, "and we can say that on several levels of analysis."

Finally, the X-ray spectroscope found silica and oxygen to be the additives mixed with the Daschle spores as a coating—silicon oxide. Amerithrax had put powdered glass into his anthrax. Major General Parker said that tests had turned up no signs of aluminum—a main building block of bentonite. "If I can't find aluminum," he told reporters, "I can't say it's bentonite." And if there was no bentonite, Iraq had not made the letter anthrax. Tommy Thompson, D. A. Henderson and other HHS officials, and the FBI saw Iraqi anthrax close-up. Parker brought them six tubes of orange anthrax simulant powder from Al Hakam. Crude and lumpy, and mostly bentonite, it looked nothing like the Daschle spores.

It looked more and more as if Amerithrax was a domestic terrorist.

"We looked for any shred of evidence that would bear on this, or any foreign source," a senior intelligence official said of an Iraq connection. "It's just not there."

PUBLICLY, WHITE HOUSE officials made no mention of the failure to find an Iraq-Amerithrax connection. That would be tantamount to a declaration of war. Instead they intensified focus on the United States. Amerithrax might not be one of the nation's enemies; he might be one of their own, someone the scientists aiding the FBI might know. "Like many people, when the case of anthrax emerged so close to September 11, I couldn't believe it was a coincidence," Tom Ridge said. Because of the timing, he had logically assumed that the anthrax attack came from a foreign nation, but as no one unearthed any evidence to confirm his initial suspicion, Ridge began to rethink the problem. "But now, based on the investigative work of many agencies," Ridge said, "we're all more inclined to think that the perpetrator is domestic." Ari Fleischer, speaking for the White House, agreed. "The evidence is increasingly looking like it was a domestic source," he said.

A domestic terrorist after the events of 9-11 was an unholy thought. But as they looked back over the last two months, the detectives realized Amerithrax had acted in a very "un-terrorist-like" manner. He went out of his way to make certain his letters did minimal damage. He taped the seams of his envelopes to prevent powder from escaping. He enclosed the spores in a pharmaceutical fold, warned the recipients the contents were anthrax, and even suggested a medication. Terrorists would have used an antibiotic-resistant strain such as the one Dr. Alibek had developed for the Soviets at their Stepnogorsk facility in the late 1980s. They would have used a more efficient delivery system. An envelope is an extremely crude device for spreading infectious aerosols. As one bioterrorism expert, Michael Osterholm of the University of Minnesota, put it, someone was firing a "powerful bullet through an ineffective gun."

Among the reasons administration officials now considered the source of the anthrax to most likely be domestic were these: Apparently, Amerithrax personally knew Dr. Assaad, the scientist at Fort Detrick that he tried to implicate. He had access to a U.S. Ames anthrax strain that was identical to U.S. weapons labs material. He chose the political targets of American conservatives.

The most promising evidence against Amerithrax was the anthrax itself, which federal scientists and contractors were still studying. The FBI counted on catching the killer through marker genes that would identify the age of the anthrax. If they could unravel the DNA of the strain they could trace it back to the facility where it had been made. However, virtually no specimen remained after the tests for follow-up studies. What the authorities needed toward the end of October was an unopened letter from Amerithrax. Unknown to them one was available—somewhere in the mail system and hot as a nuclear reactor. The post office continued to fine-tune its emergency response.

"In postal facilities when a suspected anthrax-containing parcel is found," the USPS ordered its district and senior plant managers, "follow procedures listed in MI 860-1999-3, *Emergency Response to Mail Allegedly Containing Anthrax* and your local Emergency Action Plan." Designated personnel were to examine the scene to determine if an emergency existed, then tape off the area. In event of "Possible Room or Area Contamination by Airborne Gas (dust, fumes or vapors introduced into the air with criminal intent)" workers were to turn off any local fans or ventilation units, leave the area, close doors behind, and call the Inspection service, police, and Hazmat team. The USPS advised in a seven-page letter, "Any powder or granulated substance is suspicious at this time . . . unless the contents are readily identified . . . do not try to clean up the powder. Do not do anything to create a dust cloud. If possible gently cover the spill with anything." Compounding the situation was an ink-drying processing many businesses used that left a residual powder on mail. In a small office setting, all people in the immediate area were to be listed and all contaminated clothing sealed in a plastic bag as soon as possible. In a large plant setting, workers were to shut down equipment, keep others away, and contact the immediate supervisor.

USPS Chief Operating Officer Pat Donahoe recommended to district managers that carriers scan for any powdery substance around the ledge of the customer mail deposit door *before* they opened a collection box. Should they find traces, they were to block customer access to the chute, secure the area, and watch for any individual loitering nearby. If they opened the collection box and found suspicious mail *inside*, they were to put any pulled mail back, then close and lock the box. If they identified a dangerous substance *after* placing mail inside the postal truck, they were to cover the hamper, close all windows and doors, and lock the vehicle. "If you become suspicious of an accepted piece of mail, do not handle it. Isolate it and cordon off the immediate area. Report the incident to the supervisor. Retain any surveillance tape and label it with date and time."

Capitol mail began to back up. Anthrax was found on the machinery at the military base that sorts mail for the White House. Authorities implemented elaborate procedures—treating mail with radiation—to protect Congress and other federal institutions from biological warfare.

All mail sent to key federal institutions (identified by zip codes 20200 through 20599) was routed through privately run facilities in Lima, Ohio, or Bridgewater, New Jersey, where it was treated with radiation, then trucked to D.C. The sanitized mail was sorted and examined by postal inspectors for signs that "may jump out as being suspicious." Postal workers at a station on V St. NE clipped corners off some envelopes to search for powder. Then the mail was transferred to congressional sorting facilities such as the Suburban Processing and Distribution office in Gaithersburg where Senate mail underwent additional screening by Capitol employees. The House employed a separate firm, Pitney Bowes, to screen its mail. There was official remorse and backpedaling because authorities had given the wrong advice to postal workers in the line of fire.

Twice a day, at 3:00 A.M. and at 3:00 P.M., the CIA and FBI prepared a Threat Matrix Index. This highly classified report enumerated the most dependable terrorist threats from around the world. They averaged between forty and one hundred. A report at 3:00 A.M. on October 27 indicated Al Qaeda would try to outdo the 9-11 attack. White House and Justice Department officials took it seriously, calling the threat "the most serious we've seen." Another top intelligence official said accounts were "hyped."

*   *   *

153

ON THURSDAY, OCTOBER 25, the USPS ordered environment testing of its processing and distribution centers. That afternoon a friend saw Kathy T. Nguyen on the No. 6 train in Manhattan. The moon-faced woman wore a wide, round hat. She had wide lips, a broad nose, neatly penciled brows, and hair not quite as black as her penetrating eyes. She was sturdy-shouldered with high cheekbones. A photo of her in her youth showed an exuberant, curly-haired girl who loved to dance. Though barely into her sixties, she favored black and lace, like a widow (though she was only divorced), and tiny pearl earrings. And like the Manhattan Eye, Ear and Throat Hospital where she stocked the operating and recovery rooms with supplies, she was antiseptic, well-organized, and businesslike.

The Vietnamese immigrant, complaining of a headache and flulike symptoms, had left her job in the medical supply room in the hospital basement early. Ms. Nguyen made her way home to the Bronx apartment where she lived alone. The next day, despite feeling worse, she returned to work. Over the next two days, she developed fatigue, chills, chest pain, and a cough productive of sputum which became blood-tinged.

On Saturday, Josefa Richardson, a neighbor and close friend, left several messages on Nguyen's answering machine. All went unreturned. On Sunday, October 28, Nguyen, short of breath and muscles aching, called David Cruz, her building superintendent, and asked a favor. "Would you drive me to the hospital?" she said. Cruz immediately got her to the Intensive Care Unit at Lenox Hill Hospital, a white- and pastel-colored building near Central Park in Manhattan. Dr. Shane Dawson was the surgery resident on call that night. The ICU doctor noted the following:

> Heart rate 110/min and respiratory rate 38/min, with room-air oxygen saturation of 92% by pulse oximetry. She was awake, alert, and completely oriented. She had prominent jugular venous distention at 60 degrees. She had a history of hypertension. Serum chemistries and coagulation studies were normal.

Ms. Nguyen required oxygen delivery by a nonrebreather mask to maintain adequate oxygenation. Her chest X ray was initially interpreted as showing:

pulmonary venous congestion with bilateral pleural effusions. Therapy for congestive heart failure was initiated, but an echocardiogram in the emergency department showed normal ejection fraction. There were no substantial wall motion abnormalities, only a small pericardial effusion.

Her doctor changed her therapy to levofloxacin for atypical pneumonia. But Nguyen's respiratory status worsened. She was intubated and put on a respirator in an eighth-floor room.

Also on Sunday, the nation's postal facilities flew their flags at half-staff in honor of Morris and Curseen. The two Brentwood workers had been buried over the weekend. Not far from Brentwood, at the Brookland Station, workers held a two-hour candlelight vigil in their honor. A three-peaked circus tent, striped broadly like the American flag, billowed in the darkness of the Brentwood parking lot. It was a temporary home for the displaced Branch 142 letter carriers. In the D.C./Baltimore area 2,211 employees were tested; 6,250 were on medication. Of forty-six facilities tested, including Maryland and Virginia, three had been closed. All seventy employees of the Southwest Post Office at 45 L Street were told to report to the Anacostia Station for work. Mail delivery in D.C. for customers in Zip Code 20034 was to resume the next morning.

On Monday, October 29, bilateral chest tubes were placed, and 2.5 liters of serosanguinous fluid were drained from Nguyen's right side. Doctors took another liter from her left. Then her preliminary tests came back.

A young surgeon on the ninth floor exclaimed, "Holy shit, this looks like anthrax!" Nguyen's blood cultures and pleural fluid (taken twenty hours earlier) had grown *B. anthracis*. Nguyen had inhalational anthrax, but nothing linked her infection with the other anthrax cases.

"This wasn't Tom Brokaw or Senator Daschle," said Dr. Dawson. "She was just a lady who goes home and buys her groceries. When I realized she somehow contracted it going about her daily life, that's when it hit home. Everyone's scared. No one knows."

Though her regimen was changed to ciprofloxacin, rifampin, clindamycin, and ceftazidime, Nguyen's clinical condition progressively worsened. Her chart now read:

A bronchoscopy showed hemorrhagic mucosa throughout the entire tracheobronchial tree, friable and collapsible airways, and purulent secretions in multiple segments bilaterally. A CT scan of the chest showed massive mediastinal bleeding, thickened bronchial mucosa.

Also on Monday, employees at Brentwood, Southwest, and Trenton had their ten-day regimen of precautionary treatment antibiotics increased an additional fifty days and the USPS changed its recommendation from Cipro to the less-expensive Doxycycline. Vince Sombrotto met with the Trenton letter carriers, New Jersey Branch 380. Like their Brentwood brothers and sisters, they operated out of tents. In the New Jersey/New York area, 6,128 mail handlers had been tested or were now on medication. At 11:00 a.m., the USPS released its latest national update: 8,800 postal workers tested, 13,300 on medication, and of 202 mail processing and distribution centers tested so far six had been "temporarily" closed. Six mail handlers with either cutaneous or inhalational anthrax were still hospitalized. Two hundred and ninety two postal facilities had been evacuated as a result of 7,309 threats, hoaxes, and suspicious mailing incidents. Postal inspectors had arrested eighteen individuals for anthrax-related hoaxes and placed another fourteen under investigation. The good news was that the number of anthrax hoaxes had dropped to 587 a day and was still falling. The get-tough policy was working.

But the unions were still in a turmoil. A postal Branch Worksheet asked:

> Did management violate Articles 3, 5, 14.1, 14.2 & 14.3, 19 of the National Agreement and the respective sections of the JCAM when they failed to investigate, abate and respond to PS Form 1767 Report of Hazard, Unsafe Condition or Practice within the same tour of duty in which the report was received? Did management violate Section 19 of OSHA when it failed to maintain an effective safety and health program?

On Tuesday, October 30, Sombrotto testified before the Senate Governmental Affairs Committee on the anthrax crisis. "We cannot allow the Postal Service to be intimidated," he told a packed Senate hearing room. "The bottom line here," replied Committee Chairman Joe Lieberman, "is the Postal Service is at the heart of this nation's critical infrastructure and is one of the foundations of our quality of life." Sombrotto applauded Postmaster General Potter, who also testified, for so swiftly assembling a union-management anthrax task force. "Despite Sombrotto's comments on management's actions," said the *Postal Record*, "he told the committee some things had caused concern, noting that officials acted quickly to test and provide antibiotics to U.S. Senate employees after anthrax infected employes in the office of Senate Democratic Leader Tom Daschle, but initially refused to test letter carriers in New York City who had delivered mail to locations of anthrax infected individuals. Only after the NALC intervened were the tests done."

Kathy Nguyen died Wednesday, October 31, of anthrax "indistinguishable" from the spores in Amerithrax's other victims' lungs. Autopsy findings included hemorrhagic mediastinitis. Immunohistochemical staining confirmed the presence of anthrax in multiple organs. Lenox Hill was briefly shut down for testing.

The FBI placed an urgent call to the Pentagon, sharing the most recent analytical data and informing them of the latest victim. In retracing Nguyen's steps, the investigators hoped to learn where she had contracted the bacteria. Over weeks that would stretch into months, they would interview 232 of Nguyen's coworkers, 27 of her neighbors, and 35 of her friends. Gradually, over weeks, the Anthrax Task Force reconstructed the last two months of her life. The Anthrax War had begun. On the front lines were the nation's postal inspectors, a group of professionals who had been anonymously toiling on the country's behalf for hundreds of years.

STRAIN 13

Poison Packages, Lethal Letters

THE ANTHRAX TASK Force was composed of the FBI, CDC, local police, and U.S. Postal Inspectors, the government's oldest law enforcement organization. The United States Postal Inspection Service, the investigative arm of the post office, harkens back to July 26, 1775, when Ben Franklin was appointed the first Postmaster General and the U.S. Postal Service was born.

In 1792 Congress imposed the death penalty for stealing mail. During the War of 1812, postal inspectors known as "surveyors" spied on the British fleet and reported ship movements. Sixteen years later, one of the inspectors, Noah Webster, published his dictionary. Postal Inspector Robert Cameron once got after Billy the Kid, suspecting the fast gun of robbing mail from stage coaches.

The inspectors are the Postmaster General's "special agents, his eyes, his ears, and his hands." Of all the federal agencies fighting crime, the Inspection Service has a matchless calling—to guard the sanctity of the United States mails and at the same time to prevent the use of the mails for criminal purposes.

These iron men of the post office recognized no statute of limitations. They never closed a case on a fugitive until his capture or death. Thirties' crime boss "Dutch" Schultz once lamented that anybody would have to be "plenty stupid" to commit a crime against the Post Office. The agency's formidable investigative powers and resources were brought to bear on any violators of postal statutes. Postal Inspectors are so feared that once, when thieves burglarized a department store that also housed the community post office, the crooks drew a chalk line between the commercial and postal areas. On the postal side of the line, they printed in chalk: "Inspectors, we didn't cross this line."

Postal Inspectors were the first government agents to be issued "Tommy guns" (Thompson submachine guns). They still carry firearms as they make on average fourteen arrests a day, execute federal search warrants, and serve subpoenas. During "Operation Avalanche," a coordinated strike between the FBI and postal inspectors, a hundred child molesters, suspects in child sexual exploitation, and pornographers were nabbed. They arrested 1,500 drug trafficking and money laundering suspects. Beginning in 1971, the agency became one of the first to hire female agents. They tracked con men, forgers, patent medicine and medical quacks— anyone who dealt in lies and half-truths. They hounded robbers, murderers, kidnappers, bomb and poison mailers to the ends of the earth. They investigated mail robbery, mail fraud, blackmail letters, and extortionists. Fraud on the Internet, in cyberspace, is cyber crime, but becomes mail fraud when payments for illegal schemes are received via the mail. Any blackmail, extortion, or poison pen letter that contained a threat of death or bodily harm automatically brought in the FBI. It hadn't always been that way.

For decades the post office had battled for more effective laws to deter one of the most despicable crimes committed against the American public—murder by mail. Up to the time where death resulted because of a bomb or substance sent through the mails, the matter was subject to state jurisdiction. The Inspection Service had long felt that matter belonged in the federal courts.

On January 23, 1957, Maurice H. Stans, deputy Postmaster General, sent the Speaker of the House of Representatives a new legislative proposal to amend Section 1716, Title 18, United States Code, and increase the penal provisions applicable to cases where death or injury results from the mailing of articles. The bill, approved by the Senate and House on September 2, 1957, became Public Law 85-268. President Dwight Eisenhower signed it the next day, revising the law on placing deadly substances in the mails. The new act provided the death penalty or life imprisonment for any offender if such an offense resulted in death.

Back then there were 950 postal inspectors, each charged with two hundred specific duties. In modern times there were only nineteen hundred postal inspectors to cover forty thousand post offices and twelve thousand smaller branches and coin-operated facilities. In Trenton alone, the Amerithrax case involved forty-seven post offices and seven hundred collection boxes feeding mail into the Hamilton Township sorting center. Trenton lies along the wide Delaware. During the Revolutionary period it had been the national capital for little over a month at the end of 1784. Had that meant something symbolic to Amerithrax?

Locating anonymous extortionists like Amerithrax might be the most difficult job the Inspection Service encounters. The Postal Inspection Service estimated that the average American would receive at least three anonymous poison pen letters over a lifetime. Anonymous letters—whether libelous, poison pen, targeting the famous, defamatory, spiteful, practical joking, racist, or obscene—all take their toll.

Though given a modern twist in its avenue of delivery by Amerithrax, poison by mail had been a long-standing form of murder. Postal inspectors knew it well. Poison, in its truest meaning, is a substance introduced into the body in small quantities (a teaspoonful or less) that produces a morbid or deadly effect. Drugs and other poisonous substances which can be inhaled exert their toxic effects with astonishing rapidity. The transfer of the toxin to the lungs can be made directly to the bloodstream and from there to the brain in only a few seconds. In the postal inspectors' experience, poisoned mail was usually sent by women. Could the anthrax mailer be a woman?

Years ago, postal inspectors J. A. Callahan, M. V. Saylor, and J. R. Stokes of the Atlanta Division caught such a case. It began in Charleston, South Carolina, on Wednesday, November 19, 1952, the day a small parcel arrived at a home. The parents were at work so their seventeen-year-old daughter unwrapped it. Inside was a box of candy—bonbon caramels, molasses, and coconut-vanilla-raspberry.

A note on top read: "Hello, folks. I am on my way to Jacksonville, Florida. I will see you soon. Love, Gracie." Assuming "Gracie" was a friend of her parents, the teenager gobbled one piece, then a second. The candy had "a very disagreeable taste" and smelled like garlic. She spat the second piece out and, cautioning her younger sister not to touch it, stored the box in the refrigerator. When her parents got home, her mother sniffed the candy. It reminded her of Rat-Nip, an over-the-counter poison they had in their own home.

The daughter, suffering from a burning sensation in her throat, abdominal pain, and an intense thirst, vomited. The vomitus contained blood. Most terrifying of all, it glowed in the dim light of the bedroom. The daughter was rushed to the hospital where she was treated. Analysis by a chemist showed the candy contained phosphorus. Three grains of yellow or white phosphorus is generally regarded as a fatal dose. Once absorbed into the bloodstream, it has a slow reaction and the fatal period may vary from two hours to several weeks. Often, phosphorus's lethal effects cannot be determined for up to ten days. It is a poison not excreted by normal body functions since it cannot be dissolved in liquid. Taken in sufficient quantity, it causes complete disintegration of the liver.

Like inhalational anthrax, phosphorus poisoning has a honeymoon period. If death does not follow within a few hours, the patient seems improved for a time, only to become jaundiced as the liver degenerates and the victim gradually sinks. Only prompt hospitalization saved the daughter from lasting ill effects.

Inspectors Callahan, Saylor, and Stokes, polite, noncommittal and composed as concrete posts, examined the package wrapping. The package had been mailed from St. George, South Carolina. The name "Gracie" was unknown to the family, but was in feminine handwriting. After his wife left the room, the husband admitted he suspected who'd sent the poisoned sweets. He'd met a waitress named Nan at the D & D Cafe while working on the Savannah River "H" bomb project at Barnwell, South Carolina, a city near St. George. They had gone on three dates before he returned home to his wife and family.

"Just innocent episodes and forgotten," he said. "I'm not accusing Nan," he said, "but maybe she did kind of take my friendship seriously. She's married, too. Got a kid. Well, she's the only person I know of who lives near St. George. If Nan did send the candy, I have only myself to blame. I'm just thankful that my daughter is all right."

The inspectors traveled to Barnwell to see Nan, Mrs. Nancy Coyle. She denied sending the package, but provided samples of her handwriting.

The handwriting on the wrapping and her exemplars were sent to the Washington laboratory of the Inspection Service for comparison.

Meanwhile, the dispassionate inspectors asked the cafe owner to keep tabs on Mrs. Coyle. She asked another waitress to throw away a box of stationery in the glove compartment of her car. The waitress put the box in the trash, but told the owner, who retrieved the box and its contents and notified the inspectors. They discovered, impressed on the bottom of the stationery box, a perfect copy of the note which had accompanied the poison candy. When Mrs. Coyle used the bottom of the box as an improvised writing table, she had applied sufficient pressure to make an impression of her writing in the cardboard.

When confronted, she confessed, but could not explain why, only vaguely claiming, "He done something to me." She pleaded guilty in court and was sentenced to three years' probation. United States Judge Williams told the inspectors the case represented "such an abnormal situation that I can't understand it. It's a crime an ordinary person would not conceive of."

Was the anthrax killer after revenge or did Amerithrax have a darker, more rational motive than "He done something to me"? And what of Amerithrax's threatening notes, with their racist tinge (anti-Semitic and at the same time anti-Arab); what of his helpful medical suggestions?

And so, in the absence of new forensic clues, postal inspectors fell back on traditional shoe-leather methods. They visited hundreds of households that received letters mailed through the Trenton sorting hub around the same time as the letter to Senator Daschle had passed through. The postal inspectors' goal was to get people to remember where the mail came from. This way, they might be able to trace which neighborhood the particular bin of mail that included the poisoned letters came from.

In Trenton, the Task Force interviewed residents and began swabbing mailboxes for clues to the source of anthrax-laden letters posted in September and October. Residents in Ewing Township were shown photos of the known and surviving letters and asked whether they recognized the handwriting: "Have you noticed anything suspicious lately?" "Do you know of any chemists living among your neighbors?" "Have you seen any cars with out-of-state licenses?" "Do you routinely leave outgoing mail in your personal mailbox for letter carriers to pick up or do you typically drop your letters in a public box?"

Some residents kept mail picked up at the post office weeks earlier unopened and double-bagged on their back porches. They planned to wait until it was safe. But anthrax spores were hardy and lethal for roughly seventy years. Investigators swarmed over the neighborhood after skin anthrax was diagnosed in a mail carrier, Teresa Heller. Agents hoped to trace the sources of any contaminated letters she may have handled. They had seized several mailboxes in the past few days.

Meanwhile police and the CDC under Dr. Stephen Ostroff's direction searched Kathy Nguyen's one-bedroom Bronx apartment. Entering the sturdy, black-trimmed metal door, they swabbed every surface. Biodetectives vacuumed all her clothes looking for spores. Agents poured over her phone records and inspected her regular post office, her usual laundry, and her favorite grocery store, the Freeman Grocery on Freeman Street. She was a churchgoer at St. John's Chrysostom Church, so they tested that too.

Using Nguyen's subway fare card, police traced her path around the city as she commuted to work from the elevated Whitlock Street Station, taking the No. 6 to the East 86th Street Station. She often traveled the subway to Chinatown. The Department of Health analyzed every subway station she passed through or frequented. Had she been infected by someone she passed?

Over a four-day period in June 1966, Army researchers traveling by train smashed glass lightbulbs filled with *Bacillus subtilis variant* along the tracks of the three main north-sound underground lines in mid-Manhattan. The Institute's anthrax exercise included the Seventh and Eighth Avenue trains. Forceful tunnel winds propelled clouds of fine gray dust, five to three microns in size, out subway entrances, contaminating the city from Times Square to the Bronx. This was confirmed by sampling devices and sensors at the far ends which measured the spread within as a succession of speeding trains endlessly transported germs from one station to the other through pulverization and suction. The Institute also secretly released clouds of *Serratia marcescens* (SM), an anthrax substitute, into the New York City subway. SM germs grow as red-colored colonies that can be effortlessly detected.

The Institute's own classified report, "A Study of the Vulnerability of Subway Passengers in New York City to Covert Action with Biological Agents, Fort Detrick, Maryland," concluded that "A large portion of the working population in downtown New York City would be exposed to disease if one or more pathogenic agents were disseminated covertly in several subway lines at a period of peak traffic." This became a plot element of Richard Preston's widely read 1997 novel, *The Cobra Event*. In April 1998, journalist Laurie Garrett quoted former White House health advisor D. A. Henderson in *Newsday*. "Suppose that somebody throws a little bit of anthrax into the subway," he hypothesized. "When do we decide that it's safe to go back into that subway? The answer is, nobody knows." Was Amerithrax a domestic scientist who had read the Institute's report and been inspired to release spores into the New York subway system? The Institute's classified tests used one of the routes that Nguyen traveled. Initial sampling tested negative for anthrax in elevated stations and underground stops along the No. 6 line and Nguyen's other frequented routes, but there were seven hundred miles of tunnels. Through the New York subway, the bloodstream of the city, or through the mail stream, it was startling how easily anthrax contamination spread.

Because Ms. Nguyen was older, she might have been more susceptible to the disease. Perhaps she picked up one or two spores from a more hardy individual who had tracked them into the subway line. Medical investigators examined the storeroom at Manhattan Eye, Ear and Throat where she had worked. Her job site and coworkers all tested negative for anthrax.

Agents wondered if Nguyen was only the first of thousands in an invisible aerosol spray attack on Manhattan. "So far," they mistakenly thought, "there are no other new cases." Nguyen's apartment was near to the triangle formed by NBC, CBS, and ABC, where victims, including an infant, had been infected by cutaneous anthrax. The *New York Post* sat just south of NBC and north of the Morgan General Mail Facility where spores had also been found. In fact Morgan General, which had processed all the media anthrax letters, also provided postal service to and from the hospital where Nguyen had worked.

In light of Morris's and Curseen's deaths experts realized that high-speed sorting machines could shake highly refined spores from sealed envelopes or force them through the large-pored paper. Postal inspectors explored the possibility of cross-contamination in the Nguyen case. She might have been infected by exposure to a secondhand letter—a definite possibility. By checking computer records left by letter bar codes, inspectors listed the letters that had sped through the sprawling Hamilton Township sorting machines around October 9.

One anthrax letter had gone through at practically the same moment as a letter sent on to the Bronx. However, postal records were vague on exactly which address the letter had been sent to. According to the *Daily News*, that letter was mailed in "the close neighborhood" of Mrs. Nguyen, although not directly on her postal route.

Health workers visited two addresses in the Bronx to see if they could find and test the letter, said Sandra Mullin, a New York Health Department spokeswoman. No letter was found, though interviews were conducted at the two addresses. "No one remembered a letter with a postmark from Trenton," Ms. Mullin said. Police found no one at either address who had fallen ill and so they had reached another dead end.

Dr. Timothy Holtz, a preventive medicine fellow at the New York City Health Department, said, "We will likely never know." Mayor Rudolph W. Giuliani said, "There are still no new pieces of evidence that give us any real hypothesis on how she contracted it."

They *never* found a single spore or any other clue to how Ms. Nguyen became infected. No one has ever been able to determine how she came in contact with anthrax. Nguyen's death and the unknown source of anthrax might have been the missing piece in the puzzle. Could she have known Amerithrax in his everyday guise?

Amerithrax might not have reckoned with the retentive minds of mail carriers. They knew every foot of their assigned territory. Postal carriers in every nook and cranny of the nation, trodding routes that total approximately 2.5 million miles and carrying billions of pounds of mail, comprised a powerfully effective dragnet.

Decades ago, Seattle Mayor Ole Hanson received a bomb through the mails, but his chief clerk caught it in time. Next, in Atlanta, Georgia Senator Tom Hardwick had one delivered to his home. When a servant opened it, the package bomb blew off her hands. Postal inspectors assigned to both cases suspected there were more than two bombs moving somewhere through the mails.

A clerk in the parcel-post division of the New York post office, Charles Caplan, was troubled as he read his evening paper. A description of the lethal bombs (brown-paper wrapping, the return address of a big New York department store) tugged at his memory. Where had he seen such a package? Hurrying to his post office, he discovered sixteen identical packages on a shelf where he had placed them because of insufficient postage. They were addressed to Judge Landis of Chicago, Justice Holmes of the Supreme Court, Postmaster General Burleson, Attorney General Palmer, Commissioner of Immigration Caminetti, Secretary of Labor Wilson, and other officials. Postal inspectors ferreted out thirty-six more. They never caught the man who mailed them. Was that how the Amerithrax case would end?

DAVID HOSE, A fifty-nine-year-old contract employee at the U.S. State Department mail-sorting facility, was working at the diplomatic mail-sorting location in Sterling, Virginia, when his facility received some mail from Brentwood which had accidentally been routed there. Sometime around October 22, 2001, he became ill with drenching sweats. Over the next two days he developed fatigue, severe myalgia, fever, chills, headache, nausea, vomiting, abdominal pain, and a cough with scant white sputum. He had substernal chest pain.

When Hose arrived at a local emergency room, his respiratory rate and blood pressure were normal. So was a complete blood count. A chest X ray was initially reported as normal, but the doctor took blood cultures anyway. He thought Hose had a viral syndrome, and discharged him with a prescription of ciprofloxacin. Hose took one dose that night, but his vomiting, fatigue, and headache worsened. Vision from the corner of Hose's left eye was distorted. His wife noticed he was intermittently confused.

After seventeen hours of incubation, his blood cultures grew gram-positive bacilli. The blood isolate was subsequently identified as *B. anthracis*. Hose was contacted and hospitalized. At admission he appeared ill and had trouble breathing. His chest X ray showed widening between his lungs. Computed tomography of his chest showed:

> mediastinal adenopathy with evidence of hemorrhage, small bilateral pleural effusions, and a suspected small pericardial effusion. His vital signs were: temperature 38.2°C, heart rate 108/min, respiratory rate 20/min, blood pressure 121/60 mm Hg, and oxygen saturation 94% on room air. WBC count 9,500/mm3 with 81% segmented neutro-

phils, 9% lymphocytes, and 9% monocytes, hematocrit 48.1%, platelet count 196,000/mm3, normal electrolytes and creatinine.

Hose was prescribed intravenous penicillin and rifampin in addition to the ciprofloxacin he was already taking. His temperature rose to 39°C. Subsequently, the doctor added vancomycin and discontinued penicillin.

In the meantime, Norma Wallace was very ill. She had been given a 50 percent chance of survival. Her enlarging left-side effusion required chest tube placement. A right chest tube had earlier been placed. The only good news was that Patel's fever had resolved and her other symptoms had begun to improve.

The next day, as the Supreme Court Building was ordered closed for testing, Hose developed gastrointestinal bleeding, which required a blood transfusion, endoscopic injection, and cautery of gastric and duodenal ulcers. On October 28, Hose's fever peaked at 39.4°C and then decreased to 38.3°C.

The country was becoming better prepared. Local health agencies began looking for spikes in the colored graphs they drew daily. For early detection, when hours, even minutes count, they looked for jumps in clusters of symptoms, rather than particular disease diagnoses. The number of dead cats and dogs found in the city streets each day acted as a "syndromic surveillance."

This became the bioterrorism alarm system for the understaffed, underfunded health departments. Epidemiologists began tracking orange juice sales and increases in sales of over-the-counter flu remedies. They collected electronic data from ERs and pharmacies, monitored 911 calls, and observed store surveillance videos, counting how many times people sneezed. They poured over school attendance data and calculated the number of children absent from school. They listed cases of sniffles, colds, coughs, aches, and pains—all early signals of a massive bioattack.

During the first three weeks of the anthrax outbreak, Maryland had three confirmed cases of inhalational anthrax. Eighty-five other possible cases were now being investigated. In Maryland they established two alerts: a yellow alert, which meant a hospital's emergency room was so busy that ambulances were to take patients elsewhere unless they were too unstable to travel; and a red alert, which meant that beds were filled except for those requiring intensive care or cardiac monitoring.

Since various federal officials sometimes offered contradictory advice, hospitals, clinics, doctors, and agencies in charge of emergency disaster planning monitored frequent e-mail advisories from the Health Alert Network. This network linked local and state health departments with the CDC. The undermanned CDC looked desperately for signs of chemical or biological releases, but had scant scientific understanding of how anthrax spores might behave.

"We all must do our part to enhance the security of the workplace," Chief Postal Inspector Ken Weaver advised postal workers. "Make security a part of your daily activities. Wear your identification badge and challenge unidentified individuals you observe on postal property. Keep doors locked at work. Be alert for indications of trouble and report any suspicious activities or suspicious packages to Postal Inspectors or local law enforcement officials. Lock your postal vehicles and secure the vehicle keys at all times. It's important for your safety, the protection of the vehicle and for securing the mail . . . Let's be careful out there."

The U.S. Surgeon General David Satcher admitted "we were wrong" not to respond more aggressively to tainted mail. "Some of us thought we were bioterrorism experts," Satcher said. "We have learned how little we knew." On October 27, 2001, more anthrax contamination was discovered in a House mailroom. Senators, in a closed meeting, decided to stay open as proof that while Congress could be contaminated, it couldn't be intimidated. The move infuriated the House. And while a letter they only suspected existed had not been found, no one else had grown sick. Or so authorities thought.

People were dying of anthrax from an unknown source. There were rumors of a government coverup. Doctors were boning up on anthrax and stockpiling vaccine. There was a nationwide panic. The President was telling people to go about their everyday lives, but at the same time be ready for an attack. Hazmat-suited medical teams were striding through quarantined buildings like extraterrestrials. Unbelievably, this had all happened before.

The worst anthrax outbreak had happened not in the United States, but in the former Soviet Union. It involved aerosolized anthrax such as that which killed Bob Stevens. Dr. Alibek spoke of an outbreak in 1979 in the big city of Sverdlovsk, when ninety-six victims were stricken with inhalational anthrax. Experts were still studying the epidemic, which was shrouded in government secrecy. U.S. figures estimated a thousand fatalities. Alibek thought the figure was closer to 105 deaths. "What is certain," he said, "is that it was the worst single outbreak of inhalational anthrax on record."

In the heart of a thriving metropolis, the Russian army had been secretly manufacturing one of the most deadly strains of anthrax. Afterward, the anthrax powder developed in their doomed city would travel a tortuous route around the world. Was this where Amerithrax had gotten his deadly powder?

The worst anthrax epidemic in a modern industrial nation had been called a "biological Chernobyl" (after a 1986 explosion at the Ukrainian nuclear plant). It showed what could happen in such a disaster in America, a cautionary tale of the dangers of secret and illegal science.

The Leahy letter had last been seen flying in the direction of the State Department mailroom that had sickened David Hose and which fed three U.S. embassies. Spores spread internationally to the U.S. embassies in Vilnius, Lithuania, and in Pakistan. On their path to the Capitol, the letters to the senators had cross-contaminated letters to another foreign embassy. That embassy was in Yekaterinburg, Russia, which had only recently reverted to its old White Russian pre-Revolutionary name. Back in April 1979, the city had been called Sverdlovsk.

Irony of ironies, that the missing anthrax letter should have been flitting along the mail route to Sverdlovsk, the site of the greatest biological weapons accident in recorded history. Sverdlovsk offered a cautionary tale for America. Whether it would be the nation's fate remained to be seen. It was an abject tale of horror beyond horror.

STRAIN 14
Anthrax City

"Then something woke you. What woke you up?
Did you dream? What was it?"
"I woke up and heard the lambs screaming. I woke
up in the dark and the lambs were screaming."

— *THE SILENCE OF THE LAMBS*

BEFORE BLEATING LAMBS grew silent in villages south of Sverdlovsk, a cloud hung over this churchless city of a million. The city was
perched in the eastern foothills of the Ural Mountains 880 miles east of
Moscow. From its highest bluff, Sverdlovsk peered down upon the Iset
River. Rich deposits of manganese, nickel, chromium, bauxite, and coal
studded the surrounding hills.

Walking along wide boulevards just before sunset on Friday, March
30, 1979, you would have passed dusky wooden houses that gave way to
the towering shapes of office buildings and multistory apartments. Materials for road building and construction jammed the streets. A fine dust,
rising from ditches, lifted on the southeasterly evening breeze and dusted
your tracks. Following the wind through the center city, you would have
come to towering universities and riverside parks and, at last, the outskirts.

On the way you would have spied a hundred indications marking the city as a Soviet industrial treasure—machine factories, ceramics plants, ironworks, lumber mills, and railways—especially railways. All but 13 percent of Sverdlovsk's income flowed from military production. The industrious citizens built tanks, nuclear rockets, and other armaments. Some of their endeavors were shrouded in secrecy—even from themselves.

Strolling the broad streets of the southwest section you finally would have been brought to shadowed Compound 19. Originally, the complex had been outside the city, but urban sprawl had encircled it. An ornate ironwork gate (opened and closed electronically) guarded the entrance. Beyond the gate, ten-foot-high, double barbed-wire fences defended a secret inner zone of high-security labs. Within stood huge fermenter vats and drying devices. Towering structures bristled with vents and smokestacks. Refrigerator units, concrete storage bunkers, and special rail lines crowded the interior. Not even the head of the local KGB knew that bustling Compound 19 was the Fifteenth Directorate's primary biological arms production facility.

There was something familiar about the secret city of Compound 19, and no wonder. During an August 1945 sweep of Manchuria, the Soviet army had captured Japan's infamous Unit 731 germ factory. Stockpiled there were fragmentation bombs loaded with nine hundred pounds of anthrax. Unit 731 had experimented with dysentery, cholera, plague, and anthrax on U.S., British, and Commonwealth POWs. The Japanese air force had scattered millions of bubonic plague–carrying fleas over Chinese cites, triggering mini-epidemics and seven hundred deaths. After the war, the U.S. shielded Unit 731 from war crimes prosecution in exchange for germ warfare documents. The Soviets had no need. They already had them, along with blueprints that by 1949 allowed them to construct an exact copy.

By 1979, Sverdlovsk's anthrax plant operated twenty-four hours a day to produce the most powerful strain ever known. But the powdered anthrax spores floating in Compound 19's filtered air were a strain different from any that had ever existed before. In 1953, at the Soviet Union's Microbiology Research Institute at Kirov (Russia's four leading military labs were Zagorsk [Sergiyev Posad], Kirov, Sverdlovsk, and Strizhi), a defective reactor accidentally spilled live liquid anthrax spores into the city's sewer. Army workers disinfected the sewers, but an unknown quantity spread to sewer rats. Rodents do not die from the infection, though they can carry it. The bacteriological facility performed regular disinfections after that, yet the disease continued to thrive underground.

Three years later, Vladimir Sizov, Kirov's senior-scientist army researcher, suggested a team descend into the sewers to discover if anthrax was carried by the rats hiding in the drains. The filthy maze of tunnels was an ideal environment for the survival of Norway or black rats, a heavy, energetic breed. One of the rodents captured in the sewers had developed a new strain, far more virulent than the original escaped spores. More rat catchers dropped down and trapped the infected offspring of the rats. They brought them to the surface to be killed and dissected. As Sizov had suspected, the rats had incubated a naturally selected form of new anthrax. Strain 836, as he called the unusually tough and lethal spore, having survived years in the darkness and putridness of the sewers, had mutated into super anthrax. The army immediately ordered Sizov to cultivate Strain 836 for installation in SS-18s targeted on Western cities. Sizov sent Strain 836 to Compound 19.

THREE SHIFTS OF vaccinated military technicians in gas masks and protective rubber suits separated fermented anthrax cultures from their liquid base. Carefully, they dehydrated them in dryers until they had been converted into cakes. When the bacteria are dried, they form tiny protective anthrax spores that can be converted into beige- or cafe au lait–colored powder. These cakes were carried on an internal conveyor belt and dropped into rotating steel pulverizer drums, crushers in sealed units filled with steel balls. The grinding balls were specific to the size of spores needed. The cascading balls milled the cakes into a fine, airborne powder, which exited the base of the drums to be packed into sealed containers. Afterward the drum and container exteriors were decontaminated with high-pressure hoses and heavily chlorinated water.

Pressure gauges were constantly monitored as experiments were carried out in hermetically sealed rooms. Inside an aerosol chamber two to three cubic meters in size (large enough for two monkeys), technicians conducted vaccine experiments. They "challenged" animals with a spray of five millimeters of an anthrax suspension containing five billion spores. Before venting the contaminated aerosols through special filtered channels, the air from the chambers underwent two disinfecting processes. But two washes of hydrogen peroxide (at 30 percent strength) do not obliterate anthrax spores.

Thus, the still-contaminated air was funneled through Petrionov filters of special synthetic fiber. Each filter, twenty-four inches in diameter and nearly four inches thick, was surrounded by a metal rim that clamped over an exhaust pipe. All that stood between the outside world and Strain 836, the most virulent strain of anthrax ever made, were two round filters. Technicians changed them once a week, but this Friday evening something went wrong.

After each shift the huge drying machines were briefly shut down for routine maintenance checks. During a checkup at the anthrax production unit, two workers removed the primary filter to the exhaust system attached to the drying and milling equipment. They discovered a blocked air filter. Although the filter was to be exchanged with a new one immediately, it was not. Heedlessly, the crew chief neglected to have the filter replaced, but scribbled a note for his supervisor before going home: "Filter clogged so I've removed it. Replacement necessary." Lt. Col. Nikolai Chernyshov, supervisor of the afternoon shift that day, in a hurry to get home, should also have recorded information about the defective filter in the logbook for the next shift, but did not.

When the nightshift manager came on duty, he studied the log, saw nothing unusual, and gave the command for the next shift to start up again. A technician in the anthrax drying plant, unaware that the exhaust no longer had a filter, commenced the anthrax production cycle. During the post-experiment phase, a smoky fine dust containing microscopic anthrax spores and chemical additives erupted through the exhaust pipes and into the crisp night air.

A plume the color of dark mustard unfurled silently in the sky. It dissolved as it glided down and became pinkish, then invisible as it vanished like steam. The weapons-grade anthrax spores were blown unseen by the night wind in a southerly direction from Compound 19. Between 1:00 and 4:00 A.M. human victims in Sverdlovsk were exposed to a lethal emission of aerosolized anthrax. A flock of pigeons flew through the cloud unscathed. The earth dusted. The cloud rose higher. How many aerosol spores had been released? How much would it take to kill?

The smallest estimate of what could have been released was two to four milligrams: invisible but still considerable—billions of spores. The estimated amount of the actual release was seventy kilograms, an amount that could seriously infect tens of thousands of square miles. A release of fifty kilograms of anthrax over an urban area of five million people would result in 250,000 deaths. Even as little as a gram of aerosolized anthrax, with its trillion spores, could have caused the Sverdlovsk outbreak, according to experts at Dugway Proving Grounds in Utah. The Defense Department settled on ten kilograms as the figure. The release could have been 150 times higher.

The accidental release continued for several hours before a worker noticed the missing filter. At once the shift supervisor shut the machines down. A new filter was installed, but by then it was too late. Several pounds of deadly powder had been pumped through an air duct. Though an unseen shadow hung over Sverdlovsk, no one from Compound 19 alerted city officials. No one notified the Moscow Ministry of Defense headquarters of an accidental aerosol anthrax emission.

The wind increased, steady and unbroken by gusts. In late March 1979, wind direction in Sverdlovsk was variable. This Friday night the direction was dead southeast. The first causalties were walking and talking only a few hundred yards downwind of Compound 19. Odorless anthrax aerosol settled over nearby Compound 32, a self-contained military garrison balanced on the southern edge of the secret anthrax processing plant.

Compound 32 had been built in the 1960s to shelter a couple thousand troops and their families. The accidental emission hit the military personnel from 19 hard and troops at 32 harder. They were soldiers who happened to be near open windows, in the streets or catching a drink at a bar. Anthrax was the "burning wind of plague" that begins Homer's *Iliad*: "but soldiers, too, soon felt transfixing pain and pyres burned night and day."

An auxiliary worker, Dmitryevich Nikolaev, took a deep breath. He would be dead in ten days. The slaughtering machine ran on, cold-blooded and impersonal. Within a week nearly all of those who breathed in the night air would be dead. "And each had an individuality of his own, a will of his own, a hope and heart's desire . . ." They had done nothing to deserve the plume's icy touch.

Beyond Compound 32's barracks and apartments stretched a blue-collar neighborhood: homes, schools, factories, shops, and residences. They comprised the Chkalovskiy *rayon* (district), the southern tip of Sverdlovsk. Old and older, male and female, but three-quarters of the victims were men. The median age was forty-two. But why were nearly all middle-aged men fatally infected? The oldest, Nikolaev, was a sixty-year-old grandfather; the youngest, a woman, just twenty-four.

Was the contagion selective in some way? Of course, some of the men were already susceptible. Some had problems with their immune systems or suffered from asbestosis, siderosis, or tuberculosis. Some were heavy smokers. Fifteen harbored spores in their lungs for three or more weeks before falling ill. There were no children among the epidemic's victims. Few children played outside so late on a Friday night and their stronger immune systems protected them.

The cloud drifted further southward, the densest area of spores forming a shape like a baseball bat, a discernible band of infections marking the map of Chkalovskiy. The clubbed end hung over the hinterlands. Beyond lay a ceramics plant, peaceful farmland, the lambs, and their unsuspecting owners. The bat shape widened to a triangle, its point at Compound 19 and its base a half-mile wide. Wedge-shaped, it traveled southeast over Chkalovskiy at an average rate of about fifteen kilometers per hour.

Death passed over roughly seven thousand people within its boundaries. Spores fell on a large block of five-story apartment buildings on the boulevard bordering Chkalovskiy *rayon*. Two residents there were infected—"Fate waited in their path or theirs in Fate's." Another unlucky twenty were working near the military facility or the ceramics factory to the southeast. An additional twenty-six were home or working in local industries within the same area.

The plume closed on a ceramics plant less than a mile away from Compound 19. It drifted along dusty Poldnevaya Street. The tall smokestack of the pipe factory stood in the direct path of the spore cloud. The cloud touched a huge gated complex of buildings with paths leading from one to the other—the ceramics factory. For decades the factory had made industrial pipes, bathroom fixtures, dishes, teapots, and tiles. Its tile shop fired four types of clay, including green clay aged by microbial action. A conveyor belt propelled wet ceramic squares into a furnace. Behind the tile facility lay the boiler room. To the left of the entrance and west of the tile room stood a three-story, block-long building.

A huge, rundown structure with gaping holes in its walls hugged the northeast edge of the plant—the pipe shop. Its cavernous interior was filled with engines, kilns, troughs, catwalks, gantries, and mazes of machinery. Pipes and conduits ran every way. On the top level, rows of high, large windows faced northwest in the direction of Compound 19. Warm air, heated by the ovens below, rose. The upper air was smoky in spite of a draft and several broken windows.

The overheated air rolled like a wave as it met incoming current carrying the fatal spores. They drifted through the gaping windows of the overheated factory and were trapped. Because of the inversion layer, some of the spores stayed aloft for a considerable time. Eventually, though, they drifted down on the pipe shop workers below. Now the time of disaster had come; the men would not survive another week. Unaware of jeopardy, factory workers inhaled lethal gusts of air. Speridon Viktorovich Zakharov, forty-four, was one of those.

In other parts of the factory, more employees were becoming mortally infected. Maintenance men driving trucks drove right into the invisible plume. Spores were inhaled by a man who drove an electric car inside the factory. A pipe fitter, a pipe welder, and a clay mixer were dead and did not know it. Officer Vladimir Sannikov, innocently trapped in a lethal swath of air, enjoyed a late snack at the cafeteria adjacent to the loading platform.

Ten of 150 workers would die—almost a 7 percent fatality rate. Even an unimaginably small quantity posed a substantial threat. The inhalation of eight thousand spores is required to fatally infect half of an exposed population.

Across the street from the ceramics plant, a man was finishing a new family bathhouse. The cloud did not touch him. Near the ceramics factory, Anna Petrovna Komina, a strong-featured woman with dark hair and deep-set eyes, sat in her home on Ulitsa Lyapustina. The house numbers on her street were not in order, but the invisible plume did not become lost. Anna lived in a small cottage with a muddy yard and a small gate, but the rods and threads did not open the gate. They had no need. There were two pigs in the backyard, but they were untouched. There were several steps, but the bacteria walked up them as if paying a visit. The plume did not wipe its shoes on the doormat as is the local custom.

Silently the "burning wind of plague" entered a little parlor with day beds. A small French door led to another room with a table, four chairs, and a breakfront with china behind glass. Anna neither smoked nor drank nor suffered from serious illness, but now the time of disaster had come; the fifty-four-year-old woman would not survive another week.

Like puffs of cannon smoke the cloud traversed the Chkalovskiy district, forced southward by the March wind. It would travel many miles before disseminating. As it dispersed, a less concentrated cloud of spores drifted invisibly over six small villages further south in Syserskiy *rayon*, infecting livestock with its silent hiss. Animals began to sicken in Abramovo, the village farthest southeast of Sverdlovsk.

The next morning, Mrs. Lomovtsev, an Abramovo village resident, awoke and left her tin roof cottage. Since the ground was snowless, she led her single sheep around back to graze in the large field behind her house. The sheep was still healthy in the evening, though a little muddy. On Sunday morning, the first day of April, it was dead. After she buried the carcass at the town dump, Mrs. Lomovtsev heard that her neighbors, the Krutikovs, had also lost a sheep. They butchered it and ate pies from its meat. Yet, no one in the family fell sick, possibly because the meat was well cooked.

All weekend Sverdlovsk emergency rooms at Hospitals 20 and 24 were filled with patients suffering headaches, dizziness, chills, and fevers. Most were sent home by doctors who mistook the initial symptoms of anthrax as flu. On Sunday evening, another neighbor of the Lomovtsevs, Yuriy Kostarov, lost a white ram. Its whiteness had altered to a leaden blue; its legs were sticking in the air. Mrs. Kostarov had sheared the ram before it fell sick and stored its white wool in a can. The local vet told the Abramovo villagers the disease might be anthrax and had the Lomovtsevs' sheep dug up and burned.

There was a nervous lowing in the fields—as if the herds sensed something. A plump lamb frisking about in the flock at morning, by evening was refusing to eat. At dawn on Monday, the farmer found the lamb's carcass cold and stiff, belly distended and blood oozing from its anus— blood that had turned ghastly black. Then the same thing happened with another sheep and another until there was a field of dead sheep. Other hoofed animals began to die.

The blackened blood of a dead cow or bull stained the earth, blacker still where it drained into the ground like crude oil. Whatever the sickness was, it was spreading. Bristled hogs, some white, some black, some brown, and some spotted, made low squeals and agonizing grunts in their pens, but remained curiously untouched. But the farmer himself, and a shepherd, and a hides dealer, sickened and broke out in horrible boils—or, more horribly, choked out their last breaths in a breakneck pneumonia.

On Wednesday, five days after inhaling spores that caused the onset of what seemed to be a mild cold, dozens of patients in the city rushed to hospitals with more severe symptoms: quick, powerful flu with vomiting, chills, and high fever. Some had breathing difficulties, higher fevers, and blue lips. Six patients were admitted to Hospital 40, a central facility located north of Chkalovskiy. But doctors, not knowing of a secret military biological facility in town, were still puzzled. They diagnosed the disease as pneumonia, but as more and more blue-lipped patients straggled in, their panic grew. The region faced an unknown infectious disease.

The victims with the earliest onset of disease were Anna Komina and Aleksandra Volkova. "My mother often walked home," Anna's son said, "to fix the noontime meal for us, instead of having us eat in the cafeteria. Her symptoms—faintness, dizziness, trouble breathing—began then she seemed to get better." Speridon Zakharov was too sick to go to the ceramics factory on Friday, April 6, a week after the accidental release. He went to work the next day, only to collapse. Distinctive dark swellings along his chest and neck marked the onset of inhalational anthrax. His body erupted with massive, excruciating blisters, turning his skin black and leathery. His lungs filled with fluid. He was rushed to Hospital 20 where he died.

On Sunday, April 8, Anna went completely into failure. The first doctor called to her house lacked intensive care equipment and rang the emergency medical center for an ambulance. Two medics labored for five hours to bring Anna's blood pressure up to a safe enough level to transport her to Hospital 20. The earliest cases—Mikhail Markov and Vera Kozlova—had come from Hospital 20 in the southeast section of Chkalovskiy. One doctor suggested plague as the cause of Anna's illness, another smallpox. Everyone rejected cholera as the answer. But the recent cattle cases came to mind—was it anthrax?

Sick people choked Hospitals 24 and 20. Hospital 40's five-hundred-bed infectious disease wing was designated the centralized care facility. Patients with high fevers and breathing problems were rushed to Hospital 40 for special screening and intensive care. Autopsies were done there too: four patients had been dead on arrival ("as if struck by lightning") and thirteen had died at home. Meanwhile, Anna slipped into a coma.

She died on Monday. Soldiers scrubbed the walls of her hospital room, stripped the hospital bed, bathed her corpse in chemical disinfectant, then transported her body to Hospital 40 where it was held for five days. The embargo prevented her relatives from performing the traditional Russian washing and dressing rituals and from holding a wake. In the interim, public health workers visited her home and gave tetracycline pills to Anna's son, Yuriy, and his wife, but not to their infant.

Anthrax-tainted meat might explain the outbreak, but Anna's family had bought no meat from private or black market sources. Though they all ate the same food, only the mother became ill. "Why her?" said her son. "Why her if from infected meat? Our house was disinfected, bed linens taken away." By truck, Anna's coffin was clandestinely transported from the hospital directly to the cemetery and buried in chlorinated lime. Her family learned of the burial on a tip from hospital staff, but police at the gate barred them from entering. Section 15 of the Eastern (Vostochniy) Cemetery was declared off-limits. Anna's husband died soon after with a broken heart.

Bodies on metal gurneys lined the halls at Hospital 40. More were stored in a cold-room next to the white-tiled autopsy room. On Tuesday a female doctor performed the first autopsy. Because there were so many rapid unexplained deaths, victims were laid out three at a time on long soapstone tables. Orderlies screwed wooden blocks, neck supports, into the soapstone for the autopsies. A wide shallow groove on all four sides of the tables normally channeled blood to floor drains, but those were plugged to contain the disease. A tray of instruments, an adjustable round lamp, notebooks, and a black hose for cleanup completed their equipment.

The postmortem of the third case, Vera Kozlova, revealed massive internal hemorrhaging. It puzzled the pathologist to see infection in the lymph nodes and lungs and, significantly, hemorrhaging in the small blood vessels of the brain membrane—producing a so-called cardinal's cap. She knew that such bloodied brains were caused by anthrax. But from where?

Materials from the autopsied corpse, a blood culture from another dying patient, and the pathologist's notes were forwarded to Moscow bacteriologists for evaluation.

Each of forty-two bodies studied showed hemorrhagic destruction of the thoracic lymph nodes and hemorrhagic inflammation of the mediastinum, the area between the lungs. The route the white blood cells take in transporting anthrax spores out of the lungs is directly to the thoracic lymph nodes. Eleven patients showed necrotizing anthrax pneumonia.

Spread of hemorrhagic lesions in the intestines of all but three of the victims was caused by the spread of bacteria through the bloodstream directly from the gastrointestinal tract, not from tainted meat infecting the gut. Lesions in the mesentery lymph nodes were noted in nine of the autopsy cases as coming after inhalatory infection. They died at home, in the street, and in ambulances, either misdiagnosed or with a sudden onset of severe symptoms. Two bodies had been sent home by mistake, then retrieved.

That afternoon, Dr. Vladimir Nikiforov and his assistants arrived in Sverdlovsk to arrange medical responses to an apparent ongoing epizootic south of the city. Outside public health crews, still not certain of an anthrax source, entered Syserskiy *rayon* to investigate. A "bushel" of Moscow veterinarians entered Abramovo and discovered seven sheep and a cow dying. Three of the sheep tested positive for anthrax. The doctors demanded the ears of a calf that had died. Two sick sheep were slaughtered in Rudniy village. Sulfamides, penicillin, or tetracycline, which reduced the death rate from gastrointestinal anthrax to 5 percent or less, were dispensed to villagers.

The emergency team disinfected Mrs. Lomovtsev's house and yard with chlorine, ripped out floorboards in her shed, and hauled away a wooden walkway covering the mud in her yard. They did the same at the Kostarovs' next door, then nailed a quarantine sign on both houses. Health workers, actually KGB agents, descended on the Kostarov family that night. They questioned Mrs. Kostarov "like a spy or a criminal," and confiscated the ram's wool she had stored in a can. Because she had handled the wool, they forcefully vaccinated her on the hip. A Moscow investigator asked Mrs. Krutikov, who had lost the first sheep in Abramovo, "Who sent this bacteria to you? Where did you get it?" and acted as if they suspected her of plotting to kill livestock.

On April 12, the Moscow microbiological experts confirmed anthrax was the source of the outbreak. Two days earlier, they had injected materials from the last autopsied corpse and a blood culture from a dying patient into white mice and guinea pigs. All the test animals had died of anthrax blood-poisoning. Vets quarantined the area and set up checkpoints. Moscow senior health and military officials flew over the site by helicopter, but refused to enter the danger zone. In the countryside, burning of all animal carcasses was now supervised. Formerly, villagers had burned sickened animals in the local quarry, or buried them in the forest, or left them in the streets to be eaten by dogs. Hundreds of stray dogs were rounded up and shot as "a danger to public health."

Ambulance drivers worked daily with Hospital 40, and local hospitals and clinics screened patients. By April 15, response to the epidemic was in operation around the clock, extending from neighborhood to city to oblast offices. Volunteers brigades commenced a house-to-house community-wide vaccination campaign to distribute antibiotics to victims' families and to disinfect homes. At the ceramics factory, doctors inoculated workers three times with a "pistolet," a jet-pistol injector. Vodka was used to reduce adverse reactions to a traditional Soviet STI vaccine. After the first injection, a huge ulcer appeared on one worker's upper left arm. "At the time," he said years later, "the authorities said it was for anthrax. But now I know it was bacterial warfare from Compound 19." Anna's son agreed. "It came through the air—from Compound 19," he said.

However, few officials in town suspected Compound 19 was the true source of contagion. Those who did depended on the army for their livelihood and cooperated. The Soviet military seized control of the area and posted sentries in the immediate neighborhood of Compound 19 to keep intruders away. The plant's floors were ripped up; its plastering removed. Soldiers in gray-green protective suits and gas masks took soil samples, sprayed streets, sidewalks, and trees with disinfectant, and laid down topsoil to cover contamination.

Gen. Valentin Yevstigneyev, an immunologist, said of Moscow's handling, "They isolated the camp and put it into quarantine. They immediately decided that all the infection came from there, you see. The security organs and the sanitary services created such an atmosphere of secrecy and intimidation around the population that there was no longer any doubt about it."

On the first of May, decontamination really began. The local Communist Party boss, learning of a hazardous materials leak, ordered firemen to spray roads, trim trees, and hose down roofs and walls with caustic solutions, especially near the ceramics factory because so many had died there. Soldiers disinfected Hospital 40's autopsy room with buckets of chloramine and burned records and pathologists' reports. When the KGB came to retrieve the autopsy materials used at Hospital 40, a cleaning woman, Maria, refused to let them in to search a locked cabinet where the records were kept. She so intimidated them, they never came back for them. Thus valuable clues to the outbreak were retained.

In Abramovo, soldiers paved contaminated dirt roads with asphalt—making it the only asphalted village in the Urals. Tainted topsoil was dredged up by bulldozers and dumped in pits. KGB officers, pretending to be doctors, visited the homes of victims' families with falsified death certificates. To further hide the presence of pulmonary anthrax, they confiscated records at Compound 32 and displayed photos suggesting victims had contracted intestinal anthrax, the rarest form. The government printed flyers that read: "Stay away from 'unofficial' food vendors." Un-inspected meat and feed were confiscated and burned.

By mid-February 1980 there were low-level reports in the West of a thousand estimated deaths. Two to three hundred military personnel may have died. Moscow denounced U.S. allegations of an outbreak as "an epidemic of anti-Soviet hysteria." The Soviet invasion of Afghanistan had President Jimmy Carter taking a harder line toward Moscow and tension had grown between the two countries.

The CIA knew the Soviet defense minister had made an emergency visit to Sverdlovsk in April 1979. And U.S. spy satellites had photographed burning bodies, decontamination trucks, newly paved roads, large numbers of Soviet military and roadblocks in Sverdlovsk. On June 12, 1980, the Soviet news agency TASS declared only that there had been a "natural outbreak of anthrax among domestic animals" in the Sverdlovsk region. "Cases of skin and intestinal forms of anthrax were reported in people, because dressing of animals was sometimes conducted without observing rules established by veterinary inspections. All patients were treated successfully at local hospitals." Moscow lived in fear that Western inspectors would show them in violation of the 1972 Biological and Toxic Weapons Convention, which the Soviets had been the first to sign and ratify. It prohibited such research as done at Compound 19. They concocted a near-perfect cover story—

A meat-processing center near Sverdlovsk was claimed to have ground up waste products to make bone meal, but failed to properly sterilize them. This oversight had resulted in anthrax-contaminated bone meal. Next, the bone meal was mixed with grain and other slaughterhouse products to make combined feed. One or two days before the outbreak, the meat-processing plant delivered 2,121 tons of combined feed to the local farms around Sverdlovsk. At one state farm where a small load of this feed had been received, an unvaccinated breeding bull became ill and died within a day. The same feed was delivered to local collective farms.

Once their livestock became sick, farmers butchered them, gave some meat to relatives, and black-marketed the rest as raw or processed meat (cutlets and mincemeat). Two black market vendors just outside Sverdlovsk were arrested and imprisoned on charges of selling bad meat. More anthrax-contaminated meat was confiscated on April 22, 1979, from "an unknown citizen" who had attempted to sell it in the open market. Many of the victims were ceramics workers, because most of the bad meat had been sold at the ceramics factory. It was simply "a minor, routine public health problem—due to poor food controls." The government's official tally was ninety-six stricken, sixty-four dead.

A similar infected meat epidemic had occurred fifty-two years earlier 150 miles northeast of Moscow in Yaroslavl. Twenty-two of the twenty-seven victims were men, all bachelors. All died within the first week. First, the victims developed lesions at the base of their tongues and had difficulty swallowing. Then they were overcome by nausea, vomiting, fatigue, and appetite loss. Severe abdominal pain preceded fever, severe cramps, bloody diarrhea, and signs of blood poisoning. As the deadly infection ran its course, each victim's temperature declined sharply. A sudden and unexpected cardiac collapse was preceded by a sudden chilling of the limbs, a bluish or purplish discoloration of the skin, and a rapid thready pulse.

Doctors diagnosed influenza or mild gastroenteritis, but cooked sausage sold by vendors near their railway station workplace proved to be the source of a meat-borne anthrax infection. The same bacterium will behave differently depending on how it enters the system. Spores entering the digestive tract through contaminated, undercooked meat cause intestinal anthrax, which has an incubation period of one to seven days.

Anthrax of the gastrointestinal tract strikes the gut as bacteria and toxins eat away at the intestinal lining, spread to nearby tissue, and prompt an immune-cell attack. From intestines, immune cells carry microbes to lymph nodes, which in turn become inflamed. Fatality rate is from 25 to 60 percent, but GI anthrax is so rare that the effect of early antibiotic treatment on the case-fatality rate has yet to be established. The Soviet government insisted that intestinal anthrax from natural causes (contaminated soil) had occurred in Russia 159 times between 1936 and 1968.

Thus, tainted meat was always the common hypothesis for Russian anthrax outbreaks. It was Russia's "national disease," so prevalent in Siberia that Soviets called the cutaneous form the "Siberian ulcer." The sprawling rural areas of czarist Russia and the former Soviet Union had among the world's highest levels of recorded anthrax incidents. In czarist times, outbreaks of Russian anthrax hovered around fifty thousand animal deaths per year, twelve thousand human skin infections, and over three thousand human deaths per year.

There had been major outbreaks in Germany in the fourteenth century and in central Europe and Russia in the seventeenth century. The modern history of anthrax contains accounts of "wedding banquet" scenarios in Iran, Kazakhstan, Siberia, and various African countries. In these cases, meat not cooked enough to kill anthrax bacteria is shared by a large group. Soviet history made an intestinal anthrax outbreak seem logical. The cover-up fooled the West for years.

But contaminated feed could never have been the cause of the 1979 outbreak. There was no meat-processing factory near Sverdlovsk. And, in fact, on May 27, 1992, Boris Yeltsin, president after the Soviet Union ceased to exist on December 31, 1991, acknowledged in an interview with a Russian paper that the 1979 Sverdlovsk outbreak had stemmed from an accident at a military facility.

One fact did seem puzzling, however: Sverdlovsk's epidemic had occurred over seven weeks. How to explain the long duration of the outbreak? If it had resulted from an accidental release of deadly aerosolized spores into the wind from Compound 19, wouldn't the deaths show a single spike, a common point of exposure? After developing the disease, shouldn't the victims have perished within two to seven days? The long duration of the epidemic might lie in the capacity of anthrax spores to remain dormant in the lungs for extended periods.

"We couldn't understand why people continued to die," said General Yevstigneyev. "We assumed that this was a quick, onetime exposure and that our mopping-up would be completed in a few days, but there were deaths for a month and a half after the release."

According to Ken Alibek, a leading Soviet plague expert, "The cover-up was responsible for turning what began as a medical emergency into a small epidemic." He added that antibiotics promptly administered would have saved lives if the thousands of Sverdlovsk residents had been given antibiotics and vaccinated immediately after the first cases were reported. The first two weeks had been the worst, with two-thirds of the victims falling sick and dying by April 16. Yet after a week the anthrax deaths still continued. New victims arrived at the hospital covered with black ulcerous swellings under the skin. The deaths of the remaining third were spread thinly over the next month—suggesting a second epizootic in Syserskiy *rayon*.

As fresh fields were plowed and new gravel pits dug, animal outbreaks flared as if from nowhere. Decontamination raised invisible clouds of dust that still retained the tough, virulent spores. The action of spring floods spread spores that had settled after the initial release. Cleanups spread the re-aerosolized anthrax spores further through "secondary aerosols," raising them into the air to be rebreathed by new victims. That explained the long duration of the outbreak.

Of the three Soviet centers for anthrax production, Perza, Kurgan, and Sverdlovsk, Compound 19 had been the only one active. In the spring of 1988, scientists from Sverdlovsk were ordered to dispose of Compound 19's legacy: tons of anthrax bacteria, enough to destroy the world's people many times over. They set out to destroy the anthrax, but how? They had made the anthrax spores too hardy, too nearly indestructible. The anthrax, stainless-steel canisters of lethal pink powder, was packed onto two dozen rail cars and transported in secret. America had not heard the last of Strain 836. The final result would make Amerithrax look like a piker.

STRAIN 15
Cipro Fever

ON WEDNESDAY, OCTOBER 31, 2001, the same day Kathy Nguyen died, the U.S. rejected a UN resolution offered by France to condemn the anthrax attacks on grounds it could have been domestic terrorism. The French were skittish about any questions of Iraq's involvement in the anthrax mailings. Not only had France supplied fermenters and anthrax cultures from the Pasteur Institute to Al Hakam, but in 1980 had built an animal vaccine plant, Al Manal, on the outskirts of Baghdad. Constructed of bomb-resistant concrete, Al Manal was actually a BSL-3 virus and toxin factory. It produced nine thousand cubic yards of weapons-grade botulinum toxin, enough to kill every person on earth a thousand times over. After the Gulf War all of it vanished. The toxin has never been recovered.

Investigators established that the bacterium that killed Nguyen was virtually identical to germs found in letters to the New York media and Senator Daschle. The following day, the Florida anthrax was publicly confirmed to be of the same origin—a variant of the so-called Ames strain. This made officials at Iowa State University (where the Ames strain had been perfected) very nervous. Their collection numbered over a hundred vials of anthrax, spanning seven decades. Their oldest strain was from 1928. The academicians notified the FBI that, for security reasons, they planned to destroy the university's huge bank of spores. When the FBI neither approved nor explicitly objected, the cultures were destroyed on October 10 and October 11. With their loss went potential genetic clues to Amerithrax's identity. A dispute arose later among biologists. They argued that the rush to destroy the spores probably eliminated crucial evidence about the anthrax in the letters. Martin Hugh-Jones, an anthrax expert aiding the federal investigation, said, "If those cultures were still alive, they could have helped in clearing up the muddy history." Dr. James A. Roth added, "Now we'll never know."

Wisdom told the searchers they were dealing with a "nutcase" who could only be caught through good old-fashioned policework and shoe leather. But Amerithrax had left the FBI with scant clues. All of the letters were photocopies. None contained any fingerprints. The plastic tape on the envelopes was a mass-marketed variety. FBI laboratory analysts matched the serrated ends of the strips of cellophane tape used to seal the anthrax letters. That meant that whoever had sealed the letters had torn off successive strips of tape from the same roll without leaving any fingerprints. The paper on which the letters were written was an average size, though folded and trimmed. The marks left by the photocopier were carefully studied. The envelopes were prestamped and widely available at any post office.

Agents poured over scientific literature to learn who had the knowledge to make anthrax. They questioned manufacturers and marketers of biochemistry equipment Amerithrax might have used. They sought out places that sold specialized machinery needed to make anthrax. They compiled lengthy lists of anyone who might have manufactured, tested, transported, stored, or thought about anthrax.

President George W. Bush and his advisors reached out to Hollywood directors for ideas since their outlandish movie thrillers were coming true.

The newest flashpoint in the hunt for Amerithrax was the examination of government research institutions and contractors that had the Ames strain and know-how to turn it into lethal powder form. The wrinkle in this was that these were the same scientists the FBI had counted on for scientific advice from the earliest days of the investigation. "It puts us in a difficult position," a senior law enforcement official said. "We're working with these people and looking at them as potential suspects."

On November 1, Postal Inspector Weaver complained that managers and employees alike were "becoming increasingly nervous because they aren't getting timely follow-up information, or in some cases, no information at all, about suspicious mailpieces that postal inspectors are removing from postal facilities." The same day *USPS NEWS Talk* reported:

> The masks are coming . . . In testing, the slightest instantaneous filter penetration is measured. The respirators are certified with the intent that particles as small as 0.3 microns will be captured. They are nearly 100 percent efficient at capturing the smallest of particles including anthrax spores in the micron range. Employees supplied with either FFP [filtering face piece] have been advised on proper fit and use to ensure maximum efficiency. A video airing every fifteen minutes on PSTN also teaches employees how to properly apply and fit the FFP to your face. It is important to know that neither respirator is intended for use in a suspected or known hazardous substance release situation.
>
> 'The removal is part of our ongoing investigation as we search for clues as to who is sending anthrax through the mail,' Weaver says. Weaver wants to reassure employees that none of the letters and parcels checked by the Inspection Service or FBI hazmat teams so far have contained anthrax. They have either been hoaxes or mailpieces containing some benign substance. On many occasions, when the mail is removed it is cleared and returned to the mailstream relatively quickly.

The first of November was a busy day. Agents were interviewing and polygraphing hundreds who had access to anthrax stored at the Institute, while agents were storming the home of Aziz Kazi, a Pakistani-born budget official for the city of Chester, Pennsylvania. "They hauled away dozens of boxes of his belongings and questioned him for hours about a mysterious liquid he had been seen carrying out of the house," *Newsweek* wrote. "It turned out the family dishwasher had backed up and Kazi was bailing out his kitchen." Another lead had fizzled.

Agents in Texas were watching an Egyptian man fingered by a jailhouse snitch, who had overheard the man talking with associates about delivering the contents of a "brown envelope." When the agents followed him to the airport and covertly searched his luggage, all that was inside the "brown envelope" were insurance papers. One hundred and fifty British consulate staff members were evacuated in New York after a woman in the visa department opened an envelope with white powder. It had been mailed from Glasgow on October 17 and addressed in black felt-tip pen to the British Consulate General.

The next day FBI Director Mueller admitted the government had no idea who was behind the attacks. He asked the public's help to analyze the handwriting samples on the anthrax letters. Gov. Gray Davis warned California citizens that the state's six biggest bridges might be destroyed by terrorists during rush hour between November 2 and November 7. Around San Francisco Bay, commuters left early as they tried to beat the rush-hour bombs. Tom Ridge told senators that he hoped eventually to be able to grade alerts—like smog alerts in the summer. But it is difficult to measure raw tips from unreliable sources.

The Postal Service increased its reward for information leading to the arrest of those responsible for the anthrax attacks. A direct-mail advertising company, Advo, donated $250,000 to the reward fund, which had now reached $1.25 million dollars. Amerithrax had single-handedly almost crippled the direct-mail business. People were afraid to touch their mail. A federal judged ordered a mail-processing center in Bellmawr, New Jersey, to stay closed until he could study a complaint by the postal workers' union. The union believed that the facility might not be free of anthrax. Who could blame them?

Jake Wagman of the *Philadelphia Inquirer* reported that the Bellmawr processing facility had opened and shut down multiple times and that "Several government agencies converged on the facility." Wagman also wrote of the mistakes they made—"from cleaning the wrong machine to miscalculating by several million pieces the amount of mail delayed by the scare." The wrong mail sorter was decontaminated, leaving actual anthrax-tainted equipment in operation for three days. Dozens of employees used it to sort millions of pieces of mail.

On November 3, Postmaster General John Potter finally said what everyone had been thinking. "There are no guarantees that the mail is safe." Within hours of Potter's statement other officials and experts followed in agreement. The next day more traces of anthrax were discovered in New York and Washington, followed later by more and more findings as cross-contamination spread the invisible anthrax. Scientists admitted that while they knew bacteriology, they knew nothing about how mail is handled or the size of envelope pores. The administration's crisis management team stepped in, but didn't do much to clarify matters.

On November 5, Attorney General John Ashcroft warned that America could come under attack at any time—but he did not know when or where or how exactly. He did not know what anyone could do about it. At the week's end, the alert was extended indefinitely. One month after the death of Robert Stevens, the nation's first victim of intentional murder by anthrax, new tests at the quarantined AMI building revealed a pattern of pervasive contamination that mystified investigators. Such findings pointed to an extremely dangerous kind of anthrax preparation, with small particles that could easily float in the air. The CDC recommended heightened surveillance for any unusual disease occurrence or increased numbers of illnesses that might be associated with terrorist attacks.

Postal officials denied to the *New York Times* that the letter described by Thomas Morris Jr., the Brentwood mailworker who had died on October 21, was responsible for infecting him, saying it had been turned over to the FBI after discovery and had tested negative for the deadly microbe. When Morris's 911 tape was released to CNN on that day, the Postal Service made the statement that it "grieves the loss of Mr. Morris." The Postal Service defended its handling of the anthrax outbreak, shifting blame to the federal Centers for Disease Control and Prevention, which had told the Postal Service its workers were safe. "From the day the [Daschle] letter was opened until Mr. Morris's death, public health authorities unanimously assured the Postal Service that workers in the Brentwood Road facility were not at risk."

Postal Service senior vice president Deborah Wilhite told the *Times* that her agency was familiar with the letter and did not think it was the source of Morris's anthrax. She said a supervisor gave the letter to a postal inspector who gave it to the FBI to be tested for anthrax contamination. "It tested negative," Wilhite said. She explained that supervisors at Brentwood told employees about the negative results "in a standup talk."

Suspicion grew that the letter to Senate Majority Leader Tom Daschle opened in his office had been the source of the infection at the Brentwood facility. It just hadn't been proven yet. And what of the millions of other letters that passed through Brentwood—not yet sent for decontamination, not yet examined for anthrax outbreak? Since the first contaminated letter was traced to Florida in September, an estimated fourteen thousand workers had been treated with Cipro or other antibiotics. Thousands of others had been tested and tested negative.

Though ER doctors caught most of the cases early, the anthrax mailings demonstrated how ill-prepared the government was in the face of a massive bioterror attack. Dark Winter, a CIA computer-generated biological exercise, had been carried out at Andrews Air Force Base the previous June. Former CIA director James Woolsey, advisor David Gergen, and health-policy expert Dr. Margaret A. Hamburg had gathered together with twenty-four other decision makers to test their ability to contain a simulated smallpox attack. According to the simulation, patients in Oklahoma, Georgia, and Pennsylvania came to hospitals complaining of aches, fevers, and strange rashes. The organizers realized how little they knew about containing such an attack.

Earlier, in March 2000, Project TOPOFF had conducted a simulated plague outbreak in Denver. Within a week a hypothetical plague had spread to other states and as far away as Britain and Japan, with an estimated two thousand deaths. Both military drills demonstrated a lack of crucial information and sufficient vaccine supplies. During both the Dark Winter and the TOPOFF exercises, health care facilities were overrun and in each it was unclear who was in charge.

President Bush, letting Tom Ridge handle the anthrax problem, approved new funds for smallpox vaccines and security at the Postal Service. Bush may have gotten a military vaccination for anthrax, since he said flatly, "I don't have anthrax." The next year he would get a smallpox inoculation. The President publicly discounted the 9-11 terrorists as the originators of the anthrax letters. If a state were behind the mailings, he said, that state was Iraq.

"WE FEEL WE need to be accommodated in a more human fashion by the government and the Postal Service," complained Steve Bahrle, president of Local 308 of the National Postal Mail Handlers Union. The Route 130 post office, closed and scheduled for decontamination in the fall, was not scheduled to reopen until spring 2003. Hamilton had been closed for decontamination since October 21. Parts of both the main Princeton post office, called the Carnegie Center in West Windsor, and a smaller post office on Palmer Square in downtown Princeton were closed briefly for the removal of anthrax found there. "These three centers," said Dan Quinn, a spokesman for the Postal Service said, "were determined to be a possible route mail from Princeton could have traveled."

After the Postal Service vacillated for several days on whether to expand its anthrax sampling, it finally tested for the presence of anthrax spores at three postal centers in New Jersey. The postal workers' union said it was pleased with the decision to conduct wider testing, logical because mail from boxes in Princeton was routed through the three centers before it went to either the Edison or the Eatontown center for further processing. However, the Postal Service's indecision created confusion among postal workers and rekindled their anxieties.

Panic buying of Cipro continued. Sixfold runs on the broad-spectrum antibiotic caught wholesalers by surprise. The State Department ordered U.S. embassies to buy and stockpile three-day supplies of ciprofloxacin. A preventive vaccine was available to the military, but not yet approved for the general public. The U.S. Department of Health and Human Services assured the public that "under emergency plans, the government would ship appropriate antibiotics from its stockpile to wherever they are needed."

Thirty-two thousand Americans were on Cipro; at least, that many prescriptions had been written for the costly antibiotic. Black market Cipro must have accounted for many more. People self-prescribed the drug after buying it over the Internet or abroad. Online, an anthrax "prevention pack" sold for nearly three hundred dollars. Bayer AG, the German pharmaceutical leader that holds the patent on Cipro, had been combating possible moves to override the copyright. Bayer announced it would immediately increase production of its Cipro by 25 percent. Sales rose by 1,000 percent, at a cost of seven hundred dollars for a sixty-day supply. But the huge sales had their downside.

Widespread and indiscriminate overuse and prescribing of such a potent drug could lead to more deaths from antibiotic-resistant infections than from the bacterium itself. Because Cipro was such a young drug, only fourteen years old, it could eliminate bugs that had developed resistance to older medications. Overprescribing any antibiotic breeds pathogens that can resist it and can make people vulnerable to other infections—gonorrhea, typhoid fever, meningitis, septicemia, and hospital-acquired pneumonia. Cephalosporins are the only antibiotic class to which anthrax is naturally resistant.

"Here we have a situation where a very important broad-spectrum antibiotic is massively used," Dr. Chris Willmott reasoned, "and we have the risk that more people can develop drug-resistant complications, which could lead to death, than would have actually been killed in the anthrax attacks." Willmott, a professor at Leicester University in central England, cited Johns Hopkins research scientists who had modeled the impact of five thousand prescriptions of Cipro. The results of their study demonstrated that the drug would have prevented fewer than ten cases of anthrax. "At the same time," said Willmott, "about two people per hour in American hospitals are dying of complications of drug-resistant bacteria. That equates to about seventeen thousand people a year. The frenzy whipped up regarding Cipro as the only cure for anthrax led to widespread and unnecessary self-prescription of ciprofloxacin. It remains to be seen if there is a significant increase in resistance-associated fatalities resulting from this unregulated misuse of a vital antibacterial drug."

The FDA recommended against Cipro as the first drug to treat any suspected case of inhaled anthrax. Most infections, though, could be handled with penicillin or tetracycline once anthrax spores were evaluated by the lab. In place of Cipro, the CDC recommended doxycycline, a member of a different class of antibiotics.

"Unless you have handled a package containing a powdery substance," experts warned, "there is no reason to be tested or stockpile Cipro (taking the cure without the disease). Overuse will exhaust its power against a range of bacterial menaces. If you think you've been exposed, call a doctor or your local health department. This will give emergency response workers a better chance of tracking down the source of exposure. Get the test—labs quickly diagnose anthrax by testing blood or nasal passages. Stay the course if prescribed Cipro, most respond to tetracycline [tetracycline and fluoroquinolones in children can have adverse effects and must be weighed against the risk for developing life-threatening disease] and penicillin—sixty days of medication or thirty days of meds and a series of three vaccinations."

Cipro's negative side effects include interaction with theophylline for asthma, GI distress, and, in patients under eighteen, the drug might disrupt the formation of cartilage. Pregnant women and children were advised to avoid Cipro.

After anthrax was found at Dan Rather's office at CBS-TV, federal investigators began tracking anyone who had gotten a prescription for Cipro. It was difficult to believe that Amerithrax hadn't taken the drug in advance to guard against accidental infection. As agents began tracing anyone who had sought prescriptions for Cipro in the weeks before the anthrax mailings, the effort quickly bogged down.

"Do you know how many people take Cipro in this country?" a frustrated official said, explaining that Cipro is used to treat a variety of ailments. Next, the FBI looked to the over one thousand companies that sold equipment that could be used to process the deadly spores. And they examined those that could have profited in some way from attacks—the makers of Cipro tablets or heavy investors in Bayer stocks. Amerithrax might have purchased stock in an effort to profit from the attacks. Fuad el-Hibri, a Lebanese foreign national with ties to Saudi Arabia, was one of Cipro's major investors. All but four of the 9-11 terrorists had been Saudis.

The USPS provided customers with bulletins such as: "What Should I Do if I Receive an Anthrax Threat by Mail?" They suggested: "Do not handle the mail piece or package suspected of contamination. Make sure that damaged or suspicious packages are isolated and the immediate area cordoned off. Ensure that all persons who have touched the mail piece wash their hands with soap and water."

Some of the top experts, though, said soap and detergent substances could increase the virulence of anthrax spores. They recommended to first wash hands and all unprotected skin with water for at least twenty seconds and avoid the use of soap until the spores were removed. "Notify your local law enforcement authorities," continued the USPS bulletin. "List all persons who have touched the letter and/or envelope. Include contact information and have this information available for the authorities. Place all items worn when in contact with the suspected mail piece in plastic bags and have them available for law enforcement agents. As soon as practical, shower with soap and water. Notify the Center for Disease Control Emergency Response at 770-488-7100 for answers to any questions. The mail is safe! People shouldn't stop using the mail because of these isolated incidents. The simple act of paying attention to incoming mail will go a long way in keeping it safe and viable. Everyone, in the mailing community, as well as the American public, should exercise common sense." They advised all Americans to monitor their mail and be suspicious of any unexpected envelopes with stains or odors. Not since the Unabomber had caused changes in air travel and the way we mailed packages had such an advisory been issued.

In a flyer addressed to "Postal Customer" and illustrated with a thirty-four-cent stamp showing a waving flag and the legend "United We Stand," the Postmaster General soon advised: "The U.S. Postal Service places the highest priority on the safety of our customers and employees and on the security of the mail.

"Please see the other side of this card for information about safety and mail handling. We want you to know we are doing everything possible to make sure the mail is safe, and we need your help. Your security and peace of mind are paramount to us."

The other side read, in stark black lettering,

What should make me suspect a piece of mail?

- It's unexpected or from someone you don't know.
- It's addressed to someone no longer at your address.
- It's handwritten and has no return address or bears one that you can't confirm is legitimate.
- It's lopsided or lumpy in appearance.
- It's sealed with excessive amounts of tape.
- It's marked with restrictive endorsements such as "Personal" or "Confidential."
- It has excessive postage.

What should I do with a suspicious piece of mail?

- Don't handle a letter or package that you suspect is contaminated.
- Don't shake it, bump it, or sniff it.

The USPS advisory was simple:

STOP!!! DO NOT OPEN!

"Does Your Package or Envelope Look Like One of These?" The bulletin, in full color, pointed out envelopes with unknown or no return address, too much tape, or unusually thick or heavy letters. If a package arrived marked with a threatening message, they advised, do not open; leave it and evacuate the room, keep others from entering, and notify the FBI and state police and your supervisor. "Contact your local FBI office," the bulletin concluded. "Ask for the Weapons of Mass Destruction Coordinator or Duty Agent. Tell the FBI you have a possible threatening letter or package. If it is aerosolized turn off local fans or ventilation units. Close door. Shut down the mail-handling system in the building."

It was the lack of symptoms that frightened most folks. A person who breathed the white powder in from a letter may feel fine for a week, then develop flulike symptoms: cold or flu with fever, tiredness, mild cough, or chest pain. This initial period was followed by a second phase with breathing problems and shock coming after several days. This second phase was characterized by acute respiratory distress, sepsis, and acute hemorrhagic mediastinitis causing the widening seen on chest X rays as a ghastly shadow. By this stage, the infected person had received a death sentence.

Investigators still had more questions than answers. Why had the purity of the anthrax improved? Was the terrorist learning as the attacks went on? Stealing anthrax from several different sources? Increasing the potency as time passed in a malicious demonstration of his capabilities? Or had all those extra passes that the Daschle letter took through postal sorting machines like No. 17 crumbled the contained anthrax into smaller, more floatable bits? The only sure thing was that investigators were mystified.

Why had the killer chosen anthrax? Was the disease something he felt comfortable with—was it within his area of expertise? *Bacillus anthracis* had a unique appeal for those attempting to show their power or to even a score.

The investigators were reduced to counting on shows like *America's Most Wanted* and a huge reward to incite a snitch to come forward.

Though congressional office buildings had been shut down for decontamination, other buildings that had received anthrax letters had inexplicably remained open. However, ABC News's New York and Washington offices, CBS News, and CNN suspended mail while their systems were reevaluated and safety measures put in place. J. P. Morgan Chase even issued an internal "anthrax advisory."

Then there were those postal workers who thought Bush was purposely holding back information as a cover-up or to avoid panicking the public. America's vulnerability had never been more revealed. Officials from the Postal Service and CDC were sharply criticized for failing to test postal workers at the Brentwood facility sooner, as cross-contamination spread the invisible anthrax to State Department offices worldwide.

If anthrax spores could escape through the ten-micron pores in the paper fiber of a typical envelope when squashed by a postal sorter, secondary contamination was a possibility (though this would not be confirmed immediately); the deadliest clumps of anthrax spores are one to five microns across. Few germs could survive so virulently on a paperbound journey.

B. anthracis needs no food or water and is probably the only pathogen so hardy. Viruses that live only in living cells cannot survive without food and water. A vial of Ebola-poisoned blood could be mailed, but would not be the surreptitious killer that anthrax is by the time it reached its destination. Sarin or VX, liquids, would evaporate before the envelope was sealed. Anthrax was formidable, yet could be neutralized with existing, though expensive, machines.

The impact upon the beleaguered post office was nightmarish. Everyone wore nitrile gloves and certified filtering face pieces (FFPs). The National Institute for Occupational Safety and Health (NIOSH) divided N-95, N, or P-100 FFP particulate respirators into three levels of filter efficiency and three categories of resistance to filter efficiency degradation. The "N" in N-95 meant the filter had been tested with sodium chloride particles under "worst-case" conditions—very high air flows, extremely high dust concentration and using extremely small particles neutralized to enhance maximum penetration. The "95" meant the filter blocked out at least 95 percent of the particles. The P-100 elastomeric mask would do the best job of protecting against bio-agents. The CDC also suggested that exhaust hoods be placed over the mail-sorting machines and that mail facilities and vacuum cleaners be outfitted with HEPA filters. Any public building with a HEPA-equipped ventilation system became a more difficult target for Amerithrax or any bioterrorist.

Simple respirators could filter out most of the anthrax particles, but there was always the danger of spores slipping around the sides. Through rain, heat, gloom of night, and anthrax, the postal handlers kept one eye on the in-boxes and the other on their masks. They scrubbed their hands with soap and water every two hours during their tour, washing and breathing and waiting every moment. A postal equipment repair company in Indianapolis discovered spores; then a Kansas City mail center that processed a tainted letter tested positive. Twelve Topeka postal employees were exposed, but tested negative for anthrax. Later, thankfully, so did 166 of their coworkers.

Worried branch-office workers handled potentially lethal mail as brave soldiers. One recalled the case of a homemade bomb. It had exploded in a mail pouch at the main New Orleans, Louisiana, post office, injuring two mail handlers. The parcel had been addressed to the police department. Just a bomb. Those were the good old days. With trepidation the nation's postmen and -women scrutinized every package and letter they picked up. Postal workers, thrust unexpectedly on the front lines, could only take so much. They handled 680 million pieces of mail every day. But the brave soldiers shouldered their bags and trudged on. Before new approaches to handling mail began to take hold nationwide, postal employees faced the burden of keeping their workplace safe from lethal letters and doing their job. They could screen for bombs, but no real systems of detecting biological agents on mail had been developed. But it wasn't as if the country hadn't been trying.

Since World War II, the U.S. had been investigating biodetection systems. Most methods involved the exposure of vials or petri dishes containing laboratory-grown cultures to air samples from a suspected target area. A field monitoring device used during the Gulf War took between thirteen and twenty-four hours to make a positive identification. The Biological Integrated Detection System (BIDS) cut the time to thirty minutes and was able to determine the presence of anthrax, plague, botulinum toxin, and staphylococcus enterotoxin B.

The CDC had been ordered to evaluate the sensitivity of the commercially available rapid, hand-held assays for *B. anthracis*. They reported that the CDC did not have enough scientific data to recommend the use of field assays at this time. Data provided by the manufacturers indicated that a minimum of ten thousand spores is required to generate a positive signal. This number of spores would suggest a heavy contamination of the area, but a negative result would not rule out a lower level of contamination and experience had shown, as in the case of Kathy Nguyen, that very many spores were not necessary to cause death.

Americans asked themselves what kills anthrax. Microwaving mail to kill the spores doesn't work. Microwaves heat by exciting the water molecules, but there are very few in a fluffy sample of the most dangerous kind of anthrax. Clostridium botulinum forms spores, but they're anaerobic—oxygen in air kills them. Steam kills spores in from one to ten minutes because a moist heat is a better killer than dry heat. Fumigation on the spores can be performed with ethylene or propylene oxides or paraformaldehyde gas. Ironing envelopes before opening was a good idea, as long as there was a cloth between the iron and the letter. The spores, in their thick, hard shells, resist most radiation except gamma irradiation.

The Postal Service was also investigating ways to kill anthrax spores before they reached mailboxes across the nation. Irradiation was the most promising technology—it tore apart an organism's DNA without harming paper mail. However, gamma radiation made hand-held computers completely inoperable. Electron beam irradiation, which operated in the range of 55 kGy (a measure of gamma radiation levels), irreparably damaged semiconductors, "smart" credit cards with embedded chips, contact lenses, compact flash memory cards in digital cameras, and pharmaceuticals. The USPS began working to devise new procedures to sanitize the mail, yet not damage sensitive items like film. One of the admonitions of the FBI was not to open any letter marked DO NOT X-RAY.

Electron-beam radiation, a stream of electrons bombarding a target, could penetrate mail to a depth of a quarter-inch. X rays drive even further. In February the Postal Service would truck mail from Brentwood and Hamilton sorting centers to the Titan Corp. irradiation facilities in Lima, Ohio. First letters, then flats and packages, would be sterilized with electronic beams. Over December, January, and February, the service arranged to buy irradiation machinery for "targeted areas" like Washington and New York postal facilities. To treat mail from the nation's thirty-eight thousand post offices would require 250 new distribution centers. Postmaster General Potter said at the end of October 2001, "This new technology won't be cheap, but we are committed to spending what it takes to make the mail safe." The irradiation machines cost about $2.5 billion.

By June 2002, Bridgeport, New Jersey, would have its own X-ray machine to sterilize mail.

The post office planned to use the most highly sophisticated technology available—polymerase chain reaction. PCR, or "molecular photocopying," could detect anthrax in mail as it was sorted. Unprocessed mail is dumped into mechanical lifts. The lifts move the mail onto conveyor belts where individual pieces of mail are "pinched" and placed on high-speed sorter belts. As the pinch is made, a vacuum draws air from the mail along a two-foot strip. Every half hour the air samples are tested. Anthrax and other bacteria have specific DNA signatures and PCR uses specific enzymes to magnify minute amounts of DNA and make a definite DNA equivalent. In the event of a biohazard, the supervisor monitoring the system shuts down the post office, the workers are given antibiotics, and Hazmat crews cleanse the building.

PCR technology was still being analyzed for adaptation to high-speed sorters, but by the following fall, the Postal Service was prepared to sign a $200 million contract to install the systems at nearly three hundred facilities across the nation. PCR can be automated to detect biohazards without waiting twenty-four hours for a lab analysis. Both the available prototypes grabbed air samples sucked from the mail and analyzed them for biohazards.

The USPS also decided to spend $9 million on a PCR pilot to test which of the two competitive firms had the best system. An additional $10.5 million was earmarked to repair some of the $25 million in damage to the Church Street post office in Manhattan, and another $500,000 to complete the plan to protect against bioterror attacks. The seven hundred displaced Church Street carriers who had delivered the Twin Towers mail were working out of makeshift quarters, sixty blocks from Ground Zero. Carrier Emma Thorton's route had been Tower One, a route so big it had its own Zip Code—10048. "It was like my own little town in the sky," she said. But those 16,000 addresses no longer existed.

During the year following the anthrax mail attacks, the Postal Service purchased eight "e-beam" machines for $40 million to irradiate and kill bacteria on mail. Four machines were designated for Brentwood and the other four were to be installed at a site not yet determined.

As a deterrent, an "identified-mailer" initiative, under review by the Mail Security Task Force, would allow the post office to track the mail back to the sender. Mail involved in that system would not have to go through the sanitization steam process that damaged and delayed the mail. They needed a system that would vacuum up air near the mail and feed it through a filter to capture any harmful bacteria. A continuous dust vacuuming and air filtration system was needed at all mail sorting, processing, and distribution facilities. This would keep a constant flow of air playing across the mail and directed away from the mail sorters, through the equipment and into filtration units. Inside the filtration units the air would undergo two stages of filtration. The last stage would use HEPA (high-efficiency particulate air) filters.

Other technology to detect and identify mail biohazards had been suggested. The most promising were a biological indicator strip that would change color in the presence of toxins in envelopes and air monitors that would trigger a second confirmation tester to establish an actual threat. On the drawing board was an automated mass spectrometry system that would constantly monitor the air and identify the invisible enemy moving over the postal workers in waves.

All of the safety improvements were at the mercy of funds to be appropriated. Postmaster General John E. Potter asked Congress for $5 billion, half to go toward irradiation technology to kill anthrax bacteria. Congress set aside $500 million to help the Postal Service safeguard against bioterror attacks. The Postal Service planned to spend $245 million to retrofit its high-speed sorters. Another $35 million would go to decontaminate and reopen the Brentwood and Hamilton Township sorting and distribution centers. This was the agency's "number one priority."

The Postal Service was in dire financial waters. They faced an annual loss of $1.65 billion. There had already been two rate increases in 2001, now there was a request for a third. Rate hikes were only a stopgap measure. Potter was concerned that users of the mail would be burdened with these extra costs through the price of postage and that could threaten the foundation of universal postal service. On November 8, while testifying before the Senate Appropriations subcommittee, he projected a fiscal 2002 deficit of $1.35 billion. The USPS had just spent $100 million on gloves, masks, and antibiotics, unanticipated expenses related to ensuring employee safety. Most of the money in a $20 billion terrorism spending bill had been used as bailout money for insurance companies and airlines, those hit hard by 9-11. The USPS had already received $175 million from the multibillion emergency fund.

"The Post Office was bleeding and now it's hemorrhaging," said Robert Wientzen, president of the Direct Marketing Association. Direct mailers were worried. They were afraid that people would toss out their catalogs unread because of anthrax fears. John Potter looked on the bright side. He suggested that consumers might be more responsive to direct mail because their "heightened awareness" would cause them to read direct mail more closely. Behind the scenes the postal inspectors dredged for clues.

STRAIN 16

Monsters of the Mail

EVER WONDER WHY postal inspectors always show up at airplane crashes? It's because planes carry mail. Inspectors are inextricably involved with any form of transportation that moves the mail. There were precedents for Amerithrax. There had been a number of Masters of Terror by Mail; the Unabomber was one. Another was George Metesky, "the Mad Bomber," who terrorized New York City from 1950 to 1957 by planting thirty-two bombs. In an anonymous letter, the Mad Bomber revealed that the Consolidated Edison Power Company had been responsible for his contracting tuberculosis. This valuable clue led to his capture.

Dr. James A. Brussel, a New York psychiatrist and author of *Case Book of a Crime Psychiatrist*, sometimes served as a consultant to local police, never more so than on the Mad Bomber investigation. Brussel created a near perfect portrait of the bomber through the first use of a profile. His contention was that the bomber, who held New York in a grip of fear unequaled until Son of Sam and Amerithrax, was an Eastern European immigrant in his forties. Dr. Brussel believed the bomber lived with his mother and wore a neatly buttoned, double-breasted suit. Metesky was dressed just that way when he was arrested. Apprehended on January 22, 1957, Metesky was found criminally insane and incarcerated in the New York State Mental Hospital. After his release on December 12, 1973, the lifelong bachelor (he turned down a marriage proposal from a pen pal while in jail) spent his last years caring for his ailing sister, Mae. Dr. Brussel's portrait of the Mad Bomber was the first and last time a psychological profile worked to such perfection—with one exception.

"The best example of profiling in history," former FBI profiler Candice DeLong said, "was the profile done on the Sacramento Vampire Killer, Richard Trenton Chase, in 1978. The profile that was developed was handed out to the police. They went door to door in the neighborhood where a missing car was found. The second victim's car was seen leaving the scene by the neighbor. That was the entire family that Chase had slaughtered. They had a bright red station wagon. There was only one in the world that bright a color and they had it. The neighbor who was waiting to hear from them to join them for a day at the zoo looked out her window. It was a half hour after the time for them to call. She sees their car going down the street and thinks, 'What's that all about?' She walks across the street and finds them all slain. Here's what we have to go on: the offender must have arrived on foot and then he stole his victims' car. And of course the baby was missing, the eighteen-month-old baby.

"They eventually found that car about a mile and a half away parked very haphazardly with the back end of the car kind of out on the street (like I park a car). That particular neighborhood was residential, commercial, and storefront. Robert Ressler and Russ Borpagel, one of my instructors at the Academy, both FBI people, developed a very specific profile—approximate age twenty-five to twenty-eight years old, white male, thin and emaciated, unkempt, lives alone in rental property, does not drive, would be described by others as 'weird,' tends to stay to himself,—unmarried, unemployed at the time—now that's a profile.

"And they took that profile and they went door to door in the neighborhood where the car was found. They also said in the profile that they thought the offender would be living within 250 yards of where the car was parked. They saturated the neighborhood and actually said to people, 'We're looking for somebody like this—know anyone who might fit that profile?' More than one person said, 'You know, that sounds a lot like Richard.' 'Who's Richard?' 'Well, he's this weird guy who lives by himself, is probably mentally ill.' The profile also said the person would probably be mentally ill and have a long history of mental illness. 'And he's kind of a nice guy. He loves animals. He's always asking people for puppies and kittens.' 'Where does Richard live?' 'Why, right over there.'

"So they did a little investigation and found that a guy named Richard Trenton Chase was renting an apartment in a particular neighborhood. He had been a schizophrenic since he was sixteen, in and out of facilities until the family finally kicked him out when he was twenty-one. He becomes a ward of the state. In those days people were not forced to take medication. He had been arrested six months prior to the Sacramento Vampire Murders by the Reno County sheriff. He had been living in the woods trapping animals. They checked his psychiatric records. They noticed that in some of the nurses' notes they had mentioned that they had found him on the grounds of the hospital trapping animals in nets and drinking their blood.

"His delusion, which he suffered from since his original schizophrenic break at age sixteen, his delusion was that his blood was being turned into mud by spaceships and by the soap scum on the soap dish in the bathtub. He had to replace his blood or he would die. For many years he would replace it with the blood of animals. He finally escalated to people. He did not torture his victims. He shot them immediately between the eyes and then he would attempt to get their blood through evisceration. In the first victim's home, he drank it at the scene. The second victim they found a bathtub full of water and blood. He bathed in it.

"He shot the baby in the bassinet and took the baby with him. He also attempted to drink blood by eviscerating the female of that family— the mother, an eight-year-old boy, the grandpa, and the infant. Only the female was mutilated, mutilation of course postmortem. He was compelled by his delusions to do what he did. Enough people put him with the profile to point the police in the right area. They did some background. They watched him carefully, then they made an anonymous phone call one night. 'Hey, Richard, the police have surrounded you and they're coming to get you,' and just hung up the phone. He had no idea who was calling. What do you think he did? He hung up the phone. His door opens and they watch him run out with a box. He trips and out of the box is tons of evidence from both crimes. This is the best example of profiling doing what it should do."

DeLong was anxious to see what the Amerithrax profile would look like.

Between July 1976 and August 1977, a serial killer stalked New York lovers' lanes and byways. He shot thirteen young men and women. In a letter to the police he christened himself the Son of Sam. David Berkowitz, who worked as a mailman, was the killer. He sent letters to New York columnist Jimmie Breslin that included clues to his whereabouts and identity, even his motive. Son of Sam called himself "the Wicked King Wicker." Berkowitz lived on Wicker Street and his neighbor Sam's dog supposedly told him to kill.

In the Bay Area Zodiac case, the hooded killer's long series of letters eventually became his motive in a cat-and-mouse game with the police, a game of outdoor chess.

Not a few of history's mail-writing monsters were men of science. One such was Jack the Ripper, who penned at least two taunting letters to the press (many were copycat letters written by the press themselves). Jack was thought to be a doctor because of the anatomical knife work he did on his victims. His eviscerations showed at least a rudimentary knowledge of medicine. Dr. James Gull, the Queen's physician, was a leading suspect in the Ripper case. Dr. Neil Creme, another Ripper suspect, enjoyed sending his victims poison and imagining their death throes.

Ted Kaczynski, the Unabomber, was a doctor of science, a brilliant mathematician who mailed bombs to his competitors in the computer field. He used stamps with a symbolic meaning known only to himself and bought in bulk years before his crimes began. He manufactured his own bomb components, made his own chemicals, and stripped the store-bought batteries of their metal coverings so they could not be traced back to him.

In the annals of the U.S. Postal Inspectors, those stalwart eyes and ears of the post office, is a case in which batteries tripped up a mail bomber who was also a doctor. One of the great successful hunts for a murderer by mail and one of the postal inspectors' triumphs, the story went like this:

In 1957 rules for handling unexploded bombs in transit called for immersing them in oil, not water. In some explosives, calcium phosphide is present and phosphine gas is formed when water strikes it. As soon as this gas reaches air it bursts into flames and sets off the bomb. Oil eliminates this hazard, as well as a short circuit touching off electrical detonators or igniting fulminate of mercury caps.

Curry Thomas, a socially prominent Cape Charles planter, stopped at the post office to pick up a package, a belated wedding gift. Before he and his wife reached home, he untied the parcel, removed the paper wrapping, and raised the lid of a strong corrugated carton. His wife glimpsed a small mousetrap inside. She heard a snap, then a crackling noise. "Throw the package out the car window!" she screamed. When dynamite in sections of pipe sealed with iron end caps detonated, the force turned the steel to shrapnel, which exploded in every direction. Neighbors a mile away heard the blast. Curry died instantly, and his wife was rushed to the hospital.

Postal inspectors B. B. Webb, J. E. Sentman, and C. H. Burrows of the Washington, D.C., division caught the case. They fine-combed the wreckage of the death car and rooted out a tiny coil of wire from a mousetrap, small fragments of steel pipe, iron caps resembling shrapnel, tiny pieces of corrugated pasteboard that had housed the mousetrap-type bomb, a loop of twine, a two-inch piece of wire, and a torn fragment from the label of a dry-cell battery. It was marked "—dio 'C' battery" and "—atteries, Inc." Decades later, the Unabomber would go as far as manufacturing his own tools and parts from scrap so they would be untraceable.

The postal inspector's job was to find out the source of the materials and who had purchased them. They fabricated an exact replica of the unexploded package and showed it around post offices. They hoped an alert clerk might recognize the kind of wrapping paper and string used on the parcel or recall whether a gummed sticker was used or the exact position of stamps affixed to the parcel. Anything they could learn would be a help.

The clerk at the Cape Charles post office did recall the package had been postmarked Richmond, Virginia, and of course the name of the sender. He'd thought it odd that sender and addressee had identical names. So did the inspectors. There was no "C. F. Thomas" living in Richmond. Since Mrs. Thomas still could not talk, Webb began a search for a motive.

Webb learned that Dr. Hege, a prominent (and married) dentist in Mount Airy, North Carolina, had been smitten with Mrs. Thomas before her marriage. When she met Curry Thomas at a party, Dr. Hege refused to accept that he had lost her. He broke down and cried when her proposed marriage was discussed. Hege deluged her with special-delivery letters saying, "If I can't have you, no one else can."

Hege and his wife attended the wedding, but he didn't kiss the bride. The postal inspectors interviewed the bespectacled dentist with a reputation for "quiet respectability." During their second talk with Hege, he denied his jealousy, but admitted sending special-delivery letters. However, he had an alibi for the day the bomb was mailed from Richmond, 250 miles from Mount Airy. Dr. Hege claimed he and a friend, Ed, left Mount Airy at 6:00 A.M. on the day of the mailing for a two-day fishing trip. They traveled through the mountains by way of Hillsville, Galax, and Fries Road Junction in Virginia. They reached a fishing camp on the New River on the North Carolina side of the state line between 3:00 and 4:00 P.M. Ed insisted to Webb that he and Dr. Hege did not visit Richmond. The fishing camp owner corroborated his story. Webb, Burrows, and Sentman were still not satisfied. The friend's version too closely followed Dr. Hege's. No one had seen them from the time they left Mount Airy until they reached the fishing camp.

Finally the inspectors traced the torn battery label to a Cleveland firm. It had come from a dry-cell radio battery of a type sold only to hardware stores. Five sales of such batteries had been made in North Carolina, one to a Mount Airy hardware store located on the ground floor of the building that housed Dr. Hege's office. The hardware proprietor didn't recall selling such a battery to Dr. Hege, but one clerk remembered selling him two sticks of dynamite. Dr. Hege had told him he was buying it for his brother, a farmer. At a plumbing firm, Dr. Hege had purchased two steel nipples, two pieces of iron pipe five inches in length, and four iron caps for the pipe. He had paid in cash and no record of the transaction existed.

A rope firm in Auburn, New York, recognized the loop of twine used to secure the parcel as their product. A shipment had gone to a dental supply house at Winston-Salem which had included some of the twine in a mailing of dental supplies to Dr. Hege less than a week before the bomb murder. Dr. Hege was their only customer in Mount Airy.

Mrs. Thomas, now speaking from her hospital bed, refused to speculate on who mailed the bomb, but did describe the parcel and its measurements. Postal inspector G. T. Bleakley, an expert in reconstructing dummy packages, set to work. He tied his replica at both ends with a loop of twine similar to that recovered at the scene of the bombing. Bleakley pasted white typewritten address stickers on the face of the parcel so it looked just like the original. He exhibited the dummy to all receiving clerks employed at the main post office in Richmond and at six classified stations. None recalled accepting a similar package at any time.

Next Bleakley showed the replica at the various contract stations throughout Richmond, stations set up in stores for the convenience of the public in outlying districts. Many years later the Unabomber would use such stations to avoid detection when he mailed his bombs. At Station No. 22, located in a city dry-goods store, the clerk recollected accepting a package like Bleakley's. It weighed nine pounds, carried the name "Thomas" in its return address, and was addressed to a "Thomas" at Cape Charles. His description of the sender matched that of Dr. Hege. Later Bleakley located other witnesses who had seen the dentist in the area. When Dr. Hege was arrested, he berated the postal inspectors for being fools. "Do you really think you have anything against me?" he said. When Webb briefly outlined their case, Hege lapsed into sullen silence.

A confession wasn't needed. Hege's friend, Ed, and the fishing camp owner confessed to false statements as to the time of Dr. Hege's arrival at the camp. They had reached the camp early in the evening, not late in the afternoon. Ed admitted that Dr. Hege *did* stop several times en route to open the trunk and check tools he thought were rattling. After parking in the Richmond business district, he stopped at the dry-goods store. Before entering, Dr. Hege looked into the trunk once again, but Ed didn't think he took anything into the store, though he wasn't watching him closely. When he returned twenty minutes later, Hege gave him no reason for going into the store. Leaving Richmond, they headed for the fishing camp at high speed to make up for lost time.

The case never came to trial. Dr. Hege committed suicide in his cell by cutting an artery in his wrist, slashing his arms, and severing his jugular vein with a broken lens from his eyeglasses. Mrs. Thomas, crippled for life as a result of the explosion, left Cape Charles to take up residence elsewhere.

STRAIN 17

Return to Sender

ON NOVEMBER 8, 2001, a senior official confided that though a few to a half-dozen individuals had been aggressively investigated, federal investigators had so far ferreted out no one who could remotely be deemed a serious suspect in the anthrax mailings. "Still, the more you are out there, the more things bubble up," the official said. But when reporters asked if recent news reports of a possible Amerithrax suspect were true, the official replied, "I only wish that was true. We run out every lead and we give these people a real hard look and real hard shake before we take them off the screen. There have been people who we have placed a little higher priority on than others. But then they fall off."

In the weeks after the attacks, agents tried to cobble together a psychological profile of Amerithrax. Foreign terrorist? Disgruntled scientist? A member of Al Qaeda? Had some lunatic used a vial of anthrax developed in the former Soviet Union or Iraq? When several promising leads came up short the FBI turned to profiling, at best "a rough science."

The Amerithrax profile, called a "behavioral assessment" by the FBI, was released in a briefing on November 9. "I was back East when the Bureau profile of the Anthrax Killer came out," said former FBI profiler Candice DeLong, "and so MSNBC had me all day. I was sitting in the chair commenting. I thought that particular profile was weak. I was embarrassed when this profile came out. I was embarrassed to say I was an

FBI profiler. Anybody who had been paying attention to the case could have come up with that. There really haven't been a lot of really good profiles come out of Quantico since John Douglas and Hazel Wood left. Sorry to say it but it's true.

"[This profile] is taking what we know about Kaczynski after he was caught and applying those behaviors to the Anthrax Killer. Kaczynski, as we know, was nonconfrontational one-on-one. He would be passive-aggressive in his criminal behavior and send his bomb through the mail. This profile is applying that concept to the Anthrax Killer and I don't necessarily agree with it. I can't see that at all. I went over the profile again and once again I found myself laughing. It's probably the weakest profile ever put out by the FBI and they should be embarrassed. They should be embarrassed."

The attacks were carried out by someone with access to a well-equipped lab—a scientist—someone who might work for the government. The anthrax was finely produced to spread quickly through the air, not the sort of thing an amateur could create. Experts suggested how Amerithrax might have gotten around this. He could have hired on at a lab, as a student or technician, and gotten a starter culture.

"We all use student workers who are eighteen or nineteen," says Martin Hugh-Jones of Louisiana State University. "Most of them don't even have any background you can check." For decades the government had imposed greater security restrictions on nuclear scientists than on scientists in the biodefense field. More vetting was required to operate a school bus than to work with dangerous pathogens like anthrax. But if Amerithrax was a *psychopath*, that could create difficulties: for psychopaths are skillful at concealing their true personality.

"In contrast to the simple schizophrenic, a psychopath is outgoing and articulate," wrote Robert Kessler. "A psychopath will actually kill someone and then sit where the police drink coffee and listen." Howard D. Teten, the father of profiling at the FBI National Academy, once told Kessler that the psychopath "gets a great thrill from hearing the police discussing how this crime happened. This gives him a great sense of superiority, that he knows something they don't know, and they'll never figure it out. If they stop investigating, he may commit another crime to get the police going. He may even write them a taunting letter"—and often go back to the crime scene.

The FBI profiler decided that their quarry had above average intelligence, preferred skilled work, and was sexually competent. The power over his victims (in this case an entire nation) might be his sexual stimulant. Amerithrax was organized and knowledgeable (he did not contract the disease while preparing his anthrax letters). He was probably an older sibling who drank before committing a crime. He had social skills and after his crime might change jobs or leave town.

The FBI profile sketched a picture of Amerithrax as a science loner with a grudge against society. "Based on the selection of anthrax as the 'weapon' of choice by this individual," the analysis stated, "the offender is likely an adult male. If employed, he is likely to be in a position requiring little contact with the public, or other employees. He may work in a laboratory. He is apparently comfortable working with an extremely hazardous material. He probably has a scientific background to some extent, or at least a strong interest in science. The anthrax killer is a male loner with a scientific background and lab experience . . . a man who feels comfortable in the Trenton area where the letters were postmarked."

DeLong thought Amerithrax drove to Trenton twice to make the authorities think he lived in that area. "Let's not forget what Kaczynski did," she said. "He went twenty-nine hours on a bus to San Francisco just to mail one of his bombs. The Anthrax Killer is a very smart guy and so was Kaczynski. He's going to put a lot of distance between himself and those postmarks. As for 'probably an adult male'—well, that's going out on a limb. I am on record, having spent all day—this came out on Friday, and I was in the chair at MSNBC in New York all day Saturday—I probably did five or six hits in an eight-hour period. I'm on record saying that not only is it a white male, without question it is someone over thirty-five and probably someone over forty who has advanced degrees, a lot of letters after his name, possibly Ph.D., possibly M.D.

"Why? Because this is a sophisticated crime. This is not a kiddy-crime. The person attempted to make himself look childish and immature by the handwriting and by the message. The message tried to pin this rap on Islamic extremists. To me the person was trying to disguise who they really are. So the fact that they tried to make themselves look like Arab extremists tells me it's an American—and a homegrown one.

"The misspelling of penicillin was a deliberate attempt to make himself look dumber than he is, which tells me he is smart and educated. He mentioned the wrong medication for anthrax and that too was deliberate. Just like when Kaczynski mentioned 'We are a group.' Ted Kaczynski put himself in jail, right where he is today."

Profilers thought the evidence pointed to a person who wanted to send a message and show off his talents, not necessarily to kill. Yet after Bob Stevens died, Amerithrax had mailed even more deadly letters. Some of the letters warned the recipient to start taking penicillin. On the other hand, the strain Amerithrax had selected was not a drug-resistant strain, but one treatable with common antibiotics.

The FBI's profile stated that Amerithrax "has likely taken appropriate protective steps to ensure his own safety, which may include the use of an anthrax vaccination or antibiotics [such as Cipro] . . . has access to a source of anthrax and possesses knowledge and expertise to refine it . . . possesses or has access to some laboratory equipment, i.e., microscope, glassware, centrifuge, etc." The evidence indicated that Amerithrax had access to a sophisticated laboratory between the two mailing dates and used it to refine the pure anthrax mailed to the senators.

Various specialists believed Amerithrax could have weaponized anthrax in a basement lab for as little as twenty-five hundred dollars. Others disagreed. "Just collecting the stuff is a trick," said Steven Lancos, executive vice president for Niro Inc., a leading manufacturer of spray dryers, the likeliest tool needed to weaponize the attack anthrax. The FBI studied the catalogs, trying to visualize Amerithrax's lab. He would most likely have among his instruments a flash drying system—a Flash Jet Dryer or the Fluidized Bed Dryer, known as the Quick Dryer. He might have a jet mill—a horizontal-type mill or the single-track version or a vertical-type jet mill or the complete jet milling package system or the Co-Jet System for small-quantity processing. On November 9, Boston agents visited Sturtevant Inc., in Hanover, Massachusetts, which manufactures jet mills.

"Even on a small scale," said Lancos, "you still need containment. If you're going to do it right, it could cost millions of dollars." He believed that whoever weaponized the spores was "operating at the outer limits of known aerosol technology. The anthrax mailer needed a powder that could negotiate the U.S. postal system without absorbing so much moisture that it would cake up. At the end of the trip, the coated spores had to be light and supple enough to fly into the air with no delivery system beyond the rip of the letter opener through an envelope. Their extremely small size gives them an aerodynamic quality and their high surface area allows them to readily trap moisture, acting as a natural desiccant."

The most likely method of constructing the coated spores would be to get fine glass particles—a special kind of silicon dioxide, "fumed silica" or "solid smoke"—and combine them with spores in a spray dryer. "You would need a chemist who is familiar with colloidal silica," concluded Lanos, "and a materials science person to put it all together, and then some mechanical engineers to make this work; probably some containment people, if you don't want to kill anybody. You need half a dozen, I think, really smart people . . . some experience with aerosols and . . . a lot of anthrax to practice on." Silica nanopower, superfine powdered glass, was available on the Internet. It would cause the spores to crumble apart.

According to the FBI psychological portrait, Amerithrax "has exhibited an organized, rational thought process in furtherance of his criminal behavior . . . is a nonconfrontation person, at least in his public life. He lacks the personal skills necessary to confront others. He chooses to confront his problems 'long distance' and not face-to-face."

The FBI believed that Amerithrax might hold grudges for a long time, "vowing that he will get even with 'them' one day. There are probably other, earlier examples of this type of behavior. While these earlier incidents were not actual anthrax mailings, he may have chosen to anonymously harass other individuals or entities that he perceived as having wronged him. He may also have chosen to utilize the mail on those occasions."

"This thing about [how] he's probably written nasty letters in the past," said DeLong, "that's right out of the Unabomber. It's just describing everything Kaczynski did to the UNSUB [Unknown Subject of a criminal investigation] of the anthrax case."

He is " 'standoffish' and prefers to be alone rather than in groups," continued the profile. Amerithrax "prefers being by himself more often than not. If he is involved in a personal relationship it will likely be of a self-serving nature." He may have shown a "passive disinterest in the events which otherwise captivated the nation."

The profile suggested that his pre-offense behavior, following the events of 9-11, may have made him "mission oriented." He may have "exhibited significant behavioral changes at various critical periods of time throughout the course of the anthrax mailings and related media coverage." He may have become "more secretive" after the mailings, exhibiting an unusual pattern of activity. He may have started taking antibiotics "unexpectedly."

" 'Secretive,' it says in the Amerithrax profile," said DeLong. "Once again they're comparing him to Kaczynski. I found a contradiction where the profile says 'pre-offense behavior.' 'Additionally he may have displayed a passive disinterest in the events which otherwise captivated the nation.' But in the post-offense behavior they suggest he was extremely interested in what was going on, more than the average person, and it contradicts. This is just utter nonsense, this profile, or at least silly. They say he altered his physical appearance. No. No one knows he committed this crime. Let me tell you who alters their appearance. It's men who go into a woman's house and rape and murder her and they live in the neighborhood. They might be associated with her so if they have a beard they shave it. This guy knows nobody knows he did this, why would he alter his behavior?"

Clint Van Zandt, a twenty-five-year veteran of the FBI and former supervisor of the agency's criminal profiling unit, was now a private consultant. He too saw parallels between the anthrax attacker and Ted Kaczynski, the Unabomber. Amerithrax was "cut out of a similar bolt of cloth as the Unabomber, who did it for purposes he thought were greater than himself. Kaczynski tried to warn about the dangers of technology," said Van Zandt. He additionally saw comparisons to Oklahoma City bomber Timothy McVeigh. "McVeigh tried to warn about excesses on the part of government," Van Zandt said, "and the anthrax sender, I believe, did it because he felt the United States was not responsive [to the threat of bioterrorism]."

The FBI conjectured Amerithrax was "likely an older man, a loner living in the United States who has substantial scientific and laboratory skills. He has no ties to organized terrorists, but sought to use the September 11 terror attacks as cover for the mailings." He may have altered his physical appearance and demonstrated "pronounced anxiety, atypical media interest, and noticeable mood swings."

"This profile of the anthrax killer isn't going to point to anyone," continued DeLong. "Here are the things that are on target: 'probably works in a laboratory, has access to anthrax'—duh!—and 'scientific background.' Anybody could figure that out. A social worker did not commit this crime," she said scathingly. "We're talking about somebody who knows how to handle deadly anthrax. Also the person has the expertise to refine it; well, that's possible, but my understanding is that the FBI also said it wouldn't take a Ph.D. to refine this. That if you had twenty-five hundred dollars of centrifuge equipment and whatnot, you could do it in your basement. 'Organized, rational thought process.' Absolutely."

The FBI said the UNSUB may have become more withdrawn, shown an unusual absenteeism, an "unusual level of preoccupation," and changed his sleeping and eating habits. He may have been especially manic during September 18 and October 9, 2001, the time the anthrax letters were mailed. The FBI had to ask—did he show any reaction to the deaths and illnesses of nontargeted victims?

As the investigation into the airplane attacks wound down, Van Harp, an assistant director of the FBI in charge of the Washington field office, had practically his entire office of 659 agents working on the anthrax letters. Special Agent Arthur Eberhart, overseer of the Hazardous Materials Response Unit, formed two squads of ten agents each—Amerithrax 1 (run by John Hess) and Amerithrax 2 (run by David Wilson)—that took up half the seventh floor. Amerithrax 2 utilized the talents of a CDC epidemiologist, Dr. Cindy Friedman, and a Navy anthrax expert, James Burans.

"It is highly probable, bordering on certainty," advised FBI profiler Jim Fitzgerald, "that all three letters were authored by the same person. Letters One [Brokaw] and Two [the *New York Post*] are identical copies. Letter Three [Daschle], however, contains a somewhat different message than the other letters. The anthrax used in Letter Three was much more refined, more potent, and more easily disbursed than in Letters One and Two.

"In the past the public has helped the FBI solve high-profile investigations that involved writings by coming forward to identify the author, either by how he wrote or by what he wrote. We are asking for the public's help here again in the same way. Leads from the public will play an integral role perhaps in identifying this individual."

The FBI hoped the new profile might lead to a replay of their 1996 capture of the Unabomber, a case Fitzgerald worked. But in actuality it was a tip from the public, not the profile, that snared him. The Una-bomber's brother and sister-in-law had recognized his writing style in a lengthy manifesto and tipped the FBI through their lawyer. Kaczynski had been the biggest loner of all.

STRAIN 18

Anthrax and Old Lace

ON NOVEMBER 9, 2001, after sixteen days of intensive treatment David Hose was discharged from the hospital. On October 30, his white blood cell count had peaked at 31,300/mm3. The next day, an "enlargement of the right pleural effusion required thoracentesis and removal of 900 cc of serosanguinous fluid," but he had survived. He returned to his Winchester, Virginia, home to convalesce, but as he attempted to regain his strength through physical therapy, he had little energy. "I'm just so tired," lamented Hose, a complaint echoed by the other survivors.

Postal worker Leroy Richmond was discharged from the hospital the same day as Hose. Richmond now suffered from memory problems. His wife, Susan, initially believed he was just getting old, "But it's not normal for him, in the middle of a conversation, to say he can't remember what the questions were." Richmond put up a front, trying to be "brave and strong." He agreed to a series of memory tests to regain some of his mental acuity.

Norma Wallace, released from the hospital after eighteen days, returned home. Like Richmond, she often found herself losing her train of thought in midsentence. Wallace resumed her correspondence courses for a B.A. in literature. Studying might aid her memory. "That's one reason why I stick with school," she said. "It forces me to focus and try to remember." Like the other inhalational anthrax survivors she suffered from joint pain in her shoulders, hips, and ankles. She might not ever be able to return to work. Wallace was so exhausted, she had to do her chores in twenty-minute segments, then take a rest.

Her coworker Jyotsna Patel had chronic fatigue too, along with the same joint pain and memory loss. She had been hospitalized for eight days. She only received a diagnosis of inhalational anthrax on October 26, the day she was discharged on a course of doxycycline. After her return home, she often woke up screaming in the middle of the night from nightmares. "The frustration is she is not getting better at the rate she should be," her husband, Ramesh Patel, told reporters. "What makes me really mad is they still haven't been able to find out who did this." That Amerithrax remained at large only intensified the victims' stress.

The sole exception was Ernie Blanco. "I feel good," he told the press. "I remember everything. I feel 100 percent fine. Honest to God, you won't believe me, but I almost feel better than before." Experts wondered why the others were not back to normal and why an elderly man had recovered so completely. Was the reason partially emotional? Wallace, Patel, Richmond, and Hose might be experiencing post-traumatic stress syndrome because the acts were those of a terrorist. The intense media attention was another emotional consequence.

Meanwhile, some of the injured postal employees reached out for compensation for their injuries in the line of duty. On November 9, the Office of Workers' Compensation Programs explained to workers about anthrax and OWCP coverage.

This Office has received a number of inquiries. Unless and until you have been diagnosed with anthrax or possible anthrax exposure you will not be entitled to benefits under the Federal Employees' Compensation Act. [The OWCP] has no statutory authority to pay for routine screening or preventative services, because the Federal Employees' Compensation Act only provides for medical treatment of an actual injury or occupational disease. However, preventative care can be authorized by OWCP when there is probable exposure to a known contaminant, thereby requiring disease-specific measures against infection.

Currently the USPS and CDC provide necessary medical testing and time on-the-clock to receive this screening in offices that are suspected of infection under regulations set forth in 5 U.S.C. 7901. If you are not an employee in any of the offices under investigation, any testing or time off of work that you incur getting tested will be at your own expense and on your own time. Bills should be submitted to your health insurance carrier and time off should be charged to annual or sick leave. Please note that a positive test today will only support that you were not recently exposed. Regular testing would be required to support a clean bill of health . . . When a Federal employee tests positive for anthrax exposure, and this exposure likely occurred in the workplace, a claim can be submitted to OWCP. The office can authorize payment for the treatment rendered to prevent illness.

Doctors had little to go by when faced with treating patients for inhalational anthrax. Their slim folder of studies was limited to the odd cases of millworkers who had inhaled spores from contaminated wool long ago. Little was known about anthrax's long-term effects. The CDC's scientists avidly studied blood samples from the Capitol Hill victims, attempting to understand the disease and develop improved anthrax vaccines. Their theory was that anthrax produces toxins that could impact nerve tissues. Because of Hose's contamination and that of the State Department mail center, officials suspected another anthrax letter existed— somewhere. It had just been announced that four more facilities in New Jersey had tested positive for anthrax, two more in Pennsylvania, one in West Windsor, and a second regional processing center in Bellmawr. All were linked to Hamilton in some way.

"This is a learning curve for everybody," said a senior FBI official. "Every single day, if not hourly, we're all learning something about this. If you take several weeks back, the learning curve, we were all behind it."

President Bush spoke in Atlanta to assure Americans that the Postal Service had acted effectively to deal with the anthrax attack. Noting that some three billion pieces of mail had been processed since the attacks, the president praised "a whole new group of public servants who never enlisted to fight a war, but find themselves on the front lines of a battle nonetheless: those who deliver the mail, American's postal workers." As Thanksgiving approached, letter carriers stood out as "beacons of normality in a sea of confusing and contradictory warnings."

On Monday, November 12, Dr. Jerry Weisfogel, a doctor working in

Kendall Park, New Jersey, told a television audience that he may have been the first person infected with anthrax. His symptoms (mainly a sore with a black scab) had appeared a week before the terror attacks of 9-11, but were diagnosed at a hospital as being meningitis. Kendall Park was near Franklin Park, the town mentioned on the Daschle letter's return address along with a nonexistent "4th Grade, Greendale School." There was a Green*brook* School in Weisfogel's town that only went to the fourth grade.

"It obviously made me think that there may have been some local connection between where my office is," Dr. Weisfogel said, "and wherever the perpetrators of the anthrax mailings are." He wondered if Amerithrax might have been in his office. "Have I come across patients from countries who might be doing this? Yes." He told ABC he may have had a brush with the anthrax attacker, but the government had ignored his story. It's "a possible lead" in a case with almost no leads, he said, other than a trail of anthrax infections and spores reaching all the way back to New Jersey. The next day, after the CDC became aware that Weisfogel had told his story to *Good Morning America*, the agency tested his blood for anthrax antibodies. He was told it could be weeks before the results of the tests were available.

Letterborne spores had spread far more widely than anyone could have predicted and continued to defy expectations. The inhalational form of anthrax took twenty-five hundred to ten thousand spores to seed a pulmonary infection. Even a dozen bacterial spores could cause cutaneous anthrax if they got into a small cut. Traces of anthrax were found at four more New Jersey post offices and linked to Hamilton, which remained closed.

"We learned a lot," said John Nolan, deputy postmaster general, at a briefing at the Postal Service's L'Enfant Plaza headquarters in Washington. He explained the Daschle letter, which passed through the Hamilton facility on October 9 on its way to the Hart Senate Office Building, had provided the most information so far. That letter might have been responsible for seven illnesses—three workers at Hamilton in the sorting area (two who contracted inhalation anthrax and one the cutaneous form) and four workers at Brentwood processing facility, who contracted inhalational anthrax. Two other workers had become sick, but experts still didn't know how. One was a resident of Hamilton Township who developed cutaneous anthrax, but had no connection with the post office.

Mail began to be treated like toxic waste. Compared to the same period in the previous year, the U.S. Postal Service's revenues were down 4 percent. Even Federal Express and United Parcel Service took a hit. Many consumers began to handle bills electronically and to use faxes or e-mail more. Many were just not opening their mail.

Joe Holiday, a Branch 142 mail carrier, had delivered mail for thirty-four years, eleven months and five days. "There's no point in me panicking. Somebody's got to deliver the mail," he said. While carriers wore gloves and masks when putting up the mail, they didn't do so on the street. "What message would that send to our customers?" Holiday asked. "I've got to look and be careful and check every envelope" before putting it through a slot into someone's home. "That's my job, my duty."

"In some ways," said a suburban D.C. letter carrier, "it's like the public just noticed us. Now they don't take us for granted." Carriers were left notes from their customers, a few signed only by their zip code:

Our community, and many others would like to thank you for your hard and courageous work . . . No matter the circumstances you have pursued your duties and proved to the world that you are strong, brave and ready to take on anything . . . We hope this letter has shown how much America thinks of you and your families. Your friends of Takoma Park."

To our mail carrier: In these difficult and sad times, we just wanted to let you know that we appreciate and admire the job that you and your colleagues are doing. We are all in this together and we will get through it together! Thank you and God Bless, Marisa and Vinny.

A twenty-two-year veteran of Massachusetts Northeast Merged Branch 25 said, "More people are actually touching you, giving you a pat on the back, telling you 'good job,' 'be careful,' 'God bless.' I even had one older lady on my route come out with a bunch of plastic gloves that she wanted me to wear to keep safe."

Branch President Jerry DePoe wrote a letter to the mail carriers too:

For the past month you have put your life in jeopardy simply by doing your job. Letter carriers will not allow a faceless coward to keep them from their rounds. Open message to all terrorists—letter carriers are not afraid of you.

Anthrax scares still swept the country. At a time of national terror and mourning, anthrax-laced letters had added to the panic. Across the nation any spill of mysterious powder closed freeways and halted flights. Authorities offered a $1.25 million reward leading to Amerithrax's arrest. Emergency response teams and the National Guard ran drills simulating how they would respond to a chemical disaster attack. The government strengthened management of medical stockpiles. There was designation of a new cabinet-level position for Homeland Security to integrate government-wide efforts.

Then an aged widow in Connecticut's Housatonic Valley became another puzzling mystery. Anthrax had gotten into her lungs too. Ottilie W. Lundgren fell ill a week before Thanksgiving. The ninety-four-year-old widow rarely left her cozy Oxford home and yet somehow, mysteriously, had contracted a deadly disease. Her hair was white as a blue-tinged snowdrift. Her face was creased with innumerable wrinkles set off by small gold earrings. The first symptoms appeared November 14—fever, cough, and chest discomfort. She was suffering the same as Morris, Curseen, Stevens, and the others who had inhaled infectious anthrax spores. The early signs gave way to respiratory failure, "hemodynamic collapse and thoracic edema." The headlong trajectory of inhalational anthrax could only be blocked if antibiotics were administered before the first symptoms appeared.

Thousands of microbes multiplied in a few hours. They teemed venomously in what, for her age, had been robust tissues, choking her arteries and turning red blood a sinister black. The green sticks and tangled skeins of anthrax threads were like the needles and yarn of her knitting. A widened mediastinum showed on her chest radiograph.

Mrs. Lundgren's illness was as mysterious as Nguyen's. Where and how had she inhaled the fatal spores? She was the only person in her town to become infected, though individual susceptibility was always part of the anthrax equation. Researchers in anthrax bioweapons recalled one super test-chimpanzee surviving one huge dose of anthrax after another before finally succumbing. Eventually even the most hardy succumb.

A CDC team investigating her house discovered several bags of rotting garbage. She rarely took out her trash. If Amerithrax had mailed the widow a letter, as he had Brokaw and Daschle, then it probably was still there. It wasn't. What mail there was tested clean. In fact medical detectives never found a single anthrax spore in Lundgren's home. They still suspected her mail was the source. Past experience told them as much. But how to prove it?

Investigators pored over data from the Southern Connecticut Processing and Distribution Center in Wallingford, the sorting facility closest to Lundgren's house. But they could find no record of suspicious letters addressed to her, said Dr. David L. Swerdlow, a CDC epidemiologist involved in the work. Wallingford had first been tested with dry cotton swabs on November 11 as part of nationwide testing for anthrax. Results had been negative.

Dr. Kenneth Dobuler of the Griffin Hospital in Derby questioned Lundgren on Wednesday, November 21, the same day Wallingford was retested with wet swabs. The results were negative again. "I asked whether she had come in contact with domestic or wild animals, whether she'd been gardening," said Dr. Dobuler. "I asked if she'd opened any suspicious mail. But my interview with her was unrevealing." She died the same day.

Her case was so bewildering that experts began to wonder if they really understood the disease at all. The FBI and CDC began backtracking Lundgren's movements outside her home. Would the enigma of her death lead back to the sender? "What about the diner where she used to eat?" locals suggested to them. "And wasn't there an anthrax outbreak on a nearby farm fifty years ago?" Tough, durable anthrax spores could easily last that long. That theory led them nowhere.

Three investigators visited the Nu-Look Beauty Parlor, where Mrs. Lundgren had her sparse white hair processed, and took dry and wet swabs from the parlor, then a clinic she frequented. The trio returned to their car to find they had locked themselves out. State police were summoned to open it for them. Next they made an intensive "grid-search" of her home for the letter. Eventually they took 449 samples from her home and thirty-three other places she sometimes visited. As tests continued on clothing and other belongings from Mrs. Lundgren's home, Connecticut's state epidemiologist, Dr. James L. Hadler, reported that none of Mrs. Lundgren's first-class mail had passed through contaminated postal centers. On November 25, Wallingford was retested a third time and no spores were found.

Then it was learned that some of the bulk mail that went to Lundgren's Oxford home had traveled through the postal center in Trenton. Could mail bound for Connecticut have been contaminated in Trenton, and then tainted machines in Connecticut? Could postal inspectors track such a large volume of bulk mail, find that needle in the haystack?

Investigators had a new tool. The automated postal machinery (which sorted 95 percent of flat mail automatically) could track first-class mail. Bar codes, printed on the back and front of every piece of mail as it was canceled, registered the time and place it had entered the system. Each letter gained a digital identity at each sorting hub, one that could be precisely tracked backward or forward. In looking for the attacker, the FBI and the Postal Inspection Service, using digital printouts, hoped to discern which postal route the letter had come from. They looked for any patterns in letters that had spun through the Hamilton Township center about the same time, but no patterns emerged. Bulk mail was so completely automated that none of its mailhandlers became infected. The best opportunity to use the data came only after Mrs. Lundgren fell ill, before Thanksgiving.

Until now, no one had used the data stored on magnetic tapes in the thousands of sorting machines in the nation's 362 regional sorting centers to do anything other than locate lost letters. Conceivably, the data could allow them to identify the tens of thousands of letters that passed through the Hamilton center within an hour or so of each of the known anthrax mailings.

Some officials pressed for release of that information, saying it could help people avoid exposure to anthrax. But others said such publicity would unnecessarily alarm communities that received mail that only theoretically held anthrax traces. But postal officials and experts at the CDC later found this unnecessary. Testing of 284 post offices and mail sorting centers (those thought to be at greatest risk among the nation's tens of thousands of postal centers) so far revealed only twenty-three tainted with anthrax. Most had just traces of contamination.

All those sites had been decontaminated with bleach except for the two big sorting centers where the assault began, in Hamilton Township and Washington, hubs that were shut down and quarantined a month earlier. In the CDC's "Morbidity and Mortality Weekly Report," analysts estimated that eighty-five million letters passed through the Hamilton Township and Washington hubs when both had "widespread environmental contamination" from spores sloughed off by the anthrax letters. Yet no new cases of skin or lung infections had emerged among the ten and a half million people served by those two hubs. Cross-contamination of as many as five thousand letters in the eastern U.S. may have caused the deaths of Nguyen in the Bronx and Lundgren in rural Connecticut.

"Despite this very low risk," the report said, "persons remaining concerned about their risk may want to take additional steps such as not opening suspicious mail, keeping mail away from your face when you open it and not blowing or sniffing mail, as well as washing hands after handling letters and making sure to discard envelopes."

"It's been frustrating and unsettling," said Connecticut Governor John Rowland. "You can't figure out the source, so there's no finality."

On November 27, investigators in New Jersey reexamined the Hamilton postal sorting machines that had handled the letter Amerithrax mailed to Senator Daschle. Aided by the computer bar codes, they looked at all letters that had whisked through the sorting machines at the same time. Only one letter went to the part of Connecticut where Mrs. Lundgren lived and died, a letter to the John Farkas home in Seymour, three miles from Mrs. Lundgren's Oxford home. That letter was processed in a New Jersey mail center within fifteen seconds of a contaminated letter. And as that letter made its way to Seymour, it passed through the Wallingford plant on October 11. When a team first went to the Farkas home, no such letter surfaced. But it was found shortly thereafter, and wiped with a swab. One spore took hold in a petri dish and blossomed into an anthrax colony. The Seymour letter retained enough anthrax to mark its route and offer a possible explanation of how anthrax could have reached and killed Ottilie W. Lundgren.

Investigators returned to Oxford's local post office. On November 28, they conducted extensive retesting at Wallingford, this time with high-powered vacuums instead of dry and wet swabs. The new tests revealed anthrax spores on four of sixteen sorting machines. Evidently, a letter contaminated in a sorting machine in New Jersey had tainted a postal bin in Wallingford that cross-contaminated a letter sent to Mrs. Lundgren in Oxford. More than 1,000 local postal workers were put on a 60-day course of Cipro. One sorting machine that handled mostly bulk mail still had three million spores clinging to beneath it a month after tainted mail had passed through. One of fifty-two columns of mail bins tested positive for spores. The contaminated bin was the same used for Mrs. Lundgren's mail route. The four hot sorters were tented and misted with clouds of bleach. Afterward, all four tested negative as did the floor area surrounding them.

Paul Mead, a CDC epidemiologist at the Wallingford center, said the investigative team wanted to complete "a trace forward and a trace backward" of any contaminated mail found there. But tracing postmarked and bar-coded letters was easier than tracing prepaid bulk and commercial mail, which carried no postmark or other "unique identifiers." "We have to look at other ways to track that mail forward," Mead said. "We're working with the Postal Service to come up with innovative ways to do that."

Federal and state epidemiologists continued their crash course in postal routing and sorting. The discovery of spores bolstered the possible theory that Lundgren had contracted the disease through a tainted piece of bulk mail contaminated by the letter to Seymour coming into contact with the Daschle letter.

The discovery of the single spore on a letter a few miles from Mrs. Lundgren's home did not completely answer the question of how she could possibly have inhaled a lethal dose of anthrax spores. No contamination was found in her home or at any of the places she visited regularly. State and federal investigators in Connecticut continued scouring post offices and the Wallingford sorting center for other clues.

Some 80 percent of Lundgren's mail was junk mail, and she made a practice of tearing it in half before throwing it away. This might have caused spores inside the paper fibers to be flung into her face. Ironically, on October 31, 2001, the USPS had told its employees: "Direct mail does not fit the suspicious mail profile." In 2000 the USPS had earned $64 billion in revenue, half from third-class junk mail direct marketers. Scientists estimated that the mail contamination had been slight, with too few spores to infect most people. Studies in animals had suggested that a person would have to inhale thousands of spores to become ill. But Mrs.

Lundgren may have been especially vulnerable to the disease because of her age. It may have taken very few spores to infect her. However, her death also meant that estimates of what makes a lethal dose of spores were not applicable to everyone. What she and Nguyen had in common was that both had been older. As in Russia, during the 1979 accidental anthrax aerosol release, older citizens were struck down at a higher rate than others. The parade of illnesses of postal workers who had been nowhere near sorting machines and the deaths of two women who had never touched an anthrax letter were the most puzzling questions of all. Secondary contamination was a barely possible explanation for the death of Ms. Nguyen.

Martin Blaser, chairman of medicine at the New York University Medical School, and Glenn Webb, a Vanderbilt University mathematician, coauthored a mathematical model to predict the course of future letter-borne anthrax. Focusing only on anthrax-laden envelopes was a mistake, they said. From published accounts, Blaser and Webb developed a model that included mailboxes, entry post offices, regional sorting centers, destination post offices, and final destinations. Webb estimated that the letters probably contained one trillion spores. As they made their way through the mail stream they contaminated other letters. Their model graphically demonstrated how the anthrax spread throughout the mail system.

"We hope there won't be any further outbreaks," Blaser told the press, "but if there were, this could help us identify the populations at risk and might help us move more quickly to find the source of the initial exposures. What was particularly disturbing was the woman in the Bronx, because there was no clear way in which she got the anthrax. But as soon as the Connecticut case came up, I had a pretty good hypothesis about what was going on—cross-contamination carrying a low dose of the microbe." Webb added, "The original letters were extremely dangerous, but there was also great danger from cross-contamination."

On December 9, eleven days after Wallingford tested positive for anthrax, employees and union management at the facility would be told that only "trace amounts of anthrax" were discovered on three machines and "a fourth machine was more heavily contaminated." Not until March 2003 would Connecticut postal workers learn the truth. A sorter was tainted with over three million spores. In the meantime, based on the misinformation, some workers had stopped taking Cipro early. "We were just outright lied to," John Dirzius, regional president of the American Postal Workers Union, told Dan Davidson of *Federal Times.com.* "We were hailing them as heroes and presented them with awards, all the while they were making jackasses out of us. If Dr. Hadler had never made a comment in the press, we never would have found out about this. They would have thought they could get away with it. We are pursuing legal action. We intend to file a reckless endangerment suit against the Postal Service. And we never received an apology. All we ever got was the cold shoulder. They are not even talking to us." The USPS thought decontaminating the facility and sealing the contaminated machinery was sufficient to deal with the concentration of spores. Retesting would concentrate on ceiling surfaces and air ducts where spores could collect in the dust and be stirred into the air.

Senator Lieberman asked the GAO to investigate the USPS's response to the Wallingford facility's contamination. "Based on the information given to me," he wrote, "I am concerned that there may have been a failure by public health officials to disclose to postal workers and others all the information that was available regarding the actual level of contamination of the Connecticut facility." The senator wanted to know who knew what when. In the case of Brentwood, the national union learned about the result of that plant's anthrax decontamination only after it was reported in the press. Their experts had not been allowed to review the raw data. An employee group, "Brentwood Exposed," complained of "scant and infrequent" information from the USPS and sought to make changes.

There might have been many other misdiagnosed cases of anthrax in the nation than suspected. The CDC's Dr. Jeffrey Koplan reported, "It's conceivable that our heightened surveillance has picked things up that wouldn't have been there before. [But] we have to pursue this vigorously as potentially related to these other criminal acts." Because the CDC's surveillance had turned up no new anthrax cases since Mrs. Lundgren's, they believed that any further risk from the mails was minimal—barring a new round of letters from Amerithrax.

The steady increase in postal automation was a double-edged sword. On one hand, it allowed postal inspectors to backtrack letters. On the other, the higher sorting speeds had led to a more vigorous passage of spores from letter to machine to letter. The whirling sorting machines, shaking, pounding, and compressing, were akin to adding anthrax to a blender.

Once the nature of the anthrax preparation became evident, "it was very chilling," said Patrick Donahoe, the Postal Service's chief operating officer. The Postal Service added filtered vacuum hoses to its equipment to cleanse the air. It ceased using pressurized air hoses to clear dust from sorting machines. Investigators repeatedly said there was something particularly deadly about the spores sent to Senator Daschle, but the strain of anthrax in all the incidents was the same.

The FBI pinned its hopes on determining which of the hundred plus genetically distinct strains of anthrax were sent through the mails. Many types of anthrax were held at microbiology labs across the country. Three FBI agents with Ph.D.'s in the sciences were collaborating with experts to narrow the universe of possibilities of the five million genes in a strand of anthrax.

STRAIN 19

Dead Letter

SEVERAL WEEKS BEFORE Mrs. Lundgren became ill, FBI agents and EPA Criminal Investigative Division personnel gathered to consider the monumental and dangerous task of combing 280 barrels of unopened mail addressed to and collected from Capitol Hill. The letters had been sequestered after the anthrax letter was opened in Senator Daschle's office. Agents hoped a second letter—which the infection of Hose, at the State Department mail facility, suggested must exist—might be inside the quarantined congressional mail. That letter, which would later prove to have been mailed the same day as the Daschle letter, October 9, 2001, from Trenton, New Jersey, might contain an even finer and more highly volatile powder. Its spores were uniformly small and more deadly.

It took more than a week to find a spot to open the quarantined mail. Few building owners were willing to allow anthrax operations to be performed on their property. It took FBI and EPA personnel two more weeks to transform a Springfield, Virginia, warehouse into a "hot zone." Hazardous materials (Hazmat) experts built a special interior containment unit and associated structures. Once inspectors approved the unit's structural integrity, the EPA set about designing the work space and developing sampling procedures to minimize risk of exposure to any heavily contaminated mail.

Negative air pressure ensured that spores would not escape. Intake and exhaust air was screened with HEPA filters, exhausting air faster than it was let in. Dust control trapped all particles down to the microscopic size of anthrax spores. Four air samplers monitoring the air inside and outside the containment area also helped measure the number of airborne spores. The hot zone also had a "cold zone," or decontamination area—an outer work space with outer air exhausts. The system worked so well that, during the entire operation, no spores were ever detected from air samples collected there.

Before commencing, scientific and forensic experts had to create an entirely new protocol to analyze the sequestered congressional bags for anthrax contamination. This clever strategy for finding a single "hot" letter inside 635 plastic trash bags eliminated the need for hazardous materials teams to sift and paw through each piece of mail.

They based the method used to search through the mountain of mail on classic microbiology techniques. Time-consuming sorting by hand unnecessarily exposed workers to high concentrations of spores. And they might be fooled visually. There was no reason that another anthrax envelope would look the same as an earlier one. During a manual search the real letter might be overlooked. Under the EPA's scheme, workers only had to sample 635 plastic bags, not tens of thousands of individual letters.

What they knew about the Daschle letter suggested that they should be looking for spores rather than letters. Clearly, the Daschle letter made numerous people sick. It had contaminated large areas wherever it went. Therefore, they reasoned that a trash bag containing a similar anthrax-loaded letter had to contain a gigantic number of spores. Those could be sampled to find the anthrax letter.

On Saturday afternoon, November 10, 2001, Hazmat workers from the FBI and EPA began sampling bags of congressional mail. Inside the hot zone, contamination was quite high. People were fearful and sweating though everyone wore personal protective equipment and respirators as they sorted and sampled. People would not become contaminated unless they handled a hot bag. Any worker's exposure was further monitored by taking samples directly off their clothing. Spores were automatically detected from all the hot zone samplers when a particularly "hot" bag was handled. They moved slowly. Spores become airborne with ease.

Each bag, sampled in turn, was jostled around to mix up any spores present. Then a simple, easily mastered swabbing technique was used by the workers. A swab was inserted into a small hole in each of the plastic bags and wiped around the inside. Sampling through small holes minimized the release of any spores present into the work space. After the swab was withdrawn, the hole was sealed with duct tape, and the swab was used to inoculate a petri dish containing a particular solid growth medium.

The inoculation of petri dishes with swabs was a very sensitive technique. Theoretically it could detect a single spore, as it had in the Farkas household. In this case the technique was actually too sensitive for the Hazmat search. The maximum number of spores that could be identified with this method was about three hundred. If more were present, the resulting colonies would become too crowded to count. This left little leeway to distinguish samples that produced one hundred colonies on petri dishes from those that may have contained many, many more than three hundred. The searchers decided to use a second sampling technique to determine whether or not there were large differences in contamination levels between bags.

Normally, swabs are packaged and transported to the laboratory where they are then used to inoculate the culture medium. The brilliance of the EPA plan lay in inoculating the medium at the scene. This step greatly reduced the workload on the laboratory and diminished the time needed to obtain results. The bacteria started growing as soon as they touched the petri dish. By the time the cautery reached the Naval Medical Research Center for analysis early the next morning, any with spores had already produced visible colonies resulting from the growth of the anthrax bacterium on the culture medium. Now the spores could be quickly identified by the experienced laboratory workers at NMRC.

Bag sampling by FBI personnel continued all day Sunday and into Monday, November 12. So far they had detected contamination in only about sixty bags. The swabs from about fifty bags revealed only trace contamination. Seven produced greater than one hundred bacterial colonies from a swab and were considered "hot." By Tuesday, all sampling results were back from the NMRC lab.

On Wednesday, November 14, personnel met and identified the bags that would have their air sampled and mail sorted. To be cautious, all bags that produced greater than twenty spores from the swabbing method were sorted by hand. These bags were handled in biological safety cabinets because of the increased risk associated with opening the bags and handling contaminated mail. Safety cabinets use directed airflow to prevent contamination from escaping while work is being done inside of them.

Air sampling began, as did the sorting of some bags that had tested "cold" for anthrax. For the second sampling method, air was drawn out of selected bags for two minutes each and bubbled through water. The water would accumulate spores over time, which could then be counted, no matter how many there were. This method proved to be much less sensitive than direct plating onto petri dishes, but it turned out to be more discriminating. Spores were detected in the air of only three bags. Finding the letter that had sickened David Hose at the State Department annex was crucial. An unopened piece of Amerithrax's anthrax-tainted mail might be their only hope to catch the murderer of five people by inhalational anthrax and attempted murderer of uncounted others, including an infant. One bag produced about one hundred spores; another, three hundred; and a third bag, between nineteen and twenty-three thousand. The difference between this last bag and all the others made it clear that, if there was just a single anthrax-loaded letter, it had to be in that bag.

At 5:00 P.M. on Friday, FBI and EPA Hazmat personnel searched the last bag in one barrel of unopened congressional mail. It was leaking anthrax spores "like a sieve," said one Army scientist. Approximately three-quarters of the way into the bag, they unearthed an anthrax-contaminated letter. It was in pristine condition, wrapped in tape, and addressed to Senator Leahy. It had been trapped by the Capitol evacuation and subsequent, though delayed, quarantine of mail.

"As you know," Van Harp commented from the FBI's Washington field office, "on Friday, November 16, 2001, we recovered a letter addressed to Senator Leahy in the Russell Senate Office Building from a large quantity of mail that was quarantined from the Capitol Hill complex. We believed at the time that because of the lettering and the initial test results there may have been anthrax in it similar to the Senator Daschle letter. We sealed it, secured it, had it delivered to Fort Detrick, and since that time we have been very deliberate and methodical in developing a methodology to examine—to open and examine—the letter."

Thus began a painstaking analysis by a number of laboratories. The deadly envelope presented a number of problems for the FBI and Army scientists. How could they open it without destroying the invaluable microbial contents or infecting the technicians? On November 20, they took a sample of the plastic evidence bag that contained the still-unopened letter. That sample alone contained enough for more than two lethal doses. Only after the envelope was decontaminated could the Leahy letter be removed and examined for its message. Then the paper could be studied for fibers, fingerprints, watermarks, photocopier gripper marks, and human DNA and the spores subjected to physical and chemical analysis.

For more than two weeks, government and private scientists consulted to decide how to open the letter. Experts from the scientific, public health, and law enforcement communities worked closely together to develop protocols and procedures to preserve the evidence. The U.S. Army Medical Research and Materiel Command Center was to oversee the analysis. Their goal was to save as many spores as possible in order to identify the strain and source of the toxin. They were determined to give experts as much to work with as possible. Most of the spores within the Daschle letter were spilled and lost when opened by an aide. The rest had been used up during testing. "The Leahy letter is the most intact piece of evidence we have," said FBI spokeswoman Tracy Silberling. "It may be the only complete opportunity we have to study this stuff in detail."

FBI forensic experts intended to open the letter according to a carefully orchestrated protocol. First they brought in high-tech lab equipment to redirect the air currents and reduce the tendency of the anthrax to waft about in the air like a gas. Over two days, they conducted dry runs in BL-3 on a "body-double." This was a replica of the envelope wrapped in tape like the Leahy letter. Never had any murder investigation put so much planning into the simple process of opening a piece of mail. "The U.S. Army and the FBI . . . know the sample is precious," said Maj. Gen. John Parker, commanding general of the center overseeing the analysis. "They want to make every study count toward the end of linking the sample to the perpetrator."

The Army's consummate anthrax scientist, John Ezzell, had been vaccinated against anthrax multiple times. So on December 5, the day set to open the letter, he would not be wearing a protective suit, only a surgical mask and gloves. Support technicians Dr. Jeff Teska and Candi Jones wore double gloves and moon suits with oxygen respirators. An FBI forensic expert would be there. As in the past, other FBI personnel had to be content to remain outside and photograph the proceedings through the thick glass window. Photographing the lightweight anthrax wouldn't be easy. The evidence was too fragile, immaterial, and "floaty."

For the last two weeks the original letter had been impounded in a locked, low-humidity refrigerator. The long-missing envelope was opened in a negative pressure glass containment box in the BL-3 facility. Dr. Ezzell stuck his arms through metal-cuffed gloves and unscrewed the sealed metal canister. The unopened envelope was inside. Ezzell carefully slit open a seam in the Leahy letter with a surgeon's scalpel, then began scooping out particles bunched at one edge of the envelope. The grains of highly refined anthrax were enough to kill one hundred thousand people. The scientists would not comment on any characteristics of the material until a battery of tests was completed.

It would be another three months before the FBI collected anthrax strains from suspect labs for comparison. Then a number of sophisticated scientific and forensic examinations could begin. Ezzell would dole out tiny single amounts upon request, but the material was as valuable as radium and crucial to any future criminal prosecution against Amerithrax. However, the envelope and letter could immediately be decontaminated and rushed to the FBI labs for further forensic analysis.

As suspected, the letter to Leahy was a photocopy of the letter sent to Daschle, hinting at escalating danger. He no longer warned the openers to take penicillin, but said flatly, "You die now." Amerithrax, whoever he was, had to be filled with hate. It showed in his letters.

"I have to tell you that after the Leahy letter was discovered," former FBI profiler Candice DeLong said, "that I decided unequivocally that the offender was a homegrown American. Up to that point I was willing to consider the possibility of state-sponsored terrorism, although I thought if this were state sponsored there would be a whole lot more dead people than there were. After the Leahy letter, that pushed me over the border. I'm pretty up on politics, and I vaguely knew who Daschle was. He wasn't a household word. I didn't know who Leahy was. He was definitely obscure. So how did the offender pick them? An Iraqi agent wouldn't have picked these two. They would have picked Kennedy. They would have picked the highest profile politicians we have not living in the White House at the moment.

"Amerithrax picked two obscure and liberal targets. This guy picked Leahy for a reason. Patrick Leahy for me is the key as to why this is a homegrown American who has really got a bone to pick with Leahy and Daschle. He knows of these people and of their politics. There's something about Leahy's politics he doesn't like. Possibly the motivation of the anthrax killer was to shake up our senators and make us more secure, then that makes sense."

STRAIN 20

Poison Letters

"WHILE THE TEXT of [the Amerithrax letters] is limited," the FBI reported, "there are certain distinctive characteristics in the author's writing style. These same characteristics may be evident in other letters, greeting cards, or envelopes this person has written. We hope someone has received correspondence from this person and will recognize some of these characteristics. All of the letters were photocopies and none appeared to contain any fingerprints." No fingerprints meant that Amerithrax had worn gloves. The plastic tape on the envelopes, a mass-marketed variety, was the type of surface that usually offered good clues—carpet fibers, hairs, dust, and prints. Amerithrax left none. However, all the tape had been cut from the same roll. The paper on which the letters were written was an average size. The envelopes were prestamped and widely available. A human breath can leave DNA on a sheet of paper that could be detected through PCR. The FBI believed that Amerithrax had worn a breathing mask because there was not a trace. The marks left by the photocopier were carefully studied, but revealed no clues.

Postal inspectors took anonymous letters as a matter of course. Their history was a rich one and contained many successful hunts for poison pen writers and poison by mail. The letters themselves had been their best clue. Years ago, New York City police discovered the body of a bride who had committed suicide just after her wedding. An anonymous letter crumpled in her hand alleged her husband was a bigamist. The accusation was untrue. Five other brides received similar letters. The trail led back to a young woman in a New York suburb who confessed to writing the letters. She targeted her victims after reading the marriage notices in the newspapers. She defended her actions, saying they had found the happiness to which she was entitled.

In College Park, Georgia, an Atlanta suburb, letters accusing daughters and wives of sordid sexual behavior started arriving. Inspector J. A. Callahan, who'd handled the Charleston, South Carolina, poisoned candy case, examined the letters. They were all typewritten in uppercase letters and mailed from Atlanta and suburban East Point. The letters brought domestic havoc to the two fashionable communities. Callahan studied the letters and listed all errors in sentence structure and misspelled words.

He wrote down all references to places, happenings, individuals, or incidents known only to a few people. Grouped together and properly considered, his list was invaluable. In the Amerithrax case, the killer had misspelled penicillin. The San Francisco Zodiac had spelled words correctly and incorrectly in the same letter. Misspellings also gave a frightening tone to any letter, as did the uppercase lettering.

Callahan made photostated copies of several poison pen envelopes and distributed them to all mail carriers serving the College Park and East Point areas. "Keep a sharp watch for similar typewritten envelopes during your collections," he ordered. After several weeks, a carrier named Brown of the East Point post office turned in a letter that appeared to be written on a typewriter like that used by the poison pen writer.

Callahan sent it on its way, then tracked down the addressee, Nellie Jo Barfield, a divorced woman. Callahan filled her in. "I received that letter," she said, "but I didn't know there were others. I thought I was the only one." She explained that her former husband, Fred O. Barfield, who lived with his seventy-six-year-old mother in College Park, had started sending her "filthy, obscene, and highly objectionable letters" after their divorce. "There were others, Mr. Callahan, but I destroyed them," she said. "If the letters weren't bad enough, he would call me on the telephone and use the same kind of language. It's been like a nightmare. I've been sick—sick of wondering how to get away from him." "What motive would your husband have for writing such letters?" Callahan asked. "He

239

is mean and spiteful, that's why," she said. "He likes to make people squirm and suffer."

Barfield denied writing the letters. He denied he had a typewriter even though Callahan fished one from under Barfield's bed. In the end he agreed to a typewriter test. The document examiners in the bureau of the chief inspector identified Barfield's typewriter as the one used. When Callahan dictated the letters to Barfield, the suspect "repeated every misspelling with deadly accuracy." Faced with such evidence, he admitted writing the letters, but refused to clarify his motive. Though Barfield complained to the president of the United States and two Georgia senators—by typewritten letters—he was found guilty.

Some poison pen writers pieced their letters together with type snipped from magazines and pasted down. In 1956, a series of such collage postcards were mailed to the medical director of a Boston hospital and to the mayor. A surveillance photo taken by Boston division postal inspectors assigned to the case caught a Boston physician as he mailed some of the postcards to his immediate superior. The doctor wanted to defame the character of his superior because he felt better qualified for the position.

What the postal inspectors began to look for in their search for Amerithrax was some event prior to the mailings that would have been a catalyst to him. Perhaps he had been passed over for a promotion or fired. They knew Amerithrax did not select victims randomly. He deliberately chose NBC News, the *New York Post*, and Senators Daschle and Leahy as targets.

The FBI noted that "these targets are probably very important to the offender. They may have been the focus of previous expressions of contempt which may have been communicated to others, or observed by others." The FBI had done considerable work on the characteristics of the letters: Amerithrax made an effort to identify the correct address, including zip code, of each victim, just as the Unabomber had with the series of homemade bombs he had mailed. But the Unabomber got some titles and addresses wrong because he had worked from an out-of-date reference in a small-town library in remote Montana. That eventually was a clue in his capture.

* * *

Letter 1
One page, handprinted letter
Transmittal envelope, also similarly handprinted
Addressed to "NBC TV—Tom Brokaw"—No return address
Postmarked Trenton, NJ 09/18/2001 (Tues.)

Letter 2
One page, handprinted letter
Transmittal envelope, also similarly handprinted
Addressed to "NY Post"—No return address
Postmarked Trenton, NJ 09/18/2001 (Tues.)

Letter 3
One page, handprinted letter
Transmittal envelope, also similarly handprinted
Addressed to "Senator Daschle—509 Hart Senate Office Building"
Return address—"4th Grade, Greendale School, Franklin Park, NJ"
Return address zip code—"08852"
Postmarked Trenton, NJ 10/09/2001 (Tues.)

Letter 4
One page, handprinted letter
Transmittal envelope, also similarly handprinted
Addressed to "Senator Leahy—433 Russell Senate Office Building"
Return address—"4th Grade, Greendale School, Franklin Park, NJ"
Return address zip code—"08852"
Postmarked Trenton, NJ 10/09/2001 (Tues.)

1. The author uses dashes ("-") in writing of the date "09-11-01." Many people use the slash ("/") to separate the day/month/year.

2. In writing the number one, the author chooses to use a formalized, more detailed version. He writes it as "1" instead of the simple vertical line.

3. The author uses the words "can not," when many people prefer to spell it as one word, "cannot."

4. The author writes in all upper case block-style letters. However, the first letter of the first word of each sentence is written in slightly larger upper case lettering. Also, the first letter of all proper nouns (like names) is slightly larger. This is apparently the author's way of indicating a word should be capitalized in upper case lettering. For whatever reason, he might not be comfortable or practiced in writing lower case lettering.

5. The names and addresses on each envelope are noticeably tilted on a downward slant from left to right. This may be a characteristic seen on other envelopes he has sent.

6. The envelopes are of the prestamped variety, the stamps denoting thirty-four cents, which are normally available directly from the post office. The stamps were preprinted suggesting that the mailer feared saliva on a licked stamp could be used to confirm his identity. They are not the traditional business size envelopes, but the smaller size measuring approximately six and one-quarter inches by three and one-half inches.

Criminal profilers concluded on the basis of emerging patterns that the wording of the anthrax messages appeared to be the work of a native English speaker trying to throw suspicion on Islamic terrorists in an effort to disguise his identity. This antisocial loner had some odd mannerisms in his speech and handwriting. The writer may have been a Muslim terrorist like the 9-11 hijackers. "Allah is great" is not a common expression. It was more common for a Muslim to say "Allahu akbar," which means "God is great."

ON DECEMBER 3, 2001, surviving Brentwood postal employee Leroy Richmond was coming up against a stone wall. The USPS, though "deeply troubled" by the two deaths and lingering illnesses at the Washington mail facility, rejected Richmond's $100 million damage claim. They said the agency could not "legally compensate him" beyond the workman's compensation payments he was already receiving. Richmond began legal action, telling the *Washington Post* that the Postal Service's action was consistent with the indifference he and other postal workers had encountered since the attack.

By December 5, 2001, the day the Leahy letter was opened, Van Harp had learned so much about anthrax, he might qualify for degrees in microbiology. Instead, he continued leading the FBI investigative team in the manhunt for Amerithrax. Trace amounts of anthrax spores had been found at the Federal Reserve Bank Building that same morning, another cross-contamination. At least the Leahy letter would give the FBI a whole series of new leads. The letters were all written by the same person, possibly a lone disaffected American scientist trained in biochemistry and with access to a U.S government lab.

Harp explained on the FBI website that the bureau had "enlisted some of the best minds available" to create the methodology involved in locating and opening the Leahy letter safely. "But the science really drives the investigation and the analysis," he said, "and we can't hurry that. But, we also wanted to be careful to be able to maximize our ability to examine both the letter and the contents of the letter. But, also this has never been accomplished or been required to be performed before and on top of all the other considerations, both the safety and health and the science, we have one other, that is the forensic and investigative. Ultimately, the results of what we do have to be admissible in court.

"There were a number of precautions that were taken very deliberately, and that was to maximize again our ability to analyze and benefit from this letter. It was opened under a controlled secure sterile environment in which we controlled motion and air. Again in an abundance of caution for the safety, the health, and to maximize whatever may be in that letter. Our objective—we hope to learn in the final analysis, literally, who did this and how they did it. And these examinations are critically important because we feel they will provide investigative leads to help bring this investigation to a conclusion because we do have five homicides we believe and at least thirteen other attempted homicides.

"So, every bit of information, every bit of evidence, and every additional bit of information and evidence are critically important—and it may help bring resolution to this investigation," Harp said. At this time the FBI was focusing on a military contractor that worked with the CIA. They were also interested in nonmilitary individuals who had received anthrax vaccine within the last year. Investigators, intent on keeping the American public focused on the case, reminded them that the reward was up to $1.25 million. "Anyone who thinks they may know something," Van Harp said, "should contact their local FBI office or police department."

As the Leahy letter was being slit open, two leading bioweapons experts, Richard Spertzel and Ken Alibek, were speaking before the House International Relations Committee. Spertzel now lived just outside Frederick, Maryland, and a few minutes' drive from the Institute. The two experts disagreed about the level of expertise required to make the letter anthrax, but agreed that it had probably not been obtained by using the production techniques of either the former Soviet Union or the defunct American germ weapons program.

Dr. Spertzel dismissed the FBI Amerithrax profile as "a lot of hokum." The letter anthrax was "not the kind of thing you mess around with in a university lab unless you don't like your fellow students. This is not the work of a graduate student in microbiology. I don't think that an individual is capable of doing it." Preparing anthrax particles so small and concentrated, he added, would endanger people nearby and perhaps expose the culprit himself. Dr. Alibek, who said he had seen Polaroids of the anthrax from one or two of the letters, thought it could have been homegrown. He assumed those who had produced it could have been a terrorist band of "not very highly trained professionals."

On December 8, Senator Daschle said the anthrax mailer was probably someone with a military background. The anthrax genome (the full amount of DNA in a cell, which contains the complete genetic code of the organism) is among the least variable and least genetically diverse bacteria known. There were less than two hundred genetically identified strains, a fraction of the diversity found in other bacteria. DNA testing could determine the anthrax's source. The race to break down the genetic code of the mailed anthrax was on.

On the same day two agents paid Joseph Farchaus a visit at his home about fifteen minutes outside Trenton, New Jersey. Farchaus had once worked for the Institute in Maryland. The last paper he published just before he left the infectious diseases institute was about converting anthrax into aerosol form. The FBI questioned him, gave him a lie test (which he aced), and spoke with his New York attorney, Donald Buchwald. They never got back to him again. Not so with other suspects on their domestic list.

Four days later, the press broke the story that the U.S. military had recently developed anthrax in a highly lethal powder form although they claimed to have kept track of every bit of it. The FBI was investigating government and private contractor labs possessing the Ames strain of anthrax as well as individuals who had access to them.

As the FBI considered the Leahy spores, the most unadulterated evidence they had, they tried to determine their age. Under a microscope older spores, naturally, "look wrinkled." However, varying the drying methods could make newer spores appear old. The dating of the spores was reportedly done with the same radiocarbon analysis commonly used by archaeologists to determine the age of ancient artifacts. Biologist Jennie Hunter-Cevera, president of the University of Maryland's Biotechnology Institute, later told the *Washington Post* that the FBI analysts didn't necessarily have to use the radioactive carbon 14 isotope, which decays in organic materials.

"Instead," she said "isotopic analysis could compare the radioactivity ratios from the isotopes of several elements to get an age. Carbon 14 dating is sometimes suspect for recent objects because the atomic testing of the 1950s created higher levels of carbon 14 in the air while increased use of fossil fuels has enriched the air with more inert carbon. The exact scientific process the FBI has used with the Leahy letter has been kept secret, but among microbiologists the news that this technique was bearing fruit began to leak out . . . The FBI appears to be getting good scientific advice."

The Ames strain anthrax spores mailed to Capitol Hill were no more than two years old. The age of the spores cast doubt on the hypothesis that the spores could have been stolen from a lab decades earlier, saved in dry storage, and used in September and October. Amerithrax had a recent or current connection to a sophisticated modern lab and could make a new batch anytime he wanted. In its dried spore form, a bacterium can lie dormant for years.

"The secret of spore longevity is to package it in the absence of humidity," said biological defense consultant Bill Patrick. "When the agents pick up moisture, the particle size grows, the powder deteriorates, and the agent loses the qualities that make it a potent weapon." When the spores are kept dry they are remarkably resilient.

Investigators now focused on determining the rate of genetic mutation across generations of bacteria, hoping to backtrack the mailed spores to their lab of origin. This method, though, was not immediately producing results, because the genetic variations might not be dramatic enough. Since the FBI now believed that Amerithrax was a disgruntled domestic scientist with the high level of expertise needed to culture, mill, and weaponize the spores, they began to reinterview and give polygraph tests to any scientists with sophisticated knowledge of anthrax.

On December 17, White House spokesman Ari Fleischer said it was increasingly "looking like it could be a domestic source." Two days later, ABC News reported that a scientist who was fired twice from Battelle was the focus of an FBI investigation. On December 20, the FBI emphatically declared that the fired scientist was not the focus of any investigation. Meanwhile something had to be done about the anthrax spores inside the Hart office building. There was talk of installing high-density particle filters in the building's ventilation systems.

While the experts disagreed on the level of expertise required to have made such material, there were a lot of nuts out there, who not only had access to bioweapons like anthrax but had tried to use them domestically.

In 1972, the Order of the Rising Sun, an American fascist group, obtained eighty pounds of typhoid bacteria cultures they planned to feed into the water supplies of several Midwestern cities.

In 1984, Antelope, Oregon, was hometown to a free-love commune headed by Bhagwan Shree Rajneesh, an Indian guru. To influence a local election in a private zoning dispute, the religious cult committed a crude form of bioterrorism on September 9. This first bioweapon attack in the U.S. struck a stable community of ten thousand in the spectacular Columbia River Gorge, near Mount Hood. Seven hundred and fifty-one people in The Dalles, the county seat of Wasco County, mysteriously began suffering from nausea, severe diarrhea, chills, fever, and dizziness. No one died, but forty-five were hospitalized. Bill Patrick, flown out from the Institute, examined the cult's compound and discovered a germ incubator there. Growing germs was as easy as brewing beer.

The cultists had contaminated ten restaurant salad bars, including Shakey's Pizza, with salmonella. Patrick knew salmonella well, having

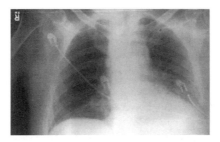

1. Initial chest X ray (Case 1) showing prominent superior mediastinum and possible small left pleural effusion.

(Credit: Center for Disease Control)

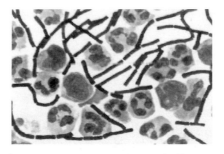

2. Grain stain of cerebrospinal fluid (Case 1) showing B. anthracis.

(Credit: CDC)

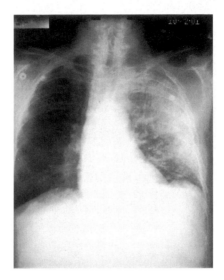

3. Chest X ray (Case 2) showing diffuse consolidation
consistent with pneumonia throughout the left lung.
There is no evidence of mediastinal widening.

(Credit: CDC)

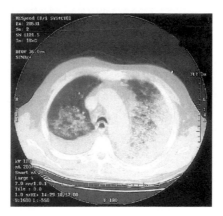

4. Computed tomography of chest (Case 2) showing
bilateral pulmonary consolidation and pleural effusions.

(Credit: CDC)

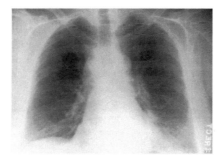

5. Chest X ray (Case 7) showing mediastinal
widening and a small left pleural effusion.

(Credit: CDC)

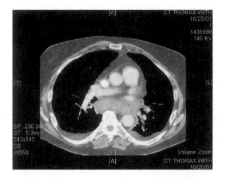

6. Computed tomography of chest (Case 7) showing mediastinal adenopathy and small bilateral pleural effusions.

(Credit: CDC)

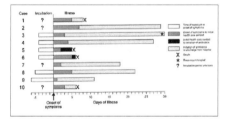

7. Timeline of 10 cases of inhalational anthrax in relation to onset of symptoms, October through November 2001.

(Credit: CDC)

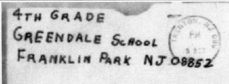

09-11-01

YOU CAN NOT STOP US.
WE HAVE THIS ANTHRAX.
YOU DIE NOW.
ARE YOU AFRAID?
DEATH TO AMERICA.
DEATH TO ISRAEL.
ALLAH IS GREAT.

8c.

4TH GRADE
GREENDALE SCHOOL
FRANKLIN PARK NJ 08852

SENATOR DASCHLE
509 HART SENATE OFFICE
BUILDING
WASHINGTON D.C. 2051

20510/4103

8b.

4TH GRADE
GREENDALE SCHOOL
FRANKLIN PARK NJ 08852

SENATOR LEAHY
433 RUSSELL SENATE OFFICE
BUILDING
WASHINGTON D.C. 20510-4502

20520+4502

8a.

8a–8g. Images of anthrax envelopes and letters.

(Credit: FBI)

Tom Brokaw
NBC TV
30 Rockefeller Plaza
New York NY 10112

10112+0002

8d.

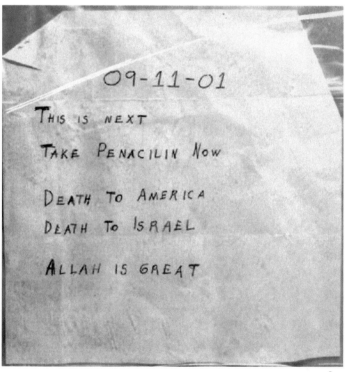

8e.

EDITOR
NEW YORK POST
1211 AVE. OF THE AMERICAS
NEW YORK NY 10036

8f.

09-11-01

THIS IS NEXT

TAKE PENACILIN NOW

DEATH TO AMERICA
DEATH TO ISRAEL

ALLAH IS GREAT

8g.

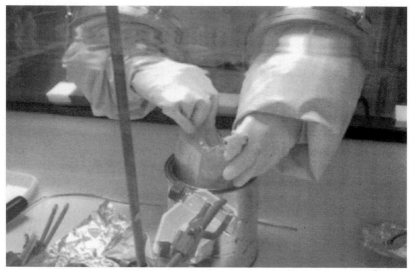

9a.

9b.

9a–9d. Photographs of the Leahy letter's opening.

(Credit: FBI)

9c.

9d.

10a.

10b.

10a–10e. FBI and Environmental Protection Agency personnel working to identify anthrax-contaminated mail at the containment facility.

(Credit: FBI)

10c.

10e.

10d.

11. In October 2001, a Trenton, New Jersey, hazmat team undergoes decontamination after inspecting a possible anthrax letter.

(Credit: AP/Wide World Photos)

12. New York Mayor Giuliani, given conflicting scientific information,
stalks from NBC after announcing to the press that
Tom Brokaw's assistant has been infected with anthrax by mail.

(Credit: Reuters/Brad Rickerby)

13. On October 12, 2001, investigators from the FBI and CDC check out a suspicious anthrax letter at the *New York Times*. It would turn out to be a cruel hoax.

(Credit: REUTERS/Peter Morgan)

14. On a blistering Sunday morning, August 11, 2002, Dr. Steven Hatfill delivers a polished speech outside his lawyer's Alexandria, VA, office. With passion he defends himself after being characterized as a "person of interest" by the FBI.

(Credit: AP/Wide World Photos)

15. FBI agents fill a van with items seized from Dr. Hatfill's apartment near the gates of the Institute at Fort Detrick, MD.

(Credit: Alex Wong/Getty Images)

16. FBI agents begin draining a brown, tear-shaped pond northwest of Frederick, MD, in their hunt for equipment Amerithrax might have used in the anthrax mailings. Diving searches in the area took place in December 2002 and January 2003.

(Credit: AP/World Wide Photos)

once investigated the bug as a weapon at the Institute. The same company that sold the Rajneeshees their salmonella had also sold the University of Baghdad and the Iraqi Ministry of Trade three types of anthrax, five strains of botulinum, and other pathogens as part of legal global commerce.

In 1985, a small group of American neo-Nazis was arrested with thirty gallons of cyanide they were hoping to use to poison the water in New York and Washington, D.C. Thousands of people would have died, but the group did not "cross the line" and use the weapons.

Getting anthrax to kill is considerably harder than it looks. Turning pathogens into weapons of mass destruction is hugely difficult. Many technical roadblocks stand in the way. A cult in Japan had come closest to getting anthrax to work in a domestic inhalational anthrax attack.

STRAIN 21

Anthrax Neighborhood

OVER FOUR STRAIGHT days in June 1993, a foul stench descended on an eastern Tokyo neighborhood. Residents who had survived World War II described it as "the smell of burning flesh." Small birds dropped from the sky. Plants wilted. Pets grew ill. Neighbors lost their appetites. Clouds of steam settled on their cars and left stains with the same noxious smell. Residents complained to the local ward office that a "horrible odor" was coming from a tower atop a nearby eight-story building. Inspectors went to the Aum Incorporated building. They got few answers. "The smell is from a mixture of soybean oil and Chanel No. 5," members of a sect who used the building told them. "It is burned to purify the premises." The matter was not pressed.

The sect's leader, Shoko Asahara, was a stocky, bearded, icy-eyed guru with flowing black hair that came down to his shoulders. Half-blind, all mad, he claimed to possess supernatural powers. Six years earlier, Asahara had used his fortune (amassed from a chain of meditation centers) to establish a doomsday cult—Aum Shinrikyo ("Shining Truth"). In the spring of 1992, he recruited disciples from the ranks of biologists, doctors, and high-tech computer experts. Using a combination of brainwashing, electroshock, and designer drugs (LSD, truth serum, and methamphetamine), he manipulated some of Japan's brightest students and scientists into joining his billion-dollar battalion of New Age zealots. Asahara professed "a

248

paranoid combination of Eastern beliefs and the Judeo-Christian idea of Armageddon" that appealed to his ten thousand followers.

Every action of Aum went to realize Asahara's vision of the end of the world through weapons of mass destruction, like anthrax. Early on, he forged ties with Japanese crime syndicates. Crime and poisons had a history in Tokyo. On January 26, 1948, a man had entered the Shiina-machi branch of the Teikoku Bank in Japan and identified himself as a physician with the Metropolitan Tokyo Health and Sanitation Authority. "An epidemic of dysentery is raging," he told employees, "and this medicine will protect you."

He induced them to swallow a bitter solution in teacups. Within minutes, ten were dead and four others were writhing on the floor. The "medicine" was actually deadly potassium cyanide and the "doctor" a poisoner making his third attempt at bank robbery. Seven months after the poisonings, police arrested an artist, Sadamichi Hirasawa, for the murders.

Inside the Aum building was a modern biolab—flasks, test tubes, beakers, glass evaporators, Bunsen burners, digital equipment, glass tubing, ceramic grinding bowls. Microscopes stood on the counters, flanked by refrigerator units and incubators. Stacked against the back wall were cans of peptone, a protein used for culturing bacteria. Aum, with a treasury of more than $300 million, had invested lavishly in gear for its six labs. The cult's experienced biologists had taken graduate courses in modern universities and obtained seed stocks from rogue governments in Aum Shinrikyo's worldwide quest for chemical and biological weapons of mass destruction.

The cult tried to culture botulinum organisms from naturally contaminated soil obtained in the wild. In April 1990, Aum had sent three trucks with compressors, vents, and special spraying devices to disseminate unseen clouds of botulinum toxin at Japan's biggest airport, Narita, and at U.S. naval bases at Yokohama and Yokosuka. Possibly, the wind dispersed the toxin. Or the strain was not sufficiently virulent. The attacks produced no casualties and thus U.S. intelligence remained unaware of them.

On June 9, Asahara found himself unable to obtain the laser gun he needed to vaporize the Japanese Parliament. Instead he sent his trucks to pipe clouds of botulinum toxin around the Imperial wedding of Japan's

Crown Prince Naruhito to Masako Owada. He intended to disrupt the marriage and capture the government during the panic. Asahara had gone along on the mission, but, halfway through, panicked. He feared toxin was seeping into the car. Commanding the driver to halt, he jumped out. The startled cultists continued on the mission. In a last-minute change of plan, they sprayed downtown Tokyo with botulinum instead. Nobody got sick. The cult hadn't gotten a virulent strain.

Aum was desperately trying to develop anthrax weapons, but was having difficulty getting beyond practice runs with a nonlethal strain.

Bacteria such as anthrax, when fed little more than yeast extract, proliferate in a lab dish. Experts advised that "growing *anthracis* is hardly more difficult than growing sourdough starter, but turning bacteria into spores, hardy, dominant spores that keep for years, the only form hard and stable enough to be spread, requires several tricky steps."

Asahara's experts had to be able to shock the bacteria with heat or chemicals and still not kill them in the process. The group also had trouble finding a virulent strain of *Bacillus anthracis* starter germs from which to make a biological weapon. Both the Iraqis and the Rajneeshees of Oregon had obtained some of their most lethal strains of anthrax from the ATCC, the American germ bank's huge library of microorganisms. Asahara ordered pathogens from ATCC for thirty-five dollars, the same amount Iraq had paid for their germs. Aum additionally picked up strains of tularemia and Venezuelan equine encephalitis once targeted for weaponization at nearby Fort Detrick.

Asahara's main lab emptied into a hermetically sealed preparation room that in turn opened onto the roof overlooking the neighborhood. On the rooftop was what appeared to be a gigantic cooling tower. Actually, it was an industrial sprayer, fitted with a powerful fan. Aum's chemical-suited scientists revved up a steam generator and poured in their solution of anthrax spores. To mount a germ or chemical assault, the terrorists needed to culture the pathogens in vast quantities and "weaponize" them, and this was the most difficult part.

There was never any indication that Aum scientists managed to produce the dried anthrax spores favored for efficient distribution, growing germs and refining them into a slurry that could be sprayed as an aerosol. Because they had only scraped anthrax off their culture dishes and sprayed it, they were using only "harmless glop." Nevertheless, the cult moved heavily into the production of anthrax spores and botulinum toxins, even conducting experiments with aerosol devices and radio-controlled drone aircraft for spraying targets as Iraq had done before the Gulf War.

And so one morning in June 1993, Asahara's men turned on the sprayer fan and waited expectantly. It was their fourth attempt in as many days. Within moments, toxic steam began billowing from the rooftop tower. Attempting their anthrax attacks from the rooftop during the day guaranteed that sunlight would kill off many of the pathogens. Ultraviolet light in sunshine degrades anthrax spores within minutes.

The cultists, however, managed to slightly sicken some neighbors in close proximity to the cult's eight-story building. While crop dusters and helicopters weren't the only way to spread anthrax, a rooftop was not a particularly good substitute. Despite local complaints in the neighborhood, no reported cases of anthrax developed. However, while Tokyo doctors might have misdiagnosed the less deadly, skin-borne cutaneous version of the disease, it was unlikely they would have missed the swelling and high death rate that accompanies inhalational anthrax. Aum also may not have properly incubated the spores prior to release. This meant that, somewhere in that neighborhood, anthrax spores might still be out there waiting for the right conditions to become active and infect again.

While biological weapons are relatively easy to produce, the successful dispersion of such weapons depends on a series of physical and atmospheric conditions that are beyond the biowarrior's control—calculating optimal wind direction and then waiting for it, properly rigging spraying devices, and the risk of contamination and death from one's own weapon. The very unpredictability of biological weapons make them not particularly expedient to terrorists.

Agents such as anthrax can be mass produced, but have to be dispersed over the targeted area at the proper altitude. Winds have to be blowing in the right direction. The variables involved in such an attack make a predictable outcome less likely for a terrorist. Asahara had vast talent at his disposal, yet couldn't produce a terror weapon from pathogens. His failure demonstrated that making weaponized anthrax work as a biological weapon of mass destruction was harder than experts had claimed. Aum's nine failures in nine attempts demonstrated the difficulty of actually deploying biological weapons to cause mass casualties.

The fact that weaponizing anthrax was rarely successful made Amerithrax's accomplishment all the more amazing.

Earlier, Aum Shinrikyo had approached a Connecticut manufacturer to buy an interferometer, a device used to make very accurate measurements of small objects. Since it could be used in the manufacture of nuclear bombs, the export of such equipment was restricted. The manufacturer notified the U.S. Customs Service and foiled the plot. Asahara also had sent his zealots to Zaire's "hot zone" the previous year to acquire Ebola virus and failed at that. The cult's repeated attempts to carry out biological attacks had yet to be successful.

The promise of apocalypse, though, resounded with post–Cold War Russians, who had endured so long with nuclear threats. Asahara bought a Moscow radio station and attracted ten thousand Russians into Aum Shinrikyo. He forged relationships with the KGB and Russian military. Aum's training grounds ranged from Germany to Australia to the former Yugoslavia and Taiwan.

In July 1993, Asahara's agents drove to the Japanese Diet and Imperial Palace to emit a colorless vapor filled with neurotoxin from a van. The Sterne strain they used was a weakened form of anthrax used to make animal vaccines. It was impossible to turn such anthrax germs into a biological weapon. They could have gotten better strains from more than fifteen hundred microbe banks around the world.

The greatest obstacle to bioterrorism is disseminating the pathogen. In spite of their education, Asahara's scientists did not understand the basics of germ dissemination. Powders are hard to work with. Pumps with powders are even harder. Nozzles clog, jam, and backfire, and crop-dusting pilots know this very well. Aerosolizing germs and spraying powder "through a tiny nozzle poses severe engineering problems," said Col. David Franz, former commander of the Institute.

And so they failed.

In 1994, a sarin gas attack in the provincial city of Matsumoto killed seven. Dozens were injured. The deaths were blamed on a local resident who had supposedly produced sarin while trying to make home-brewed pesticides. But producing sarin is an exacting process and can't be done accidentally. Sarin, a nerve agent developed during World War II by the Nazis, is odorless, colorless, and deadly like anthrax; and like inhalational anthrax, it causes respiratory failure. The local man was arrested, though the attack, a dry run, was later linked to Aum. A success of sorts.

Eight months later, during the rush hour, an Aum cultist descended into Kasumigaseki Station, a major hub for the nine million that traveled Tokyo's nearly four-hundred-mile-long subway system. He left behind three briefcases containing battery-driven dispensers connected to vinyl tubes. They were to be activated by a passing subway train and disperse a fine mist of home-brewed sarin. Among the thousands of commuters were those who worked at the nearby government ministries and Tokyo police headquarters. Asahara failed once more.

Five days later, on March 20, 1995, five members of the Aum Shinrikyo cult entered the Tokyo subway system during the Monday morning crush. All five clutched sharp-tipped umbrellas. Each concealed a vinyl bag. At 7:45 A.M. they boarded five high-speed trains at different ends of the underground. At 8:15 A.M. the five trains converged upon the city center of Kasumigaseki. On board, the cultists punctured their plastic bags with their umbrellas and exited the subway platforms at Kasumigaseki. Each bag was filled with a chemical solution of 30 percent sarin. Within seconds, sarin can destroy the nervous system of any living being within a hundred feet. A dozen people were suddenly dead. As the invisible gas drifted through the five trains, 5,500 commuters began rolling in agony and clutching their throats.

Asahara, who must have seen too many James Bond films, fled to his elaborate hideout inside an extinct volcano. He was arrested at his Mount Fuji enclave, cowering behind steel doors, on May 16.

The U.S. officials had been in the dark about all of Asahara's terrorist ambitions. John O'Neill, the FBI's chief counterterrorism official, said, "We received no information [before the subway attack] from the Japanese National Police." Gordon C. Oehler, chief of the CIA's Nonproliferation Center, said it was up to local authorities to detect cults like Aum. "The world is full of very crazy organizations that have designs against the U.S.," he said. "You are certainly welcome to argue that, quite frankly, we have not followed religious cults around the world and we do not have right now the resources to be able to do that."

"If biological weapons are as likely to be chaotic and catastrophic as some people think, why have they been so infrequently used?" asked political scientist Leonard A. Cole of Rutgers University. Cole had written extensively about terrorist threats by biological, chemical, and nuclear means. "On a theoretical level, one could create a scenario that would be horrible," he said, "but it is far less predictable that all the factors will produce the terrorist's desired effect."

Yet throughout the U.S. there was a significant fear about all parameters converging to produce a devastatingly deadly biological attack.

On June 21, 1995, President Bill Clinton signed a secret directive on counterterrorism. This was the fruit of an intensive two-year review begun after the WTC bombing. Presidential Decision Directive 39 delineated the agencies that were to play the lead roles in handling terrorist incidents: the State Department overseas and the FBI inside the United States. Clinton ordered the Federal Emergency Management Agency to update its planning for "terrorism involving weapons of mass destruction . . . The United States shall give highest priority to developing effective capabilities to detect, prevent, defeat and manage the consequences of a nuclear, biological or chemical materials or weapons use by terrorists."

President Clinton had warned at the end of 1994 that the potential use of biological weapons by terrorist groups or rogue states represented "an unusual and extraordinary threat to the national security, foreign policy, and economy of the United States." His Executive Order 12938 made it illegal for Americans "to help any country or entity to acquire, design, produce, or stockpile chemical or biological weapons and place the country in a state of emergency." The order was amended in 1998 to include penalties for "trafficking in equipment that could indirectly contribute to a foreign germ warfare program."

BUT HOW COULD the nation protect itself from a threat that was tasteless, odorless, and often invisible? Bioterror was no longer a hypothetical threat, but a real one as dangerous as nuclear war. The Amerithrax case had become as much a detective story as a warning of future danger. The FBI profilers assembled the usual motives—Amerithrax, like the Unabomber, might be seeking revenge against those who had somehow passed him by. His motive might be envy, profit, revenge, love, or advancement. It could be a story of a man who used tragedy to further his own career. Experts recalled the analogy of the fireman starting fires in order to put them out and be a hero. Was some anthrax expert doing something similar? With so many thousands of scientists who had anthrax knowledge or so few who knew how to weaponize it, the search now focused on the source of Amerithrax's equipment.

Dr. Craig Smith, an infectious disease specialist at Phoebe Putnam Memorial Hospital in Georgia, told *Newsweek* of the difficulty of connecting and even finding Amerithrax's equipment. "So many of these machines are dual-use," he said. "The same small, sealed milling unit used for producing pharmaceuticals can be used to weaponize anthrax. Fermenters can produce antibiotics as well as bioweapons. Culture media can grow bacteria for vaccines as well as weapons." The FBI's wisdom was that Amerithrax didn't use an everyday lab where he was employed. It would be too dangerous to produce it there.

At this point investigators still were not totally certain whether the source of the attacks was foreign or domestic. If they could find a genetic fingerprint they could pinpoint the lab and country that had produced it. Clues from the physical and biological properties of the anthrax sent through the mail may point to a source and hence to a suspect. The FBI was currently looking closely at twenty scientists on a short but ever-changing, list.

All of Amerithrax's letters had contained the same strain of anthrax. It corresponded to the Ames strain in the Northern Arizona University database. NAZU's was labeled the "reference strain." It was one of the more virulent strains used in research to "challenge" vaccines and has since been sent to hundreds of research and defense facilities in the United States and Europe for study. They could track the bacteria from its beginning before it was altered into Amerithrax anthrax. The Ames strain was originally isolated from a cow in Texas in 1981.

STRAIN 22

Anthrax Cow

THE COW CHEWED gravely under the Texas sun, tossing her head to jerk up clumps of grass. A breeze rustled the yellow pasture and ruffled her short-haired coat. There came the dry rattle of parched grass. She gave a whisk of her brown tail in the stifling heat and swallowed. The life cycle of the anthrax strain that would infest the nation's mail twenty years in the future had begun.

The cow was grazing in a spore-laden pasture tainted with droppings deposited by sick horses, cows, and goats. Anthrax grew naturally in that earth. Herbivores like this cow acquire it directly from contaminated soil. Under the blazing sun one afternoon in 1981, the cow became infected while foraging for food. But how could microscopic bacilli live in such aridness? How could any bacteria survive over seventy winters and seventy inferno-like summers without food or water? How could it exist in the fields in such extremes of heat, cold, and dryness?

Relative temperature, along with varying blood and soil conditions, had determined whether the spores would form or not. Once formed, the durable spores are resistant to temperature extremes and dehydration, and are devilishly difficult to obliterate. They can remain dormant, deadly, and capable of growth for twelve years. Outdoors the spores tend to stick to the soil components and do not easily re-aerosolize. Indoor spore accumulations are more airborne.

The cow had ingested anthrax spores in the softened food she was rechewing. The swallowed cud underwent further chemical breakdown in one of the four compartments of her stomach. After water was absorbed, the food entered the "true stomach" where juices further digested the material. From the stomach to the intestine, where digestion and absorption were completed. In an hour, ellipse-shaped spores had begun to germinate. The living anthrax cells absorbed nutriments from their environment.

In the warmth of the cow, the microorganism swirled as chains of two to eight bacilli surrounded by a large capsule that contained polyglutamic acid. An extracellular toxin breached the cow's germ defenses. The microbes, accumulating and bunching, produced edema and hemorrhaging throughout as they made endless copies of themselves. Her bloodstream became a river of poison. Her spleen grew big and black and soon was engulfed by quivering bamboo-like rods and serpentine threads.

The cow grew feverish as the swarming sticks and threads leaked tissue-destroying poison into other organs. She went into shock, twitching and shaking, her nostrils splaying. Circumscribed cutaneous carbuncles appeared throughout her body. In swine similar lesions are found only in the throat. There came a sudden apoplectic attack of secondary shock, an immediate crash. Death occurred a few moments later. In animals, death from anthrax came as suddenly as a bolt of lightning. Animals had been known to die standing up.

On his rounds, the rancher found the animal suddenly dead—carcass cold and rigid, legs in the air, and belly distended. Golden-yellow fluid streaked with red oozed from her nostrils—anthrax sputum exudate. Blood from her anus and other orifices was ghastly black. The bacteria of putrefaction from the intestines in the decomposing carcass multiplies without free oxygen. The intestinal bacteria were doing cleanup work, killing off the anthrax bacteria. Tissues from animals dead of anthrax, fresh or putrid or dried or a year old, can only produce anthrax when they contain bacilli or the spores of bacilli.

The real danger lay in the watery blood spilling from the animal, blood now more dangerous than the decaying carcass. The anthrax bacteria needs its host to die in order that the disease may continue. Spores never form in an animal while it is still alive. They only appear after it has died, and then only when kept very warm. As the tangled blood came into contact with oxygen its microscopic outlines grew dim and faded as the bacteria returned to protective spore form. With the blood, spores drained into the warm ground to take up residence. They would wait patiently to reactivate into ordinary bacilli once more.

Spores are heavy and don't travel easily by air. And so they waited where they fell until the right conditions for incubation presented themselves. One day the farmer would disturb that patch of stained earth as he plowed a new field. Or a road would be laid, or a flash flood would rush over the spot. Then, the spores would be ingested or breathed or get into a cut to begin their life cycle again—from spore to bacterium to bamboo-like rod and back to tough spore.

A veterinarian arrived on the scene. He knelt and studied the cow. The cow's sudden death and bloody fluid oozing from every orifice told him he was dealing with splenic fever (anthrax). That infectious, persistent disease was serious business, able to wipe out herds of cattle and sheep, and thankfully rare.

Vets advise that any animals that die of anthrax must be destroyed immediately. If they cannot be burned, they should be buried deep in the ground, where the earth is so cold that the bacilli cannot turn into long-lived spores. The poet Virgil knew that fact two thousand years ago. In his advice to farmers in 29 B.C., he wrote in *Georgics*:

> The rivers and thirsty banks and sloping hills echo to the bleating of flocks and incessant lowing of kine. And now in droves she deals out death, and in the very stalls piles up bodies, rotting with putrid foulness, til men learn to cover them in earth and bury them in pits.
>
> For neither might the hides be used, nor could one cleanse the flesh by water or master it by fire. They could not even sheer the fleeces, eaten up with sores and filth, nor touch the rotted web. Nay, if any man donned his loathsome garb, feverish blisters and foul sweat would run along his fetid limbs, and not long had he to wait ere the accursed fire was feeding on his stricken limbs.

Bacillus anthracis is one of mankind's oldest known diseases—a daily risk to Bronze Age herdsmen and hunters who were exposed by killing and skinning wild sheep. It had been one of the plagues of medieval days. "Our fields are cursed," peasants whispered in the green mountains of Auvergne. No flock could venture there without sheep dropping until carcasses covered the hillsides like sunflowers. The farmers and horse doctors of Europe had long held strange beliefs of anthrax's mysterious power.

Wild and domestic hooved, grass-eating animals carry it. Herbivora—cattle, sheep, pigs, horses, antelope, and goats—eat spores with forage as the Texas cow had done. Humans with close contact with infected animals or animal products—butchers, tanners, and farmers—become infected through abrasions. Or they might inhale spores from wool and hides or drink contaminated water. In instances of those who consume tainted meat, the bacteria burrows into the digestive tract. (Intestinal anthrax, though, accounts for less than 1 percent of all anthrax cases.)

As the vet studied a culture from the Texas cow under a microscope, he saw the familiar chains of bacilli. They were never found in the blood of healthy animals. His text said:

> *Bacillus anthracis,* the etiologic agent of anthrax, is a large, gram-positive, nonmotile, spore-forming bacterial rod. The three virulence factors of *B. anthracis* are edema toxin, lethal toxin and a capsular antigen.

However, the polyglutamic acid capsule was lost on an artificial medium like his glass slide. Bacteria isolated from the cow was mailed to Ames, Iowa. Ames lies below Boone and a hundred miles west of Cedar Rapids in the "land where the tall corn grows." At this time, Iowa farming had suffered a sharp economic downturn and many farms had been lost and lay burning in the sun. The lab where this natural type of anthrax was cultivated, the U.S. Agriculture Department's National Veterinary Service Lab, was inside a burned-colored, low-slung complex surrounded by equally burned and flat farmland.

The CDC's lab was at Fort Collins and work on the sample was begun there. In off hours, a researcher at Iowa State University studied drops of the cow's blackened blood. It was a common virulent strain, but he worked magic with it. Eventually that bacterium would be used in every antibiotic and vaccine study and be the staple of research for years to come.[10] Live spores of attenuate virulence form an effective vaccine for

---

[10] In addition to the 1981 Texas cow strain, only one other Ames isolate was ever reported—from a Texas goat in 1997 and of a type that was not used in the anthrax mailed by Amerithrax.

cattle and other animals. A cell-free protective vaccine was shortly produced for use in humans, a sterile filtrate created from a culture of *B. anthracis.*

President Eisenhower spoke in Iowa in 1954 to a crowd of twenty-five thousand. Iowa was as central to American politics as it is central in American geography. From the Ames heartland, the bacterium began its travels. In 1981, it was sent to Texas A&M for further study, and from there to the Institute, a key player in the nation's biowarfare program. When the sample reached the Institute, it was mistakenly attributed to the USDA lab in Ames. They just jotted down the postmark "Ames" and so hereafter it was called the "Ames strain."

The Ames strain reproduced very rapidly in the right environment and thus was an excellent strain for research. The Institute distributed offspring of the Ames strain of anthrax microbes to as many as twenty labs in the U.S. and abroad. Amerithrax later got his anthrax from one of them. But which one?

The Institute sent a sample of the Ames index strain to the Canadian defense establishment at Suffield (Lab 1), the University of New Mexico (Lab 2), the Battelle Memorial Institute (Lab 3), and, in 1982, the Porton Down Centre for Applied Microbiology and Research in the United Kingdom (Lab 4). Porton Down was the British biological warfare lab and the first to refine the Ames strain.

Porton Down was set in southern England at an old chemical warfare proving ground deep in the Wiltshire countryside. Wiltshire was famous for Stonehenge, an arrangement of ancient stone slabs once used as an observatory. Porton Down itself was rows of square, flat-topped, three-story concrete buildings. The repellent, forbidding grounds were as empty of life as condemned slums.

Each row was a quarter-mile in length, with two hundred yards separating the rows. The five hundred yards between the slablike buildings and the electrified boundary fence was completely open. There were no trees, bushes, or shrubs, "not even a clump of flowers." Everything was kept low so no man could hide behind anything. Alsatian man-killers and Doberman pinschers patrolled the fifteen-foot-high outer barbed-wire fence. Electrified, it sloped outward so drastically that the top was four feet out of line with the foot.

In the summer of 1942, Porton Down began testing biowarfare agents.

They proved it was possible to grow anthrax, pack it into a shell, transport it hundreds of miles, and effectively explode it over a precise target area. During World War II, they dropped the West's first anthrax bomb, a twenty-five-pound prototype, on rugged 550-acre Gruinard Island. The bomb hit amid several dozen tethered sheep at one end of the scenic isle three miles off the northwest coast of Scotland. Most of the sheep perished immediately. The survivors were slaughtered. The remarkable durability of anthrax spores, though, was the main problem with using the disease as a weapon. Safety conditions were so poor the anthrax on Gruinard Island rendered the island uninhabitable for forty-five years.

The British tried everything. They defoliated ten acres of contaminated areas, stripping the land with defoliants. Porton Down scientists, using a dilute solution of 30 percent formaldehyde in two thousand tons of sea water, sprayed down the island to a depth of six inches. After deep-soil sampling revealed persistent organisms, they resprayed with eighty tons of formaldehyde. Then they used bleach, but that had to be in contact with spores at least two minutes. Next they tried paraformaldehyde gas, glutaraldehyde, hydrogen peroxide, and peracetic acid, but none stayed in contact with spores long enough.

In 1943, Porton Down planned to use anthrax spores released by five-hundred-pound cluster bombs, each holding more than a hundred small four-pound bomblets containing spores. Tests demonstrated that each cluster bomb produced an effective aerosol concentration that covered one hundred acres from impact area. In the end the British simply charged ordinary cattle cakes with anthrax spores and kept a stockpile of five million cakes that were never used.

In 1997, Porton Down sent the Louisiana State University a sample from its freezer. The strain obtained by LSU had been refined. The paperwork noted that the Ames strain had been "cured of the pXO1 and pXO2 virulence plasmids." This would be important later. The Porton sequencing project, begun in 1999, was funded by grants from the U.S. Office of Naval Research, the National Institute of Allergy and Infectious Diseases (NIAID), the Department of Energy, and the United Kingdom's Defense Sciences Technology Laboratory. The anthrax was marked "10-32," meaning number ten of thirty-two samples.

In 1999 a police investigation was begun into some of the Porton Down experiments. Between 1939 and the 1960s Porton Down scientists exposed twenty thousand unknowing volunteers to nerve gas and other biological and chemical agents. The volunteers were led to believe they were helping to find a cure for the common cold. Years afterward they began suffering from unexplained maladies.

As of January 31, 2002, Fort Detrick was one of about twenty research facilities known to possess the strain of anthrax bacterium that was used in the attacks in September and October. Which of the twenty known to have worked with the Army's strain was the one from which the terrorist's microbes came? Only four labs in the U.S. might have the capability for weaponizing anthrax—three were at U.S. military labs and one was a government contractor.

What had emerged from the investigation so far was that the anthrax originated not in some Afghan cave or Iraqi laboratory, as first feared, but at one of a handful of other labs involved in defensive U.S. biological warfare research. The Institute was one of those labs and one with a dark secret.

STRAIN 23

The Undeclared Enemy

IN JUST TWENTY years, the Institute secretly made American citizens the victims of more intentional biological infections than Amerithrax ever did. Between 1949 and 1969, the Institute at Fort Detrick conducted 239 simulated biological weapons tests in urban areas using "relatively" harmless bacteria. Entire American cities were clandestinely sprayed with mild germs so the Institute could assess the likely impact of deadly pathogens and their ability to spread through urban centers. Those unwitting subjects totaled in the hundreds of thousands, if not millions. Prisoners at the Ohio State Penitentiary were among those exposed. Five thousand five hundred service members participated in the covert tests as willing or unknowing subjects.

In 1949, the Institute carried on "top secret" biological tests within the Pentagon to see if air-conditioning units and ducts were vulnerable. A minute amount of biological warfare stimulant inserted into just one air-conditioning unit was rapidly distributed throughout the world's largest office building. If it had been a real pathogen, large numbers of people inside the building could have easily been incapacitated or killed.

In the early 1950s, the CIA cruised around New York City in a car with a modified exhaust pipe that sprayed bacteria over much of the city. Their results were so impressive that Japanese terrorists later used the same device in Tokyo.

The germ scientists also chose San Francisco in which to conduct domestic vulnerability trials. Theoretically, a minesweeper or an enemy submarine surfacing off a major U.S. port could secretly release germs at sundown and escape undetected. Between September 20 and 26, 1950, two Navy minesweepers cruising two miles off the San Francisco coastline sprayed the Bay Area six times, exposing eight hundred thousand residents in a 117-square-mile area to clouds of *Serratia marcescens*, an anthrax substitute. At the time Fort Detrick thought that SM germs were relatively innocuous.

However, three days later patients with SM infections began appearing at local hospitals. Eleven patients at Stanford University Hospital came down with SM infection and one, Edward J. Wevin, died. If live bioweapons had been released by the cruisers, the death toll would have been devastating. The Army continued testing with SM until February 1951 when they returned to San Francisco to test advanced dispersal methods by spraying supposedly harmless *Bacillus globigii* all over the Bay Area. *Bacillus globigii* is a relative of the anthrax bacterium and is often used as an anthrax simulant.

Between 1952 and 1953, the U.S. military biological warfare simulants were released all over America and parts of Canada. The Army staged open-air experiments above populated areas from Minneapolis to San Francisco, imposing infections as far away as twenty miles. Soaring planes sprayed clouds of fluorescent particles (inorganic zinc cadmium sulfide) over populated areas of Fort Wayne, Indiana, rural Maryland, and Leesburg, Virginia.

During "Project Saint Jo" 173 dry runs with noninfectious wet germs were made over St. Louis, Minneapolis, and Winnipeg just sixty miles north of the Canada–United States border. Since the three cities were similar in magnitude and climate to key Soviet cities, it enabled the Army to establish how clouds of bacteria drift and decay in the environment and to figure out how Russian cities could best be attacked with anthrax germs. Anthrax simulants rained down on the Canadian citizens of Winnipeg, capital of Manitoba and Canada's main grain market. Because of the small amounts inhaled, no illnesses were ever connected to the secret aerosol bombardment.

In the summer of 1955, the main U.S. test facility at the Dugway Proving Grounds in the Utah desert commenced Operation CD-22, Project

Whitecoat, called so because there were so many medics. Until 1973, they conducted 153 tests. Dugway, some eighty miles from Salt Lake City, Utah, was six hundred buildings spread across thousands of acres of desert, cactus, and hardscrabble. A large complex designated Life Sciences Lab was a compound of ten buildings. There were sheds for disinfecting equipment and rooms for conducting animal autopsies.

Thirty Seventh-Day Adventist soldiers, human guinea pigs, were tied to chairs a half-mile from the center of a circular test grid. Five sprayers in the grid each held an ounce of Q fever slurry. Cages of test animals were scattered all around the men. Like anthrax, Q fever is found in sheep, cattle, and goats and like anthrax the organisms multiply in the lungs. Q fever is not fatal, but it is incapacitating.

The conscientious objectors were volunteers. Though refusing to bear arms, they had agreed to be the subjects of the first American trial of actual germ warfare agents on human beings. The vaccinated volunteers and animals waited a week through a number of false starts. Finally, on the night of July 12, a fine aerosol mist of *Coxiella burnetii* emerged from the sprayers and drifted downwind to infect the test subjects. Afterward, the Army learned that a 5 mph breeze did not spread the mist far enough, while a 30 mph wind degraded the agent.

On another occasion they used the Institute's giant one-million-liter aerosol testing sphere on a thousand soldiers in a sealed chamber. Volunteers also gathered around the ball's periphery, donned face masks, and breathed in mists of Q fever germs through rubber hoses connected to the ball's chamber. Those infected with the moderately mild disease contracted chills, blinding headaches, coughing, muscle and joint pain, trembling, diarrhea, weight loss, and visual and auditory hallucinations. They got fevers of up to 104 degrees F. Congestive heart failure was one of the side effects. Though one in a hundred die from Q fever, during this test every one of the volunteers survived.

The newest jet fighter, the sound-breaking F-100 Super Sabre, bled germs into the air over the wilds of the Utah desert. Rigged for nuclear bombs, the F-100 had been refitted to scatter liquid germs. Mechanics had strapped a tank of *Coxiella burnetii* onto the plane's belly and connected it to special nozzles that spewed germs. As the jet streaked, the wind broke the aerosol up into particles fine enough to penetrate human lungs and stick to the wet membrane there. The wet germs were so effective that the pilot became infected when he left his jet before it was decontaminated. The test proved that fifty kilograms of C. *burnetii* dumped from an aircraft upwind of a population center would kill 150 people and incapacitate 125,000 citizens.

In 1956 Camp Detrick was renamed Fort Detrick, but those in the know still called it the Institute. In the same year, under Bill Patrick, the Pine Bluff Arsenal was remodernized and refitted to make weapons from bacteria and store infectious viral agents in bulk. The Army had cut Pine Bluff Arsenal out of fourteen thousand acres deep in the wilderness of central Arkansas. At a cost of ninety million dollars, they constructed a ten-story building and ten giant fermenters. In early 1954, the Pine Bluff virus plant (X1002) had gone into operation to mass-produce biological agents. The 858 scientists and technicians working there eventually added anthrax to the mass-production line.

In 1957, the Army initiated Operation Large Area Coverage. That operation would measure the feasibility of contaminating huge sections of the nation with agents dropped from aircraft and rooftops and dispersed from speeding cars. Since fine fluorescent powders—cut down to one micron—covered tens of thousands of square miles under favorable winds, the Army was able to blanket thirty-three urban and rural areas from border to border and coast to coast. The "Honest John" rocket, the first U.S. missile to carry a biological warload, was surpassed by the "Sergeant" missile, which increased the available range for biological rockets to seventy-five miles. Spray tanks on fast-moving planes delivered a wet slurry, but after 1963, viable dry agents became the U.S. goal.

In June 1966, the Army released SM into the New York City subway tunnels, allowing a succession of speeding trains to transport germs from one station to the other through suction. It worked so well, Aum's Japanese doomsday cult later used the technique to kill in the Tokyo subway, but with nerve gas instead. In 1969, the Army had figured out how to convert anthrax to a usable dry bioweapons agent. They knew how to protect organisms from decay after spraying. They developed the ability to freeze-dry large amounts of liquid agents and how to fortify agents with unique chemical properties that would keep them stable and virulent during spraying.

The biowarriors at the Institute realized they would have to aerosolize the anthrax germ to be effective. They produced five thousand anthrax bombs, but even the most effective released only 3 percent of its spores; the rest got blown into the ground or vaporized by the heat of detonation.

They worked on anthrax for killing enemy troops and to do that they had to encourage the anthrax bug, appropriately gun-shaped and hardy enough to remain viable for decades. The Institute used heat and chemical shock to force the rod-shaped bacteria to convert into spores. Upon being inhaled, the spores would transform back to rods and establish infections.

Between 1962 and 1969, as improved live agents developed by the Institute became available, their scientists made Dugway obsolete as its testing ground for anthrax. In its place the Army sought out a larger-scale venue for testing. Johnston Atoll fit the bill—four coral islands in the central Pacific Ocean 720 nautical miles from Honolulu. They code-named the exercise "Shady Grove." Invisible biowarfare agents released at night from a spray tank mounted on a low-flying F-105 Navy jet infected three hundred personnel with a whitish spray dispersed at intervals downwind.

In the mid-1960s, the Army conducted test runs to see how their germs behaved in extreme conditions. Thirteen trials in the dry, blazing climate of the Deseret Testing Center in Utah measured the decomposition rate of liquid Q fever and tularemia aerosols on animals. Four large scale secret cold-weather experiments held in the Alaska wilderness demonstrated how the same germs behaved in frigid conditions. The tests measured the cover rate and decay rate of aerosol bacteria. In cold conditions germs ranged farther and lasted longer than in the desert and atoll tests. However, the Alaska tests also exposed soldiers in protective suits to VX, which was the military's deadliest nerve agent. Nearly forty years later, the Pentagon acknowledged that some soldiers engaged in chemical and biological testing may not have been fully informed about the secret Alaska experiments. This was also the case with other soldiers tested in Florida, San Francisco, and Hawaii, and at sea. Some of these tests also used VX.

Experiments on U.S. troops in Hawaii additionally used a hallucinogen developed as a chemical weapon. Uncounted numbers of civilians in Hawaii and Alaska were also unaware they were being saturated with relatively mild bacteria meant to simulate anthrax germ weapons. And between 1932 and 1972, the Tuskegee Syphilis Study conducted by the federal government withheld medical treatment from poor, black men in Alabama for experimental purposes. The Tuskegee men were not told they had syphilis and were not treated for the illness, though penicillin had become available. More than one hundred died from the disease and related complications.

In the late 1960s, twenty-two microorganisms were under study and there were plans to weaponize hemorrhagic fevers such as the Machupo virus and Rift Valley fever. Toward the end of the decade, public anger over biological and chemical arms brought pickets every day to Fort Detrick, Maryland.

The Institute's scientists were looking into possibilities presented by genetic engineering when their program was dealt a fatal blow. Twenty-five years after a presidential advisory board launched America's experiment with biological warfare, a panel appointed by President Nixon recommended killing it. The tests were abandoned in 1970.

In September 1990, Fort Detrick conducted its most ambitious "defensive" anthrax experiment. An anesthetized rhesus monkey, in a rubber-lined Plexiglas box, was sprayed with an aerosol dose of Vollum 1B, the same anthrax strain later sold to Iraq. The particles of the mist measured one micron, perfect for lodging in the lungs. A specially designed ventilation system kept the air pressure in the glass box slightly lower than the outside air. The negative pressure kept the anthrax germs inside to infect other test monkeys.

Col. Arthur M. Friedlander, chief of the bacteriology division at Detrick, conducted this and other monkey experiments that demonstrated that inhaled anthrax spores deep in the alveoli of the lungs could take up to fifty-eight days to develop into the lethal bacterial form. Hundreds of dead monkeys at Camp Detrick proved it. A 1956 British article stated that anthrax spores could remain dormant in test monkeys for as long as a hundred days after aerosol exposure.

Colonel Friedlander hypothesized that large doses of antibiotic administered for a month would vanquish the disease, and Dr. Alibek's experience at the Soviet facility at the Stepnogorsk, a couple of years earlier, bore that out, when a technician who had been accidentally infected recovered with this treatment.

Three of the six groups of monkeys at Camp Detrick were treated for thirty days with penicillin, doxycycline, or ciprofloxacin. Monkeys treated with daily antibiotics survived into the fourth week while most of those in control groups died. The antibiotics were not always effective; thus they were not a complete solution; and they had to be administered within twenty-four hours of contracting anthrax, a disease with no early warning symptoms.

Both antibiotics and vaccines can be defeated using widely known genetic engineering techniques to create resistant anthrax strains, or select naturally occurring anthrax strains, and at Vector in the former Soviet Union such a strain had been tested and perfected. The U.S. was anxious to get its hands on it in order to come up with a vaccine that would be effective against it.

STRAIN 24

The New Year

THE GOVERNMENT AWARDED Ashland Incorporated of Covington, Kentucky, and Sabre Oxidation Technologies of Odessa, Texas, the
contracts for fumigation of the Hart Senate Office Building. Sabre, the
main contractor, operated five thousand generators around the globe, similar to the ones it would use on the Hart Building and, later, the massive
Brentwood Postal Facility. The Hart Building was the first large structure
in the nation's history to undergo decontamination from anthrax.

Throughout November and December, the teams had poured over detailed engineering drawings and used scientific models to simulate air currents inside the Hart Building. To remove anthrax from the building would
entail bleach disinfectant, dust removal, the removal and decontamination
of any equipment, replacement of heating and air-conditioning filters, gas
fumigation, and HEPA filtration. First the Hart Building was sealed and
all possible escape routes plugged.

The entire building had been closed on October 17 and more than
half the senators relocated to temporary quarters. On December 1, 2001,
technicians pumped Senator Daschle's sealed office full of chlorine dioxide
gas. After traces of anthrax were discovered in 9 of 377 environmental
samples, a second fumigation was done. In the interim, computers and
files from his suite were packed and driven to Richmond, Virginia, where
they were sanitized with ethylene oxide. Liquid and foam forms of chlorine

dioxide and HEPA filters were employed in the offices of eleven other senators. Congressman Mike Pence was one of three members of the House whose offices had been contaminated.

Throughout most of January 2002, men in space suits pumped yellow-green chlorine dioxide gas into the 100,000-cubic-foot office building. The gas can kill anthrax spores when injected into a sealed environment with a humidity of 75 percent. That humidity level softens a spore's shell and allows chlorine gas to penetrate. Maintaining a minimum temperature of 75 degrees Fahrenheit helps the gas interact with protein and DNA.

It took multiple rounds to cleanse the huge edifice because ventilation blockages disrupted humidity levels needed to ensure the effectiveness of the gas. Whatever they learned during the Hart cleanup would next be applied to the massive Brentwood fumigation, a far more daunting and complicated operation. Any suspected areas, ceilings, joists, and carpeting, were vacuumed free of dust using HEPA vacuums. The collected dust was sealed in drums for disposal. The contaminated Senate building (the Hart Senate Office Building) and other Capitol Hill offices were cleansed of anthrax at a cost to the EPA of $42 million. Health authorities were still studying how to sanitize the main mail-sorting facility in Washington. By January 22, staffers would be back at work inside the Hart Building once more.

Soon after returning to their offices, sixty employees in the Hart Building began complaining of dry eyes, dry throats, and pounding headaches. Another seventy-three Senate employees reported headaches, skin rashes, and dry mouth. Officials first considered flu and colds as the probable cause. After all, the symptoms were flulike, but then so were those of anthrax. Had trace amounts of anthrax spores somehow survived the rigorous decontamination or was it something else? "We take these health complaints extremely seriously," said the Office of Compliance. "These are the unknowns." What was making the employees sick? Many Hart staffers complained of a chlorine smell. Were there leftover contaminants from the chlorine dioxide treatment? But skin reactions were also epidemic. Of the 750 mail handlers at the V Street NE station in D.C., 87 had become sick. Those unpacking cardboard boxes and plastic bags containing e-beam irradiated mail from Lima and Bridgewater facilities reported similar symptoms as those in the Hart Building—burning eyes, sneezing, nausea, breathing problems, and itching hands. The illnesses might be linked. By the end of January, the USPS was irradiating 350,000 items of federal mail a day and reassuring its mailroom workers that irradiated mail was safe. But complaints of fumes and illness continued. The adverse reactions might be from irradiated mail.

Finally, they hit upon a solution. The answer lay in the plastic bags used to hold the mail during the radiation process. Unhealthy levels of carbon monoxide and some volatile compounds were released when the plastic was exposed to radiation. The process also caused the mail to release ozone and carbon monoxide. In response, engineers determined that a diminished dosage was enough to kill spores. They lowered radiation doses by nearly 40 percent and held the treated mail in a venting area for longer than a day. As for the skin irritations, the irradiation process made paper drier which meant employees handling the mail would encounter more dust and thus have drier skin on their hands.

At the beginning of the year metropolitan Washington got a $292 million congressional appropriation to upgrade emergency preparedness. The District's share was $154 million earmarked for fourteen municipal departments. Four hundred million more in biodefense funds were due over the next two years.

"After September 11th, if we did nothing else, we needed to communicate better," said Margaret Kellems, deputy mayor for public safety and justice in charge of biodefense for the District. The fire department bought a new hazardous materials unit equipped to handle biological, chemical, and radiological events. The District had not had its own Hazmat capability since 1998. The city got new protective gear, traffic light upgrades, video camera technology for managing traffic flow, pathogen-testing equipment, and a mobile lab.

The post office now offered citizens more advice in red, yellow, blue, and white: "Keep the Mail Safe. You can screen your mail before opening. Ask yourself: Is it from someone I don't know? Does its return address appear legitimate? Is its weight unusual for its size? Is it lopsided or uneven? Does it have oil stains or a powdery deposit? Is it sealed with excessive amounts of tape? Is it marked with restrictive words like 'Personal' or 'Confidential'?

"If You Receive Suspicious Mail: Don't handle it if you suspect it's contaminated. Don't shake or sniff it. Don't try to clean up powders or fluids. Isolate it by covering or placing it in a sealed envelope or plastic bag. Keep others away from the area. Wash your hands for five to ten minutes with soap and water [advice some experts disagreed with]. Call 911 or your local law enforcement authorities and the U.S. Postal Inspection Service.

"When Sending Mail: Double check the spelling of names and correct titles. Avoid using excessive amounts of tape [the anthrax letters were taped and the Unabomber's packages were excessively taped] or sending odd-shaped packages. Alert the addressee prior to sending unexpected packages or out-of-the-ordinary packages." Yet the Unabomber often wrote his victims in advance of his infernal devices: "You will be receiving a package."

As for the postal workers, their union wrote them:

Certainly we want to be sure that every piece of mail we deliver is "clean," free from anthrax spores or any other deadly biological agents that could harm the public. And we want a safe working environment for ourselves and our fellow postal employees. We want to be sure what happened at the Brentwood facility in Washington . . . never happens again. Anywhere . . . But a perfectly safe working environment and a safe mail system will not be achieved overnight. Evil or deranged killers are loose, and they have demonstrated their willingness to attack innocent citizens through the dispersion of deadly germs. Keep on keeping on—and carrying on . . . You are out there on the street, delivering to every home and business in America despite the awful fears of anthrax. . . . Letter carriers are quiet heroes, helping America to regain its faith in the future.

At 11:30 A.M. on January 3, 2002, a delayed envelope bearing a London postmark was finally received and opened by a congressional staffer in Senator Daschle's temporary quarters. It had been mailed in late November, but was caught up in the tons of Capitol mail undergoing irradiation cleansing. No one could fathom how a letter containing suspicious white powder and a "threatening note" had managed to slip by unopened.

Hazmat-specialized Capitol police in protective gear arrived within ten minutes. Senator Daschle, who had been at work in another suite, was quickly relocated to a more distant room. He remained there until police had conducted two field tests. The U.S. Navy biological defense program first created the field tests in 1996. They had been available commercially for about two years. Rapid field tests cost as much as one hundred dollars and work along the lines of a home pregnancy test. A surface is swabbed and placed in a liquid. That liquid is then squirted onto a paper strip laced with antibodies that will react with organisms. The appearance of a line denotes a positive test while the absence of a line is considered negative. The devices have a low threshold of sensitivity.

Designed to detect the spore-forming bacterium *Bacillus anthracis*, it also detects other forms of *bacillus*-type organisms. The presence of other chemicals can also compromise the test. Suspect powders are sent to a CDC-approved laboratory. The test can grow anthrax spores in a specially prepared soy-based medium within six hours with a final determination available in twenty-four hours.

Anthrax spores are still detectable even when rendered inert by radiation. The tests ruled out anthrax, active or irradiated, as ever being in the London letter. "Everything about this points to a hoax," said authorities. "Whoever mailed the letter apparently attempted to mimic the handwriting on the envelope of a previous [anthrax] letter to Senator Daschle."

The anthrax mailed to Daschle had an extremely narrow-size range and had been processed to a grade of one trillion spores per gram—fifty times finer than anything produced by the U.S. bioweapons program. In fact it was ten times finer than the finest known grade of Soviet anthrax. How had Amerithrax achieved such an "extraordinary concentration" with his anthrax and at the same time given his energized spores such an astonishing mobility in the air?

The physical properties of the very pure, finely powdered spores were characteristic of the secret U.S. processes for producing anthrax. The optimal process, actually several processes, had been created by Bill Patrick, inventor of a sophisticated form of anthrax and chief of the abandoned U.S. offensive biological weapons program. Patrick held five secret patents on the technique and would only say of his process that it involved a combination of chemicals. As far as U.S. authorities knew, there was no evidence that any other country possessed the formula. This suggested, more than ever, that Amerithrax was a domestic terrorist.

Under the microscope, the anthrax appeared to be unmilled. But reports on this were at odds with various experts who had studied the small sample the government had. Milled anthrax spores are identifiable because they contain debris. A milling machine is used to grind down clumps of spores to their most infectious size. The optimal U.S. process does not use milling. The toxin that Amerithrax mailed was identified as a strain that had been originated in the U.S. and created within the last two to three years. It had not been genetically modified. They had learned that from the Florida attack. Had it been grown in liquid medium or on petri dishes? A "coating" on the Daschle spores (to eliminate static charge so the particles would float and not clump) was also indicative of the secret U.S. weaponization process. The Daschle letter contained a special form of silica used in the U.S. process, and not bentonite as used by the Iraqis.

When Lockheed technicians first heard anthrax-laced envelopes were surging through the mail stream, they began accommodating existing military sensors, sampling devices, and filters to serve homeland defense. By January 14, they had constructed an inexpensive mail biohazard detection system. Instead of killing the anthrax, the Lockheed setup ventilated the air around the letters and sampled it to detect any harmful biohazard. The system potentially removed 99.97 percent of contaminants that were greater than 0.3 microns in diameter. Last October 27, SureBeam Corp. had won a contract from the USPS to provide them with e-beams to eliminate anthrax bacteria.

The FBI narrowed the focus of its investigation to employees of U.S. military laboratories. On January 17, genetic analysis began at Northern Arizona University in Flagstaff on Ames strain samples from the suspect labs winnowed down through analysis from twenty to eight. They were the Institute at Fort Detrick; the United Kingdom defense establishment at Porton Down; the Battelle Memorial Institute; Louisiana State University; Pine Bluff Arsenal in Arkansas; the Salk Center in Swiftwater, Pennsylvania; the U.S. Army's Dugway Proving Ground; and Northern Arizona University itself. All the labs possessed identical anthrax stocks that matched the letter anthrax. Tests would continue until the end of the month.

A complete sequence was also being determined for the genome of both the anthrax in Florida and the Ames strain to which it corresponded. This work was done under government contract by the Institute for Genomic Research, a private nonprofit organization.

On January 20, the *Hartford Courant* revealed in an exclusive story that anthrax might be missing from the Institute, the nation's premier biological defense lab facility. The Institute had failed to adopt strict safe-guards against the theft of lethal viruses and bacteria. During the early 1990s twenty-seven biological specimens, including several anthrax spec-imens and the virus that causes Ebola hemorrhagic fever, went missing. A search turned up all but three. The only remaining one containing anthrax bacteria had been rendered harmless.

The Institute defended its security policies and stated no evidence ex-isted that any of its hazardous microbes had been stolen. In the last four months safeguards had been intensified in line with the National Institute of Health's guidelines.

Joby Warrick of the *Washington Post* told the story of Army bio-defense researcher Richard Crosland. "No one asked questions," Crosland told the *Post* about lax security at the Institute. "You could literally walk out with anything [at Fort Detrick]. Crosland "had kept scrupulous notes about the frozen (botulinum toxin) crystals he kept in his lab."

A single gram of them could wipe out a million people. For eleven years, he logged every shipment of toxin received and accounted for every molecule. However, not once during his career, and not when he left, did anyone check to see what he was carrying. Labs are poor at keeping track of their inventory. Security is poor. For a government scientist getting hold of anthrax was not hard. One U.S. government lab in Utah had covertly manufactured a small amount of weapons-grade anthrax since the early nineties. Reports revealed that anthrax like that used by Amerithrax had been grown secretly at the Institute and taken to Dugway to be weapon-ized. Another secret Army project involved the construction of bomblets for delivery of anthrax in defiance of the BTWC.

Someone could "just put a Baggie in his coat and walk out of a lab with the stuff," said Crosland. Was the mailable anthrax already prepared before Amerithrax made up his mind to send it? Preparing and delivering anthrax was the tough part—the mailer would contaminate himself and his work area. The man would need a "clean room" or sophisticated home lab. The finely milled powder floats off glass slides before it can be gotten under a microscope. Getting the stuff into an envelope and not everywhere else took extraordinary skill. The FBI privately had developed a theory of how Amerithrax may have done this. It had to do with why the letters had gotten wet. Did Amerithrax do the weaponizing himself? "Biological agents can easily be obtained," said Ron Atlas, president of the American

Society of Microbiology. "A survey of nearly fifteen hundred U.S. academic institutions indicated that 22 percent work with pathogenic microorganisms and toxins that could be used in biological weapons development."

CIA research on biological production exemplified itself in Project Jefferson, a study of classical germ agents. The Institute's Project Clear Vision was an attempt to see into the future of biowarfare and reproduce a Soviet anthrax bomb. In 1998 the Pentagon began a project to see if it could manufacture bioweapons using material available on the commercial market. A year later, agents in the Pentagon's Project BACHUS (Biological Activities CHaracterized by Unconventional Signatures)[11] spread out across the nation to buy pipes, glassware filters, a fermenter to breed colonies of anthrax, nutrients, and a secondhand milling machine to grind down spores to the most infectious size. By the summer of 2000 their $1.6 million budget had equipped a mini-bioweapons plant at the U.S. Nevada Test Site where there existed a series of underground tunnels for testing the durability of biological and chemical components. By January and February 2001, ten months before the first anthrax letter, the modest plant was able to produce *Bacillus thuringiensis*, the same biopesticide made at Iraq's Al Hakam, and another powdered anthrax simulant that could be weaponized by the addition of anthrax spores.

The agents manufactured two pounds of simulated anthrax (the bacterium *B. globigii*) to stand in for the deadly one. In an investigation in February 2001, it was learned that labs were exchanging microbe samples, including anthrax, without reporting the transfers to the CDC as required by law. The investigation concluded that departments lacked sufficient federal oversight. At one DOE facility, scientists experimented with anthrax bacteria for years without anyone being notified. Though no one had been harmed (as far as was known) the lapses could have placed the public at risk.

According to former Institute scientists, lab workers until recently could have slipped away with live microbes without being challenged. There was little or no accountability, nor stringent inventory controls over the pathogens and toxins used—a standard practice at private labs. "No one checked," said one microbiologist. "It was easier to get some-

---

[11] A group of agents with the Science Applications International Corporation (SAIC).

thing out of Fort Detrick than into it." Scientists worked "covertly" on unauthorized projects and technicians were coming in on weekends for off-the-books assignments and sometimes bringing their girlfriends. "It wasn't just a matter of [lax] security," said a scientist granted unsupervised access to secure biohazard labs. "There was absolutely no security."

"It was a concern to me," said Dr. Assaad, "that these scientists were being allowed access not only to lethal [microbes] but to knowledge and information." He complained that "shenanigans had been going on at the lab." The Army's policy of recruiting foreign researchers from China and the former Soviet bloc to work in some of the Institute's most secure labs was troubling. Foreign scientists, selected for their expertise with deadly microbes and as leverage against an aging workforce, had unrestricted access to secure lab facilities. They worked at the Institute for months. It was not uncommon to find them working nights and weekends. The FBI's operating theory was that the Institute was the anthrax source and that an insider took the spores to another location to prepare the letters.

And so there was anthrax at the Institute, apparently of the letter strain. And it was possible that it had been stolen from there—not bought, although the same germs had been for sale in the past for research.

Eubacteria, the microbes that cause infectious disease, reproduce asexually and rapidly. Not only are they nucleus-free, but they have a genome that is a single circle of DNA. Only a few U.S. labs had the ability to tease apart subtle genetic variants. It was hoped they could compare them to strains from around the world and determine if the strain was common in U.S. livestock or used in U.S. labs or weapons development.

Scientists had already traced the bacterial lineage of the Ames strain that killed Stevens and the others back to an anthrax-infected Texas cow in 1981. The FBI had focused with particular attention on former and current employees and insiders with access to laboratories and research facilities that had samples of the Ames strain of anthrax, the type contained in the letters. Because of the strain's virulence, it was parceled out to labs in the U.S. and other countries like Canada to help them test vaccines. The researchers needed to discriminate between the various stocks of Ames to see if they could pinpoint the laboratory of origin.

One federal laboratory sequenced the DNA of several individual genes in various Ames stocks and failed to discover any real differences between the Florida and Porton Down samples. Since all Ames stocks came from a single source, the bacteria were essentially members of a single large clone, as alike genetically as identical twins.

Now the hunt for Amerithrax was headed for truly uncharted ground—the rarified atmosphere of bacteriological DNA.

STRAIN 25

Anthrax Tiger

BY JANUARY 26, 2002, scientific investigators were pinning their hopes on identifying the source of the bacteria by comparing it to a collection of nearly one hundred anthrax strains gathered from around the world. The strains were curated by Martin Hugh-Jones at Louisiana State University, and molecular biologist Paul S. Keim of Northern Arizona University. Dr. Keim, Dr. Hugh-Jones, Dr. Paul J. Jackson of the Los Alamos National Laboratory, and other scientists had come up with a genetic identification test for anthrax strains, similar to the DNA fingerprinting test used in human forensic cases. They discovered eight markers, or points of genetic difference, that they made the basis for distinguishing one anthrax strain from another.

Because the Ames strain had been widely distributed to labs in the U.S. and overseas this recognition proved of little help at first. When Dr. Keim still could not distinguish between the different stocks of Ames anthrax, he set about trying to develop more markers. To help in the search for new markers, the National Science Foundation asked the Institute for Genomic Research (TIGR) in Rockville, Maryland, to decode the full DNA sequence of the anthrax bacteria recovered from Bob Stevens, the photo editor who died in the Florida attack. TIGR, founded in 1992, had sequenced the complete genome of the first living organism in 1995. Before the attacks, TIGR had started sequencing a nonpathogenic derivative of the Ames strain of anthrax from Porton Down.

In January, TIGR added the bacteria isolated from the Florida attack to its sequencing task. The idea was to tease out subtle divergencies between the two genomes that might identify the source of the attack strain. TIGR also had an Ames strain sample from Dugway in Utah.

Working independently of Dr. Keim, TIGR was already sequencing the full genome of the Ames strain owned by Fort Detrick's laboratory. TIGR was already making good on its $200,000 National Science Foundation grant. TIGR specialized in microbial genomes and was in the process of determining the sequence of chemical building blocks in the DNA of the anthrax bacterium. TIGR had started the project two years earlier at the behest of the Office of Naval Research and the British Defense Evaluation and Research Agency.

TIGR was also negotiating for a second grant to sequence the full genome of other strains of anthrax and of other samples of the Ames strain to speed up the investigation. Having the full sequence of several Ames stocks might help pinpoint the source. Under Dr. Timothy D. Read, who headed its anthrax genome sequencing, TIGR expanded its anthrax sequencing and mapped the bacteria recovered from the Florida strike at AMI, the attack strain. The TIGR scientists used a sample of the Ames strain obtained from the British biodefense laboratory at Porton Down in England, which in turn had received it a decade earlier from the Institute at Fort Detrick and modified it in 1998 and 2001. TIGR compared the sequencing of the Florida anthrax isolate to its nearly completed sequence of another Ames-strain isolate obtained from the Porton Down sequencing project.

Read looked for DNA differences throughout the bacterium's genome. "Because the two bacteria studied are of the same strain," said Dr. Read, "it's like taking two first cousins from a remote village, determining their differences, and then trying to differentiate the whole human race based on those differences." TIGR focused on the main chromosome of the highly monomorphic bacterium, a large ring of DNA now known to contain 5,167,515 DNA letters holding information for 5,960 genes. The bacterium contained two tiny rings of DNA known as plasmids. Plasmids carry the genes essential for the Ames strain's virulence. The plasmid's

DNA had already been decoded several years earlier by scientists at the Los Alamos Nuclear Laboratory. Read and his team found it generally identical to the other mailed anthrax except for the rare errors made in copying the five million units of DNA that compose its genome, its complete set of heredity information. DNA's long double-helix resembles a spiral staircase with four types of nucleotide bases comprising its steps. Human DNA consists of four billion of these steps.

TIGR scientists discovered several points of difference between the Porton Down Ames strain and the Florida Ames strain:

1. Single unit changes (Single Nucleotide Polymorphisms, or SNPs) in DNA.

2. Variable repeats (Variable Number Tandem Repeats, or VNTRs, where the same tiny sequence of DNA units are repeated a few times. The variable regions are the type of differences used for human DNA fingerprinting.

TIGR scientists sent their list of DNA differences to Dr. Keim, who began analyzing the Ames strain samples in his collection and new Ames samples the FBI had just given him to find out if he could now distinguish among them. A comprehensive collection of Ames samples would increase Dr. Keim's chances of identifying the exact lab that produced the attack strain. He had an enormous number, but a few Ames samples remained outside his collection at private and foreign labs. The Defense Research Establishment at Suffield in Alberta had the Ames strain. The Canadians had converted an agricultural experiment station into a government testing area for anthrax. However, they had received no FBI requests for samples and the agency soon rectified that.

In September, Defense Research and Development Canada (DRDC) had produced a classified paper that demonstrated how a single anthrax letter with slits in its envelope could poison the mail system and kill swiftly through the air once opened. The Canadian report may have been circulated at the Institute just before the first anthrax letters were mailed on September 18. On October 4, as Bob Stevens lay dying at JFK Hospital, the letter was widely released by e-mail throughout the U.S. scientific community.

Dr. Read said the current plan was for Dr. Keim to test each Ames stock in his collection at the points of difference TIGR found on the anthrax genome. Each sample was to then be graded as to how close it was to the Florida attack strain and two Porton Down specimens. The index strain the Institute sent to Porton Down in 1982 and 2001 had been cured there of the pXO1 and pXO2 plasmids. That gave TIGR a before and after reference. The two preparations of genomic DNA sent to TIGR, Porton 1 and Porton 2, had been grown from the Institute's original frozen culture and prepared in a lab at the University of California at Berkeley for the new test. Because the Porton isolate was cured of the pXO plasmids, TIGR was only able to compare the Florida plasmids against the *Bacillus anthracis* Sterne strain in pXO1 and the Pasteur strain in pXO2. This data could not be used to infer a higher mutation rate in pXO2 because the Ames strain is more closely related to Sterne than to the Pasteur strain. The Florida isolate contained a mixture of both orientations. If one of Dr. Keim's stocks was nearer to the Florida specimen than others, that would point to the lab that provided it as the likeliest source from which the perpetrator stole or grew the attack anthrax.

The anthrax fingerprinting test (which looks for unique patterns of repeating DNA) now had over fifty markers to work with. The test could differentiate between the letter germs and the various samples of the Ames strain. Although the test itself can be completed in hours, "quality control measures" expanded out the required time. Read hoped to learn Dr. Keim's preliminary results in a week or two. He waited anxiously. TIGR worked with Keim to use the new markers to analyze six anthrax isolates that initially had appeared to be indistinguishable from the original Ames strain based on existing genotype information. The new markers allowed the scientists to divide the six Ames isolates into four different categories.

If successful findings were publicized they could tip off Amerithrax, worried an FBI official. He was unwilling to give Amerithrax "a road map" to the investigation. Dr. Claire M. Fraser, TIGR's director, said that Dr. Keim's findings of whether the genetic differences pointed to particular laboratories might remain secret at the FBI's request; TIGR's own results, however, would be openly published the following month. "We are working on a draft of the paper now," Dr. Fraser said. "Nothing TIGR has done will be censored by the FBI." That was not the case with Dr. Keim, who was dying to talk about what he had learned.

In late January and early February, agents from the Baltimore, New York, and Washington FBI field offices visited the Institute. They conducted inquiries over a number of days, then asked about a former scientist who had returned in 1999 and taken away discarded biological safety cabinets. Reached at his job with a defense contractor, the scientist admitted that, with Army permission, he had taken three biosafety cabinets that were being discarded. He said they were for use in a classified Defense Department project. He considered the questioning to be part of a routine effort to exclude people with the knowledge to mount a biological attack. "I think they had a profile," he told the *Baltimore Sun* later. "They had a bunch of people on the list. They have to rule people out. . . . I certainly didn't appreciate getting called in. No one likes that. I'm one of the good guys."

By February, Ernie Blanco was back handling mail at AMI's new office in Boca Raton and FBI agent Van Harp was e-mailing forty thousand members of the Washington-based American Society of Microbiology. In his letter, Harp requested help in discovering if one of their members could be Amerithrax. He explained that the FBI was looking for a single person with lab experience and a clear and rational thought process. Amerithrax had appeared to be very organized in the production and mailing of his letters. "It is possible this person used off-hours in a laboratory or may have even established an improvised or concealed facility comprised of sufficient equipment to produce the anthrax," Van Harp wrote. "It is very likely that one or more of you know this individual." Unless Amerithrax was a brilliant amateur.

In the months to come, a large number of U.S. scientists and biowarfare experts would reject the FBI's theory that a disgruntled American scientist prepared the spores and mailed the letters. "In my opinion, there are maybe four or five people in the whole country who might be able to make this stuff, and I'm one of them," said Dr. Spertzel.

"And even with a good lab and staff to help run it, it might take me a year to come up with a product as good." Spertzel and other experts would suggest that the FBI might reexamine other theories—state-sponsored terrorism, weaponized spores stolen or provided by an accomplice from an existing, but secret, biodefense program.

Spertzel believed that developing a weaponized aerosol so sophisticated and virulent as Amerithrax's required scientific know-how, technical competence, and unfettered access to expensive equipment—capabilities beyond a lone individual's.

By February 6, 2002, more than 1600 suspicious mail items had been checked by Postal Inspectors. There had been 569 evacuations of post offices, 72 recent anthrax hoaxes, and 11 convictions. Sometimes the task of protecting the mail staggered even these iron men. Seven hundred million letters coursed through the mail stream each day, 207 billion pieces each year.

ON FEBRUARY 12, 2002, Dr. Keim made a startling statement at a national conference on microbial genomes in Las Vegas. Dr. Keim said he had distinguished between stocks of the anthrax strain kept in different laboratories. The method should help tell which laboratory's stock of anthrax was closest to that used by Amerithrax. That could limit the search to people with access to that particular laboratory and its store of anthrax. Dr. Keim succeeded by analyzing a site on the second of these plasmids called a poly-A tract.

Ames stocks held in different labs varied in the number of A's, one of the four units of DNA, contained in the poly-A tract. The number varied from eight to twenty-five, the exact number depending on which lab provided the Ames sample. On the basis of the poly-A test, Keim distinguished between the Ames strains held in four laboratories (Porton Down and three labs he did not name), and in a natural Ames isolate taken from a goat that died of anthrax in Texas in 1997. Marker stretches of DNA were tested then against five other samples of Ames anthrax. The goat sample differed at four markers, showing a divergence among anthrax lineages. Two differed at one marker, "a stretch of repeated adenines on pXO2, one of the two DNA plasmids that give anthrax its virulence."

"It may be the most polymorphic site in the genome," Keim told *New Scientist*. Strain A can immediately be ruled out as the attack strain as it is missing a plasmid (a short ring of DNA) and is nonpathogenic."

Dr. Keim's agreement with the FBI prevented him from listing the labs. One could guess. The reference Ames in Keim's collection came from a freezer at Porton Down, which in turn had gotten it from the Institute. Another was a culture that came directly from the Institute, and the third from the Dugway Proving Ground in Utah. When TIGR published its paper in May everyone would know.

On February 22, civilian workers at the U.S. Army Reserve Command headquarters at Fort McPherson, Georgia, discovered a suspicious package with a "white powdery substance" inside a plastic sandwich bag. Field tests indicated that anthrax might be present, but since such tests can provide false positives, six people who handled the package were sent to the hospital for decontamination. "We're going to treat it as if anthrax is present." Most of the military personnel had been inoculated with the anthrax vaccine, but not the civilians. While Atlanta's CDC conducted further tests, the building was locked down for five hours. Two hundred people trapped inside were permitted to leave when the powder proved to be harmless.

Three days later, federal authorities subpoenaed documents and anthrax samples from U.S. scientific labs to narrow their search through genetic analysis. White House spokesman Ari Fleischer said there were several suspects but declined to elaborate. "The FBI has not narrowed the list down to one," he said. "I wish it were that easy and that simple right now." Fleischer said President Bush wanted the case resolved quickly, but "also wants the FBI to take its time and build a case that would stand in court, that is thorough, that is conclusive." He reported that the source of the anthrax was definitely domestic and of the so-called Ames strain of *Bacillus anthracis*; the suspect probably has or had legitimate access to the bio agents in a lab and the block handprinting on the envelopes was "chosen by design" to throw off investigators.

Fleischer was asked, "Well, is the suspect an American, and is it a scientist from Fort Detrick that is being looked at out of the group?"

"All indications are that the source of the anthrax is domestic," Fleischer replied. "And I can't give you any more specific information than that. That's part of what the FBI is actively reviewing. And I just can't go beyond that . . . Obviously, anybody who would engage in that type of terrorism through the mail puts people in a position where it becomes very difficult not only for them, but for local communities, for all the people who were affected by all the hoaxes that followed those attacks. But I think the federal government responded as well as it could, given the knowledge the federal government had, as quickly as it could."

"What's the sense here about the pace of the investigation?" asked a reporter.

"Obviously, the person who did this is very smart," said Fleischer, "has employed means that are very difficult to track. The pace of justice is a methodical one. And that's the effort of the FBI, and the President believes the FBI is doing a good, solid job."

"Does the White House feel the government has a full handle now on the inventories of anthrax at universities, at military facilities?" asked a reporter.

"To the best of all the information that we have received here," said Fleischer, "that was never a question. The military laboratories, other laboratories accounted for their anthrax."

The FBI doubled its reward for the capture of Amerithrax to $2.5 million for information leading to the arrest and conviction of the bioterrorist. The *Washington Times* quoted unidentified law enforcement authorities and biochemical experts as saying one of the suspects was believed to have worked at the Institute and had been fired from government jobs.

The next day, the FBI conducted tests with swabs to detect the presence of anthrax spores in the homes, offices, and vehicles of about a dozen people with the attributes Fleischer had listed. All of them were cleared of suspicion after the tests came back negative. The tests were conducted with the consent of those under investigation and did not require search warrants.

The searches took place amid burgeoning concern on Capitol Hill over an apparent lack of progress in the probe. There were no firm suspects, despite thousands of interviews. Investigators claimed they kept a fluid list of about twenty who were under scrutiny at any time. No one had remained on the list more than a month. It was frustrating not to have a target yet. "It's not stalled . . ." said one investigator, "but there are no easy answers or instant gratification."

At the Institute, agents conducted hundreds of interviews. One agent, assigned there full-time, supervised a hastily formed library of anthrax strains. Investigators now knew which labs possessed live cultures of the Ames strain. All but three of the labs were in the U.S. The FBI flew agents to a Canadian defense lab with anthrax stocks. More visits were scheduled to British and French research agencies.

Nine research groups were helping with the analysis of Amerithrax's lethal powder. Experts peered at the genetic structure of the bacteria, looking for chemical and physical clues that would reveal exactly where the poison was manufactured. Tests to this point had shown a match between spores used in the attacks and a strain of anthrax used in U.S. biodefense since the mid-1980s, the Ames strain. The FBI had already e-mailed forty thousand members of the American Society for Microbiology asking for aid. Now they sent letters to a half-million New Jersey residents appealing for their eyes and ears. It would be ironic if Amerithrax was captured because of a letter.

FBI and outside scientists continued their examination of the large repository of anthrax spores from the attacks. Highly sophisticated tests kept a snail's pace to allow for elaborate protocols that would ensure that the analyses were scientifically accurate and legally defensible. "You can't be in a hurry on this stuff," one official said. Only Leahy's letter contained enough anthrax to permit extensive testing. The FBI commissioned a series of sophisticated forensic experiments by outside laboratories to try to determine when, where, and how the anthrax had been produced.

In Washington, D.C., the quip was that mail was so slow that only anthrax mail was being delivered. One congressman complained that, due to the irradiating and sterilization of mail, he was only now, in February, getting his Christmas cards. "I'm not sure this irradiation of mail does any good. My suggestion is that if you have anything to send to Washington, D.C., send it by e-mail." Senators had their mail opened for them and photostated for reading. At no time did they touch the originals.

When postal officials caught up with the mail, there was a string of unusually late deliveries—overdue bills, holiday wishes, business mail, vehicle registrations, parking tickets, jury summonses, and passports. An invitation to a christening on November 18 finally arrived. One couple's three-thousand-dollar wedding ring, mailed to a jeweler for their tenth anniversary by registered mail in October, had not yet arrived. Somewhere in the system a mail-order suit had gone missing. The irradiation and redistributing of one million pieces of mail quarantined inside Brentwood had delayed everything. Above all, the mail had to be kept safe for the public and for the postal workers.

The CDC had also contracted a number of private labs to work through the backlog of thousands of environmental swabs. Investigators hoped the processed specimens would give them an idea how far anthrax spores had spread at contaminated sites.

On Thursday, February 28, a technician at a Texas laboratory cut his jaw while shaving. The next day, he began working on some of the spores collected the previous fall from the Amerithrax letters. He was not wearing gloves (in violation of CDC protocol) as he moved vials of spores from a cabinet into a freezer. At some point he touched his face. While workers at labs who regularly handle anthrax specimens are usually vaccinated against the disease, none of the forty workers at the Texas lab had been.

Over the next three days, the technician's shaving cut became larger. He developed a low-grade fever and a swelling on his neck. When an unusual skin lesion festered, he went to his doctor, who swabbed the sore. He gave the swab to the technician, who brought it back to the private lab to analyze. A test told him he had developed cutaneous anthrax. On antibiotics, he spent five days in the hospital recovering. It was the first known anthrax case in the United States since the anthrax-by-mail attacks.

More than five months after the first envelope from Amerithrax was postmarked in Trenton the FBI finally issued new subpoenas to the labs in North America and Europe that had been identified as having live cultures of the same general strain of anthrax used by Amerithrax. The subpoenas demanded samples from each facility.

The labs were still analyzing the anthrax spores mailed to Leahy. FBI Director Mueller defended the sluggish pace of the Amerithrax investigation. Allegations from some scientists that the FBI was fumbling the case were "totally inaccurate," he said. He had begun his FBI tenure a week before the terror attacks in New York and Washington. "Because of the unique nature and form, it takes some time. We are going to have to come into court and explain to the jury the process we went through to identify this individual and, if there is a match, the scientific procedure to make that match." The FBI, he said, had not focused on any group of biodefense laboratories and had not ruled out a terrorist connection, though FBI profilers now believed the culprit was not connected to international terrorists.

Mueller dismissed recent comments by scientist Barbara Hatch Rosenberg who contended that the FBI likely knows who Amerithrax is, but is "dragging its feet." Dr. Rosenberg, a professor at the State University of New York at Purchase and an expert on biological weapons, was a specialist on the treaty banning bioweapons. She told UPI that samples like anthrax posted to researchers must be mailed in three-layered packaging, consisting of sturdy, watertight containers to prevent leakage. "Most, if not all, bags, envelopes, and the like are not acceptable outer shipping containers," the CDC wrote at the time. Dr. Rosenberg said, "The CDC had given some thought to the prospect anthrax could leak during mailing and certainly they knew [the Daschle letter] was not packaged according to prescription." The Postal Service's previous policy, issued in 1999, called for evacuating the building upon discovery of a suspicious letter. In Dr. Rosenberg's articles, "Analysis of the Anthrax Attacks," posted on the Federation of American Scientists website in January and February, she theorized that the FBI knew Amerithrax was an insider with "hands-on experience" and that the number of their suspects was under fifty. In an interview reported in *Salon*, she said, "This guy knows too much, and knows things the U.S. isn't very anxious to publicize. Therefore, they don't want to get too close."

On March 6, the National Academy of Sciences endorsed the Pentagon's controversial anthrax vaccine as a safe and effective treatment. The NAS said it was effective and safe enough to be used by high-risk people against inhalational anthrax. It presented no higher incidence of adverse reactions than other vaccines in common use. The NAS said it was "unlikely" that any natural or bioengineered strain of anthrax could evade the antigen produced by the vaccine and still produce a toxin lethal to humans. This was a vote of confidence to BioPort Corp., the embattled company that had needed more than three years to bring its manufacturing practices into compliance with the FDA before resuming making vaccine.

On March 21, Theodore J. Gordon, D.C. deputy director for public health assurance, felt they were "nowhere near" ordering a prefumigation of the commercial areas fringing the Brentwood mail hub. The project was still "embryonic." Thomas G. Day, vice president of engineering for the Postal Service, said the same thing: "If there's any message I want to give you it is that we're going to make sure we get it right, so that there is an effective treatment and [Brentwood] is effectively decontaminated. We are absolutely committed to getting this done, but we need to get it done right." Two days later the grand strategy to cleanse Brentwood was laid.

On April 9, intensive lab tests of Amerithrax's "wispy white powder" demonstrated it followed a recipe commonly used by U.S. scientists. They were narrowing the suspect labs. The FBI refused to name the chemical used to coat the trillions of spores to keep them from clumping together. Previously authorities had disclosed that the anthrax powder contained silica—a chemical used in the U.S. germ warfare program in the 1960s. "The powder's formulation was not routine," said one law enforcement official. "Somebody had to have special knowledge and experience to do this." Months of lab analysis of the anthrax spores suggested that Amerithrax did not merely copy U.S. techniques or those used in the former Soviet Union or Iraq. More than ever the government was convinced that Amerithrax was a U.S. scientist with highly specialized training and skills and with access to a government lab. "If anything, this has narrowed our focus," said one investigator.

On April 19, an Institute worker tested positive for anthrax exposure after a researcher on April 8 noticed a biological deposit on a flask inside an anthrax testing lab. This lab was not connected to the FBI Amerithrax inquiry. Subsequently, spores were discovered in the hallway and administrative area despite strict rules on the handling of the agent. The worker, though immunized against anthrax, began taking antibiotics as a precaution. The Pentagon said, "The presence of the spores appears to be highly localized based on negative results from sampling of surrounding areas."

The Postal Service gave an informational standup talk to Brentwood workers and updated the decontamination status. Six months after inhaling anthrax spores six mailworkers who'd survived the deadly anthrax attack had yet to make a full recovery. Experts wondered why they were not back to normal. Five of the six experienced memory loss and trouble concentrating, fatigue, and frequent exhaustion that required daily naps.

The day after tests isolated an anthrax spore in material collected for analysis, scholars from the Brookings Institution released a new report. The study, "Protecting the American Homeland," estimated a million people would die if terrorists launched a biological attack that widely dispersed anthrax and other agents. It recommended that the Bush administration concentrate homeland security efforts on terrorist scenarios that have the potential for causing the greatest number of deaths, economic loss, and psychological damage.

Tom Ridge's national strategy was already devoted to "high consequence" scenarios. But administration officials warned that appraising threats and allocating probabilities is tough. Some terrorist cells are obscure and terrorists frequently shift tactics. Since it is impossible to guard against every probable kind of attack, resources should be used to guard against nuclear, chemical, or biological terrorism and conventional large-scale attacks on airports, seaports, nuclear and chemical plants, and stadiums.

"We really should be focusing on potentially catastrophic attacks, meaning large numbers of casualties or large damage to the economy," said the report's author Michael E. O'Hanlon. Meanwhile the Department of Health and Human Services continued stockpiling smallpox and anthrax vaccines.

A widespread biological attack against shopping malls or movie theaters could cost $250 billion. The White House sought $38 billion in the fiscal 2003 budget for homeland security: over $10 billion for border security, nearly $6 billion to defend against bioterrorism, and over $700 million for new technology—a down payment in a multiyear plan. An emergency spending bill passed in January had added an extra $2.5 billion to President Bush's biowarfare defense budget. The Brookings scholars considered $45 billion a year closer to the mark.

The Army scientists could not get over how Amerithrax's mailed anthrax had grown more potent from one letter to the next. Was he making gradual improvements through experimentation, ratcheting up the potency of his germ powder? "It could be that the final steps of the processing were done in steps," a senior government official said. "You take it so far, and take off a bunch. You go further, and take off another bunch."

So far the measured FBI inquiry had consumed millions of hours in interviews, detectives' time, and lengthy neighborhood sweeps. The detectives still had no idea who was behind the tainted letters. Increasingly, the Bureau looked to science to unravel the mystery. When they learned the exact genome of the strain, the agents could narrow the search for the laboratory from which the anthrax sprang. The deadly powder could have been made in any of thousands of biological laboratories—with the right starter germs.

The analysis of the contents of the Leahy letter was proceeding with glacial pace. They were learning the science as they went along. The technicians wanted to be positive none of the lightweight, but extremely valuable, evidence was lost, corrupted, or misinterpreted. Authorities said,

"We had to assure ourselves that we had a quality program." A senior Bush administration official expressed sympathy for the FBI because the inquiry had grown so scientifically complex. The FBI lacked advisers skilled in the subtleties of germ weapons. "They're having to review a lot of the initial takes on things," he said. "There's an evolving picture. The Bureau has gone back to scratch to invent the science."

At least the investigators could do deeper analyses because of the relatively large amounts of powder in the Leahy letter. The amount of anthrax inside the other tainted letters was just 0.871 grams, less than a pat of butter. One trillion spores present in one gram of letter anthrax had been easily contained within a one-ounce (twenty-eight-gram) letter. Such an envelope could theoretically hold a million lethal doses easily dispersed to sleep and wake, hibernate and reinfect for longer than the life span of a man.

Amerithrax had to have made his anthrax stable and durable enough to survive its delivery system and small enough to infect the lungs of his victims. Weaponizing it would have involved nutrient media, perfect temperature, and lots of time. Federal experts investigated whether the anthrax powders had electrostatic charges and chemical coatings meant to increase dispersal, potency, and shelf life.

On April 26, the USPS began precautionary random testing in the D.C. area and found that seventy-one postal locations showed the presence of *B. anthracis*. On April 29, the Office of Personnel Management closed its mailroom after new tests found one anthrax spore in a batch of material collected for analysis. On May 2, four days of tests began which would prove negative for anthrax. This was the same day anthrax cleanups began at the Wallingford, Connecticut, facility and there was an anthrax scare in St. Louis. On Tuesday evening, May 7, the Federal Reserve Board detected traces of anthrax spores in twenty pieces of business and commercial mail. Since October's attacks, the Fed had processed all its mail in a secure trailer in the courtyard outside its downtown headquarters.

Every piece of the Fed's mail was irradiated by the Postal Service before it arrived at the trailer where it was subjected to random testing. Although this procedure kills anthrax spores, U.S. Postal Inspector Daniel L. Mihalko said it does not preclude the possibility that dead spores could produce a positive swab test. Screeners wearing protective suits found more the next morning. False positives had proven fairly common during the anthrax scare, but the twenty letters were rushed to the lab for further analysis anyway. Fed spokesman David Skidmore did not know when test results would be available. On May 8, the cleanup contract for Brentwood decontamination was signed, with a goal of finishing within ninety days.

Thursday, May 9, a call went out for a blanket vaccination program for all U.S. mail handlers to counter any further outbreaks. On the same day, TIGR researchers, led by Timothy Read, Claire Fraser, and chief of bioinformatics Steven Salzberg, posted their findings in the *Science Express* paper. They reported that comprehensive comparison of the Porton Down and the Florida letter anthrax isolates identified slight differences in their DNA that could be used as genomic fingerprints in future analyses.

STRAIN 26

Anthrax Paper

IN A PIONEERING use of genomics as a tool for the forensic analysis of microbes, TIGR had finished decoding the genome of the anthrax bacteria used by Amerithrax. On the Science Express website researchers said they had isolated the strain used to contaminate mail at AMI, discovering that it was related to the Ames strain. Anthrax DNA had more than five million unique genetic components that had to be compared.

"In different labs over twenty-one years," said Fraser, "they have developed mutations [unique to each lab] in their DNA sequence. And these are the regions we are focusing on, regions that are different, because that gives us the information we need to try to distinguish one from another." Fraser was a member of a National Research Council panel drawing up a report about how scientific research can help counter bioterrorism.

Because anthrax shows little genetic variability, it made fingerprinting the organism difficult. TIGR had identified sixty new, unique genetic difference sites in the genome that helped investigators eliminate some labs and concentrate on others. The new genetic markers distinguished the anthrax isolate used in the previous fall's bioterror attack in Boca Raton from closely related anthrax strains. Those main differences include what the scientists described as four "high-quality" single-nucleotide polymorphisms (SNPs)—differences of a single DNA base—between the sequenced chromosomes of the Porton Down and Florida isolates. Most of those differences were found in the plasmids—circular units of DNA that are separate from the chromosomes that contain most of the organism's genetic material.

Of those sixty markers, Fraser said, eleven could help researchers discriminate between the Florida sample and others. Previous genetic-marker analysis had focused on a limited number of DNA segments, rather than the entire genomic sequence. According to TIGR, "Specific attributes of the DNA of anthrax bacteria used in the Florida attack show the genetic fingerprints of the bacteria."

They detailed their findings to the FBI. Genome sequencing of the bacteria used by Amerithrax would allow researchers to recognize the varieties should another attack occur and help scientists develop a new vaccine and a speedy means to detect infection. "Genome-based analysis will provide a powerful new tool for investigating unexpected disease outbreaks—whether they are bioterrorism attacks or natural outbreaks of more familiar pathogens," said Fraser.

Dr. Read and his team planned to publish the integral sequence of the anthrax bacillus genome in a scientific review by the end of the year. He predicted that at least fourteen other strains or isolates of anthrax would be decoded in 2003, in cooperation with Northern Arizona University, which has twelve hundred isolates of the bacteria archived. "Building a comprehensive database of information related to gene content . . ." read their paper, "and inversions in the genomes of important pathogens will allow investigators to quickly pinpoint the isolate that is most closely related to an outbreak strain." A database like that might deter future attacks.

To support its claims TIGR posted four sets of anthrax data:

1. the set of all assembled "contigs" (contiguous small segments of the genome) of all sizes

2. the set of individual sequences that were used to create those contigs

3. a file containing the quality values (estimates of error rates) for each individual sequence

4. a set of one thousand base pair regions centered on each SNP to allow other scientists to identify and test the markers on other anthrax strains

Sequence data from the *B. anthracis* research were also placed in the Genbank repository.

New Scientist revealed that the two reference strains that appear identical to the attack strain most likely originated at the Institute at Fort Detrick, Maryland, and Dugway Proving Ground in Utah. The new work also showed that substantial genetic differences can emerge in two samples of an anthrax culture separated for only three years. This means Amerithrax's anthrax was not separated from its ancestors at the Institute by many generations. A handful of mutations arose some time after the bacteria left Detrick—very subtle differences, but it was now indisputable that the mailed microbes were direct descendants of germs developed at the Institute.

The difference between the Dugway strain and the attack strain was not great—thirty-six adenines in a row, instead of thirty-five. The detailed genetic analysis of the anthrax letter bacteria revealed "minuscule but consistent differences between the terrorist strain and the nearly identical strain developed by the U.S. Army at Fort Detrick." The FBI might pinpoint the exact lab, but not who there absconded with the microbes or to whom that person may have passed them along.

Friday, May 3, the FBI began analyzing the strain of anthrax mailed and comparing it to strains from around the world. Building an all-inclusive database of the genomes of important pathogens would allow investigators to quickly distinguish the isolate that is most closely related to an outbreak strain and calculate the age of the terrorist substrain.

On Monday, May 20, frustrated FBI agents tried to narrow the hunt for Amerithrax further. They began administering mass polygraph tests to current and former employees of the Institute, Dugway Proving Ground, Pine Bluff Arsenal in Arkansas, and the Salk Center in Swiftwater, Pennsylvania. Anyone who hadn't taken a polygraph test would be asked to voluntarily submit to one. "It's nothing we can force them to do," said one official. "But it's an effort to work through this list with a little more specificity." The latest list consisted of over two hundred domestic scientists and lab workers who had had contact with the Ames strain used in the attacks and descended from stocks developed at the Institute. Some would be reinterviewed.

Senate and House bills anticipated spending $3 billion per year on anti-bioterrorism efforts, roughly the amount appropriated for the current fiscal year. Funds to finance first-year operations had been approved after the 9-11 terrorist attacks and subsequent spore-tainted letters were received on Capitol Hill. The bioterrorism authorization bill established a framework for allocating the money. It included provisions to prevent, detect, and treat terrorism-related health threats.

"Because of this bipartisan legislation, Americans will be able to sleep better at night in the knowledge that our nation is taking the steps necessary to protect them and their families against the deadly threat of bioterrorism," said Senator Edward M. Kennedy, who cosponsored the Senate version of the legislation with Senator Bill Frist.

The bill called for tighter regulation of labs and bioweapon materials workers, new record-keeping requirements, safety improvements at animal research labs, and vaccines and antibiotics stockpiles to protect against biological and chemical weapons. Funding was increased for state and local health officials to help them prepare for bioterrorism attacks, research on prevention and treatment, and grants to help hospitals prepare for treatment of victims. It required community water systems serving more than three thousand people to conduct vulnerability assessments, tighten security, and prepare emergency response plans. In case of an attack on a nuclear power plant, expanded supplies of potassium iodide would be made available to communities near the plants to handle contamination.

On May 29, the House and Senate negotiators agreed on the final version of legislation to make certain of a sustained, all-inclusive effort to bolster the nation's defenses against bioterror attack. The bill, calling for initiatives to prevent and detect terrorism-related health threats, won swift approval from Congress. The following day, the FDA, responding to the threat of anthrax, adopted new rules to speed approval of new bioterror medicines. The FDA said that it would allow companies to base their new drug applications on animal testing alone when assessing whether a drug is effective. Previously, a drug's effectiveness had to be tested on humans before the FDA would allow it on the market. "The terrorist attacks of last fall underscored the acute need for this new regulation," said Lester

M. Crawford, the FDA's deputy commissioner. "Today's action will help make certain essential new pharmaceutical products available much sooner—those products that because of the very nature of what they are designed to treat cannot be safely or ethically tested for effectiveness in humans."

Janet Woodcock, director of the FDA's Center for Drug Evaluation and Research, said use of the new rule, which the agency considered "urgently needed," would be limited. Woodcock said the FDA has "been struggling in a number of cases to persuade applicants to go forward" with drugs to treat biological, chemical, and nuclear attacks. It would still take a year or more for companies to design, undertake, and complete their animal studies. It was unethical to expose a human test subject to potentially lethal or permanently disabling agents, making it impossible to test a drug's effectiveness against biological and radiological threats.

The FDA has already approved Cipro use against bioterror. It received "fast track" approval against inhaled anthrax based on both animal tests and human studies of how it behaved in the bloodstream. Steve Lawton, chief lawyer for the Biotechnology Industry Organization, said the new rule is an "absolutely appropriate and necessary tool to combat terrorism . . . It's a terrific combination of patriotism and opportunity and there are a lot out there ready to respond."

"Federal agencies have come under fire," wrote the AP, "for failing to realize that the postal workers at Brentwood were at risk for anthrax even after an anthrax letter was disclosed on Capitol Hill and treatment had begun for Senate staffers." On June 7, Judicial Watch, a conservative watchdog group, sued the Bush administration for access under the Freedom of Information Act to documents about the previous fall's anthrax attacks. The chairman of the group, Larry Klayman, had previously asserted that top officials might have known the bioterrorist attack was coming. He said some White House staff members had begun taking Cipro the night of September 11, before the anthrax attacks began. "We believe that the White House knew or had reason to know that an anthrax attack was imminent or underway," Klayman said. "We want to know what the government knew and when they knew it. . . . One doesn't simply start taking a powerful antibiotic for no good reason. The American people are entitled to know what the White House staffers knew nine months ago."

"We did not know about the anthrax attacks. Period!" countered Gordon Johndroe, a White House spokesman. He did not know why staffers were given Cipro, but guessed it was "a precautionary measure in the early hours of September 11, before the situation could be fully assessed." In October 2001, press reports said that White House workers, including President Bush and the staff accompanying Vice President Dick Cheney, had been taking Cipro nearly a month before anthrax was detected on Capitol Hill. There was a biological alarm at the White House on November 18, but it proved to be false.

"The American people deserve a full accounting from the Bush administration, the FBI, and other agencies concerning the anthrax attacks," said Klayman. "The FBI's investigation seems to have dead-ended, and frankly, that is not very reassuring given their performance with the September 11th hijackers." Judicial Watch said records showed the decision was made not to close Brentwood after the anthrax attacks began because it would have cost the post office a half-million dollars per day. Judicial Watch was seeking a criminal inquest into the U.S. Postal Service's handling of the anthrax contamination and presented documents to a federal prosecutor that it said proved postal and government officials knew anthrax spores had leaked from a letter sent to Daschle into the Brentwood Processing Plant but neither warned workers nor shut down the site.

"The government does not have the right to injure people, to harm them, and that's what [officials] did through their action and inaction," wrote Klayman. "While Capitol Hill workers received prompt medical care, Brentwood postal workers were ordered by USPS officials to continue working in the contaminated facility. Health officials have said they did not realize then that anthrax could have escaped a sealed envelope." Klayman said the mistake goes beyond a bad judgment call. "They deliberately withheld information," he concluded. "The political elite, they'll be protected from day one. The ordinary folks will be treated in a lesser fashion."

On June 11, President Bush signed legislation in a Rose Garden ceremony that provided over $4 billion for drugs, vaccines, training, and other initiatives to deal with a bioterror attack. It committed $1.6 billion to states to help with emergency preparedness. "Biological weapons are potentially the most dangerous weapons in the world," he said. "Last fall's anthrax attacks were an incredible tragedy to a lot of people in America, and it sent a warning that we needed and heeded. We must be better prepared to prevent, identify, and respond."

With overwhelming backing on Capitol Hill, Bush intended to use that consensus to create a Department of Homeland Security that incorporated all or parts of twenty-two federal agencies. The new department would be the lead agency in promoting research for new vaccines and antidotes, dealing with bioterrorism, and managing the National Pharmaceutical Stockpile. Bush aggressively promoted the reorganization plan, saying it would "align authority and responsibility."

Afterward, the President and Tom Ridge attended the first meeting of sixteen business, academic, and government leaders drafted by the White House for a new antiterror advisory council. "You all can play a very useful role in this process," Bush told them. "You bring a lot of heft and a lot of experience and a lot of know-how." Ridge spent an hour with the council, then dashed to Capitol Hill, where in a closed session, he briefed House members on the new department. On June 13, he held a similar meeting with the Senate.

If these had been patriotic murders, Amerithrax had achieved his goal with this legislation, though his final goal, probably one of personal aggrandizement, had yet to be achieved. Amerithrax was not running the war against anthrax, but he certainly had started it.

On Thursday, June 20, a scientific panel advised the government that twenty thousand health care workers in each state should be vaccinated against smallpox to protect them in the event of an outbreak. This would expand the use of the vaccine for the first time in nearly thirty years. Each state would designate at least one "smallpox response team" (physicians, epidemiologists, local policemen, lab technicians, nurses, and vaccinators) and choose one or more hospitals to be referral centers for possible cases. Vaccination would be voluntary. Smallpox vaccinia infected a person and set up an immune response that protected against smallpox. There were side effects and the risk of a smallpox virus attack was too meager to justify the complications that would arise from widespread vaccination. Health and Human Services Secretary Tommy Thompson said he would "review the recommendation with experts . . . as the administration works toward a policy on the smallpox vaccine."

The next day, there was a Brentwood cookout at a D.C. park to raise money for Brentwood employees' families. Their spirits were flagging. Depression was widespread. Members had received a chart listing the common signs of stress, "anxiety, survivor guilt/self-blame, grief and denial."

The EAP suggested mail handlers offer "realistic reassurance" to their children and provided these examples: "I have no symptoms and have not worked anywhere that has been exposed," or "I am taking medicine as a preventative measure because a few people in my facility did get sick. I have not been sick . . . I am going to continue to do everything I can to keep myself safe, while helping to deliver the mail."

On Monday, June 24, a National Research Council report called for "a comprehensive rethinking of the nation's antiterrorism infrastructure, underscoring the need to quickly bring existing technologies into use, accelerate new research and create a Homeland Security Institute to evaluate counterterrorism strategies. The structure of federal agencies is . . . to a large extent the result of [the] distinction between the responsibility for national security and the responsibility for domestic policy. Given this compartmentalization, the federal government is not appropriately organized to carry out a [science and technology] agenda for countering catastrophic terrorism."

The study went on to give a long list of shortcomings—lack of coordination in research on "dirty bomb" threats and "enormous vulnerabilities" in the ability of public health systems to defend against biological warfare. The report laid out challenges in developing vaccines for airborne pathogens, creating better sensors and filters for dangerous chemicals. Throughout, the NRC report lamented a lack of coordination among federal agencies and the absence of a "coherent overall strategy" to "harness the strengths of the U.S. science and engineering communities, and direct them most appropriately toward critical goals, both short-term and long."

The Pentagon announced a new anthrax vaccination policy, which reversed a plan by the Clinton administration to immunize all 2.4 million men and women in the military. Factors contributing to the Pentagon's decision were limited supplies, the cumbersome requirement of six shots spread over eighteen months (with a yearly booster), and the development of a new generation of vaccines.

The revised scheme limited inoculations to soldiers who would be deployed for more than fifteen days to areas that held a "higher risk" of biological attack—the Middle East and the Korean peninsula. The policy also committed to stockpiling 40 percent to half of the vaccine manufactured for the Pentagon for civilian use. Police officers, firefighters, rescue crews, and other "first responders" would receive shots only after expo-

sure to anthrax. The Pentagon intended resuming limited military vaccinations in June.

William Winkenwerder Jr., the assistant defense secretary for health
affairs, explained, "We remain very committed to the goal of protecting
all forces from anthrax through a variety of approaches, including intelligence, surveillance, protective clothing, antibiotics and other countermeasures. We are committed long-term to the notion of a new vaccine."
He said "roughly half" of the vaccine produced by BioPort, the nation's
only anthrax vaccine supplier, was destined for civilian use, either through
the Department of Health and Human Services or the Office of Homeland
Defense.

BioPort had been purchased four years earlier for nearly $25 million
by a group of private investors, including executives who had worked at
the plant under Michigan ownership. In 1997 the Michigan Biological
Products Institute in Lansing had put the vaccine up for bids after wrangles
with the FDA over quality control. After BioPort signed a contract with
the DoD the following year, it quickly used up the old Lansing stock. In
November 1999, the FDA approved BioPort's new vaccine and the price
per dosage rose from $4.36 to $10.64. It was continuing to rise. BioPort
president Bob Kramer said, "We're not aware yet of any policy decisions
that have been made regarding first responders. We stand prepared today
to increase our production based on policy requirements." There was some
question whether civilian emergency personnel should be vaccinated or
simply use antibiotics.

In March, the Institute of Medicine had released a report endorsing
the vaccine's safety, apparently answering complaints first raised when
veterans complained of illness after receiving shots during the Persian Gulf
War. Since the program's inception in 1997, several hundred servicemen
and servicewomen have refused to take the shots, and about one hundred
have been court-martialed for this refusal. Winkenwerder said the new
policy "is mandatory" for those who qualify.

In all, the vaccine had already been given to a half-million servicemen.
In the months to come highly trained pilots and crews in the National
Guard and Air Force Reserve would began to leave the military because
of the Pentagon's new anthrax vaccine. The General Accounting Office
(GAO) had reported adverse reactions to the vaccine at double the rate
claimed by BioPort Corp. "While many factors can and do influence an

individual's decision to participate in the military, a significant number of pilot and air crew members cited the required mandatory anthrax immunization as a key reason for reducing their participation or leaving the military altogether in 2000," the GAO said.

"Anthrax is a serious threat that our soldiers might face on the battlefield. At the same time, this vaccine has been controversial, and it has caused serious reactions in some individuals," Rep. Dan Burton, chairman of the House Government Reform Committee, would report. No research was available on the possible effects of the vaccine on older people, children, and pregnant women.

By July 2000, there had been cases of adverse reactions to the vaccine—joint pain, nausea, swelling, muscle spasms, and spinal pain. Only a month after the first anthrax letter, the BioPort contract had been in jeopardy. Then the FDA granted its long-delayed approval and the cost of one dose of vaccine climbed from $10.64 to $90.

Dr. Meryl Nass said, "The existing vaccine may or may not be effective. The one human study ever done on any anthrax vaccine was about 70 percent effective at preventing anthrax infections. The current vaccine's effectiveness, though 95 percent effective in monkeys, has not been tested in humans." Doxycycline and ciprofloxacin prevent anthrax in 80 to 90 percent of a small number of monkeys, but they may respond better than humans.

The Army understood the shortcomings of the anthrax vaccine, acknowledging the existing formulation was "highly reactogenic" and "may not be protective against all strains of the anthrax bacillus." A handful of patients had suffered serious reactions after taking the shots, including brain damage and death. Winkenwerder said while vaccinations could begin almost immediately, individuals and even quick-reaction forces like the Marine and airborne divisions would not start the six-shot course of inoculations until they were forty-five days from deployment.

Should they be deployed, they would continue injections for the next eighteen months whether overseas or not. The policy would directly affect reserve pilots regularly sent to the Middle East. In the past few years, many of those pilots had led protests against the vaccine. Officials searched for ways to reduce the number of shots to four, or even three. The Institute's Anna Johnson-Winegar, a civilian Army official who understood how devastating the anthrax bacillus could be, had very little experience with the vaccine. Only a small number of researchers at the Institute had been given it and they had shown no side effects.

Tensions between the U.S. and Iraq were heating up. The Amerithrax case put everyone in mind of their presumed stocks of chemical and biological weapons. However, during the Gulf War Iraqi warheads had detonated on impact and were poorly designed for disseminating biowarfare agents. The U.S. did not know Iraq possessed new warhead designs. It did know Iraq could use warplanes or helicopters to spray germ agents. The best way to neutralize the danger was by occupying Scud launching areas and seizing control of the skies.

The FBI had expended a lot of brain power and shoe leather trying to nab Amerithrax. They had conducted nearly six thousand interviews and served about seventeen hundred grand jury subpoenas in what FBI officials called "one of the largest operations in the Bureau's history."

Residents of Middle Eastern descent were questioned, and in some cases their homes raided by agents. Labs and pharmaceutical research facilities with the probable ability to create anthrax were looked over. Since autumn 2001, fifty U.S. bioweapons experts had been targeted for intense scrutiny and their homes and offices searched. They had been ordered to take polygraph tests and a few had been under open or covert surveillance.

"The pool of suspects contains hundreds more, including researchers of biopesticides, biopharmaceuticals, and veterinary products," said one federal investigator. "Remember, it doesn't have to be a top scientist. It could just be a good bench technician."

But the whispers that swept the scientific community concerned only one particular American bioweapons expert. FBI agents in protective gloves were about to search a former Army researcher's home in Maryland.

STRAIN 27

Anthrax Search

ON TUESDAY, JUNE 25, 2002, the FBI conducted a high-profile search. Such searches were common in the Amerithrax probe. Agents had searched apartments before, but never with so much media attention. For months, Dr. Steven J. Hatfill, a former Army researcher, had been extensively discussed by scientists, journalists, and other professionals speculating about possible domestic suspects in the anthrax investigation.

Since late January and early February, biowarfare experts in and out of government had spoken quietly (and some not so quietly) of Dr. Hatfill as fitting their profile of the anthrax attacker. Hatfill's bigger-than-life personality, and remarks he had made about the dangers of biological attacks against the U.S., made him suspicious. The previous fall Hatfill found himself on a long list of those questioned by federal authorities.

Private experts, chief among them Barbara Hatch Rosenberg, a bioweapons authority, decided Amerithrax was a federal insider. She and others believed that Amerithrax was someone who meant to warn the nation of the dangers of biological terrorism. Publicly she named no one, and though the FBI had no clear suspects at the time, Hatfill's name circulated in the scientific community on a shorter and shorter list.

More and more, the agency agreed with the view that the culprit was probably a domestic biological expert worried enough about the nation's vulnerability to germ weapons to send anthrax spores to the media, not to kill, but to alert the nation to a looming threat.

The big, muscular, and mustached virus expert was known around Washington as an outspoken advocate of bolstering germ defenses and as an opponent to the Biological and Toxic Weapons Convention. He publicly demonstrated how easily bioweapons could be created. Terrorists were the biggest threat, he suggested, not secret CIA projects. Several days after Dr. Rosenberg met with the FBI, agents approached him again and asked if they could examine his apartment and "swab the walls for anthrax spores." Hatfill showed surprise at the request, but consented to the brief search.

Agents said Hatfill had been straightforward answering questions but investigators were unwilling to declare him cleared of any suspicion because of intriguing circumstances of his past. A spokesman for the FBI, Peter Christopher Murray, said, "We are unaware of any FBI employee who has named a suspect in the anthrax deaths investigation."

According to FBI sources, Hatfill had failed questions on a polygraph examination he took the previous August at the Washington field office while applying for a job with the CIA. Hatfill seemed to fancy himself a James Bond. The post required a high-level security clearance and he must have known that it would reveal any padding of his military and academic career. The CIA lie detector test generated ambiguous results about his time in Africa and led the CIA to refuse him top secret clearance for certain projects. His security badges were lifted and he was assigned a low-level security clearance on one project. On August 23, 2001, just before the first anthrax mailings, the government formally suspended Dr. Hatfill's security clearance. Pending review, his basic-level secret clearance had also been suspended. This made agents wonder. Had he become embittered enough to do something against his own country?

But the FBI underscored both publicly and in private meetings that Hatfill was not a suspect in the case. The term "suspect" carried special legal meaning among FBI agents and federal prosecutors. Dr. Hatfill was to them just a "person of interest."

TV news crews flew above the Detrick Plaza Apartments in Frederick, Maryland. Below they saw green lawns and three-story redbrick complexes. The area was also the home of the American Type Culture Collection and the Institute, the Army's biodefense laboratories. Two investigators in Hazmat suits with respirators were at the front door of an apartment washing some equipment in a basin full of detergent. One female agent was traipsing in and out with a mask over her nose and mouth. She had been conducting anthrax swab tests on the apartment. In front of the complex, the feds had cordoned off the street abutting the Institute, where Hatfill used to work.

They stopped residents returning to their apartments and asked for ID before permitting them any further. Agents carted out videotapes, and six full black plastic garbage bags of other items. "I don't know what all the results of the search were," one agent said, "but I can tell you there were no hazardous materials found in the apartment. I don't know how much in advance he knew about the search, but he has been cooperating with us fully all along." Because the bags were plastic there was probably no anthrax inside. "You would never put anything biological in a plastic bag," said Candice DeLong, "because the heat could change the chemicals." The agents packed their treasures in the truck and left.

Hatfill had invited agents to search his Frederick apartment without a warrant and so they did. No traces of anthrax were detected. But in recent weeks, investigators' interest in Hatfill had heightened. They wouldn't say why.

"We're obviously doing things related to him that we're not doing with others," one law enforcement official said. "He is obviously of more interest to us than others on the list at this point."

Dr. Hatfill had early on been identified as one of twenty to thirty scientists with the knowledge and opportunity to be Amerithrax. The FBI first contacted Hatfill in October. The first voluntary search had been in February when agents used a high-tech vacuum on his car. As in this search, they rooted out no trace of anthrax, but unlike this search there had been no media attention.

When agents had interviewed Hatfill briefly then, they had told him that the agency was offering polygraph tests to a number of other scientists. Lie detector tests were being conducted at Dugway Proving Ground in Utah where researchers had been developing a powdered form of anthrax for testing biological defense systems. Small quantities of anthrax were routinely produced at Dugway, then shipped to the Institute in paste form for irradiation and returned. Though Hatfill had worked at the Institute only from September 1997 until September 1999, he had retained access to labs there and at Dugway until March 2001.

He had already been doing related research on contract at Science Applications International Corp., a private-sector lab defense contractor in McLean, Virginia, when his Institute grant expired. At SAIC he worked to detail the risks of biological and chemical attacks and gave presentations to employees of the U.S. military, intelligence, and other agencies.

SAIC laid Dr. Hatfill off on March 2 after reporters pursued him and because he was being investigated by the FBI. Hatfill formally left the Department of Defense–contracted firm two days later. SAIC officials would only say Hatfill was let go because of matters unrelated to anthrax. "Agents questioned targets at their places of employment to intimidate their employers and get them to fire them," wrote FBI expert Ronald Kessler. Kessler compared such harassment tactics—including phone calls, threats, and rumors—to those used by the KGB in Russia and the Stasi in East Germany.

Meanwhile, Hatfill denied any role in the anthrax mailings and expressed contempt for those who raised questions publicly linking him to the mailings. At the time he complained by phone to the *Baltimore Sun* that he had been fired from his job at a federal contractor because of incessant questioning by reporters and after a reporter questioned senior managers about him. "I've been in this field for a number of years," he said, "working until three o'clock in the morning, trying to counter this type of weapon of mass destruction, and, sir, my career is over at this time."

Hatfill had spoken with *New York Times* reporters in late May. "I've got a letter from the FBI that says I'm not a suspect and never was," he said. "I just got caught up in the normal screening they were doing, because of the nature of my job." Protesting his innocence, he rankled at the private experts who had pursued him as a suspect and castigated the FBI as having little or no "idea what they were doing." In early June, before his name emerged publicly in the Amerithrax case, he refused to show a *Times* reporter the FBI letter. "Why should I?" he snapped. "My reputation is intact. I was caught up in the first round of the investigation—so what?"

On June 26, the day after they searched his apartment, agents located and searched a mini storage unit Hatfill had rented downtown in the north-central Florida city of Ocala. An NBC affiliate and the *Hartford Courant* reported the unit was refrigerated. Hatfill had stored some of his belongings there after his parents, Norman and Shirley Hatfill, sold their thoroughbred horse stud farm, Mekamy Oaks, in 1999. The farm was about 12 miles west of Ocala and about 230 miles northwest of the Atlantic Coast city of Boca Raton. Ocala policemen assisted the FBI.

"They gave us a call and told me they were going to be serving a search warrant there," said Ocala police chief Andy Krietemeyer. Four cars, including a Chevy Suburban with tinted windows, pulled up to the storage unit. Several workers in Hazmat gear piled out and spent the day searching the unit. A Marion County sheriff's bomb squad helped agents transfer two suitcases and at least two boxes to the van. As they had at the Detrick Plaza, probers swabbed air ducts for anthrax spores. No trace of anthrax was found at either site.

Later in the day, Senator Daschle said, "I have asked for another briefing by the FBI on the anthrax investigation. I don't know if one has actually been set yet. I hope it has, because I have a lot of questions." Law enforcement officials again insisted that Dr. Hatfill wasn't a suspect in the anthrax killings.

Six days earlier, the FBI had obtained a copy of a top secret report from a defense contractor. Just after a series of hoax anthrax mailings in February 1999, Hatfill commissioned a classified report on how anthrax might be sent through the mail. At the time Hatfill was still an SAIC contract-worker, making $150,000 a year, three times what the Institute had paid him.

Under instructions from the CIA, Hatfill and another research scientist, Joseph Soukup, detailed the possible consequences of a hypothetical anthrax attack by mail. The study told how such attacks could be carried out. The details included an anthrax-by-mail scenario—2.5 grams of *Bacillus globigii*, a simulated form of anthrax, sent through the mail in a standard business envelope to be opened in an office environment. The account suggested a spoonful in an envelope—about 2.5 grams of anthrax—the amount used in the actual anthrax mailings. That had really raised eyebrows at the FBI and fueled widespread speculation among scientists that Hatfill fit the Amerithrax profile.

Hatfill did not work on the intelligence and wasn't alone in authorizing the study. According to Ben Haddad, a spokesman for SAIC, the work was done by bioterrorism expert Bill Patrick, whom Hatfill listed under personal and scientific references on his resume. Patrick was the "father" of a process for making a sophisticated form of anthrax. Haddad told the press that the study had been "misconstrued" and was "not about sending anthrax through the mail." Most of the report dealt with decontamination after large attacks.

The day after the highly publicized searches of Hatfill's apartment and Florida storage unit, the *Baltimore Sun* revealed more information about the report that spookily foreshadowed the mailborne attacks. Haddad confirmed that commissioning a study on the consequences of a hypothetical anthrax attack "in general, would not be an out-of-the-norm sort of request." Hatfill and Soukup commissioned the report internally. Hatfill's collaborator, Soukup, still worked at SAIC.

One item that pointed to Dr. Hatfill as *not* being the FBI's man was that he worked with viruses, not bacteria. Viruses are small infectious organisms that need a living cell in order to reproduce. They are usually fragments of RNA (ribonucleic acid) with no metabolism of their own. After multiplying and killing cells of a living animal, they escape through body fluids, water, or air to the cells of other hosts. The viruses of influenza are known for incessantly changing. Viruses cause AIDS, food poisoning, and the common cold and do not respond to antibiotics.

On Thursday, June 27, the FBI reported it was now focusing on roughly thirty U.S. biological warfare experts. They had searched twenty-five homes and apartments of researchers and scientists in April, May, and June. All, including Dr. Hatfill's, had been done with the owner's consent. The FBI was still administering polygraphs to more than two hundred current and former employees of the Institute and of Dugway Proving Ground. In its search for a domestic terrorist, the FBI had also questioned scientists with biological knowledge at Pine Bluff Arsenal in Arkansas and the Salk Center in Swiftwater, Pennsylvania. Law enforcement agents had issued hundreds of subpoenas nationwide and had only begun sifting through thousands of documents.

Meanwhile the spotlight remained on the "person of interest." Apparently Hatfill had some enemies in the biowarfare family. He also had some powerful friends. Bill Patrick was his mentor. Hatfill had been highly recommended to Louisiana State University by two very highly placed friends, David Franz and David Huxsoll, former commanders of the Institute. Within three days LSU would hire him as the new associate director of its National Center for Biomedical Research and Training.

Huxsoll was currently director of Plum Island Animal Disease Center, a U.S. Department of Agriculture research facility off the coast of North Fork in Long Island Sound. In December 2001, there had been a three-hour power failure on the site, popularly known as "Anthrax Island," and all three backup generators had failed. There had been concern over escaping pathogens. Right after the blackout, the facility was run by replacement workers during a five-month strike.

Anthrax Island had for decades figured in Soviet intelligence reports. Dr. Alibek knew all about it. During World War II, Plum Island was used to test biological agents. It was eventually turned into a quarantine center for imported animals and food products, accessible only by ferry. The secluded island was supposedly used to study exotic animal illnesses, including foot-and-mouth disease. No animals leave the island alive.

Officials deny that they have ever studied anthrax on Anthrax Island in spite of the popular nickname. FBI agents asked Dr. Hatfill, a former infectious-disease center specialist, if he had ever been there or worked there and he said no.

However, there was in existence a bona fide "Anthrax Island," an isle more fearsome than Plum Island or the U.K.'s Gruinard Island, still seething with anthrax after fifty years. The Soviets' Anthrax Island was a hot zone of the deadly anthrax from Compound 19 that had been tested unknowingly by the dead of Sverdlovsk. It was arguably the most deadly spot in the world and refining a product that would make Amerithrax's anthrax look tame by comparison.

STRAIN 28

Anthrax Island

SVERDLOVSK'S ANTHRAX, AS you know, was enough to destroy the world's people many times over. The Russians had carefully hidden it away from Sverdlovsk—seventeen hundred miles away at Zima, near Irkutsk. One day Army scientists were ordered to dispose of Compound 19's powder. But how? They had made the spores too hardy, too nearly indestructible. They packed the stainless steel canisters of the lethal pink powder on two dozen rail cars and sent them rumbling across the Russian and Kazakh Republics to isolated Vozrozhdeniye Island. Translated from Russian, *Vozrozhdeniye* meant "Rebirth" or "Resurrection" or "Renaissance." The island was a rebirth of sorts, at least for Strain 836.

Strain 836, the most virulent and vicious strain of anthrax (of dozens purposely developed) ever known to man had survived years in the darkness and filth of the Kirov sewers and at Compound 19 had proved to be an unusually tough spore. The Kirov anthrax refined at Sverdlovsk was becoming even more lethal. The spores were awakening to new strength. In 1987, Strain 836, a pathogen created in the Soviet Union's first anthrax factory, would be confirmed on bleak Rebirth Island.

Rebirth Island was a dismal, tear-shaped speck in the midst of a rubber-cement sea. It bobbed fifty miles off the Kazakh shoreline and twenty-three hundred miles south of Moscow. Scientists and technicians took a one-and-a-half-hour flight by MI-8 helicopter from the coastal town of Aralsk to the island. The shrinking Aral Sea divided the Central Asian countries of Uzbekistan and Kazakhstan. Two decades earlier Soviet planners had diverted the Aral's river sources into concrete irrigation canals. The sea silted over with clouds of toxic salts. The fourth largest inland sea began to shrink, while Rebirth Island expanded from seventy-seven square miles to ten times that size.

The Soviets made Rebirth Island their largest open-air bioweapons testing site. Rebirth Island, under control of the Fifteenth Directorate, became Hell's Island. In the summer it was 140 degrees Fahrenheit. The wind always blew south. Hot winds constantly blew dust off the desert test range. Like the dust at Ground Zero, it got in everyone's eyes, hair, clothes, and food.

The technical base (well guarded by a four-hundred-man battalion) was hidden a mile from town behind a barbed wire fence. One hundred and fifty scientists and soldiers lived there in six rundown buildings—scientific headquarters. Collectively, the dusty settlement and labs and test site were known as Aralsk-7. Facilities for the soldiers were a three-story housing compound on the northern part of the island, a mile from the test range. There were shelters for thousands of test animals—monkeys, horses, donkeys, sheep, rodents, rabbits, and guinea pigs.

They held tests after dark on the eighty-square-mile test range, hoping the rising sun would extinguish any ambient bacteria. Condemned hamadryas baboons were tethered to parallel rows of telephone poles evenly spaced a kilometer apart. The baboons cost five to seven hundred dollars apiece and a single experiment used nearly one hundred of them. Anthrax bomblets, small metal spheres, were exploded three miles upwind.

After a dark, yellowish cloud settled over the baboons, soldiers in protective suits collected the dead and dying animals and transported them to a holding unit for postmortems. At the site, thousands of corpses were burned and the ashes buried in mass graves. Rebirth Island became the largest burial ground of weapons-grade anthrax in the world.

Tons of Strain 836 (code-named L3 and L4) were dumped, sprayed, and detonated over Rebirth Island until the stagnant sea was a marshland of sand and cement. Birds that flew over dropped from the sky until no more birds flew over the island. As the sea all around shrunk, the island grew closer to the mainland. What would the still-deadly anthrax do to the unknowing people on land?

Of course, the Soviets tried to disinfect the island after each test. They could not. They sealed the bacteria from the test range into stainless steel canisters. At the edge of the old test range, soldiers poured bleach into them to decontaminate the deadly pink powder. Then they dug eleven huge pits and poured the sludge into the ground, burying the decontaminated spores. Analysis of soil samples from over half the anthrax burial pits on Vozrozhdeniye Island revealed that bleach-soaked anthrax spores buried there a decade earlier were still thriving and dangerous. Contamination spread into the sea. In 1972, a fishing boat went missing from the mainland. It was found drifting much later, all onboard dead from plague germs and anthrax contamination. The men had sailed too close. There was no vaccine effective against this island toxin—Strain 836, which had made its long pilgrimage from Kirov to Sverdlovsk to Rebirth Island.

Strain 836 had journeyed to a city of germs and death so shrouded in furtiveness the Soviets listed it only as a post office box number in the remote northeastern part of Kazakhstan's Central Asian steppes. The complex owed its very existence to the Sverdlovsk accident. After the disaster, production at Compound 19 stopped because of growing Western demands to inspect the facility. Of the three facilities in Russia designated as anthrax production centers in case of war, Sverdlovsk had been the only active production facility. Penza and Kurgan were only standbys, awaiting orders to activate the strains of anthrax in their vaults. In 1981 Brezhnev signed a secret decree relocating all biological weapons–making equipment and materials from Sverdlovsk.

In order to fill the production gap created by the now-discredited anthrax plant in the Urals, the Soviets upgraded Stepnogorsk, a small biological research facility a thousand miles from Moscow. In 1982, Soviet slave labor swiftly constructed a huge plant in the remote desert to develop and manufacture an improved, more deadly variant of anthrax.

The next year, sixty-five army technicians and scientists from Sverdlovsk, fearful of further contamination, arrived in Kazakhstan. The Stepnogorsk Scientific Experimental and Production Base, one of six production facilities managed by the Fifteenth Directorate of the Soviet Ministry of Defense, was capable of producing nearly ten tons of anthrax a day. Within five years, its combined production capacity reached nearly five thousand tons a year. Equipped for large-scale cultivation, Stepnogorsk generated thousands of tons of anthrax, plague, and smallpox for use in missiles and other weapons.

Stepnogorsk's pride was Strain 836, the most virulent and powerful of the dozens of anthrax strains investigated as weapons over the years by army scientists. A photo taken on May Day 1985 at Stepnogorsk showed the anthrax developers and their children holding balloons and celebrating like happy employees anywhere. Dr. Ken Alibek recalled that the following year a technician was infected with anthrax in a lab that was supposed to be sterile. He had an abrasion on his neck, one of the most dangerous places to contract cutaneous anthrax in the body.

They first treated the patient with streptomycin and penicillin, but a painful swelling erupted on his chest and spread over his body, making it increasingly difficult for him to breathe. Within three days, death seemed inevitable. In a final effort to save his life, they injected him with an abnormally high dose of antibiotics. "If treated with high doses of penicillin into the bloodstream at short intervals for a week to ten days before the first toxins are released, survival is 100 percent," said Alibek. The shock dose succeeded and the technician recovered.

During the last half of the twentieth century, as anthrax as a weapon of mass destruction began to be increasingly stockpiled by nations and terrorists, the Russians engineered anthrax strains resistant to penicillin, doxycycline, and other antibiotics. They did this by splicing in genes from naturally resistant strains of bacteria, such as *E. coli*, the common intestinal bacterium.

Stepnogorsk's Strain 836 was made three times as strong and lethal as Sverdlovsk's anthrax. During that outbreak, an aggressive treatment of penicillin, anti-anthrax globulin, cephalosporin, chloramphenicol, and corticosteroids; hydration; and artificial respiration had saved fifteen lives. The Russians not only made Strain 836 resistant to heat and cold, but developed variants that would defeat antibiotics.

It would take only five kilograms of the anthrax 836 developed at the Kazakhstan base to infect 50 percent of people living in a square kilometer or territory. The Sverdlovsk strain had needed at least fifteen kilograms to achieve the same results. Only after Strain 836 had been successfully tested on bleak Rebirth Island in 1987, did Moscow finally take Sverdlovsk off the roster of anthrax production plants.

Alibek found a more efficient way to produce the anthrax mutated by

Kirov's sewer rats and refined at Sverdlovsk and Rebirth Island. Alibek, the mastermind for decades behind Russia's experiments with bioterrorism, invented the world's most powerful anthrax. The quiet-spoken biologist had graduated from the military faculty of the Tomsk Medical Institute in 1975, where he majored in infectious diseases and epidemiology. He held Ph.D.'s in microbiology, for research and development of plague and tularemia biological weapons, and in biotechnology, for developing the technology to manufacture anthrax bioweapons on an industrial scale. Alibek's strain needed fewer spores to be effective, and delivered "more bang for the buck." His powdered and liquid formulations of anthrax were many times as lethal as the anthrax that was produced at Kirov, Sverdlovsk, *and* Rebirth Island. Alibek described his type of anthrax to author Richard Preston as being "an amber-gray powder, finer than bath talc, with smooth, creamy, fluffy particles that tend to fly apart and vanish into the air." Alibek said the particles stick to lungs like glue, just as Amerithrax's did.

Just as Fort Detrick was known by biowarfare intimates as "the Institute," Biopreparat, which ran Stepnogorsk, was known as "the Concern." Alibek called Biopreparat "the darkest conspiracy of the cold war, a network so secret that its members could not be told what colleagues in other parts of the organization were doing or where." The Concern was a civilian agency created in 1973. Its stated mission was developing vaccines, biopesticides, and lab equipment, but this was only a cover for weapons work. Joining the Concern in 1975, he was deputy chief of the agency from 1988 to 1992.

Encircled by gray walls and electric fences, Stepnogorsk presented a skyline of strange buildings and towers. The little city sat in an area denuded of all vegetation, with wide spaces between the buildings. Everything was kept open and clear so no spy could hide behind anything. And they had learned a lesson from the Sverdlovsk disaster. There was no foliage. Hosing down contaminated shrubs had caused new infections in Sverdlovsk. And Stepnogorsk was isolated from highly populated areas.

Zone 2 was the first biosafety enclosure—storage vaults, rows of seed, and industrial reactors, sealed lab windows hiding hooded technicians. The enormous autoclave in Building 221 was used to sterilize nutrient media and for the deactivation of anthrax cultures. Ten twenty-ton fermentation vats, towering four stories high and each holding twenty thousand liters of fluid, filled a building two football fields long. The vessels could brew three hundred tons of anthrax spores in a production cycle of 220 days, enough to fill many ICBMs. Building 221 alone produced more than enough anthrax to kill America's entire population.

The foreground view from Building 221, the main production site, was of a building housing aerosol explosive chambers and bunkers for filling and assembling biological munitions. Directly behind, framed by large open spaces, stood an anthrax drying facility. By the late 1980s the Concern, with a budget of one billion dollars, employed a workforce of forty thousand scientists, technicians, and support staff. Nine thousand scientists with substantial bioweapons expertise conducted experiments on roughly fifty different pathogens.

At the main Kazakhstan facility and eight satellite labs they stored eighty strains of anthrax, plague, smallpox, and cholera. They collected brucellosis and tularemia bacteria and smallpox, Marburg, and Ebola viruses. Some trials blended different agents to create superbugs or mask symptoms. Biopreparat had once employed seven hundred scientists and run fifty labs and production sites throughout the former Soviet Union. The Ministry of Defense ran four other facilities devoted to developing bioweapons. Four of those labs developed anti-crop and anti-animal agents for warfare.

At the viral research site called Vector (the Russian State Research Center of Virology and Biotechnology) hundreds of deadly genetically altered bacterial strains were stored in small glass flasks. Inside refrigerated vaults hundreds of tiny vials of freeze-dried bacteria stood on metal trays in rows. This Siberian "Museum of Cultures" contained more than one hundred varieties of smallpox, Marburg, and Ebola viruses and highly virulent plague bacteria. Vector stood in a forest clearing on the southern outskirts of Koltsovo, "an abandoned village transformed into a closed city," near Novosibirsk, Siberia. Ken Alibek, who went to Koltsovo in December 1987, proclaimed Vector the biggest, most sophisticated facility ever to refine viruses for weapons. Vector was adjacent to a huge civilian biotechnological plant, "Progress," which produced herbicides and ethanol.

Building 1 at Vector was a giant eight-story-high glass biocontainment facility designed for lab experiments with contagious viruses. It towered over all the other heavily insulated buildings and labs. Floors were divided according to pathogens. The second floor was for plague. Where the Americans had failed to produce an aerosolized plague microbe that could survive outside the lab, the Soviets had created a new, genetically improved version of the Black Death, a superbug that was resistant to heat, cold, and antibiotics. The third floor was for tularemia and upper levels were reserved for anthrax, glanders and melioidosis, and so on. Dozens of new lab and production buildings were under construction, but adequate security was becoming a problem.

Gorbachev's Five-Year Plan had funded Vector's 360-liter viral reactor, assembled by Biopreparat in western Russia to produce smallpox. In Building 6, well guarded by security police, was a smallpox laboratory, a huge aerosol test chamber, and high-containment labs where research on other exotic agents was being conducted. Buildings 6 and 6A were two adjacent four-story brick buildings housing work on Marburg and other deadly viruses.

Building 600 housed a fifty-foot-high aerosol test chamber, the Soviets' largest indoor testing facility, where they experimented with new strains of anthrax. The walls were crisscrossed with pipes delivering fresh air to workers' space suits. Grounding strips prevented static electricity buildup, which would cause accidental explosions in rooms where germ bombs and bomblets were tested. Glossy floors of epoxy eased decontamination. Underground bunkers with seven-foot-thick walls protected and stored the finished product. Inside underground filing rooms, anthrax was filtered into warheads and other delivery systems.

The collapse of the Soviet Union left behind tens of thousands of nuclear, chemical, and biological weapons and the scientists who knew how to make them. Many of its researchers were lured overseas. In 1997 Iranians visited Obolensk, the civilian-run secret State Research Center for Applied Microbiology in Russia, and tried to recruit biologists. The Iranians were interested in bioweapons for use against people, crops, and livestock. As in South Africa they were lusting after genetically engineered agents to kill or cripple selectively by race or gender. Between 1990 and 1996, Obolensk lost 54 percent of its staff to this brain drain and security deteriorated.

The U.S. learned of a new super anthrax from a 1995 conference in Great Britain. Obolensk scientists Andrei Pomerantsev and Nikolai A. Staritsin published a journal article about how they had altered anthrax's

DNA to create a super vaccine-resistant strain. They had genetically engineered anthrax by inserting virulence genes from *Bacillus cereus*, a bacterium that attacks blood cells but normally does not cause lethal disease
in humans, into anthrax microbes. Their cover story was this: "The Russian strains of *Bacillus anthracis* and *Bacillus cereus*," Staritsin said, "were
closely related and often found in soil of the same proximity. If the two
organisms naturally exchanged genes without any external intervention
Russian scientists needed to know what the result might be." A natural
gene exchange was of course a lie. What was true was that even exposed
test animals given Russia's own anthrax vaccine died when exposed to this
new strain.

Over the last eight years American officials had arranged generous
grants for Obolensk, more than twenty million dollars' worth. They were
after a sample of super anthrax to study, but arrangements always fell apart
at the last minute. The super anthrax was locked in an old Soviet bioweapons lab in the rural Serpukhov district a two-hour drive from Moscow.

In 1998, the Pentagon paid $325,000 to Russia to decipher the strain's
genetic sequence. The sequencing was done by spring 2002, but U.S. scientists still weren't provided with the data. The U.S. wanted a sample to
improve its own vaccines, but the two nations had no formal agreement
on exchanging dangerous pathogens. Russian officials failed to fulfill two
contracts in which they'd agreed to provide a sample of the altered anthrax's infectious qualities in exchange for money. They stated the sequence was subject to "Catch-22" export rules and withheld a sample.
Both nations wanted to defend against bioweapons and agreed that the
altered anthrax must not be allowed to escape. "The anthrax issue will
resolve itself over time," said the Russians. Until then, "it's locked up
tight—thanks to the American assistance." U.S. aid had improved security
at Obolensk—one million dollars for fences, a concrete wall, electronic
sensors, professional guards, cameras, and vault upgrades. At eight satellite labs there were still small problems with security.

Officials had weighed the question of whether to reproduce the
vaccine-resistant strain of anthrax made by Russian scientists for several
years. Pentagon officials needed to know if the Michigan vaccine being
administered to millions of American soldiers was effective against such
genetically modified pathogens. Amerithrax's anthrax was virulent, but
susceptible to the usual antibiotics. The Obolensk strain might be vaccine-

resistant, but it was difficult to reproduce, not very stable, and tough to keep alive.

The Concern had been able to create antibiotic-resistant anthrax by using standard recombinant DNA techniques to splice in a gene for resistance from a common microbe like *E. coli*. Why hadn't Amerithrax used such an antibiotic-resistant strain if he wanted to maximize the loss of life? What was his motive if not to kill?

ON SUNDAY, JULY 14, 2002, the U.S. took its first faltering steps toward biodefense readiness. After so many decades of neglect, experts had thought such progress would take years. The Department of Health and Human Services began distributing more than $1 billion to the states and some cities to upgrade community public health preparedness. The start-up program required communities to begin developing infrastructure: chains of command, response patterns, and communications, a condition of receiving their share of funds. In addition to the HHS money was a plan to shift $1.9 billion in research funds from the NIH to a new Department of Homeland Security. A new $420 million program was to convert metropolitan Washington and three other urban areas into showcases for the best in biodefense.

"This is the first year, and in this context, it's going to take maybe five years to build the systems and capacity," said Thomas Milne, executive director of the National Association of County and City Health Officials. "What we'll get this year is an increment of improvement, not preparedness. Not yet." The future of all the programs depended on both the 2003 budget and the way bureaucratic lines of authority were redrawn in the proposed Homeland Security Department.

"We have practice with explosions or chemical spills," said epidemiologist D. A. Henderson, principal science adviser at HHS. "The biological has been more difficult because of the misapprehension that you could deal with it the same way as a chemical incident, when, in fact, these events could not have been more dissimilar."

A concerned John H. Marburger III, director of the White House Office of Science and Technology, drafted a memo to handle a problem that had been bothersome ever since Amerithrax had begun sending his deadly letters. Anthrax field tests—widely used since the previous fall's attacks—

give fast but often incorrect results, prompting authorities to shut down buildings prematurely and hand out unneeded antibiotics. Law enforcement and emergency response personnel used the test kits whenever white powder feared to be anthrax was discovered in buildings around Washington and across the country.

Marburger's memo was sent to 250 federal and state agencies and firefighters, police, and local authorities. The White House warned them that commercially available anthrax field tests were flawed and should not be used to determine possible exposure to the deadly pathogen. The Bush administration advised federal agencies to halt purchases and cancel pending contracts with companies that produce them.

"This equipment," Marburger said, "does not pass acceptable standards for effectiveness." The CDC and the FBI's study of field tests found that discrepancies in their levels of detection made them unreliable. Designed to detect the spore-forming bacterium *Bacillus anthracis*, their low thresholds of sensitivity also detected other forms of bacillus-type organisms. The White House wanted federal and state agencies to use the "gold standard" of test methods: the microbiological culture. A blood culture test is the most definitive way to determine actual anthrax infection. It involves placing a blood sample in a culture of nutrients and then waiting a day or two to see if an anthrax colony grows.

The Bush White House kept searching for high-tech methods for detecting bioweapons disseminated in highly populated areas. President Bush visited the Argonne National Laboratory in Illinois and saw equipment that applied light one million times brighter than an X ray. This equipment projected a beam that could identify an agent like anthrax in less than three minutes.

Shortly afterward, a twenty-six-year-old Czech-born graduate student at the University of Connecticut, became the first person charged under the zero-tolerance USA Patriot Act of 2001. Anyone possessing "any biological agent, toxin or delivery system" that was not reasonably justified by "bona fide research or other peaceful purpose" could face up to ten years in prison. In October 2001, the grad student had been transporting biological spores from a broken lab freezer when he came upon some samples collected thirty-five years earlier from an anthrax-infected cow. He moved two of the samples to a working freezer and forgot about it.

A few weeks later, a coworker observed the samples in his freezer space (right next to West Nile virus samples). He tipped off the FBI and the agency added his name to a computerized government watch list. He cooperated completely with the authorities and, to avoid prosecution, agreed to community work and some restrictions on his activities. Amerithrax had accomplished one thing—anthrax labs were turned into vaults as scientists rushed to destroy anthrax samples and other deadly microbes in their university deep freezers.

A company in Coralville, Iowa, provided scientists all over the world with made-to-order DNA. When some New York scientists used mail-order molecules to create polio viruses, this increased concerns about keeping a closer watch on the DNA synthesis industry. Since 1989, the U.S. and other nations had limited the risk of bioweapons by placing controls on their cultivation and shipment. Now, for the first time, potentially deadly viruses could be built from scratch.

In the meantime, Amerithrax and his deadly letters had not been forgotten. Where was the invisible enemy? Was anthrax in the cracks of the floor? On your hands as a fine powder? Already in your lungs or lurking in the air you're about to breathe? The very mail in your hands might be your executioner. Worst of all, there seemed no defense against the unseen and unheard. Wash and wash and hold your mail away from your face and worry: when would Amerithrax strike again? If not today, then soon, and if not then, why not? Had the police gotten too close? Had he been a victim of his own pathogen and died, classified as a pneumonia victim? Had he run out of his poison or was he secretly making more this very moment? While the nation held its breath, the damage already done had to be undone.

It would be costly and dangerous.

STRAIN 29

The Anthrax Tent

SPACE-SUITED MEN WERE vacuuming rats on a sunny July day. They had to. The rodents had been scurrying inside the quarantined Brentwood Mail Facility. Though rodents don't die from anthrax, they can carry it. For weeks Hazmat crews had been snaring the rats and cleansing them with an HEPA system. And they did it on a sunny day because the burning rays of the hot sun on any escaping spores provided a natural safety net. Ultraviolet rays vaporized many of the pathogens.

Rodent control was only one of sixty-nine different sanitization procedures the cleanup teams had put in place, including sampling, gas fumigation, HEPA filtration, and bleach disinfectant. They removed dust, equipment, heating and air-conditioning filters, and debris. Since the previous October, when tainted letters bound for Capitol Hill left spores behind in the Brentwood facility and forced the mail hub's closure, the contractors and EPA had conducted daily tests. Ten thousand samples told them contamination still swarmed inside. Resurrecting Brentwood would be the most ambitious and intricate fumigation ever attempted of any biohazardous building in the nation's history.

The cleanup required flawless coordination and perfect execution. In November, teams of chemical, civil, and mechanical engineers; chemists; and environmental response experts had begun learning all there was to know about Brentwood's interior and exterior. Sabre Oxidation Technologies of Odessa, Texas, and Ashland Inc. of Covington, Kentucky, had been contracted to handle the fumigation. Sabre and Ashland were also contracted to clean the Trenton, New Jersey, mail facility next. They were joined by a third partner, Shaw E & I, who had helped prepare for decontamination of the deserted Brentwood plant since October, 2001.

The men plugged all possible escape routes. During the Hart Building cleanup there had been no problems with leaks. But only 100,000 cubic feet of the Hart Building had had to be sealed to fumigate it with chlorine dioxide gas. Brentwood had some 17.5 million cubic feet to decontaminate. Over the last three months, workers had overlaid every outside window with foil-backed foam insulation. Crews had filled all visible exterior cracks and obstructed and insulated all roof openings with foil tape and poly-sheeting.

Late Thursday afternoon, July 25, the U.S. Postal Service conducted a last-minute press conference to detail its test to pump chlorine dioxide gas into Brentwood. Chlorine dioxide, with its familiar chlorine swimming pool smell, was the only proven technology available for truly eliminating anthrax from such a gigantic structure. They knew the gas would work. The same lethal letter that had infected the Hart Building had corrupted Brentwood, and since the gas had been effective against those spores, the strain was not chlorine dioxide–resistant.

Moon-suited technicians entered an impromptu air lock of tunnels and plastic curtains to take samples and double-check the interior seals. Banks of perpetually blazing sodium-vapor lights lit their way and cast long shadows in the vast auditorium. Every floor, wall, and ceiling crack had been injected with silicone caulking or expanding foam sealant. The men had plugged roof cracks, taped over two hundred skylights, occluded vent openings and utility conduits, and stopped up all floor drains and pipe entrances. A hundred loading-dock doors had been framed and wrapped with heavy poly-sheeting.

The interior of the Brentwood plant was spookily empty. No postal employee had worked in the building since its closure on the day Thomas Morris died soon after calling for help on the phone. Mail had been repackaged and removed for irradiation. Rolling stock, mail trays and bins, even vending machines had been carted away for sanitization. Mail-processing equipment had been wiped down with a solution of chlorine bleach. Even trash was decontaminated. But sterilize as they did, spores still floated invisibly and lazily above in the dazzling lights. Sometimes they settled atop three gigantic letter-sorting machines. One of the three, No. 17, had sorted the anthrax-tainted letters Amerithrax had posted to members of Congress. To be doubly certain of eradicating the spores, the crew had erected a 29,000-cubic-foot tent over all three monster machines. The tent created a fumigating plant within a fumigating plant.

On Friday, at 10:00 A.M. sharp, the House Government Reform subcommittee convened a public hearing to debate the following week's fumigation test. One hundred and forty interested spectators showed up at Gallaudet University's Kellogg Conference. Many were postal workers reluctant to return to the infected mail facility. Christine Armstrong, a twenty-nine-year Brentwood veteran, said she would not return when the plant reopened no matter what precautions were instituted. "Who would want to go back in there?" said Armstrong, who had been transferred to a Capitol Heights postal plant the previous fall. "We have been treated unfairly from the get-go, and they have no idea what we're going through."

"Everyone's a little distrustful about going back," said Pat Johnson, president of the American Postal Workers Union, which represented fifteen hundred Brentwood employees out of a total of twenty-five hundred. "Because the employees have not been regularly briefed about the progress and procedures [of the decontamination process], they are less confident of the results," said Roy Braunstein, the union's legislative director. Some postal workers wanted the low-slung brick building leveled. Leaving it as a sealed hot spot would be unfair to the neighborhood.

"The amount of chemicals in play is very limited," reassured Peter LaPorte, director of emergency management for the District, "but this will serve as a very good test run for us." Eleanor Holmes Norton (D-DC), representing the subcommittee, urged them to take extra care. "We must take no chances at Brentwood," she said. "The Brentwood tragedy reminded us just how thin our knowledge of anthrax was . . . I say do it slow but just do it right."

Norton asked Thomas G. Day, vice president of engineering for the Postal Service, to guarantee the Postal Service would reimburse the city for expenses related to the decontamination and asked representatives from the federal CDC to undertake an epidemiological health study of Brentwood workers and the community surrounding the poisoned plant.

Postal and public health agency officials believed the Brentwood postal plant could be safely reopened several months after that summer's planned decontamination. One of the renovations would be a system to detect biological agents.

Over the weekend, the Department of Mental Health sent twenty workers door-to-door in the neighborhoods surrounding the Brentwood plant—T Street, 9th Street, V Street NE, Reed and Douglas Streets, Adams Street, Edgewood Terrace, and Rhode Island Avenue, among others. Their job was to inform residents of the forthcoming test. The Postal Service set up a toll-free information line to answer questions about Brentwood twenty-four hours a day. Guidelines developed by the National Response Team (NRT) were put in place.

On Sunday evening, D.C. police filled out a 282-yard safety zone around the building. They would remain there throughout the trial. "The test will take about twenty-four hours," explained Day. If the test was a success, a full-scale fumigation would be conducted later in the summer. Since all neighboring homes and businesses fell outside that perimeter no evacuations or road closures were necessary.

On Monday, July 29, the day of the preliminary test was, as hoped, a sunny day. Hot sun on any leaking chlorine dioxide would provide a natural safety net, neutralizing escaping gas instantly. (Though it takes longer, any gas leaks at night would still break down.) For more than seventy years, chlorine dioxide had been safely disinfecting the nation's water at nine hundred water treatment facilities. Nationwide, it was commonly used in sewage treatment systems and pulp making. "It is a chemical we understand well," Gilbert Gordon, professor of chemistry at Miami University in Ohio, said. "We know how to make it. We know how to destroy it."

Emergency management officials had carefully laid out the safest route for transporting the chemicals. On this day, only five pounds of the yellow-green chlorine dioxide would be used. Such a small amount wouldn't pose a health threat should it escape. Negative air pressure would keep the gas inside the building. While it was not a gas that would explode, at least not in the concentration being delivered, it was still too unstable to transport as a gas by truck. Instead a "precursor substance" was driven to the Brentwood parking lot in tanker trucks. Four chemicals—sodium, hypochlorite, hydrochloric acid, and sodium chlorite would be mixed at the site as needed.

A huge machine converted the chemicals to chlorine dioxide gas. The concentration would be kept far below volatile levels to reduce risk of fire. Pumping was slated to start at 9:00 A.M. But there was a delay while engineers operated remotely through the "dormant" heating system to keep a constant eighty degrees inside.

Using monitors, the engineers continuously adjusted humidity, temperature, and gas concentration. Officials had great faith that the equipment would allow them to maintain the proper relative humidity (a precise level of 75 percent without leaks), temperature (a constant seventy-five-degree minimum), and specific gas concentration levels needed for successful decontamination—750 parts per million for at least twelve hours.

Temperatures can vary, but humidity must not. That fact had been confirmed at the Hart Office Building. Humidity inside Brentwood now averaged almost 30 percent and would be raised by humidifiers as the time to inject the gas was reached. Around 10:45 A.M. the countdown began. Would the fumigation equipment be up to the task of decontaminating Brentwood and could they keep the spores and gas contained? Technicians called a halt. It would take them a little longer to get the temperature and humidity to the perfect points where the gas would be most effective.

Finally, at 12:18 P.M., the countdown began again.

At 12:20 P.M. gas began its work at a constant temperature and humidity level. The process would be repeated five times.

Chlorine dioxide gas began roaring into the deserted mail center. Funneled through a three-foot-wide main distribution pipe, it raced on to fourteen specially built "emitters" at key locations inside Brentwood. The gas, swirling to the building's center, twisted and curled into every nook. The tent that had been erected over the three mail-processing machines, including the one that had handled the anthrax letter that killed Morris and Curseen, concentrated the gas. The gas enveloped the three letter-sorters inside the tent, searching out spores with a vengeance. To expose all moving machine parts to gas, they started up the sorting machines electronically. The din could not be heard outside where men waited expectantly.

Gas hissed through a secondary pipe, three branching pleated metallic tubes side by side, which in turn branched upward from the main pipe into the sixteen "dormant" rooftop heating and air-conditioning systems.

It flowed through their vents into the building. High-speed fans, revved up by remote control, forced gas penetration to all areas. Chlorine dioxide saturated and penetrated the tough shells of the spores, which the humidity had softened. The warmth assisted the gas interaction with protein and DNA inside and killed the spores more efficiently than any human cleaning ever could.

Outside, Hazmat crews continually updated temperature and barometric pressure in the area. They studied data on wind currents and direction to estimate how any escaping gas might move. The FDA analyzed air outside the plant for traces of leakage. Ambient air monitoring provided detailed information regarding the concentrations of chemicals and contaminants inside and outside. So far everything was going as planned. It was hard to believe a little envelope that had touched another little envelope had caused all this.

A TAGA bus (an EPA van) circled the area monotonously, while the CDC took random air samples and analyzed them. The technicians squinted, even sniffed, trying to detect the slightest trace of chlorine dioxide. Electronic air-monitoring locations were set to automatically halt the test if concentrations up to twenty-five parts per billion sustained for fifteen seconds were detected outside the building.

Marcos Aquino, an EPA scene coordinator, told the press that the agency's air quality was calibrated to detect chlorine dioxide outside the building at levels as low as thirteen parts. This was two thousand times less than the levels that would have halted the operation.

People exposed to chlorine dioxide for eight hours at concentrations of one hundred parts per billion could experience, at worst, difficulty breathing, runny noses, rashes, and watery eyes. There should be no further ill effects. Air-quality monitors beyond the yellow tape surrounding the plant on Brentwood Road NE continued clicking. They had picked up no trace of leakage so far.

When the gassing was done nine hundred spore strips placed around the area (three thousand had been suggested earlier) would be removed and tested to see if the fumigation had worked. After the test decontamination the gas would be neutralized and removed.

Only harmless by-products should remain by then—natural substances such as water, salt water, and oxygen. They would be sealed in tanks and disposed of in accordance with EPA standards. This day's results would determine whether the Postal Service's fumigation equipment had been able to decontaminate the Brentwood building in a single round of gassing, the largest single fumigation ever attempted.

Theodore Gordon, senior deputy director of the D.C. Health Department, saw that everything was working perfectly. None of the chemical was found to have leaked. "We were just double-checking, making sure everything was in place and secure." After twelve hours the gas would be sucked out through scrubbers to render it harmless. Then the test strips throughout, on walls, ceilings, and floors, would be checked to see if any spores remained. Prior to final cleaning, sometime in the future, the building itself would be cleansed of all residual chlorine dioxide gas using a chemical scrubber to neutralize the remaining gas. Large-volume exhaust fans, air filters, and sensor equipment would also be employed. Once the interior was cleaned of gas, a secondary cleaning would be done. Ceilings, joists, and carpeting and any suspect areas would be vacuumed using HEPA vacuums to remove any dust.

Dust, collected and sealed in containers, would be disposed of. It would take several weeks to analyze the strips and full-scale tests would begin in late August. At that time they would place six thousand new sample strips. Another three thousand HEPA, swab wipe, and air samples had to be taken the next day.

The CDC would try to culture anthrax spores from these samples. If limited contamination was found, the contractors would go back in and surface-clean the specific spots with a wet bleach solution on all hard surfaces. If the site was not clean, they would retest until the samples showed it was.

Samples from the equipment in the tent would be collected about a week to ten days after the gassing. A detailed analysis would take an additional twenty to thirty days. If the first cleanup was a success, they would fumigate the entire building with two thousand pounds of chlorine gas created on the site by mixing about twenty thousand tons of component materials.

After chlorine dioxide gas was pumped into Brentwood during the last stage, probably in December, workers in biohazard suits would reenter the building and collect more than eight thousand test strips impregnated with spores of a nontoxic bacterium, an anthrax simulant. After the successful limited test, plans were laid at last for No. 17 to be disassembled and dumped before the reopening of Brentwood. No one would ever again feel comfortable working with the massive machine.

In December, Brentwood would be renamed in honor of Morris and Curseen.

The cost of anthrax cleanup was estimated at $22 million, but factoring in the decontamination of New Jersey's Hamilton facility still to come, the total would stand closer to $35 million or even in excess of $100 million for all the facilities. After final decontamination Brentwood could be open by April 2003. Brentwood was coming back.

Just as the decontamination had begun, in New York City reporters and editors for the *Wall Street Journal* went back to work at the world financial center for the first time since September 11. They'd been toiling at scattered offices around the city since evacuation from their offices when the World Trade Center towers crashed down. Wall Street was coming back.

At Ground Zero in New York the air was as gas-filled as the inside of the anthrax tent. It was the same all over the area. For many months after the collapse, hundreds of aromatic hydrocarbons and volatile organic compounds released into the atmosphere had been making people sick. One was extremely toxic benzene, a colorless, sweet-smelling liquid that evaporates very quickly.

A woman who lived in a small apartment in Chinatown a mile north of Ground Zero complained of acrid air seeping into her apartment. "It gets so bad you can't even sleep," she told writer Juan Gonzalez. "It's a burning smell and it stays in your apartment. I had two months of bronchitis. I was coughing so badly that all the muscles on my rib cage hurt. On one occasion, I had to go to the emergency room, so my doctor suggested I get out of there."

Almost a year after the World Trade Center collapse coated much of lower Manhattan in asbestos-laced dust, federal environmental officials announced plans to clean up and test up to thirty-eight thousand homes. EPA and other government agencies downplayed any health risk from the dust. Tests, they said, showed the asbestos did not reach hazardous levels.

A thirty-five-year-old firefighter named Bobby Stanlewicz was suffering from respiratory disease. His exposure to disease-causing chemicals hadn't ended when he left Ground Zero. He learned that, for many months, he had been working on a contaminated truck. Asbestos concentrations were as high as five times the 1 percent safety limit set by the Occupational Safety and Health Administration (OSHA). NYFD signed a $2 million-plus contract to pay for decontamination of hundreds of dust-tainted Ground Zero fire engines.

The FBI had tested 561 mailboxes in Trenton, New Jersey, looking for bacteria that would mark one as being the box Amerithrax had used in his deadly mailings. So far they had had no positive results.

In mid-August, the FBI in New Jersey began showing merchants the photograph of a man and asking if they had seen him in the area the previous fall. The identity of the man, Steven Hatfill, was not revealed to the merchants, but Hatfill was only one of about thirty "persons of interest" in the investigation of the mailed attacks, although no other names had surfaced in the media, at least not with such relentless vehemence.

STRAIN 30

Dr. Hatfill

ON WEDNESDAY, JULY 31, 2002, the day before the FBI served a warrant on Dr. Steven J. Hatfill's Maryland apartment, a reporter called his father and advised him that something big was going to happen the next day.

The next morning agents were back and rolling up their protective gloves for another search. The federal warrant served represented an escalation over the voluntary search conducted June 25. It signaled an increasingly aggressive strategy on behalf of the FBI. Shortly after 10:00 A.M., they blockaded the entrances with unmarked cars and began to search Hatfill's apartment anew. Hatfill, after saying he knew nothing about the anthrax murders, left the apartment. He was not questioned.

Agents watching his apartment earlier had seen him "pitching loads of his belongings into a Dumpster behind his apartment." They thought it might be evidence. Agents who dove into the green Dumpster found only his personal belongings, an unusual type of glove, and "other items associated with laboratory paraphernalia." Hatfill's former neighbors had reportedly already rooted through his garbage looking for artifacts to sell on eBay. The FBI bagged items in red evidence bags, filled white cardboard boxes stacked next to the trash bins, and stored it all in a silver van. But when tested for anthrax, the items would prove negative.

But Dr. Hatfill knew he was being watched and had complained to friends about it. "I'm throwing things into a Dumpster," he said later, "because I've recently accepted a job at Louisiana State University and I'm cleaning out my apartment before the move." At LSU he would design hands-on training programs for emergency personnel facing bioterrorist attacks. When Hatfill went to a Baton Rouge mall to pick up shaving supplies, he was shocked when folks asked for his autograph. He was obviously the object of a whispering campaign as an undeclared suspect in the mailing of deadly letters.

The FBI was aware that Hatfill had written a novel about a bio-attack on the White House and Congress and went right for his computer. In the afternoon neighbors saw agents carrying more cardboard boxes, plastic bags, and computer parts from the residence. The back doors of a dark blue van parked nearby were flung open and the boxes stored inside. A Ryder rental truck was backed up to the door of Hatfill's apartment. The search continued for several hours. Agents began leaving at 3:30 P.M. and by 5:00 P.M. all had left.

The neighbors weren't very surprised at the search, though Hatfill had not been living in the apartment recently, only keeping it as a residence. They had been aware of surveillance on his apartment for days and that was the way the FBI worked to apply pressure. Circulating rumors and assigning agents to keep "lockstep" surveillance had been a favorite technique of former FBI director J. Edgar Hoover. In the 1950s he had waged little wars of rumor and innuendo to intimidate "persons of interest."

Hoover launched a program code-named COINTELPRO [Counter Intelligence Program] to discredit the Klan and the Communist Party over a dozen years. Under COINTELPRO, the Bureau engaged in illegal surveillance practices, operated unsanctioned wiretaps, and committed "black bag jobs" (illegal break-ins). Rough treatment during the serving of a search warrant was another of Hoover's ploys. COINTELPRO had harassed targets by placing anonymous calls, applying pressure on the investigative targets' loved ones, and leaking information to the media.

Federal law enforcement sources told CBS News that Dr. Hatfill was "the chief guy we're looking at" in the Amerithrax probe. Visions of Richard Jewell dancing in their heads, the officials were cautious not to use the term "suspect." They said they were "zeroing in on the guy" and that he was "the focus of the investigation." FBI Director Mueller was more cautious. He said only, "We're making progress in the case, but I can't comment on ongoing aspects of the investigation." Yet, a number of things did not fit. Dr. Hatfill was not the "loner" that the FBI profile said that Amerithrax must be. Scientists who took the UN course with him at Porton Down described Hatfill as "well-rounded" and "energetic and outgoing, a super lab worker." Others said Hatfill was "arrogant and wild-tempered." This was hardly the nonassertive individual the FBI profile had conjured up. Author Richard Preston described Hatfill as a "bluesuit cowboy," because he thrived in Biosafety Level 4 and was so comfortable there he ate candy bars inside his space suit as he worked with Ebola-infected monkey blood. "He kept a strip of reflective tape on the roof of his car," reported Preston, "so that in the event of a biomedical emergency the state-police helicopters could find him."

Using investigative techniques developed in spy cases, the FBI compiled a minute-by-minute time line of Dr. Hatfill's whereabouts on days when the anthrax-tainted letters were dropped into a Trenton mailbox. Agents returned to the rented storage unit in Florida and searched again. If they found anything, they weren't saying.

The FBI continued giving current workers at the Institute polygraph tests, and that wasn't the only government or contractor lab being finecombed. At this time there were fifty people on its "persons of interest" list, but so many fell off it was constantly evolving as leads were followed, worn out, or dead-ended. The FBI said the list had to be periodically updated.

So far the FBI had been repulsed in its hunt to find a domestic suspect with scientific expertise. "Obviously, Dr. Hatfill is somebody who had access to anthrax and scientific capability," said an FBI official. "That is why we want to look at him—to either remove him from a list of potentials or add him to a list of potentials . . . Are we saying he's the guy . . . No, we're not."

But Dr. Hatfill was a virologist. "Hatfill did not work with anthrax," they once more admitted, "although like other employees, he might have had access to anthrax and other hazardous substances." The Ames strain was available at LSU, but though Hatfill had just gotten a job there, he hadn't started yet. And Hatfill's history was full of gaps and inconsistencies. His resume was "riddled with gaps where classified projects presumably belong." They looked closer.

*   *   *

STEVEN J. HATFILL, born St. Louis, Missouri, October 24, 1953, grew up in Illinois and attended high school in Mattoon. His classmates nicknamed him "Dr. Science" because of his all-consuming interest in the sciences. He was "nerdy" but funny, and an outrageous wisecracker in class. In June 1975, he graduated Southwestern College in Winfield, Kansas, where he had studied biology. During his college undergraduate years, he interrupted his degree program for eight months. At the behest of his Methodist minister, he went to work as a volunteer at an isolated mission hospital in Kapanga, Zaire.

Resumes Hatfill produced over the years asserted that he served with the Army Special Forces after college, from June 1975 to June 1977. However, an Army spokesman stated Hatfill "was never part of the Special Forces." In October 1976, he married Caroline Eschtruth, daughter of the chief medical missionary. Their marriage ended in less than two years.

In the spring of 1978, he moved to Africa, where he lived and worked for the next sixteen years. In 1979 and 1980, while he was in Rhodesia (which became Zimbabwe in 1980), thousands of black tribesmen became infected with anthrax. Some call it the first modern case of germ warfare. One of Hatfill's later papers tracked untreated disease in rural Zimbabwe.

He spent six years in Harare, Zimbabwe (then called Salisbury, Rhodesia), earning his medical degree. Before joining the Godfrey Huggins School of Medicine (now the University of Zimbabwe), records show he did serve in the military in Rhodesia during the civil war of the late 1970s when the white government fought against black insurgents. Hatfill had supposedly served in Rhodesia's Special Air Service (SAS). A later resume said this:

> Active combat experience with C Squadron Special Air Service, Rhodesia [6/75–3/78 . . . Assigned to the 2nd Medical Battalion (TA Reserve) SADF . . . Consultant Flight Surgeon to 30 Squadron Air/Sea rescue unit based at Yesterplatt Air Force Base, Cape Town . . . I served as Emergency Medical Officer for the Conradie General Hospital, Cape Town.

Dr. Hatfill also claimed to have worked with a Rhodesian commando unit, but Michael John "Mac" McGuinness, who ran the Rhodesian government's counterterrorisim operations, said he had a minor civilian role. McGuinness said they wouldn't have welcomed an American's help anyway. "We didn't trust foreigners with that sort of thing," he said. Hatfill, "cultivating a flamboyant, swashbuckling manner," was "a good person to suspect because he's off the wall," said Ed Rybicki, a biologist at the University of Cape Town. "[He] would talk about running around in the bush and throwing grenades in Zimbabwe . . . boast about shooting up the ANC's offices."

On a college biography and resume he boasted of having fought with the Selous Scouts, an elite white mercenary force that tracked and killed black rebels in the backcountry in an unsuccessful effort to maintain white rule in Rhodesia. The infamous Selous Scouts, named for F. Courtney Selous, an explorer and hunter, fought for white rule and inspired the South African special forces units. A school in Greendale, a suburb of Zimbabwe's capital city, Harare, was also named for Selous—leading to later speculation about the "Greendale School" appearing in the return addresses of the two senators' anthrax letters.

A classmate of Hatfill's recalled that, "He carried a lot of weapons around at the time, rocket-propelled grenades and stuff like that. On the weekends he'd go with the army and they would do Special Forces kinds of stuff." "He always carried a 9-mm pistol and constantly boasted about his military past," said a former colleague. Another of Hatfill's classmates, Mark Hanly, had always doubted Hatfill's claims.

Professor Robert Burns Symington, head of the Anatomy Department of the University of Rhodesia, was "the father of Rhodesia's biowarfare expertise." According to a recent story by Innocent Chofamba-Sithole and Norman Miambo, Dr. Hatfill was his student. "Symington, whom former colleagues at the then Godfrey Huggins School of Medicine have described as a 'little white supremacist,' " they claimed, "allegedly facilitated the entry into Medical School of Steven J. Hatfill, the man the FBI has now targeted as the prime suspect in the U.S. anthrax attacks last year." Hatfill used the Milnerton Shooting Association's shooting range in Table View, Cape Town. According to later reports by the *Johannesburg Mail & Guardian*, he boasted that he was a weapons trainer in the Western Cape, joining the military there in 1978, and had "combat experience" during the guerrilla war against white rule.

In 1978, Rhodesia may have been used as a human lab for anthrax. LSU anthrax expert Martin Hugh-Jones doubted that. "There's just no evidence whatsoever," he said. In 1979, an outbreak of the skin form of anthrax sickened some ten thousand people, mostly black farmers. Many in Zimbabwe today still believe it was a bioattack by the white government.

They suspected the whites had distributed anthrax spores among cattle of the Rhodesian Tribal Trust Lands, where most Africans lived, even seeded cholera into the rivers. The intent was to kill food sources of Rhodesian guerrillas while the white farms remained untouched. Before 1978, there were 13 human cases a year in Rhodesia. From 1979 through 1980, there were 10,778 human cases a year. Of these 182 died. In the entire world, about 7,000 cases were reported annually. Thousands of Rhodesian cattle were slaughtered. Anthrax spread into six of eight provinces. A drought followed by heavy rain consistently preceded an outbreak of anthrax.

"It became obvious that anthrax spores were transported over large distances—across areas where no cattle sickness had occurred," wrote experts. "No one ever learned how anthrax was delivered—the strain came from the United Kingdom. But the war is still in the earth. Spores know no side and kill with impunity. The anthrax zone is red dust and thorny scrub . . . and the stuff lasts forever. That is the evil of biological warfare."

Hatfill remained in Rhodesia after blacks won majority rule and the country was renamed Zimbabwe. Hatfill has never been connected to the Rhodesian anthrax outbreak, but it made the FBI take a closer look at his "murky background in Africa." Graduating in April 1984 from the Godfrey Huggins School of Medicine in Harare, with the British equivalent of an M.D. degree (Certificate No. 376-621-9), Hatfill went to work in South Africa. At Cape Town he obtained several master's degrees and a doctorate, before joining apartheid South Africa's military medical corps on a one-year tour of duty. He was a member of a 1986 Antarctic exploration team on the Fimbul Coastal Ice Shelf of Queen Maud Land. In a snapshot of Hatfill and thirteen other members, he is in the last row, withdrawn, hands in his pockets, sunglasses covering his eyes. He is a thin and rather romantic figure against an icy landscape, standing out against the red try-works of a trawler. In a medical school photograph he is posed almost primly, with fingers laced. He wears a droopy mustache. His dark blue eyes are intense and probing, his dark brown hair short and feathered across his brow. Hatfill seems closed up within himself. His colleagues described him as "brilliant" and "short-tempered."

STRAIN 31

Dr. Death

AFTER SERVING HIS clinical internship, Dr. Hatfill began his post-graduate work in Cape Town. A professor in South Africa recalled Hatfill as "very intelligent. Very driven. And very unconventional . . . He talked a lot about guns when he would go out to the pub." He boasted of military exploits in places like Vietnam, although public records show only short military stints. He earned three master of science degrees: in microbial genetics and recombinant DNA at the University of Cape Town (September 1988); medical biochemistry/radiation biology in a research fellowship at the University of Stellenbosch Medical School (December 1990); and hematological pathology, as a three-year residency (June 1993). Lothar Bohm, professor of oncology at Stellenbosch, said he was unpopular because "he just did not respect other peoples' lives or work or their needs in the lab. He was the kind of person who would go into the labs late at night and take pieces of equipment without asking." Female colleagues especially disliked Hatfill "because he used to invite them to 'poke and puke' parties."

Hatfill's rotating internship was at the Paul Kruger Hospital, where the apartheid-era government had an infamous offensive bioweapons program. Lt. Col. Wouter Basson, known as "Dr. Death," had single-handedly founded, developed, and led South Africa's top secret apartheid germ program.

A military doctor with a master's in chemistry and a top cardiologist, Dr. Death was project manager of "Project Coast." This was the code name for a chemical and biological program to manufacture germ weapons to cripple or kill apartheid foes. Blue-eyed, handsome, charismatic, Dr. Death answered to no one, referring to his superiors as "chicken-heads." Basson infiltrated Porton Down, the top secret bioweapons defense plant in Wiltshire, and went to Fort Detrick. Basson said the FBI contacted him about Hatfill and he told them Hatfill had no contact with South African special forces or intelligence.

Project Coast, hidden by a maze of front companies and covert science labs, had a staff of two hundred and a budget of $4.5 million. The Roodeplaat Research Laboratories (dissolved in 1993), a front for Project Coast, performed effectiveness tests to determine LD50 for more than forty-five strains of anthrax. Responsibility for the project fell to Neils Knobel, a former professor of anatomy at the University of Pretoria Medical School.

Project Coast's offensive weapons included an arsenal packed with anthrax, botulinum toxin, Ebola, Marburg, and human immunodeficiency virus, a grotesque jumble of bio-agents and delivery systems for the commission of murders. Their top program was geared to manipulate the fertility of people in South Africa on an ethnic basis. Russia had studied such ethnic weapons. Project Coast was unsuccessful in creating a blacks-only infertility virus. Science someday might be able to find a subtle combination of markers common to particular races. That might work as an ethnic weapon, but why bother? Racial mixing and an inherent ambiguity over definitions of ethnicity meant that no single genetic marker would give an attacker sufficient leverage. There were much easier ways to use germ weapons against particular ethnic groups. Anthrax or other traditional killers would be effective in spreading death. Anthrax was one of their favorites, though allegations that South African anthrax was released in Zimbabwe during 1979 and 1980 during its independence struggles have never been confirmed.

At a local game park, Project Coast collected forty-four strains of anthrax, tested for antibiotic resistance, in order to produce an antibiotic-resistant anthrax. They considered using anthrax to cripple antiapartheid leader Nelson Mandela. According to testimony before South Africa's

Truth and Reconciliation Commission, Basson's germ program claimed many lives and was even considered for use against Mandela in jail.

Three hundred assassinations, geared to small amounts of bacteria, were alleged to have been committed by them with snake venom, plague, and Ebola and Marburg viruses. They planted anthrax in the gum of envelopes and dusted filters of Camel cigarettes with spores. They laced peppermint-flavored chocolates with anthrax, tainted beer with botulinum toxin and sugar with salmonella. The injected germs into whisky and paraquat bleach, put paratyphoid in deodorant, and fitted walking sticks and umbrellas with secret spring syringes that could inject an untraceable polycarbonate ball containing ricin straight into victims. Bulgarian dissident Georgi Markov, stabbed in the thigh by an umbrella tip, had been assassinated in London in just such a manner. Project Coast operatives soaked organo-phosphate into the clothes of an antiapartheid activist to turn it into a burning cloak.

Colleagues recalled Hatfill wore a 9-mm side arm, even when making his rounds. As a medical doctor, he published more than a dozen scientific papers focused on leukemia, HIV, and the Ebola virus. Ebola is "an incurable hemorrhagic fever, drives blood and guts from every orifice of the victim's ravaged body." Medical men first diagnosed the disease in 1980 after watching it kill nine out of ten infected villagers in Zaire. The most deadly strain was named after the Ebola River, which flowed alongside the villages where it struck.

At times Hatfill listed on his resume that he had a Ph.D. in molecular cell biology from Rhodes University in South Africa. Stephen Fourie, the university's registrar, said, "Rhodes did not—repeat, did not—award a Ph.D. to Hatfill."

The Rhodesian Civil War ended in 1980, but anthrax was still in its soil, slumbering and waking and then reinfecting. Thirteen years after Zimbabwe's independence, a former senior white member of the Rhodesian Security forces admitted the use of anthrax in the war by the military. "It is true that anthrax was used in an experimental role and the idea came from the Army Psychological Operations," he said. The strategy was to blame the guerillas for cattle deaths and also deprive them of food. Allegations that South African anthrax was released in Zimbabwe during its independence struggles have never been conclusively proved. Symington moved to South Africa, where he died of a heart attack a year after joining the University of Cape Town.

The RRL was dissolved in 1993. The apartheid regime in South Africa collapsed and white minority rule ended the next year. Mandela became president. Later, Western intelligence learned that the Libyan leader, Muammar Qadaffi, was trying to hire South African scientists, including Basson, who had made trips to Libya. U.S. officials, fearing he might leave South Africa permanently, launched a politically delicate covert operation to block Basson's emigration. Now unemployed, Dr. Death could disappear at any time.

And the problem went beyond Libya. As the creator of South Africa's germ arsenal, Basson had developed a global network of covert and overt contacts. British and American representatives met with Mandela, and persuaded the president to return Basson to government service. There his actions could more easily be tracked. On January 29, 1997, Dr. Basson was arrested in possession of a thousand tablets of Ecstasy. Charged with drug dealing and several crimes in connection with Project Coast, including twenty-nine counts of murder and conspiracy to murder more than two hundred victims, he was acquitted in April 2002 of all charges by a single judge. The state, he said, had failed to prove its case. Relaxed and smiling, Basson denied all crimes.

UN reports charged that South Africa backed "dirty wars," estimating one and a half million deaths and sixty billion dollars in losses in Zimbabwe, Mozambique, Angola, and Namibia. By 1995, all evidence of South Africa's Project Coast and all dangerous substances related to it were destroyed.

Steve Hatfill left Africa in the summer of 1994 and moved to England in September. According to his resume, he spent a year doing clinical research at an Oxford University hospital as a clinical research scientist. He returned to the U.S. in 1995 where he received a fellowship for biomedical research at the National Institutes of Health at Bethesda, Maryland, and other civilian federal labs. Beginning in September 1997 Hatfill took a two-year senior research fellowship from the National Research Council (NRC) at the Institute. He had respiratory and medical clearance to conduct research on Biosafety Level 3. He worked with pathogens such as plague, anthrax, and monkeypox. In October 1997, he had taken a full course for "medical and incident consequence management of personnel exposure to anthrax, tularemia, plague, VEE, orthopoxvirus, filovirus and the SEB, BOTOX and ricin biological toxins."

He also had clearance to operate in a Biosafety Level 4 environment for research on exotic viral pathogens. His work was done in a maximum confinement lab reached through an air-lock door and decon shower. He wore a bright blue Chemturion space suit, a pressurized, heavy-duty biological space suit.

Dr. Hatfill's specialty was viral illnesses. He investigated therapeutic responses to filoviridae. Filovirus is a family that comprises only the Ebola and Marburg primate-borne tropical thread viruses. Under a microscope filoviruses show as long and stringy as befits their name, filamentous. His initial research had been on the deadly Ebola hemorrhagic fever and Marburg filovirus infection in rhesus primates. Marburg had been the first filovirus discovered. In 1967 in Marburg, Germany, and Belgrade, Yugoslavia, lab workers were infected with hemorrhagic fever after handling tissues from African green monkeys. Thirty-one cases and seven deaths resulted, but Marburg disappeared as mysteriously as it appeared, only to reappear in Zimbabwe in 1975 with the infection of a traveler. In 1976 Ebola (in four strains) came along as the only other member of the filovirus family. Dr. Stephen L. Guillot, director of the biomedical research center at LSU, later said Hatfill had impressed him as a "technically very competent individual," but not in anthrax. "Steve's expertise is Ebola," Dr. Guillot said.

Of his two years at the Institute, Hatfill's resume stated that he had gained "a working knowledge" of wet and dry biological warfare agents and their chemical additives, spray disseminators, and designs for germ weapons. His resume listed "working knowledge . . . of wet and dry BW [biological warfare] agents, large-scale production of bacterial, rickettsial, and viral BW pathogens and toxins, stabilizers and other additives, former BG simulant production methods." Anyone who knows how to grow *Bacillus globigii* and turn it into a simulant powder could do the same with anthrax. Such expertise would lend itself to the preparation of the dry anthrax powder.

During the same period, Hatfill had become focused on the dangers of a potential bioweapons attack in the U.S. He believed the nation wasn't prepared or doing enough to be prepared. In August 1997, Hatfill provided a *Washington Times* columnist scenarios for a biological attack that included "anthrax spores put into the ventilation system of a movie theater." He also mentioned a recent anthrax hoax at B'nai B'rith in Washington, D.C. He appeared on a cable TV news show, warning that anthrax could be sent through the mail. On the *Armstrong Williams Show* he discussed "The Emerging Threat of Biological and Chemical Terrorism." "He was so sure this was going to happen," Williams said. "He was emphatic." The host later commented further, "There's no doubt in my mind that he had knowledge about anthrax," adding that the FBI had questioned him about Hatfill's appearance. At a June 1998 bioterrorism conference in Washington, Hatfill showed slides of anthrax victims. In December, at Temple Beth Ami in Rockville, he enumerated the problems encountered with developing anthrax as a weapon. He spoke on the Canadian Broadcast Network and on a Voice of America Mideast broadcast about "Chemical and Biological Weapons."

On January 26, 1998, Hatfill appeared in an *Insight* magazine photo spread depicting him whipping up toxins in the kitchen. The kitchen was modern, but his bio-suit was as old-fashioned as the early anthrax suits used in Britain. Looming on the counter was a big bottle of Clorox. The article, "Cooking Up the Plague at Home," by Tiffany Danitz, began:

> National Institutes of Health researcher Steven Hatfill demonstrates how a determined terrorist could cook up a batch of plague in his or her own kitchen using common household ingredients and protective equipment from the supermarket. A homemade broth culture, based on recipes published by Louis Pasteur in the late 1800s, could be incubated in an ordinary electric oven set at a low temperature. An Army surplus gas mask, garbage bags, duct tape and dishwashing gloves complete the chemical chef's fashion ensemble. Household bleach decontaminates working surfaces.

Hatfill left out one secret ingredient for the photo story: the plague bacterium. He explained that an imaginative terrorist could collect that from a prairie-dog habitat in the American Southwest, where it is endemic. Hatfill "weaponized" his batch by pouring it into a hiker's water bag attached to a homemade sprayer. He laid out a hypothetical situation in which a terrorist in a wheelchair, highly inoculated with antibiotics, could conceal the water bag under a tracksuit and wheel through a crowded area, dispersing as he went. Hatfill had used this idea in a novel he was writing. He told *Insight* that fumes reported at Baltimore-Washington International Airport "could be a form of testing for a possible future terrorist attack—perhaps next time using anthrax."

Dr. Hatfill left the Institute for a job at SAIC. There he worked to detail the risks of biological and chemical attacks and gave presentations to employees of the U.S. military, intelligence, and other agencies. In 2000, Dr. Hatfill trained in France to become a United Nations inspector ready to hunt for germ weapons in Iraq, said Ewen Buchanan, a UN spokesman. He snared an important new job as associate director of the National Center for Biomedical Research and Training at LSU.

He was preparing to move there when on August 1, the FBI executed a court-issued search warrant.

STRAIN 32

Literary Anthrax

ON FRIDAY, AUGUST 2, 2002, the day after his Frederick, Maryland, apartment had been searched, Dr. Hatfill was on every news show: "a man who may be linked to the anthrax mail attacks," said Frank Somerville on Channel 2's *Morning Show*. "For the second time this summer the FBI has searched the apartment of Maryland biologist Steven Hatfill, a former Army researcher who once worked for the Army Institute of Infectious Diseases. The center studies biological warfare. Hatfill gave his permission for the search yesterday. Agents, however, showed up with a search warrant." . . . "I do know about him," former UN weapons inspector Richard Spertzel said. "Basically he's an Ebola virus expert and his two stints from 1997 to 1999 were to work on Ebola virus."

"We are also learning this morning," Somerville continued, "that Hatfill is on a short list of Americans authorized to go to Iraq to look for chemical weapons there and he also once commissioned a study about a fictional terrorist attack where an envelope containing anthrax is opened in an office."

FBI Director Robert Mueller declined to comment on the search. He said the FBI had not changed its profile of the likely culprit. Amerithrax was a lone domestic man with a scientific background and access to a lab. "We're making progress in the case," he said. "But beyond that, I can't comment."

Stephen Guillot, Hatfill's supervisor at LSU, announced through spokesman Gene Sands that Dr. Hatfill had been suspended with pay from his job as associate director of LSU's National Center for Biomedical Research and Training (NCBRT) at the Academy of Counter-Terrorist Education. Hatfill was placed on thirty days paid administrative leave of absence. Sands said his status would be reevaluated at the end of that period. Hatfill was to teach emergency personnel (police, firefighters, health professionals, and federal agents) how to handle germ attacks. The Army researcher specialized in helping the government devise responses to possible bioterrorism incidents such as anthrax attacks.

Friends and colleagues described Hatfill as "strange" and "charming." One called him the "Warren Beatty of science." He drove fast and piled up traffic tickets and ran through girlfriends as speedily. He made wild claims. He told one pal he had been a fighter pilot in Vietnam and had been shot down over the China Sea. He was also brilliant. "Once when we were chatting I grabbed a thick medical reference book from the library and said to him, 'Hey, Steve, can I test you?' " one former colleague recalled to *Newsweek*. "It didn't matter what I asked him: he repeated the answer as if reading the book to me." In May, Esteban Rodriguez, a supervisor at the Defense Intelligence Agency, had composed a letter lauding Hatfill's "unsurpassed technical expertise, unique resourcefulness, total dedication and consummate professionalism" in aiding the Army prepare for potential biowarfare in Afghanistan.

Dr. Hatfill was obviously highly imaginative as well. Someone leaked that he had written a novel about a bioterrorist attack on Washington. A portion of Hatfill's manuscript was obtained by ABC affiliate WJLA in Washington. "His novel was leaked," said former FBI profiler Candice DeLong. "If that leak had anything to do with anyone who was involved with that search or if it was an official leak, that was prosecutable behavior. Somebody should be in trouble for that."

Everyone was anxious to see what Hatfill had written and if it had any bearing on the Amerithrax case. It was not hard to see why Hatfill had wanted to write a biological thriller. A number of them had been bestsellers. Some had become popular motion pictures like *Outbreak*. Robin Cook had been successful with medical suspense novels like *Coma*. In Cook's 1999 novel, *Vector*, a New York City cabbie, a disillusioned Russian émigré and former technician at Sverdlovsk, mails anthrax in envelopes that explode in a puff of white powder, much as the Daschle letter did.

Over lunch one day, *New Yorker* contributor Richard Preston sketched out the plot for a novel in which a terrorist has dispersed anthrax into a metropolis. An FBI source begged him to have second thoughts and stick to nonfiction. Cook's "terrifying true story" about Ebola, *Hot Zone*, had been published in 1994 to instant success. The threat from anthrax was too real, the agent cautioned him, and it would be a disservice to the public to so graphically demonstrate its powers in print. Preston revised his story line to focus on a less plausible germ: a biologically engineered superbug.

In Preston's 1997 book, *The Cobra Event*, a CDC pathologist tracks "Archimedes," a madman who plans to detonate virus glass bombs in New York's subway. The Institute's report on the "Vulnerability of Subway Passengers in New York City to Covert Action with Biological Agents" had inspired the fictional plot. Archimedes chooses the Second Avenue subway tunnel near Chinatown, one of the routes Ms. Kathy Nguyen traveled before she became mysteriously infected with pulmonary anthrax. "One kilogram of glass shattered and dispersed in a fine cloud the size of a city block," Archimedes theorizes, "would plume out nicely in the city."

The biokiller in *The Satan Bug*, Alistair MacLean's 1962 thriller, is a derivative of the botulinus toxin. In his novel eight ampoules of deadly virus are stolen from Porton Down, fictionalized as Mordon Research Establishment, near Alfringham, Wiltshire. The villain, Dr. Gregori, has taken the Satan Bug ostensibly to blackmail Mordon into shutting down its biowarfare labs. His real aim is to loot London during a citywide panic. In MacLean's thriller, the toxin oxidizes after twelve hours' exposure and becomes harmless.

"We have refined this toxin into a fantastic and shocking weapon," says Dr. Gregori, "compared to which even the mightiest hydrogen bomb is a child's toy. Six ounces of this toxin, gentlemen, distributed fairly evenly throughout the world, would destroy every man, woman and child alive on this planet today . . . This is a simple fact. Give me an airplane and let me fly over London on a windless summer afternoon with no more than a gram of botulinus toxin to scatter, and by evening seven million Londoners would be dead. A thimbleful in its water reservoirs, and London would become one vast charnel house."

Gregori says that in Russia and Canada scientists are working to produce such deadly bioweapons. Four thousand scientists at Fort Detrick, he claims, are working on so hurried a crash program that scientists have died and "eight hundred of them have fallen ill over the last few years." Mordon scientists also have the germs for causing plague, smallpox, typhus, rabbit, and undulant fever in man; fowl pest, hog choleras, Newcastle disease, rinderpest, foot-and-mouth, glanders and anthrax in livestock.

"The Americans have calculated that even a full-scale Soviet nuclear attack on their country, with *all* the resources at Russia's disposal, would cause no more than seventy million deaths—no more, I say!—with possibly several million others as a result of radiation. But half the nation would survive, and in a generation or two that nation would rise again. But a nation attacked by the Satan Bug would never rise again, for there would be no survivors."

In its present form, Gregori claims, the Satan Bug is an extremely refined powder, like weaponized anthrax, and more terrible than the Black Death. Should he spill a saltspoon of it outside, refined to its purest and most lethal form, in a week to ten days all life would have ceased to exist in Britain. Wind, ships, planes, birds, or the waters of the North Sea would carry the Satan Bug to Europe, Gregori predicts, saying no obstacle could stop its eventual worldwide spread. "Two months," he says, two months at the very most."

Over at the FBI, Van Harp and his agents were fascinated by a thriller about an anthrax-by-mail attack on America. The revelation that one of the thirty or so "persons of interest" they had under scrutiny had supposedly written it was astounding. The plot had even raised eyebrows at the CIA. Hatfill, a biowarfare expert, was a protégé of famed microbiologist Bill Patrick. Patrick could have offered plenty of imaginative plot ideas from real life.

In 1995, at a three-day conference in Bethesda, Maryland, Patrick demonstrated "how a terrorist could mount a germ attack on the World Trade Center using a blender, cheesecloth, a garden sprayer and some widely available hospital supplies." According to Patrick a terrorist could grow enough bacteria on one thousand agar plates to produce five liters of material within thirty-six hours. All he had to do was Waring-blend the mixture and filter it through cheesecloth. The resulting home brew would be swarming with germs, about five hundred million cells per milliliter. A terrorist who aimed an infectious dose of the bacteria, about fifty cells per milliliter, through a garden sprayer at the building's air intakes would disseminate enough agent in a few minutes to infect half the people in the WTC.

Several of Patrick's scenarios dealt with an attack by *Francisella tularensis*, a germ that the Rajneeshees had ordered. Patrick had been advisor on that real-life case up in Oregon.

As for Hatfill's novel, the idea for that had been hatched several years earlier at a dinner party. A group of journalists and former military men had been standing around and the conversation had turned to bioterrorism. Pat Clawson was there. The conservative commentator was Hatfill's close friend. "We started kicking it around," said Clawson, "that it would be a cool novel to write. 'Let's have a bioterrorism attack on Washington and Congress.'" In the summer of 2001, Hatfill asked for Clawson's help finding an agent or publisher but nothing came of it.

The FBI had located Hatfill's 198-page draft manuscript in his computer hard drive during its June and August searches. Though the novel, *Emergence*, had never been published, it was on file at the U.S. Copyright Office at the Library of Congress. Roger Akers, a friend of Hatfill's, had registered it in 1998. He had proofread it for Hatfill and, with his permission, copyrighted it in both their names. A law enforcement official characterized the work as an "interesting coincidence at this point."

The novel still raised suspicions even after the plot was shown to differ from the actual attacks by mail. *Emergence* was about a biological attack that involved neither anthrax nor toxins by mail. The bioweapon used in the attacks was a bacterium, *Yersinia pestis*, which causes bubonic plague and pneumonic plague. The major symptoms of pneumonic plague are a fever and lung infection that becomes pneumonia-like after two to four days. The plague has a 50 to 90 percent mortality rate. Antibiotics such as streptomycin, tetracycline, and doxycycline are ineffective against it. *Yersinia* bacteria are one of the pathogens that terrorists might most effectively use to rapidly infect large numbers and with large loss of life. Plague was usually delivered via contaminated vectors such as fleas. Vaccines exist, but would have little effectiveness against aerosolized plague.

Hatfill's unpublished draft novel centered on epidemiologists attempting to uncover the origin of mysterious illnesses in Antarctica and then in Washington. The story opens in Antarctica, where ten members of a South

African research team die from a strange disease. "Eight years later," Hatfill wrote in his opening synopsis, "a similar disease sweeps with explosive effect through the members of the U.S. Congressional House and Senate. The nation's leadership is paralyzed and panic ensues as members of the Executive Office begin to show symptoms." The novel's villain is Ismail Abu Asifa, a Palestinian terrorist paid by Iraq to carry out a biological attack on Washington. Asifa flies into the U.S. from England, planning "to strike terror deep into the heart of the most powerful nation on earth."

Once in Washington, Asifa buys supplies for $387 to grow bubonic plague bacteria. That was "not a high price to strike terror in the government of a country this large." Hatfill's villain infects the White House with a homegrown plague, using a sprayer hidden inside a wheelchair during a public tour. The President is sickened, and within days the illness spreads to top congressional leaders. In his plot, the White House becomes the "House of Death." It's an attack so lethal that not only do members of Congress and congressional aides sicken, but "hundreds of Washington residents become ill and many die as a result."

But Asifa also infects himself and ultimately stumbles into the path of a car; he dies six days later in a hospital. "For all its wealth and power, the United States . . . was actually an incredibly easy target for biological terrorism," Hatfill wrote. Hatfill's villain "would probably have only enough time to perform one attack and observe its early effects . . . It was unlikely with his present resources, that he would be able to kill more than a few hundred people at most."

The hero is Steven J. Roberts, who has a background similar to Steven J. Hatfill's and who had visited the same places he had. Hatfill made on-target observations about how the country would react to a bioterror attack. "Even if only a single person died in the attack, the sensationalistic-seeking news media could be trusted to whip the American public into a state of near total hysteria."

Taking a leaf from Patrick's book, Hatfill wrote that "[Asifa] wanted a facility small enough so that the people inside could be exposed to a high concentration of airborne bacilli, yet important enough so that this act could hurt the United States. Only in foolish America could this be so easily accomplished."

At the book's conclusion, the United States retaliated with a nuclear strike against Iraq. But the lone terrorist in the novel used plague (like

Maclean's Satan Bug), not anthrax, and dispersed it with a sprayer, not by mail. "There's nothing similar to what has happened," said Hatfill's friend Roger Akers, who edited the manuscript. Roger Akers indicated that the book dealt with a biological attack on Congress and how the perpetrator covered his tracks.

DR. HATFILL'S CRIMINAL defense attorney, Jonathan Shapiro of Alexandria, Virginia, had represented Brian P. Regan, a retired Air Force master sergeant charged with trying to sell American secrets to foreign countries. Hatfill's civil attorney, retained after government inquiries about him intensified to an impossible degree, was Victor M. Glasberg. Glasberg told the press, "Dr. Hatfill was voluntarily debriefed and polygraphed, and voluntarily agreed to have his home, car and other property subjected to lengthy and comprehensive search by the FBI. He . . . was told that the results were all favorable and that he was not a suspect in the case."

A number of rumors (possibly as fictional as Hatfill's novel) swept through the scientific family: that Dr. Hatfill had removed cabinets from Fort Detrick that could be used to culture anthrax; that he had been inoculated against anthrax and gotten booster shots; that he had unfettered access to the bioresearch labs at the Institute after his grant ended in 1999.

He claimed to have been a member of Rhodesian special forces which were later blamed for an anthrax outbreak that killed 182 during the Rhodesian civil war. For five years Hatfill lived in Harare, Zimbabwe, near a suburb called Greendale. A "Greendale School"—the same name given as a return address on anthrax letters—was located there, near Hatfill's medical school.

And finally, there were whispers that he had an "isolated residence" described as a "remote cabin," which was in truth a safe house operated by "American intelligence" and in which he kept quantities of Cipro to protect his friends from anthrax infection. Hatfill's friends asked, "How could such stories develop a life of their own?" His closest friend, Pat Clawson, thought he knew. In mid-October 2001, both he and Hatfill attended a skeet-shooting party in George Borsari's three-story vacation house in the Virginia mountains. Clawson had previously opened a letter filled with white powder and asked Hatfill if he should take Cipro. Clawson was already taking tetracycline for jaw pain and Hatfill replied that would be effective enough. The other eight party guests naturally began talking about protection from anthrax. "I was joking with Steve at dinner," Borsari recalled. "I said, 'We're all your friends. Why don't we have Cipro?' Steve said, 'I can get it for you if you really want it, but you don't need it.' " And from that innocent remark blossomed two pieces of lethal gossip.

On Sunday, August 4, Senator Daschle, who had come out against FBI polygraph tests for senators, spoke on ABC. "Do you think the investigation into the anthrax letters that came to you and others is going fast enough?" asked Cokie Roberts.

"Well, I wish it were going faster, frankly," Daschle replied. "I'm concerned about whether or not we're going to have the opportunity to see evidence that may have been destroyed, but I know the FBI is working on it. They've been informing me as they've gone along. I just hope we can bring this to a close sometime real soon."

On Monday, August 5, Robert Kramer, president of BioPort, reported finances of the Lansing, Michigan, company were shaky. BioPort, the nation's only anthrax vaccine maker, was under the gun. The Bush administration was treading water. It had yet been able to decide how much vaccine it intended to buy. Several civilian agencies had not yet given the military budget commitments to pay for the vaccine they wanted. This kept BioPort from selling to foreign and private customers, including large multinational corporations that would now pay more than one hundred dollars a dose.

"BioPort," said Kramer, "could not sell them until it had fulfilled its contract with the military, an estimated 3.4 million doses." The Pentagon permitted BioPort to sell up to 20 percent of its annual production after it produced the military doses it agreed to buy in 1999. In July, BioPort had tossed out about 180,000 doses of vaccine, two weeks' production, deemed below-standard.

All this turmoil came at a time when Bush was vowing to oust Saddam Hussein. The U.S. believed he had stored thousands of gallons of anthrax that could be used as bioweapons. So far Amerithrax's anthrax letters had led to more than twenty thousand people taking antibiotics.

Meanwhile the hunt went on. "We're still a long way from any proof we could take to court," a senior FBI official said. The media that covered the searches of Hatfill's apartment had to have been tipped off by government leaks, just as had been done in the Richard Jewell and Wen Ho Lee cases. Nonetheless, as the Bureau proceeded, it was being exceedingly careful. The shadow of Richard Jewell stretched over the Amerithrax case like a shroud.

STRAIN 33

Loomings

RICHARD JEWELL WAS never far from their minds, as agents showed a photo of one man, Steven Hatfill, their "person of interest," around Princeton. Sometimes they could almost see the plump, affable guard lolling against a mailbox and shyly watching them. Richard Jewell got a raw deal. A quiet Atlanta security guard who lived with his mother, he had been a bona fide hero. FBI leaks snatched that brief glory from him. To this day many still associate him with a crime he had nothing to do with perpetrating. The FBI was not anxious to repeat that experience. "Richard Jewell looms large around here," remarked one FBI official. "We've got to be very careful."

On July 27, 1996, startled and shaken spectators dove for cover as a pipe bomb exploded at Centennial Olympic Park during the Atlanta summer games. One person was killed and 111 were injured. The FBI swiftly targeted Jewell, a former sheriff's officer in north Georgia and a hero of the night. The round-faced, mustached young man, working security at the A&T light and sound tower, alerted police at 12:57 A.M. to a suspicious abandoned green backpack. Twenty-three minutes later, the backpack exploded. For a while he was praised as a hero for helping to evacuate the area before the blast.

The FBI prematurely singled out the pudgy guard. Sometimes those who claim to be heroes at the scene are the actual perpetrators. They used

356

the examples of a fireman who starts fires in order to heroically put them out or a mother suffering from Munchausen-by-proxy syndrome who sickens her baby so she can nurse it back to health.

Three days after the bombing, the *Atlanta Journal-Constitution*, citing unnamed sources, printed an article (based on bad FBI news leaks) saying Jewell was a suspect in the FBI investigation. The FBI had never formally acknowledged that Jewell was a suspect. Publication of the story forced the Bureau to speed up interviews with Jewell. Agents Don Johnson and Diader Rosario drove to the apartment Jewell shared with his mother. They found it already surrounded by reporters. The agents asked Jewell to come to the field office. He hesitated. Johnson said that, with his permission, they would be videotaping the interview for "training purposes" as it contained "sound bites from a first responder." "You'll be a superstar," Johnson said.

An hour and a half into the interview, they were still going over Jewell's background when FBI Director Freeh rang David W. "Woody" Johnson Jr., the SAC in Atlanta. Johnson, averaging an hour of sleep each night, had been working eighteen-hour days since the bombing. With him, in an office down the hall from Jewell, were U.S. Attorney Kent B. Alexander and other SACs. Freeh discussed the case over the speakerphone, saying he'd thought Jewell was going to be questioned at home. He then ordered Jewell's interrogators to read him his Miranda rights (as is the case when a suspect is in custody or about to be arrested). "There's no legal requirement to read him his rights," Alexander said; "Jewell isn't in custody. Under those circumstances, there's no need to read him his rights." By Freeh's order, made "in an excess of caution," Johnson had the agents read Jewell his rights. After that, Jewell clammed up.

Publicity about Jewell mounted. The more he insisted he was innocent, the more a media circus fueled by anonymous government leaks convicted him in the press. Freeh gave orders to agents on a cell phone as they searched Jewell's apartment. They took his guns and bagged his mother's Tupperware and Walt Disney videos. Three months later, Jewell, never charged, was given a government apology and publicly cleared of all suspicion in the Olympic Park bombing. "For eighty days, I lived a nightmare," Jewell said in tears afterward. He complained that the FBI's investigation had ruined his career and personal life.

Jewell sued for damages and eventually settled his complaint against

CNN over the network's coverage of the attack. "CNN continues to believe that its coverage was a fair and accurate review of the events that unfolded following the Centennial Olympic Park explosion," the Atlanta-based network said. The settlement came the same day Jewell sued the *Atlanta Journal-Constitution* and the college where he once worked as a guard. Of the lawsuit, Jewell said he was "doing it so this won't happen to anybody else. I want them to get the story 100 percent before they put it out."

Roger Kintzel, publisher of the *Journal-Constitution*, defended the newspaper's coverage. "We believe the charges are without foundation and that we will prevail in court," he said. The suit claimed Jewell was falsely portrayed as a man with "a bizarre employment history and an aberrant personality" who probably was guilty of placing the bomb. The lawsuit also named as defendants nine reporters, columnists, and editors, along with Piedmont College president Ray Cleere and a former school spokesman. The lawsuit said that newspaper stories quoted Cleere as describing Jewell as a "badge-wearing zealot" who "would write epic police reports for minor infractions." Jewell reached a settlement with NBC (worth half a million dollars) over comments anchor Tom Brokaw made on the air shortly after the bombing.

Eventually Eric Robert Rudolph, a fugitive, was charged with the bombing, along with the 1997 and 1998 bombings in Birmingham, Alabama, of an abortion clinic and a nightclub, and an Atlanta women's clinic. At the time, Rudolph was still at large (although he has since been taken into custody on the outskirts of a national forest in North Carolina). Now the FBI was careful of who they accused and how they phrased it. They were cautious of leaks.

Another person of interest looming large was Wen Ho Lee. Born in Taiwan, the son of uneducated farmers, Lee studied mechanical engineering at Cheng Kung University. In 1964 he came to the U.S., where he earned a doctorate in mechanical engineering from Texas A & M. In 1978, he joined the Los Alamos National Laboratory, a nuclear laboratory in New Mexico, and within two years became part of the X Division, the unit that designs nuclear bombs. Lee held a Q clearance, the highest level of security clearance. His equations were used in the Persian Gulf War in 1992.

On September 25 of that same year, China detonated a small, two-point nuclear bomb. On February 23, 1994, Los Alamos hosted a delegation of Chinese weapons officials, among them Dr. Hu Side, who had been in charge of designing China's new bomb. A translator said he overheard Hu quietly thanking Lee for providing computer software and calculations that helped China complete its sophisticated bomb. Los Alamos reported the conversation to the FBI, which began an investigation of Lee. They did not use electronic eavesdropping, conduct surveillance, or search Lee's computer even though he had signed a waiver in permitting his employer to do so. The *Wall Street Journal*, without naming Lee, ran a story about an espionage investigation at Los Alamos.

In June 1995, a Taiwanese official received a document purporting to show that the Chinese had obtained the design of America's most advanced nuclear bomb, the W-88, seven years earlier. The CIA, which had suspected the Chinese of obtaining American secrets, drew up a list of Los Alamos scientists with access to the plans or who had security problems. Lee had traveled to China in the mid-1980s. Often, China focused on Chinese Americans, appealing to an obligation to aid their homeland. Chinese intelligence encountered prospects in social, academic, or professional settings. Most information was passed orally. Lee never reported such advances, though they are common, and failed to inform his supervisors about his trips to Beijing as security regulations required.

In August 1998, the FBI set up "a false flag operation." An agent, posing as a Chinese intelligence officer, attempted to lure Lee into a meeting, but since he spoke Cantonese and Lee spoke Mandarin, the advance failed. In December, Lee went to Taiwan for three weeks. When he returned, he was reassigned out of the X Division. Given a polygraph test, Lee passed, but admitted during the test that during his 1988 trip to Beijing, a Chinese scientist whom he knew called him in his hotel room and asked to meet with him alone. Lee agreed and Hu Side showed up. Lee said he did not tell him anything, but did not report the contact as required.

During questioning, the FBI threatened Lee with the fate of the CIA's Aldrich Ames, who had sold secrets about the nation's spy apparatus to the Russians for a decade. That information led to the deaths of many CIA and FBI sources. The FBI also used the examples of Julius and Ethel Rosenberg, who were executed for giving secrets from Los Alamos to the Soviet Union. They pointed to John A. Walker, a Navy warrant officer turned in by his former wife. "Whether you're professing your innocence like the Rosenbergs to the day they take you to the electric chair," interrogators warned, "do you want to go down in history with your kids knowing that you got arrested for espionage?"

On February 10, 1999, FBI polygraphers examined Lee in a hotel room in Los Alamos. "Did you give nuclear weapons codes to any unauthorized person?" he was asked. Lee said he had not. FBI polygraph examiners in Washington examined Lee's polygraph charts and reported the results were inconclusive, but that Lee had probably showed deception.

For the first time the FBI asked Lee's consent to search his office and he consented. Agents discovered that over seventy days Lee had downloaded sensitive files equal to 430,000 pages of information from the laboratory's classified computer system. He had transferred them to his unsecured desktop computer and portable tapes. Nine of the fifteen tapes were missing. Lee later said he had copied the information as a backup to his work. After his inconclusive polygraph, Lee started deleting files he had downloaded.

On March 6, 1999, the *New York Times* headlined: BREACH AT LOS ALAMOS: A SPECIAL REPORT; CHINA STOLE NUCLEAR SECRETS FOR BOMBS, U.S. AIDES SAY. Though the *Times* didn't name the spy suspect, it described him as a Los Alamos computer scientist who was Chinese American and who had failed a lie detector test in February.

The day after, the FBI conducted another interview. The next day, Lee was dismissed for failing to report contacts with people from a "sensitive country" and for mishandling classified documents found on his desk.

After languidly pursuing the investigation for four and a half years, the FBI conducted a thousand interviews and surveilled Lee around the clock. They uncovered nothing. A fifty-nine–count indictment on December 10 required prosecutors to prove that Lee acted with intent to "injure the United States or to secure an advantage to any foreign nation." The maximum penalty was life in prison. At Lee's bail hearing, Robert Messemer, a new agent on the case, said Lee had told a colleague he wanted to borrow his computer to download a "resume" but in fact, Messemer testified, Lee borrowed the computer to download more files. Messemer had stretched the truth.

"The reason I downloaded those files," wrote Lee, "was very simple and mundane. I wanted to protect them from loss in the event that LANL

[Los Alamos National Laboratories] changed the computer operating system again or experienced a computer crash—both had occurred in the past, causing serious problems for me. During those incidents, I lost some important computer codes I had written . . .

"As a code developer, it was important that I have my own copy of my version of the codes I worked on. That's because other code developers worked on other parts of the code at the same time that I worked on the hydrodynamics portion . . . If they made changes to the code, it could affect the way my subroutines operated on the code. What I wanted to do was save a snapshot of the code at a certain time. It wouldn't help me to have a copy of the code after months or years of additional work had been done on it, because I would have to reconstruct all the changes to all the subroutines that might have affected my part of the code. I might be able to reconstruct everything, but it would be a great waste of time, possibly years, when it was so simple just to have a tape as documentation of the program." As in the Jewell case, unsourced leaks had played a part in the government's rush to judgment.

Without benefit of a trial, the sixty-one-year-old Lee was imprisoned in a tiny, constantly illuminated cell. His leg was manacled the entire time. After 278 days in solitary confinement, he was given a second bail hearing. On August 17, 2000, Messemer admitted he had made a mistake. Lee had been indicted with insufficient evidence. On September 13, 2000, Judge James A. Parker finally freed Lee, speaking to him before a packed courtroom gallery. "I believe you were terribly wronged by being held in custody pretrial in the Santa Fe County Detention Center under demeaning, unnecessarily punitive conditions," Parker said. "I am truly sorry that I was led by our executive branch of government to order your detention last December. Dr. Lee, I tell you with great sadness that I feel I was led astray last December by the executive branch of our government through its Department of Justice, and its Federal Bureau of Investigation."

Lee agreed to a sentence of time served and to undergo sixty hours of debriefing under oath. He acknowledged illegally making copies of the tapes and mishandling national security data, a single felony count out of fifty-nine counts. Those had included thirty-nine counts each carrying a life sentence for violating the Atomic Energy Act and for stealing nuclear secrets with the intent to harm America. Asian American groups claimed Lee was a victim of racial profiling and the CIA raised doubts about the veracity of information showing China had stolen the secrets to W-88 in the first place.

Lee and Jewell—two cases highly prejudged by the FBI and un-proven—explained the hesitancy of the Bureau. Treatment of both had led to formal apologies and successful lawsuits.

The months-long search had been maddening. Who had committed the worst bioterror attack on American soil? He had to be smart, an expert, have access to the spores of a certain strain and the machinery to manufacture it, and have been at postal zones where they were mailed. Could he be connected to Kathy Nguyen or Ottilie Lundgren, the two victims who did not fit? Their investigation kept turning back to Hatfill. Though officials were now pointing him out as only one of "around twelve" people they were looking at, not a suspect or even a target of the investigation. The Anthrax Task Force had discovered the strain of an-thrax used and winnowed it down from a series of labs to the precise source of the contagion. Now they were about to find the mailbox the killer had used.

STRAIN 34

Anthrax Bloodhounds

ON TUESDAY MORNING, August 6, 2002, Attorney General Ashcroft, speaking from his fifth-floor suite at the Justice Department, told *The Early Show* that "Progress is being made. But until you cross the thresholds of information that will provide the basis for action, it may be that the progress doesn't mean a lot." When asked if Dr. Hatfill was a suspect, Ashcroft said, "Well, he's a person of interest . . . I'm not prepared to say any more at this time other than the fact that he is an individual of interest . . . We have important things to do and to proceed with and to comment would be inappropriate at this time." He hinted at another search of Dr. Hatfill's apartment.

A month earlier, the FBI handlers of three police bloodhounds had presented the dogs with a set of "scent packs." These had been lifted from the letters to Daschle and Leahy, which had been cleansed of anthrax spores without eliminating the sender's scent. The handlers either rubbed sterile gauze on the envelopes and exposed the scent packs to the dogs or used a scent machine. The six-hundred-dollar STU-100 device vacuumed scent onto a gauze pad directly from items a suspect had touched or worn close to the skin. The gauze pads could be preserved in an evidence freezer until needed. Bloodhounds have "noses a thousand times more sensitive than a human's" and are the only dogs whose powers of smell are admissible in court.

In the hunt for Jack the Ripper through the streets of Whitechapel, Sir Charles Warren had been ridiculed when he obtained the use of Edwin Brough's two champion Scarborough bloodhounds, Barnaby and Burgho. On October 8, 1888, in Regent's Park, London, handlers on horseback gave a demonstration of the hounds' tracking powers on ground thickly coated with frost. The bloodhounds hunted a man for a mile after he had been given a fifteen-minute head start. They were tested again that night in pitch blackness and the following morning when a half-dozen successful runs were made. Warren himself took the part of the hunted man twice. Unfortunately bloodhounds were never used in tracking Jack through the narrow East End streets.

With little fanfare, FBI agents had been taking bloodhounds to locations frequented by the twelve "persons of interest" on their Amerithrax short list. While they hoped the dogs might leap and bark, meaning they had matched the scent on the letters, they had not reacted at all. They drove the dogs to a series of locations Hatfill frequented, hoping to match the scent on the letter. Larry Harris and his bloodhounds had been flown in from California by the FBI for the Hatfill search. Earlier, the FBI had already taken the three dogs to Louisiana to aid local police in tracking a serial killer. Now they returned.

The dogs were said to have visibly reacted when brought to a Denny's Restaurant in Baton Rouge where Hatfill had eaten the day before. FBI agents also brought the bloodhounds to the Washington, D.C., apartment of his girlfriend. The dogs barked and jumped there too, as they did at places where Hatfill and two women had been. Dr. Hatfill later claimed that agents used heavy-handed tactics when they searched his Malaysian girlfriend's home. "She was manhandled by the FBI upon their entry, not immediately shown the search warrant, her apartment was wrecked while FBI agents screamed at her that I had killed five people and that her life would never be the same again," he said. Rough treatment during the serving of a search warrant had been another of Hoover's ploys.

"Now I recall his girlfriend said we pushed her around," said retired FBI profiler Candice DeLong. "Let me explain what probably happened because I've been on many searches with FBI agents. We don't push people around. The only way she would have been restrained or touched in any way is if she tried to attack any of the agents, then they would have restrained her physically. Probably would have arrested her. That didn't happen. She probably opened the door and there were ten FBI agents there and they said, 'We have a warrant for a search.' They handed it to her, let her read it, and then they went past her. I wouldn't be surprised if one of them merely bumped her and that turned into being manhandled. She was free to leave. She could stay as long as she didn't get in the way or touch anything. FBI agents are polite. We're not jackbooted thugs. It's just more hype to make them look like they're being victimized by the big bad FBI."

On Thursday, August 8, agents arrived at Hatfill's Maryland complex with three leashed police bloodhounds in tow. The handlers of the pure-bred bloodhounds—Lucy, a Southern California hound on loan, Tinker Bell, and Knight—padded toward his apartment. The closer they got, the more agitated they became. The dogs were sniffing, straining at their leashes, and barking—the telltale sign that they had sensed something. At one point they broke free and bounded up to Hatfill, who was outside the apartment sitting in his car. "They went crazy," one law enforcement source later told *Newsweek*.

When they entered his apartment, the dogs also reportedly got excited. "When you see how the dogs got to everything that connected him, you say 'Damn!' " a law enforcement official told *Newsweek*. Could dogs really pick up any scent from a ten-month-old envelope that a terrorist likely had handled with gloves? The FBI claims that usable scent has been collected from evidence three years old.

"I'm a big believer in bloodhounds," said DeLong. "I know what they can do. I've seen them do it. As I recall, the dogs alerted on a restaurant and the girlfriend's place. And the bloodhound is the only dog whose sniffing abilities can be admitted in court or put in an affidavit for a warrant. There's a famous case. A little girl was abducted from an apartment parking lot where she lived. Weeks later—this was in the Boulder area during the dry season—they brought in a bloodhound that sniffed around. It went out to the street and it stopped. The handler decided to see if the girl had been put into a car and driven somewhere. They went a few blocks and let the bloodhound out to sniff around. Every time they did, it would alert they were on the right path.

"They went down the highway miles and miles and miles with this dog and at every exit they'd stop and let the dog out. If the dog didn't go down the exit, they put the dog back into the car and continued on a straight path. The dog finally took them to a highway leading out of town. Finally, the dog alerted and went down the exit and took off on the desert, collapsing in exhaustion. It was not going to stop. You see, the cells exfoliate off your body and go out the exhaust and out the window and then eventually, those skin cells and hair cells fall to the street and that's what the bloodhounds get by with. They bring in a second bloodhound. That hound within minutes found the body of the girl.

"Weeks later, miles and miles out. The grandparents of the victim girl were so impressed they began breeding and raising bloodhounds for law enforcement. It's a wonderful story. The offender was caught and guess what—it was a neighbor. With that said about bloodhounds you can see why I put a lot of faith in them and their reaction in the anthrax case."

Despite the hounds' enthusiasm, the feds left Hatfill's apartment several hours later with nothing concrete linking him to the crime. Drew La France of the National Police Bloodhound Association told reporters that a jury wouldn't convict on dogs alone. "Have bloodhounds made mistakes? Sure." The search took place one day after Hatfill had agreed to meet with agents. Hatfill's attorney, Victor M. Glasberg, criticized investigators for obtaining a search warrant, which he said was unnecessary. He said the agents carried out the search even though the day before the raid he had left a message on the voice mail of one of the FBI's lead investigators, Bob Roth, asserting Dr. Hatfill's continued willingness to cooperate.

"It's all bogus! It's bogus!" Glasberg said. He ridiculed the idea that bloodhounds would be used that way and asked the media to check the story themselves instead of just reporting what someone else reported. "It's not fair," he said. "If the United States wants to charge anybody with a crime, they should damn well go ahead and do it in a fair manner . . . But that's different from the kids' game of telephone, bandying about allegations that get more expansive every time they're repeated, so you can't tell fact from fiction." Dr. Patrick, the holder of multiple anthrax patents, was given a polygraph and asked about Hatfill. The bloodhounds, with his permission, sniffed around Patrick's garage with no result.

IN TRENTON, THE Anthrax Task Force—made up of the FBI, CDC, and U.S. Postal Inspectors—continued interviewing residents and swabbing mailboxes for clues to the source of the anthrax-laden letters. They didn't want to frighten the neighborhood, so they tested at night. Night-time tests had been under way for three weeks, from July 23 to August 13. More than seven hundred samples collected from Trenton mailboxes during June, July, and August were currently undergoing exhaustive testing at the New Jersey Health Department lab.

The postal inspectors weren't worn out. They were used to finding a needle in a haystack. They had had their successes over the years. A Boston division inspector once left for Galveston armed only with a picture of the girlfriend of a fugitive. Calling in all the city letter carriers, he showed the photo around and asked if anyone had ever seen her. A carrier identified her as the wife of a new storekeeper on his route. The fugitive, who had set the store up as a blind to avoid detection, was arrested.

The Task Force continued analyzing the four Amerithrax letters that had survived. The Postal Service had its own labs—five identification laboratories, each serving postal inspectors in a specified geographical area. One was in the Bureau itself; the others were at Chicago, Cincinnati, St. Louis, and San Francisco. Skilled specialists made the examinations, mostly analysis of handwriting in cases involving anonymous and threatening letters, forged money orders, and checks stolen from the mails. The Bureau had compiled a book illustrating every conceivable form of handwriting, including ransom and extortion notes received through the mails. To identify two writings as the product of the same individual, document examiners must depend upon the characteristic significance of a habit based upon departures from the normal copybook patterns.

Back in 1958, the Bureau lab had collaborated with the eminent Dr. William Souder, for thirty-nine years an expert in the Bureau of Standards. He was instrumental in the development of chromatographic analysis. It is possible to determine whether two inks in liquid form are identical and often determine the brand of ink. This technology meant they would be able to match the toner used in the Xerox copier Amerithrax had used.

In the Document Section of the FBI lab, any foreign trait in the hand-printing could be detected and compared with a ready reference of foreign handwriting systems to distinguish accurately between national and individual characteristics in coping with the problem of identification.

At 3:00 A.M. on August 8, the same day the bloodhounds went "crazy" in Frederick, anthrax-bacteria field tests conducted on a single curbside mailbox on the corner of Nassau and Bank Streets in the business district of Princeton registered positive for pathogens.

It was the only positive sample taken from nearly 650 boxes tested in towns whose Zip codes began with "085" and "086." State and federal officials still didn't know if the spores had gotten into the mailbox from the plastic bin used to catch mail or from an actual anthrax letter. If it had been the reusable bin, other mail carriers would have gotten sick. Further tests would reveal if the spores matched the strain of anthrax in the letters.

By 9:00 A.M. the contaminated mailbox had been removed under cover of darkness and replaced with another box of a slightly lighter shade of blue. Only the sharpest eye could have detected the switch. The hot box was airlifted to a lab for further forensic testing. Thirty-nine boxes remained to be tested. Now the inspectors concentrated on local photocopiers. Those were checked for identifying marks. They also reviewed prescription records at local pharmacies to see if large quantities of Cipro had been prescribed.

Agents headed to nearby Borough Hall to search municipal files for tickets issued for traffic violations around the Nassau Street drop box. Son of Sam in New York had finally been caught through a parking ticket he got the night of one of his shootings. The agents specifically asked about Dr. Hatfill. A court clerk told them he hadn't received any tickets in the borough.

When recent reports in the *Sun* and other publications revealed that Dr. Hatfill had claimed a Ph.D. certificate he had not received, he offered an explanation. He had completed the work for the degree at Rhodes University in South Africa and assumed it had been granted. Later, when he learned the degree had not been awarded, he stopped listing it on his resume. But when applying for an NIH research job in 1995, he provided the Rhodes University Ph.D. certificate in molecular cell biology with his name on it, signed by the university vice chancellor and other officials.

According to Angela Stuurman, assistant to the registrar at Rhodes University, "Our parchment doesn't even look like that. It's most definitely a forgery." The university seal was positioned wrong, the vice chancellor's signature had the incorrect middle initial, and other names were made up. Victor Glasberg declined to comment on the degree, telling the press via e-mail: "We are not feeding the media frenzy on collateral issues. If you ask me whether Dr. Hatfill was standing on the grassy knoll when JFK was shot, I will give you the same answer." At least one of his resumes said he was a member of the Royal Society of Medicine, but a spokeswoman for the society said it had no records of his ever being a member.

Hatfill's embroidered claims about his accomplishments, his long residency in Rhodesia and South Africa, his bioweapons training, the loss of his security clearance twenty-six days before the first anthrax letters were mailed—no wonder the FBI, the media, and his fellow scientists were so intrigued. *Newsweek*, in debunking Hatfill's claims of Army heroics, obtained military records that showed he had joined the Marines in 1971, but was discharged a year later. He did a three-year stint in the Army, stationed in the U.S., but did not rise above the rank of private. He was never trained as a pilot. His resume said he served with Army Special Forces, but the Army had no record of that. U.S. records showed he was in America for at least two of the years he claimed to have been fighting in Rhodesia.

"We are very angry at the way they have treated this man, who has done nothing but cooperate fully with the federal authorities," said Jonathan Shapiro. "We're extremely angry at the course of this investigation and the way the United States has seen fit to trash Dr. Hatfill. We've made it clear." Shapiro conceded that the government had no obligation to keep Hatfill's name secret, but said his client was severely damaged. "Through innuendo in the public eye they have begun to destroy this man's life," he said, "his standing in the scientific community, his ability to make a living. This is absolutely wrong. This is outrageous." He accused the government, under pressure to make progress before the anniversary of 9-11, of leaking details from the affidavit submitted with the application for the search warrant, details that were supposed to be kept secret.

Glasberg rebutted some of the various claims in advance. It was rumored that Dr. Hatfill had unfettered access to the Army bioresearch lab at the Institute after his grant ended in 1999. He did not, Glasberg said. "After he stopped working there, he had to be escorted, like everybody," Glasberg said.

The FBI at first theorized that Amerithrax would have contracted anthrax and needed Cipro. Like many of the scientists at the Institute, Hatfill had been inoculated against anthrax. Hatfill claimed he had a limited number of anthrax vaccinations, including an annual booster to maintain immunity. His records said his last inoculation had been in "early" 1999. Since December 2000, he had been susceptible to anthrax. Yearly boosters are required for the anthrax vaccine to remain effective and the FBI speculated that Hatfill had taken booster shots to prevent getting anthrax at the time of the anthrax mailings.

He had not, Glasberg said. Dr. Hatfill waived doctor-patient privilege so agents could ask his doctor about his prescriptions for Cipro. Glasberg explained that Hatfill had had an infection. But if Hatfill had been exposed to anthrax, he might still have been protected. A study done in the 1990s at Fort Detrick said seven out of eight monkeys that were given two doses of anthrax vaccine two weeks apart were protected from exposure to large amounts of the aerosolized Ames strain spores for almost two years after the last dose had been given.

Glasberg answered the charge that Dr. Hatfill had taken 350-pound cabinets from the Institute that could be used to culture anthrax. The obsolete biological cabinets were moved by truck to a training site for military exercises and then blown up, Glasberg said. Fort Detrick spokesman Chuck Dasey corroborated that the biosafety cabinets were "old and nonfunctional." They had gone to the Army's Special Forces Command to help train soldiers to identify apparatus that might be found in a bioweapons facility.

"To the best of our knowledge, there isn't any Greendale School," Glasberg said. "There is a subdivision near Harare called Greendale, but there are Greendales everywhere." The Harare suburb of Greendale was an upper-middle-class neighborhood and had a Greendale grade school. He denied that Hatfill was disgruntled at losing his security clearance. At the Institute Hatfill never had nor needed security clearance, according to Dasey. Virtually none of Hatfill's work at SAIC required a clearance, Glasberg said, but the company used its revocation as a reason to fire Hatfill. He said the company has since offered Hatfill settlement payments, which he rejected, and more work, which he accepted.

Once more the FBI stated it had nothing to indicate that Dr. Hatfill was anywhere near Trenton, New Jersey, where the anthrax letters were mailed. Dr. Hatfill had called a press conference for Sunday, August 11, to address some of the charges against himself. These remarks would concern his skills and access to anthrax spores of the Ames strain and expertise to turn them into a weapon. He would also explain some of the inconsistencies in his accounts of his life.

STRAIN 35

On Dangerous Ground

AS IT APPROACHED 1:00 P.M., starting time for the press conference, the crowd filling the street shuffled their feet. They looked about or skimmed their Sunday papers as they waited. The *Times* said Hatfill had surfaced "several months ago." Other papers ran bits and pieces: "Hatfill has been focused on because of his background in biochemistry . . . Flamboyant and arrogant, with a penchant for exaggerating his achievements . . . Politics: for years complained that U.S. wasn't doing enough to prepare for a bioattack . . . feared his warnings weren't being heeded . . . wanted to prod the country into action . . . the forty-eight-year-old was not a criminal suspect, but 'a person of interest.' "

Pat Clawson took the microphone. "You're going to have an opportunity in just a couple of minutes to meet a distinguished American scientist and a great patriot, Mr. Steven Hatfill," he said with fervor. "He will make a brief statement to various media. He will not be taking any questions. His attorney, however, will be taking questions. I request that we try to treat this proceeding with some dignity and some decorum. Obviously, this is a story of tremendous national interest. Right now for the first time, the American people are going to get to see the man that I have known for the last six years, a man who is a tremendous scientist, a man who is a distinguished medical doctor, a man who is a healer and not a killer. This is not the biological equivalent of the Unabomber."

In the sweltering heat, Dr. Steven J. Hatfill took to the steps in front of his lawyer's brick-red office in Alexandria, Virginia, suburban Washington. It was Sunday, August 11, 2002, and a mob of reporters and the curious, among them FBI agents, had come to see the "person of interest." Hatfill was appearing publicly for the first time. If he thought the coverage of the search of his apartment had been a media circus, this was the real thing—helicopters and television cameras, satellite TV trucks, scores of reporters and photographers. Every word he uttered would be carried on hundreds of stations nationwide and printed in every paper.

The sun fell from his right, glinting on an American flag pin on his lapel. He was attired in a dark suit and blue shirt. The strong light emphasized the angles in his face; the lines on either side of his mouth were cut sharp. In profile, his short brown hair seemed lifeless. His chin, thrust out defiantly, was as strong as the brick building behind him. His beefy face was broad, wide as an Iowa field. His whole build, in fact, was expansive and possessed the same muscular squareness as Tom Ridge's. The two men looked, in many ways, very similar. Hatfill's nose was well formed, but pointed in profile. There were the accents of small moles on his face and thick neck. He was clean-shaven and no longer wore his trademark brown mustache. Now it was his chin that dominated the intelligent face. His brows were knitted. The lowered brows overshadowed dark eyes underscored by circles, eyes that were gunsights as they surveyed the battalion of cameras. Who could blame him for his anger? As with Richard Jewell, his case had been tried in the press. Hatfill would use the media too.

Hatfill came out swinging. He was not going to answer any questions afterward. He strode to a battalion of microphones and prepared to speak to a live national audience. He took out two typed pages. Tense, speaking in strained tones, but well composed, Hatfill began to read his statement. He was angry and sympathetic at turns as he spoke of "outrageous official statements and calculated leaks to the media leading to a feeding frenzy operating to my great prejudice." He accused the FBI of "manhandling" his girlfriend.

The statement composed by Dr. Hatfill, bioweapons expert under scrutiny for the anthrax attacks, began like this:

"Good afternoon, ladies and gentlemen. My name is Steve Hatfill," he said, his voice reedy. For many of the journalists this was the first time they had put a face with the name. "I'm a medical doctor and a biomedical scientist. I am a loyal American, and I love my country. I have had nothing to do in any way, shape, or form with the mailing of these anthrax letters, and it is extremely wrong for anyone to contend or suggest that I have."

Ardently, Dr. Hatfill told the assembly how he had devoted his professional career to safeguarding men, women, and children from the ravages of infectious disease. He was proud that he had protected the nation against the scourge of offensive biological warfare. Pride showed in his eyes.

"I am appalled at the terrible acts of biological terrorism that have caused death, disease and havoc in this great country starting last fall. But I am just as appalled that my experience, knowledge, dedication, and service relative to defending the United States against biological warfare has been turned against me in connection with the search for the anthrax killer."

He explained how last fall two FBI investigators had dropped by his office. Hatfill had considered his brief interview with them to be congenial, with the agents explaining that polygraphs were being conducted on a wide range of scientists in connection with the anthrax letter investigation. When asked if he would consent to a polygraph concerning this incident, Dr. Hatfill said he readily agreed. Later, he had gone down to the Washington field office where an onsite polygraph was administered.

"After reviewing the polygraph charts in private," Hatfill told the press, "the polygraph examiner told me that I had passed and that he believed I had nothing to do with the anthrax letters. The FBI told me they believed I had nothing to do with this incident of terrorism. In due course, following an additional debriefing, the FBI confirmed to me and to my former counsel, Tom Carter, that I was not a suspect in this case."

Hatfill told the press that at this point he had assumed that his involvement in the investigation had been completed. In February, he received a phone call from a reporter "all but accusing me of mailing the anthrax letters." Because the journalist had wanted to know precise details about a classified project on which Hatfill had previously worked, he hung the phone up on him in mid-sentence and reported the conversation to his supervisor as an improper solicitation of classified information. Two days later, Hatfill was informed by a former medical school colleague that the reporter had phoned him too.

"He all but accused me of mailing the anthrax letters," Hatfill told the throng with feeling, claiming that this same journalist afterward telephoned his employer, Science Applications International Corporation, and that shortly thereafter SAIC had laid him off.

Hatfill had been devastated by the loss of his job in March, although he stated he could understand why it occurred. After SAIC, he accepted a job with Louisiana State University to work with a consortium group of universities on important federally and Justice-funded programs for biological warfare defense. Ironically, Dr. Hatfill was called back to SAIC on numerous occasions to assist with projects he had started as well as to assist with new projects. SAIC eventually had to contract for his continued services through LSU.

"According to the *Frederick News-Post* of June 27, 2002," Dr. Hatfill continued, ". . . a woman named Barbara Hatch Rosenberg, who affiliates herself with the Federation of American Scientists, saw fit to discuss me as a suspect in the anthrax case in a meeting with FBI agents and Senate staffers. I don't know Dr. Rosenberg. I have never met her, I have never spoken or corresponded with this woman. And to my knowledge, she is ignorant of my work and background except in the very broadest of terms. The only thing I know about her views is that she and I apparently differ on whether the United States should sign on to a proposed modification of the international biological weapons convention. This was something I opposed to safeguard American industry, and I believe she favored. I am at a complete loss to explain her reported hostility and accusations. I don't know this woman at all."

As Hatfill spoke his right finger would dart out. He emphasized important points with a jab. He raised his chin skyward and pointed his finger to the heavens. He had done his share of public speaking. Obviously, he was deeply moved and had given his comments considerable thought. Originally, his speech had been much longer, but in the light of recent events he had shortened it. He said, in discussing Dr. Rosenberg, that within a few days after her reported comments in Congress, the FBI had come to his home again, requesting to look at his apartment and swab the walls for anthrax spores. This request surprised Hatfill. He knew that anthrax is a deadly inhalational disease. While previously working at

Building 1412 at Fort Detrick he had, like many researchers there, gotten a limited number of anthrax vaccinations. Hatfill stated that a yearly booster was required to maintain immunity, and that he had last been inoculated beginning in 1999.

"Since December 2000," he said, "I am as susceptible to anthrax as any of you. So I was surprised at the notion that I might have brought anthrax to my home, and would have been even amused if it was not for the fact that this matter is so grave and serious. In addition, I have two cleaning ladies with their own keys that come and go and clean. I don't know when they come there, just that things look a lot better when they leave."

Dr. Hatfill not only agreed to sign a release for a search of his apartment, but volunteered searches of his car and a small, unrefrigerated storage area in Florida where he kept some books, a few original paintings, and some other personal effects. Some news reports had maintained that the unit had been refrigerated. He told the journalists that agents had assured him that the search would be "quiet, private, and very low-key." The reality had been considerably different. Within minutes of his signing, helicopters churned the air above his apartment block and overhead television cameras and satellite TV trucks were broadcasting. He told how FBI agents and hazardous-materials technicians fully garbed in protective space suits arrived in a huge truck. Ironically, Dr. Hatfill had previously helped train one of the FBI agents who searched his apartment.

"Responding to my surprise and dismay," Hatfill told the reporters, "the agent-in-charge apologized to me, saying that the request for this swabbing and search had come from very, very high up. A written and televised media frenzy ensued and continues, with journalists, columnists and others writing, stating and repeating combinations of defamatory speculation, innuendo, and other accusations about me. Several have urged the FBI to step up its investigation of me. And indeed, last week, the FBI executed a search warrant on my residence. This happened one day after my attorneys had left a message on the lead FBI investigator's voice mail confirming my continued readiness to answer questions and otherwise cooperate. My girlfriend's home was also searched. She was manhandled by the FBI upon their entry, not immediately shown the search warrant. Her apartment was wrecked, while FBI agents screamed at her that I had killed five people and that her life would never be the same again. She was terrified by their conduct, put into isolation for interrogation for eight hours. I was horrified. The search was another media event."

Dr. Hatfill told how the very next day he was placed on paid leave from his new job at LSU. Naturally, this was painful to him, though he said once again how he understood the circumstances in which his employers had found themselves in light of the actions taken against him. As a scientist in the field of biological warfare defense, he stated he had never had any reservation about aiding the anthrax investigation in any way he could. He said that he was happy to be of assistance, as part of the price that scientists in the field of biodefense are glad to pay, a price more than offset by the satisfaction they had gained in doing work that they believed was important to the security of the country. Next, he remade an important point.

"It's true that my research expertise is in biology—for example, the Ebola virus, the Marburg virus, and monkeypox—and not bacteriology, as in the case of the anthrax organism. It's also true that I have never, ever worked with anthrax in my life. It's a separate field from the research I was performing at Fort Detrick."

He spoke of how Americans value freedom of speech and of the press, freedoms, he said, that were essential for our continued way of life. However, he added, "with this freedom comes responsibility. That responsibility has been abdicated here by some in the media and some in the government."

Hatfill said he, like all Americans, was appalled at the anthrax terrorist incident, and wished the authorities godspeed in catching the culprits or culprit. He explained to the press, listening eagerly now, that while he did not object to being considered a subject of interest by the authorities because of his knowledge and background in the field of biological warfare defense, he did object to an investigation characterized "by outrageous official statements and calculated leaks to the media." Many in the crowd agreed with that point.

Hatfill said he especially objected to character assassination and reference to events from his past. He believed that those events bore absolutely no relationship to the question of who the anthrax killer is. "After eight months of one of the most intensive public and private investigations in American history," Dr. Hatfill said firmly, "no one, no one has come up with a shred of evidence that I had anything to do with the anthrax letters." He again pointed out that he had never worked with anthrax. Strong emotions twisted his rugged features. The corners of his mouth turned down. The press knew this was high drama.

"As a substitute, the press and now the public have been offered events from my past going back twenty or more years, as if this were critical to the matter at hand. In fact, it is not. It is a smoke screen calculated to obscure the fact that there is no evidence that I, the currently designated fall guy, have anything to do with the anthrax letters."

Hatfill said he did not claim to have lived a perfect life, and like the assembled reporters, there were things he would probably have done or said differently than he did ten or twenty or more years ago. Because of modern information-retrieval technology, he said, "coupled with sufficient motivation, can lead to anyone's life and work being picked apart for every error, wrinkle, failed memory, or inconsistency. Mine can; so can yours. Does any of this get us to the anthrax killers? If I am a subject of interest, I'm also a human being. I have a life. I have, or I had, a job. I need to earn a living. I have a family, and until recently, I had a reputation, a career, and a bright professional future."

At one point he began to well up, covering his nose with his hand to push back his emotions. His nose visibly reddened and his ears crimsoned.

He next acknowledged the right of the authorities and press to satisfy themselves as to whether he was the anthrax mailer, but that they have no right to smear him and "gratuitously make a wasteland of my life in the process. I will not be railroaded!"

As he said this, his mouth became a long straight line and he spoke the last of his remarks in measured words.

"I am a loyal American. I am extremely proud of the work I have done for the United States and for my country and her people. I expect to be treated as such by the representatives of my government and those who report its work. Thank you very much, ladies and gentlemen."

He stepped back into the cool shadow of the doorway. Now Hatfill's lawyer took the microphone in the growing heat. Though Hatfill took no questions, he stood behind Vic Glasberg as the lawyer fielded some. Glasberg identified himself and said that about three weeks ago, Dr. Hatfill had come to see him about problems he was having with the press and rumors about him. Glasberg told the press that he was not a criminal lawyer, but a civil litigator, and that his client had wanted assistance on civil law.

Glasberg said that he had advised his client to step up to the plate. "The notion was that stepping forward and handing out the truth," he said, "stating what the facts were, and letting it all hang out, would be the best way to counter the misinformation, the half-information, and in some cases correct information but presented in a terrible context, that was in the process of making his life a wasteland. I told him that he would have to be—not merely crazy, but stupid—to do what I was suggesting if there was the slightest possibility that he was facing any kind of liability in relation to the anthrax matters. He said, 'I want to do it.' "

Glasberg explained how his client had written out a lengthy statement covering the time from medical school to the present. Just before the warrant on Hatfill's house had been served, Glasberg learned that he had been called by Bob Roth, one of the lead investigators on the anthrax investigation. Roth wanted to see Hatfill to debrief him again. Hatfill told Roth, "That's fine. Please call my lawyer and set it up." Glasberg said he waited for Roth's call and when it didn't come, he phoned him. He wasn't in, so Glasberg left a voicemail message suggesting that they get together between August fifth and seventh. Hatfill was leaving for Louisiana August eighth.

Glasberg said he wasn't called, except by Hatfill who informed him that the FBI had just served a warrant for searching his residence. Astounded, Glasberg called Roth and asked if he did not understand that Hatfill remained in a mode of total cooperation. "Oh, no, no I didn't understand that," he said. Glasberg got the name of the U.S. Attorney handling the case, Ken Kohl at the U.S. Attorney's Office in the District, and met with him the following week.

"Both of the *media* searches," Glasberg began, then laughed. "Excuse me . . . both of the FBI searches were major media events. . . . I will also tell you that today I was advised by ABC News that they have obtained a copy of the manuscript of the novel that Steve was working on. He was working on a novel dealing with bioterrorism kinds of things—his professional concerns. Well, they won't tell me where they got it, and I understand that you all can't leak your sources, but so far as we're aware, there is only one place that it could have been obtained: it was on his hard drive that was on his computer that the FBI seized pursuant to the warrant that was obtained with a subpoena . . . with an affidavit filed under seal, so that material seized in what is surely the most important criminal investigation internally in this country in a long while is now being leaked, and I'll be dealing with the Office of Professional Responsibility at the Department of Justice with regard to that."

Again it was driven home to the sweltering journalists and to the millions of Americans watching that Hatfill understood that he is a "biological warfare guru and that the officials have a right to be interested in him." Glasberg also stressed that as far as real substantive evidence there was none that he knew of. What he did know about, he said, was the continuing drumbeat of things that were part of his client's life ten, twenty, twenty-five years ago. Glasberg reiterated, "We don't live perfect lives. I'll tell you this, I wouldn't want people asking me what I was doing twenty-five years ago." He then agreed to take some questions, but only relating to aspects of the investigation of which he had direct knowledge. Glasberg said the investigation had been plagued by the game of "telephone" in which everybody repeats what he heard from somebody else. He specifically wanted to avoid that.

"Sir," asked a reporter, "do you have any reason to believe that a team of scientists in the biodefense community might be trying to frame Mr. Hatfill? And is Mrs. Rosenberg involved in that?"

"Steve has always held his colleagues in the highest regard," said Glasberg. Steve does not believe that anybody he worked with at Fort Detrick is implicated in this. It is a total puzzlement to him as to why these things are being vented the way they are. With regard to Dr. Rosenberg, I beg you: Speak to her. Ask her, why is she writing what she's writing and why is she saying what she's saying?"

Glasberg agreed it was appropriate for the government to have a "proper, discreet, professional, ethical, and appropriate investigation" into the Amerithrax case. He did not think the government should unload "smoke screen stuff that sells good because they don't have substance." He suggested that "no comment" was better than innuendo and that the FBI shouldn't scapegoat, shouldn't leak.

"This man has been called a 'Nazi swine,' " said Glasberg. "His daughter, who is a police officer, has had her home address posted on the Internet. His life has been laid bare for the past quarter-century. When you say the word *anthrax*, his heart jumps in this throat. So, I could not recommend [he take another polygraph test]." Asked if Hatfill had access to anthrax, Glasberg replied: "The short answer is: It all depends upon what you mean by having access. It's my understanding . . . and you can check this with Fort Detrick . . . is that the labs and the decontamination locations are separate and that he did not work in the bacteriological area. That's the answer that I can give you."

Glasberg said he knew nothing more of the case than a number of pieces published by Dr. Rosenberg on the Web and what he had read in the papers. He had found those entirely consistent with what he had read in the media.

A reporter queried Glasberg about Hatfill's history. "Was there any connection between him," he asked, "and the elementary school that is listed as the return address? Or is that just a rumor that got blown up in the press?"

"The sum total of the knowledge I have about this is the following: Dr. Hatfill lived in or near Harare, Zimbabwe, for a number of years. There is a subdivision in Harare called Greendale. He did not live there. We have attempted to determine whether there is a school there called The Greendale School. The information we have is that there is no such Greendale School. So, that is the total connection that we know. The name Greendale School was used and he lived in a city where there was a section called Greendale. I think there are several hundred, or thousands, of Greendales in the United States."

Glasberg answered a question about Hatfill's full cooperation with the FBI, and what else that entailed besides a polygraph. "Did it include writing examples that could be compared with the letters that were found?" a reporter asked.

"I do not know. He took the polygraph. He was asked to be debriefed. He was debriefed. He answered every single question. He didn't withhold a question. He was asked if his house could be searched. It was searched without warrant. He was asked if his car could be searched. It was searched. Could his storage facility in Florida be searched? It was searched. So, and the ongoing posture that he has had toward the government has been one of—tell me what you want and I'll give it to you."

Glasberg explained how he would have handled the matter if he were an investigator. His approach would have been to ask all the nice questions first, get all the information possible through cooperation, and only then ask, "Okay, sir, now how about this." To Glasberg's thinking that was the method by which you got more data. "If you hit them at the start with the nasty questions," he said, "you get resistance and they clam up. I should imagine that a more appropriate way of conducting an investigation is getting what you can without antagonizing the person you are trying to get information from. And, by the way, I should also say that, had they shown up with a warrant, it could have been kept in their pocket, just knock on the door and say, 'Dr. Hatfill, we're very sorry but we need to search your place again.' I know exactly what would have happened. He would have called me up and said, 'Vic, they want to search my place again.' I would have said, 'Let them in, go to the movies.' "

Naturally, the civil litigator was asked if he saw any similarities between Dr. Hatfill's situation and that of Wen Ho Lee and Richard Jewell. Glasberg laughed and said, "Yes . . . by way of escalated innuendo, accusation, and mudslinging in an entirely premature manner. Whether this man is guilty or innocent should be determined in an appropriate process and in an intelligent process, which permits the question to be answered. You don't take some punitive suspect and drag him through the mud and hope you've got the right guy. It doesn't end up being a good result, criminally, as Wen Ho Lee who was apologized to by a United States district judge or Richard Jewell, as those cases show."

Glasberg thought the bloodhound search was "bogus" and "untenable" because as far as he knew the process doesn't work that way since the scents were ten months' old. When asked if Dr. Hatfill had the expertise and knowledge to have carried out the anthrax attacks, Glasberg repeated that Hatfill "does not work with anthrax, has not worked with anthrax, has not cultured anthrax . . . I think the proper answer to that question is 'probably not.' But that's going to be for him and scientists to discuss."

A law enforcement official said afterward, "Some people have said this is our guy, but others have not. But if there was anything significant, we would have moved on to the next stage including further searches [and taking Hatfill in for questioning and possible arrest] . . . To be honest, we don't have anybody that is real good. That is why so much energy has gone into Hatfill—because we don't have anybody else. There is a feeling of 'where do we go now?' A lot of other people have already been crossed off the list."

The number of "persons of interest" remained constant and while some were cleared to be replaced by others, Hatfill remained on the list. Shapiro, Hatfill's criminal lawyer, also told reporters he was not going to address inconsistencies in his client's resume. "Our hands are full," he said. "We have not been concerned to address matters going back twenty-five years. We are focusing on what's happening today."

Meanwhile, MI5, the British security service, was in contact with Porton Down to find out about Hatfill's movements. Hatfill had traveled to Britain shortly before November 12, 2001, and left sometime after November 23. A hoax anthrax letter, which investigators believe may have been posted by the anthrax terrorist in London during that period, was sent to Sen. Tom Daschle.

Hatfill's travel expenses to Britain during his two-week trip were paid by the British Foreign Office. At Porton Down he trained as a United Nations bioweapons inspector so he could be on call to go to Iraq and track down anthrax and other germ weapons. During the course Hatfill worked with twenty or so other international scientists who attended the course. Inside, the scientists created a mockup of an Iraqi germ warfare laboratory. Scientists on the UN course recalled Hatfill as "well-rounded, energetic and outgoing." That type of personality certainly did not fit the FBI's suspect profile of a "loner."

Although Hatfill claimed to have had no access to anthrax during his two-year fellowship at the Institute, Fort Detrick's Dasey said, "He could have worked in proximity to someone who was working on anthrax."

And what of the doctor who told President Clinton in 1998 that he would have to place greater priority on negotiating a protocol to enforce the biological arms treaty if he wanted to stop the spread of germ weapons? She had met with FBI agents in June after months of complaining that they were failing to pursue a prime suspect who seemed to fit their own profile. The day of Hatfill's press conference the doctor told the AP, "I have never mentioned any names, not publicly, not to the Senate committee or staff, not to anyone. I have never said or written anything that pointed only to one specific person. If anyone sees parallels, that's their opinion." She added that Hatfill "has been misinformed" about her role and that she has "a certain sympathy" for him. "He may be falsely accused," she said, "and I don't think the FBI should do that publicly." Several days after this person met with the FBI, said Hatfill, agents approached him again and asked if they could examine his apartment to "swab the walls for anthrax spores." Hatfill said he was surprised at the request since anthrax is a deadly disease, but consented to the search anyway.

Ronald Kessler, an author of two books on the FBI, said Hatfill's complaints were predictable. "A lot of these claims don't make any sense," he said, adding that FBI Director Mueller's record of conducting investigations had been flawless since he took over almost a year earlier. Kessler said that if the FBI disclosed Hatfill's name, the Bureau probably had its reasons. Athan Theoharis, a history professor from Marquette University said the Bureau's conduct toward Hatfill was troubling and heavy-handed. Theoharis said if the FBI had evidence against Hatfill, it should reveal it. If not, it should have conducted the investigation quietly. "Here," he said, "you have a case of publicity that has the effect of convicting."

Hatfill told the *Washington Post,* "I went from someone with pride in my work, pride in my profession, to being made into the biggest criminal of the twenty-first century, for something I never touched. What I've been trying to contribute, my work, is finished. My life is destroyed."

STRAIN 36

The Big Heat

"MSNBC, AT THE time he had those press conferences," said former FBI agent Candice DeLong, "had me commenting right afterward on Dr. Hatfill's press conference. Talk about your righteous indignation." That evening on the *ABC World News Tonight*, Terry Moran discussed the former government scientist and germ warfare expert's passionate denial of any involvement in the anthrax attacks. "Dr. Steven Hatfill is one of dozens of scientists who have taken lie detector tests at the FBI's request," said Moran, "but the only one whose case has been discussed publicly in great detail."

Moran told how Dr. Hatfill in his first public comments had described himself as the victim of an unethical investigation and a media frenzy. From Washington, ABC's Barry Serafin had details. After keeping a low profile for months, Serafin said, "Hatfill went public today to deny any involvement in the anthrax attacks. Hatfill . . . focused on viruses, not bacteria such as anthrax." Serafin said Dr. Hatfill had allowed a search of his apartment near Fort Detrick in June, but was upset when agents returned this month with a warrant for highly publicized searches of his apartment and that of his girlfriend's. Hatfill had complained of government leaks, specifically a manuscript of a novel he had been writing. Today, part of the manuscript had been obtained by ABC affiliate WJLA in Washington. WJLA reporter Rebecca Cooper reported that Hatfill's novel envisioned a biological attack on Congress in which members of Congress, congressional aides, and hundreds of Washington residents become ill or many die. "Late today," continued Serafin, "the FBI responded to Hatfill's remarks, saying any credible allegations concerning mishandling of evidence will be investigated thoroughly. As far as the FBI is concerned, Hatfill is not a suspect, but along with others he remains a person of interest."

Brian Ross spelled out why investigators seemed to remain suspicious of Hatfill.

"In 1999, while working for a defense contractor," said Ross, "Hatfill commissioned a report looking at how anthrax might be sent through the mail. That report suggested there would be about 2.5 grams of anthrax in an envelope. And, except for the AMI letter that was thrown away, that's what was in last fall's mailings."

Ross elaborated, explaining that Hatfill did not work on the report. Under instructions from the CIA, Hatfill and another scientist, Joseph Soukup, commissioned a study of a hypothetical anthrax attack in February 1999. The work was done by bioterrorism expert William Patrick III. Ross listed some of the things that apparently intrigued the FBI about their person of interest. Some of his former coworkers at Fort Detrick were the first to tell the FBI they were suspicious of him as the anthrax mailer. Ross listed the loss of his top secret security clearance August 23, 2001 and the apparent misrepresentation of a number of items on his resume.

"Although he has claimed that he was a member of the U.S. Special Forces from 1975 to 1977," said Ross, "the U.S. Army has denied this. Army records indicate that he took part in a special forces training course but dropped out of it. Dr. Hatfill moved to England in 1994 and his CV claims that he became a member of the Royal Society of Medicine. But a spokeswoman for the society told the *New York Times* last week that they had no record of him being a member. He has also claimed to have a Ph.D. from Rhodes University in South Africa but has since removed this claim, saying there had been a misunderstanding. He was said at that time to be mad at the world, mad at the government, and many in the FBI thought that perhaps gave him the motive for some kind of revenge against the government. As well, he's known as a person who has worked around anthrax experts, although the FBI concedes he could not himself make anthrax, does not have what they call 'the bench skills' to make it."

ABC reported there was scant evidence that led to anyone, Dr. Hatfill or anyone else. The FBI had no fingerprints or DNA, and at the moment some of the thrust of its investigation had focused on other letters that were mailed with phony anthrax, including one sent from London in November to Senator Daschle.

Moran concluded with the most important statement, "We should emphasize, as Brian did, that the FBI has not formally named Dr. Hatfill as a suspect in this case." Just as the Bureau had not named Richard Jewell or Wen Ho Lee.

As agents nosed around the scientific community, one name kept coming up: Dr. Hatfill's. "In the small, insular world of germ scientists, his outsized personality stood out," wrote *Newsweek*. "He told colleagues tales of his exploits as a Cold Warrior in the '70s, fighting with the SAS troops and the notorious Selous Scouts of the white Rhodesian Army against black rebels. He claimed a brilliant career in the U.S. military, bragging to a friend that he flew fighter planes and helicopters. On his resume he listed impressive credentials, including degrees in medicine from a Rhodesian university and a Ph.D. in microbiology from Rhodes University in South Africa."

On Monday, August 12, the news was still focused on Hatfill's bold press conference. Ross said on *Good Morning America*, "Despite the attention Hatfill has been receiving, he is not believed to have the ability to make anthrax. The only person in the U.S. known to be able to make anthrax is a man named William Patrick, who happens to be a friend of Hatfill's."

THE FBI HAD taken nearly a year to test all mailboxes around Hamilton Processing Center, the fountainhead of the contaminated New Jersey mail stream. If no other boxes were found to be tainted, then all the letters had been mailed from the same Nassau Street box. United States Representative Rush Holt criticized the FBI on Thursday. "It appears," he said, "that it has taken the FBI nearly a year to test all these mailboxes for anthrax. One does not need to be a trained criminologist to know that identifying where the tainted envelopes entered the mail stream should be a primary goal of the FBI investigation. . . . I have doubt whether the FBI has even now tested all the mailboxes feeding Hamilton for anthrax."

Finally Governor James E. McGreevey announced publicly that anthrax spores had been found in a single curbside mailbox. Dr. Clinton R. Lacy, commissioner of the New Jersey Department of Health and Senior Services said the positive result on the mailbox came from full lab tests. Mail carrier Cleveland Stevenson was still servicing the mailboxes in the area, but now he was wearing gloves.

All day Monday, Postal Inspector James Britt and a Trenton detective canvassed the streets surrounding the box across from the Princeton University campus showing local shop owners and workers a color photo. "Does this person look familiar?" "Have you seen him in the area around the third week of September? In October?" "No," came the answer. All along Nassau and Bank Streets they stopped citizens and showed them a color photo of a younger and mustachioed Hatfill. "I've seen him in the newspaper," said one. "I'd love to say that I did see him on the street here but I didn't. Obviously, you are looking for some sort of connection between the two." They questioned merchants whose establishments were near the mailbox where Amerithrax had mailed his letters. Several merchants said they recognized the man as Hatfill, having seen him on television.

They spoke to shop owners a block away and around the post office. A female employee of a Palmer Square coffeeshop told investigators she recognized the picture shown to her by an FBI agent and police officer. She said she didn't know who Steven J. Hatfill was, but thought she saw the man in the photo in her shop late the previous summer. "I definitely recognized him," she said. "I remembered his face." Agents interviewed her for about three minutes and took her name and phone number.

On Tuesday, the FBI safety-packaged an additional thirty-nine swabs taken from other Trenton mailboxes and sent them to the state lab for full analysis. Mail drop boxes in New Jersey had been tested based on postal coding that recorded when items entered the mail system. The Postal Service was able to pinpoint boxes where mail originated through this coding. Agents fanned out in downtown Princeton. They paid a visit to Princeton University and took samples of all the photocopy machines throughout the institution. No anthrax research was conducted there, and the inspectors declined questioning anyone in the Princeton microbiology department.

Agents searched fruitlessly the rest of the day for a connection between Hatfill and that public mailbox. Anthony Federico, chief of the Princeton

Borough police, said he expected them to complete their rounds with the help of his officers before long. "They're just going around and talking to people," he said. Several Justice Department officials declined to say whether or not the circulation of Hatfill's picture signified an advancement in the investigation. Agents were told that late the previous November, Hatfill was in the Trenton area. He had been attending a conference with a colleague. However, detectives could not place him there any earlier, at the time of the anthrax mailings.

Pat Clawson said the FBI should either reveal why the government was interested in him or clear him. "The only thing the FBI has said is that he has a very colorful background, yet they are destroying this man's reputation," Clawson said. "Normally when you're doing a photo canvassing, you have photos of more than one person, because you want to eliminate false identifications. The fact that the FBI is using only one photo makes the entire process suspect.

"I just spoke to him," said Clawson, "and he categorically denies that he's ever been in Princeton. He couldn't find it on a map, and he doesn't even know where it is in New Jersey." Clawson didn't know where Hatfill was on the days when the anthrax letters were mailed from Princeton. The FBI apparently knew. Hatfill provided them with his diary and travel calendar in May or June.

The FBI publicly declared that Hatfill was no more or less important than thirty other "people of interest" in the investigation, but conceded that he was being treated differently. A U.S. official close to the case speaking on condition of anonymity told the AP that Hatfill's apartment was the only home searched under a warrant in connection to the case.

One senior law enforcement official said the FBI was avoiding discussion of Hatfill to prevent a "Richard Jewell" situation. Without naming him as a suspect, the FBI was making him appear as one. "When there is little evidence of wrongdoing, the FBI has to be careful," said Lawrence Goldman, president of the National Association of Criminal Defense Lawyers. "There is a general lack of sensitivity in law enforcement as to how reputations are destroyed."

Ten months after the attacks-by-mail, some of the nation's top researchers were increasingly doubtful that they would ever find evidence linking anyone to the crime. Residue of anthrax microbes had not been found during searches of Hatfill's car, apartment, Florida storage unit, or his girlfriend's home. Phillip Hanna, a microbiologist at the University of Michigan Medical School, said that over-the-counter bleach would destroy all traces of anthrax. "Chances of finding something get more and more remote [as time passes]," he said.

Lawyers for Hatfill lodged formal ethics complaints with the FBI and Justice Department, saying investigators leaked information (and his novel) about their client to the news media, violating DOJ regulations. Glasberg refused to provide details of the complaint he filed at the Justice Department's Office of Professional Responsibility and the FBI. He would only say that he had "presented certain concerns and asked for an inquiry and appropriate action." He argued that investigators had unfairly singled Hatfill out as one of about thirty, then twenty-six, and now twenty "persons of interest."

On Monday, August 19, two mail processing centers in Edison and Eatontown, New Jersey, were examined again for anthrax. U.S. Postal Service authorities began testing to see if the anthrax spores found in the Princeton mailbox had been there since the previous fall. On Wednesday, Dr. Lacy said that the chances of mail being contaminated by the spores found in the mail were "vanishingly small. I think the most important take-home message from this is that since October of 2001, there have been no new cases of anthrax in humans in New Jersey." The following day, Dale L. Watson, the FBI's counterterrorism chief, who had overseen the investigations of the 9-11 terror attacks and then worked the anthrax mailings, announced he was going to leave the Bureau. Watson had worked on counterterrorism and counterintelligence investigations since 1982. His departure came at a critical time and might hint at a larger shakeup by Mueller. "With Watson's departure, we're changing horses in the middle of a very dangerous stream," a Congressional aide said.

Hatfill's lawyer filed an ethics complaint against Attorney General Ashcroft for singling his client out and for leaking information about him to the press. The complaint characterized Ashcroft's actions as "unAmerican," accusing "the attorney general, a deeply religious Christian, of breaking the Ninth Commandment." Hatfill now intensified efforts to clear his name, filing complaints against specific agents and charging them with violating his privacy by continuing to follow and harass him and "ruining his life." Bitter and angry, Dr. Hatfill held his second press conference on Sunday, August 25. "Good afternoon, ladies and gentlemen," he began. "Two weeks ago, I reluctantly appeared before the TV cameras to defend myself against the bizarre allegations that were appearing about me in the news media dealing with last year's anthrax attacks. These allegations were fueled by ongoing leaks from the Justice Department, and those leaks continue to this day."

He explained that Justice Department representatives had confirmed to the Associated Press several days ago that there was no evidence linking him to the anthrax attacks. "Despite this lack of evidence," Hatfill said, "I am still hounded by the FBI, victimized in a never-ending torrent of leaks and general innuendo from the United States Attorney General John Ashcroft and unnamed others, all of which is then amplified and embellished by the media."

Dr. Hatfill considered this an assassination of his character and an effort on the part of the government to demonstrate to the nation that it was proceeding vigorously with the anthrax investigation. Reluctantly, he was taking a second opportunity to "look his fellow Americans directly in the eye" and declare to them that he was not the anthrax killer, that he had no knowledge of the anthrax attacks and had absolutely nothing to do with them.

"My life is being destroyed by arrogant government bureaucrats," he told the assembled press, "who are peddling groundless innuendo and half information about me to gullible reporters who, in turn, repeat this to the press under the guise of news."

Repeatedly, Dr. Hatfill singled out Ashcroft for openly naming him as a person of interest. In doing this, Hatfill claimed, Ashcroft not only violated Justice Department regulations and guidelines, which bind him as the nation's top law enforcement official, but in his view, broke the Ninth Commandment: "Thou shalt not bear false witness."

"I have never met Mr. Ashcroft," he said. "I don't know him. I've never spoken with him. And I do not understand his personalized focus on me."

Though his lawyers could find no legal definition for a person of interest, Hatfill had his own working definition for such a "prejudicial label." "A person of interest," he said, "is someone who comes into being when the government is under intense political pressure to solve a crime but can't do so, either because the crime is too difficult to solve or because the authorities are proceeding in what can mildly be called a wrongheaded manner."

Dr. Hatfill deemed himself the "serviceable target" who made it unnecessary for the FBI to produce a warm body, a person about whom mysterious questions could be raised, someone with an interesting or colorful background like himself. Once he was a person of interest, Hatfill alleged, then the government could leak appropriate rumor and innuendo to the press.

"Then they sit back," he told the reporters, "and watch an uncharged and presumptively innocent person picked apart by journalists looking for hot stories."

Hatfill said the only useful objective achieved by this was that the FBI then could be seen to be on the job. "God help us all," he said, "if the FBI's pursuit of Mr. Ashcroft's person of interest, me, represents that progress. I would like to tell you about how Mr. Ashcroft's progress has played out in my life and that of my loved ones. When you become a person of interest . . . they will make small but carefully orchestrated leaks to the press designed to drive news reporters into a frenzy, in an effort to uncover every minuscule, tiny detail of your life."

He believed the press would do most of the work for the FBI as they came up with items of personal information, no matter how scandalous or insignificant. When the *New York Times* reported that Hatfill had access to a secret cabin in the woods, the FBI questioned him about it. Then they interrogated his friend, a prominent Washington, D.C., lawyer, who sometimes invited Hatfill to dinner at his modern three bedroom home in the Shenandoah Valley in Virginia. Next the FBI had demanded to search the lawyer's house.

"A photo of the house," said Hatfill, "then becomes featured prominently on the pages of a northern Virginia daily, under a headline that says, LINKED TO ANTHRAX. Friends and neighbors of the lawyer then stop coming to visit him because they were afraid of catching anthrax or some other disease or simply did not want to be associated with the incident."

Hatfill had helped develop a biodefense training program for first responders, police and fire departments. He claimed that some reporters now suggested it was a blueprint for the anthrax attacks.

"Almost a quarter-century ago," he continued, "I lived in a city that had a suburb named Greendale. The FBI and some in media willingly linked this with a nonexistent Greendale School that appeared in the return address on the anthrax letters. ABC News even reported as a fact that I lived next door to that nonexistent school for four years. . . . My entire life history has been laid out on the Internet by reporters and conspiracy nuts. My daughter, a policewoman in Detroit, with a child, even found her name and home address published, a reckless and dangerous act that invites retaliation from criminals. It is one thing to have your alleged faults and misdeeds publicly aired because you are seeking as a candidate for a high office, but I am a private citizen, and one who has not sought the limelight."

Dr. Hatfill spelled out from his point of view what it was like to be labeled a person of interest by the attorney general. He then pointed out his problems with Barbara Hatch Rosenberg, whom he said he didn't know and had never met. "Another person I've never met or spoken to and don't know," he continued, "is Nicholas Kristof of the *New York Times*. After transparently implicating me as 'Mr. Z,' over a period of months he berated the FBI for not investigating me aggressively enough to suit him." Hatfill claimed that Kristof had never called him, asked for comment, or contacted any of his representatives before he published.

"Following my first press appearance," said Hatfill, "Mr. Kristof said, for example, that I had failed three successive polygraph examinations since January. This is a total lie. I have not taken, let alone failed, three polygraphs on anthrax since January. I had one polygraph session, which the FBI did administer to me in January, and I was told I passed and the examiner was satisfied that I had told the truth."

Dr. Hatfill asked aloud why Kristof had never called him about this allegation. He asked, "Mr. Kristof, why do you write such things? Why did you not at least check your facts? What have I done to injure you in this manner? Why do you permit yourself to be used as a vehicle to leak irreparably damaging information about me to the public?" Hatfill admitted that Kristof's statement that he was under constant surveillance by the FBI was true. But he argued that there was no reason that the information should be gratuitously broadcast, making him a pariah and shunned by his friends. He asked Kristof if it was necessary, right, or fair for him to write such things?

"The answer, of course," Hatfill said, "is that I am a person of interest."

Candice DeLong, retired FBI profiler, was so far not convinced as she listened. "The one thing that Hatfill engaged in that tipped in for me was this bullshit phony life of his," she said "that he went so far as to print on job resumes going back years—a member of Special Forces, a Ph.D. Come on, we all have a fantasy life, but to go so far as putting down degrees you don't have and military service you don't have on an application for official employment. That's pretty serious. He put himself in the hot seat when he tried to get a job with the CIA and failed the polygraph. I used to do background investigations—before you sign a federal document they ask, 'Is everything in this application true to the best of your knowledge? Don't leave out any job you've ever had.' He probably signed it 'Yes, everything's true.'

"Then when you go for your CIA polygraph, pretty much the three main questions are: 'Are you a spy? Secondly, are you in compliance with the FBI/CIA drug policy?' which means you can't have even a toke off a marijuana cigarette for the last three years; you can't have used it so many times in your life. 'Are you in compliance with the drug policy, yes or no?' And the third question is: 'Is everything on your application true and accurate? Did you leave anything out?' I bet you that's the question he actually failed. Those are the minimum questions you'd be asked by the FBI and CIA. His application was not truthful and so they washed him out. And then, his current employer was notified by the CIA that his clearance was being pulled."

Hatfill distributed copies of his lawyers' communications with the *Times* and Kristof in which he requested that the paper publish an op-ed reply from him. So far, he claimed, they had not agreed to do this

"When you are a person of interest," Hatfill said, "your home is subject to search based on statements in sealed affidavits, which your lawyers are not permitted to see. Armed with a secretly obtained government search warrant, FBI agents can enter your home with impunity and take virtually anything they want, including your car registration, your tax records, your car keys, the deeds to your house—if you have one—your apartment, rental agreements, cell phone, pagers, unused bank checks, checks made out to you but not yet cashed, clothing. They can keep these items for as long as they want, unless you go out and retain and pay a lawyer and you can convince a judge that you should get your property back. It is definitely not good to be the girlfriend of a person of interest."

Dr. Hatfill told the assembled press that his girlfriend had been locked inside an FBI car and hauled off to FBI headquarters. Prior to a long interrogation she had not been told that she had the right to leave at any time. Her requests for a lawyer were delayed and made difficult. The contents of her purse, although not on the search warrant, were examined as she was driven back to her residence. Her purse was taken from her and its contents examined after questioning. Hatfill alleged she had been shouted at by FBI agents who claimed they had firm evidence that he had killed five innocent people.

"The FBI trumpets that I am not a suspect," he said, "and the woman I love is told by the FBI . . . that I am a murderer. This is the life of a person of interest, Mr. Ashcroft. But that's not all. My girlfriend was told that she better take a polygraph examination and cooperate, or else. Her home checkbooks, computers, private papers and car were seized. As for her home, it was completely trashed, as is appropriate for the home of a girlfriend of a person of interest. Some of her delicate pottery was smashed. The glass on a three-thousand-dollar painting was broken . . . Neatly stacked boxes awaiting shipment to her new home were ripped open.

"Ladies and gentlemen, we have pictures of how FBI left this apartment, her apartment, which, at the time of the raid, was neatly prepared for a move to Louisiana, with all her belongings packed in nicely stacked boxes. This is one of the pictures. . . . She is not here today. I love you. I will not state her name here. And I ask the news media, please, for common decency, if you know it, please leave her alone. She will not make a statement."

He returned to describing a day in the life of a person of interest. Hatfill claimed he was openly followed by agents, in cars and on foot, twenty-four hours a day. The simple act of driving down to the store for a pack of gum had created a parade of FBI cars, following as near as two to four feet from his rear bumper. The FBI told Hatfill's closest friend that they had concrete evidence that he had mailed the anthrax letters and asked him to confront Hatfill in order to obtain a confession. Later, the friend tearfully asked Hatfill if their allegations were true.

"In complete violation of normal investigative procedures," said Dr. Hatfill, "the FBI have circulated only my photograph at a crime scene, a photographic one-man lineup, in an attempt to find someone to testify that they remember seeing me in the area almost a year ago."

He told the crowd that he could never win as a person of interest. His love of country and the work he had done on behalf of the nation's security had been turned against him by means of a "ridiculous suggestion" that his patriotism had prompted him to murder five innocent persons so that a statement could be made regarding the nation's lack of preparedness against a biological attack. All this reminded Hatfill of Kafka's novel, *The Trial*.

"Perhaps," he said, "that story is the source of Mr. Kristof's 'Mr. Z.' [Kafka's protagonist is named 'K.']." All the above is what it's like living as a person of interest designated by John Ashcroft. Again, the Justice Department has told the press that there is no evidence that I've committed a crime. I have to contend with a moving target of rumor, innuendo, fantasy, half-truths, and now the super-duper bionic bloodhounds that the FBI recently pulled out of a hat."

He discounted the Justice Department's repeated claims that it was making meaningful progress in the anthrax investigation. He laid out the facts in the case and asked what any of them had to do with him.

"We know," he said, "that four anthrax letters were mailed September 17 and 18, and October 8 and 9, 2001. On these days, as indeed for many weeks after September 11, I and my colleagues at SAIC were working overtime in our McLean, Virginia, office on national defense issues. My time sheets from the company, which are being distributed here, show that on these days I worked respectively fourteen hours; thirteen and one-half hours; thirteen hours; and eleven and one-quarter hours at the office. Yes, I know, it's possible that time cards could have been altered. Well, I'll tell you SAIC goes to extreme lengths to ensure this process can't happen. In addition, the FBI long ago interviewed all of my colleagues at SAIC, and each confirmed that I was, like them, continuously hard at work in the office during this entire period."

Dr. Hatfill suggested alternative methods to get around these time lines. He could have surreptitiously driven to Trenton or Princeton from the D.C. area, mailed the letters, and returned unnoticed. With luck, he might have made the eight-hour round trip in time to return to work unnoticed and exhausted and work another thirteen-hour day.

He explained he was living and working in the D.C. area during the entire time when the anthrax letters were mailed. Hatfill said that Ashcroft should know that while the anthrax letters were mailed from New Jersey and the first anthrax incidents occurred in Florida, he had not set foot in either state in September or October 2001.

"We know, by the way, that some of the 9-11 terrorists did," he continued. "The FBI's focus on me seems to have eclipsed the need for appropriate inquiry into elementary, scientific aspects of the anthrax investigation. It took the FBI seven months after the letter attacks before they turned to assistance to Bill Patrick, the top dry-powder biological warfare expert in our country. How sensible is that? What inquiries have been made into who received the Ames strain of anthrax at any time prior to the fall of 2001? Until the mid 1990s, regulation of the traffic in dangerous bacteriological pathogens was very poorly controlled and poorly documented."

Hatfill said that it still had to determine if the anthrax powder in the letters was prepared by sophisticated methods known only to select scientists or by more crude methods using information readily available on the Internet.

"Speaking of the Internet, the American people should know that the complete top-secret recipe for making smallpox into a sophisticated dry-powder biological weapon was recently posted by the U.S. government on the Internet by mistake for several weeks. Thank God the document in question has finally been removed from the Internet, but not before anyone with an interest, foreign or domestic, would have had time to view it and download it."

Like many in the Amerithrax investigation, Hatfill believed that scientific input into the hunt for the anthrax mailer had been insufficient. He illustrated this point by relating that he was the one who had suggested that the FBI could conduct blood tests on him in order to rule him out as a suspect.

"The test measures antibody levels," he explained, "which would mark either my exposure to anthrax recently or a recent anthrax vaccination, not one that I've had two years ago. At long last, the government has agreed to my proposal, and I'll shortly be providing blood samples as I originally suggested. I hereby openly request the FBI make public the full results of these forthcoming tests, their conclusions based on these tests, and the scientific basis for the tests and the conclusions."

Hatfill claimed that he had earlier offered to give the FBI handwriting samples for examination. As in the case of the blood tests, he had requested the results, including all work sheets and analyses, be made public when completed and asked the media to press for their release.

"The one certain progress that the FBI has made in this investigation," he said, "is its inability to find any evidence connecting me with the anthrax letter attacks. This is after an eight-month inquiry, and Lord knows how much taxpayer money has been poured into this effort to uncover my presumed guilt . . . If the FBI does not have me as a person of interest, then what does it have?"

Dr. Hatfill answered his own question. He said the FBI has a stalled investigation, characterized by a lack of proper scientific investigation and expertise. He criticized the Bureau's single-minded dedication to the use of "so-called profilers."

"Remember," he scoffed, "these are the folks that described the Unabomber, Ted Kaczynski, as a well-dressed manual laborer. It has a lack of the most basic understanding of the relevant biology by many front-line and senior FBI investigators. It has an investigation that is characterized by the apparent avoidance of any major avenue of inquiry, except the one decided upon by the attorney general. Most importantly, it is driven by a compelling and overwhelming desire that the FBI look good at any cost, regardless of the price in individual freedom, due process, common decency, and civil liberties. I believe that I may actually get arrested when all this is said and done and if it occurs, it will have nothing to do with anthrax. It will have everything to do with my being named the national person of interest."

This label had caused painstaking inquiry into his past and given the authorities incentive to justify massive financial expenditure and thousands of man-hours during their pursuit of him. Hatfill decried their heedless exposure of himself, their defamation of him as a murderer.

"For these reasons, even as I stand before you proclaiming my innocence of this terrible crime, I believe I shall yet pay a price for having been named a person of interest. If Steve Hatfill isn't the anthrax killer, well, he spit on a government sidewalk or littered in front of a government building somewhere, something he shouldn't have done. I should imagine that a great many Americans, including a host of our nation's political, social, and intellectual leaders [would] be at serious risk of some sort of prosecution under these circumstances."

As he concluded, he cautioned the nation against the FBI's increased powers under the Patriot Act. He wondered aloud what America would be like in a decade or two. He asked if it would be like the America he loved and would risk his life to defend. He asked the fourth estate, if the nation might someday evolve into a society where uncharged persons of interest live in fear of damaging police and media intrusion? He recited the slogan of the American Civil Liberties Union, one he never thought he would. "But I must tell you," he said, "after what I have been through, I wholeheartedly embrace its motto: 'Eternal vigilance is the price of liberty.'

"My story is not all sad and negative. I have been buoyed beyond words by the support of my family, friends, past and current colleagues, and even strangers, who, since my first news conference, have warmly greeted me on the streets or in letters. I thank my employer, Louisiana State University, for its incredible sensitivity in balancing its obvious institutional needs in light of my status as a person of interest with my own personal needs and circumstances. Thank you. As poorly as my own government and much of the press have treated me, those persons who mean the most to me have stood by me unflinchingly. For that, ladies and gentlemen, I am eternally grateful. Thank you."

MARK CORALLO, A Justice Department spokesman, said immediately after the press conference that the department would not respond to Hatfill's "personal" attack on the attorney general. "The investigation is ongoing and we cannot comment further," he said. Gail Collins, editorial page editor of the *New York Times*, said that in conversations with his lawyer on Friday she had invited Dr. Hatfill to submit a column for publication. Responding, she said, "We have confidence in our columnists."

In a letter to Senate Judiciary Chairman Patrick Leahy, Glasberg said the FBI had "violated elementary rules of fairness and decency." He also objected to the FBI's "in-your-face surveillance" that quickly became harassment.

U.S. News & World Report said, "The FBI has seized Hatfill's travel records and datebooks and new clues may yet come to light. But if now, Hatfill may be no more than a larger-than-life man whose past seems to hint at dark secrets. In the world of bioweapons research, that's not so unusual. As one insider notes wryly: There's a lot of strange people who work in biodefense. No matter the outcome, Dr. Hatfill's name should never have been leaked unless he was an actual suspect. In the end he might be another Richard Jewell or Wen Ho Lee and the most wronged man in America."

As the anniversary of 9-11 approached, the close-knit biowarfare community was still saying that a disgruntled former employee at the Institute was the likely perpetrator of the anthrax letters. A public service announcement for the 9-11 anniversary was called "Main Street." It showed a row of houses and aired a voice-over saying, "On September 11, terrorists tried to change America forever." The scene altered to one of the same houses, all now displaying American flags. "Well, they succeeded," says the announcer.

Anthrax had come like a thief in the night. Amerithrax had struck in the blaze of a busy street. Like a thief the spores were silent and almost invisible, yet as deadly, insidious, and crafty as the worst murderer. You could not smell it. It left no shadow and yet, on a microscopic level, was a living breathing creature the size of a human cell. It needed no water, no air, no food. Virtually indestructible, its life was one of birth, hibernation, and rebirth. It was virtually immortal, moving stealthily over the flagstones of every American home.

On Monday, August 26, 2002, suspicious powder spilled from a smaller-than-usual envelope opened by former Vice President Al Gore's office manager, Mary Patterson. The room where she opened the letter was quarantined and a Hazmat squad investigated. Firefighters dumped drums of cleaning solution into the sewer outside the building that housed Gore's office. Gore, on vacation in northern California with his family, phoned his staff to check up on their safety. His spokesman, Jano Cabrera, said the envelope, postmarked from Tennessee, was stamped on the back, THIS LETTER HAS NOT BEEN INSPECTED BY THE CORRECTIONS DEPARTMENT. The Department of Corrections said it was its policy to stamp letters that had not been inspected, but the wording the department uses was different from that on the Gore letter. No suspects were identified and no one was tested. The letter turned out to be a hoax.

And so a year later, were cities and communities better prepared to handle a terrorist attack involving biowarfare agents? Experts at the first meeting of the Health and Human Services Secretary's Council on Public Health Preparedness didn't think so. While national drug and vaccine stockpiles had been increased, understaffed and underfunded local health departments still lacked the ability to deliver the vaccines.

STRAIN 37

Return to AMI

AT THE DUST site at Ground Zero, high winds made a mournful benediction. The 9-11 anniversary in New York drew near. Shuttered, the tan three-story building on Broken Sound Boulevard in Boca Raton huddled behind a fence. The silent, still, and deserted AMI building was approaching an anniversary too. It had been under federal quarantine since October 7 of the previous year. AMI Chairman David Pecker said the building remained exactly the same as it was when employees were suddenly evacuated. "It's like it's frozen in time," said Pecker. "It's almost the anniversary of Bob Stevens's death and his family wants to know who's responsible. I'm hoping that they really can find something." All of the employees were off Cipro now and had been since December. Many had abandoned their medication because of unpleasant side effects. Tim O'Connor of the Palm Beach County Health Department was certain now that the mass administration of Cipro had proved to be the correct decision. "Originally," he told the press, "we were all figuring that it would be isolated to an office or a little area just in the mailroom and Stevens's desk. The fact that they found it everywhere means there's a good chance that someone else would've gotten sick if we hadn't taken those steps."

On Monday, August 26, 2002, the FBI returned, planning to spend two weeks inside the plant. Over the winter, high-tech analysis of the anthrax envelopes for fingerprints had failed to pan out. A gnawing feeling they had overlooked some clue had brought them back (as criminals often do) to the scene of the crime. The agents, convinced that evidence existed somewhere within AMI, notified the Palm Beach County Health Department that they planned to enter the quarantined building. Pecker had refused them entry until his company received a written proposal on what they intended to do. In late June, Florida Governor Jeb Bush, Police Chief Andrew Scott, and Boca Raton Mayor Steven Abrams met with the FBI to discuss the toxic building. Florida Democratic Senator Bill Nelson wanted the feds to take over and decontaminate AMI.

The FBI and the U.S. Agency for Toxic Substances and Disease Registry (a unit of the CDC focused on managing public health hazards) had prepared newly designed, disposable chemical suits with air masks and latex boots for detectives to wear inside AMI. One reason the EPA wanted to go back into the building was to further examine how the air handling system had spread the bacteria. Any lessons learned could be applied to the ongoing decontamination of the Brentwood and New Jersey mail facilities. They were still not certain how the deadly spores had spread throughout.

"Unlike other sites where anthrax hit in 2001," said Hector Pesquera, special-agent-in-charge of the Miami division, "this is a site where no letter has been found, no delivery vehicle has been found. All of a sudden there was anthrax in that building. There must be a vehicle that introduced anthrax into that place." Why was there no trail of spores leading out of the building? The FBI was resuming its search for the letter or other delivery vehicle that had carried the disease into the AMI building and fatally infected Bob Stevens. Some officials believed the letter was still there and that new techniques would allow a more complete search. There could be more than one. Most of the AMI employees thought the Lopez letter had been incinerated. That was the way the publishing house got rid of its own waste. Pesquera said in reply to a question that the new probe at the AMI building "has nothing to do with Mr. Hatfill."

"We're looking for large quantities of spores in order to chemically characterize those spores and compare them against the spores found in the Senators Leahy and Daschle letters," said Dwight Adams, assistant director of the FBI's laboratory division.

Only a month earlier AMI had tentatively agreed to the new search when the FBI introduced its plan in a meeting at the tabloids' new offices at T-Rex Technology Center. The details and logistics had been worked out and finalized a few days before the search. One day in advance, AMI saw a rough draft of the search warrant. An earlier version had authorized the seizure of "business records, computer files or other papers that might explain the motive, method or intent."

AMI was "heavily lawyered" by Williams and Connolly, a powerful Washington firm, to defend its legal rights and protect against libel suits. Its confidential informants had to be kept confidential. "It is not our desire or intention," said Assistant U.S. Attorney Kenneth Kohl, "to remove any documents, business records or other objects from the AMI building that may compromise your journalistic sources. If, at that time, you feel that any items taken during the search exceed the scope of the search warrant or the limitations imposed by this letter, you may contact me directly and I am confident that we will be able to resolve the matter to the satisfaction of AMI." Pecker got his "anti-snoop pledge" in writing, a modification of the search warrant that forbade the FBI to snoop through reporters' private files or remove notes or other unpublished material from the building. "Computers are off limits," he said.

The FBI wanted access to AMI's back issues, bound volumes of the *National Enquirer*, *National Examiner*, *Globe*, *Sun*, and *Weekly World News*. They were there in the dust of the deserted building. "Our desire is to review back issues and databases (published material only) to determine whether any past article published by AMI may be relevant to the motive for the anthrax mailings," wrote U.S. Attorney Roscoe C. Howard Jr., clarifying the earlier search warrant. AMI decided agents could search those issues, but limited the search to fourteen days.

According to Dwight Adams, the FBI would try to find letters presumably thrown out in the trash by using new techniques of microbial forensics. "The quantity of spores at each sampling location will be estimated," Adams said, "providing data for a three-dimensional map relating levels of contamination with positions in the building." The FBI was interested in those publications dating to the late 1980s and early 1990s, as well as a "file system . . . that contains hard copies of past issues sorted by topic."

In November 2001, the EPA had listed the eighty-four locations of spores found inside AMI. Seventy-eight percent of the contaminated samples were taken from the first floor and the mailroom. Sixty-six positive anthrax samples (thirty-five from desks, computers, keyboards, cabinets, and mail slots; thirty-one vacuumed from the floor) were on the first story. The last search had focused near the mailroom. Now the entire 67,000-square-foot building was to be searched.

"Last year, we were in the building for a different reason," said Pesquera. "It was not as comprehensive an investigation as the one we are planning. It was more of a public health concern investigation. This investigation will be scientifically driven for a criminal investigation," Judy Orihuela, a spokeswoman for the FBI field office in Miami, said. "Before, when we were there, we took samples. My understanding is that they want to be more thorough."

Adams listed what they wanted to accomplish. "Number one," he said, "we hope to do a very comprehensive, detailed assessment of the spore contamination throughout the entire building. Number two, a very detailed assessment with regard to the mailroom in particular. Number three, we are looking for a dissemination device, such as a letter or letters, again, to generate new leads for the investigation. And then finally, we're looking for large quantities of spores in order to chemically characterize those spores and compare them against the spores found in the Senators Leahy and Daschle letters."

Agents believed their new methods could identify the anthrax source at the site. Where was that anthrax-laden letter? Who had it been addressed to and would that knowledge give investigators a clue to Amerithrax's identity and motive? If the letter was located, said an agent, "We'll look at the postmark and work it backwards to determine the location of the initial mailing. A collection box or post office."

"So the anthrax that was there the day they closed the building is still there in spore form," said Dr. J. C. Peters. "Those letters give off spores through the pores in the envelopes and so on. We know that. And now if you go back in and quantitatively or semiquantitatively examine the environment, you should be able to trace that letter just like you would follow a set of muddy footprints over your white carpet."

They were thinking of the anthrax envelope's pores—bigger than the largest Daschle anthrax clusters. How effortlessly the powder could escape individual letters to contaminate the general mails. "It had to be one of the most porous materials," an official said of the attack envelopes. "Whether that was by chance or design, I have no idea."

The next day, Tuesday, August 27, moon-suited investigators, working in pairs, entered AMI, a return anthrax experts labeled "a prayer." Only federal agents and an air-conditioning repair crew hired by AMI had been inside since October 7. Tim O'Connor of the Palm Beach County Health Department said, "[AMI] has been virtually untouched since the incident." Agents reentered the building in coordination with a team of several dozen investigators—scientists from the CDC and the Toxic Substances Agency.

"What I have heard is there may be some follow-up activities [by the FBI] once we leave the facility," said Elwin Grant, a spokesman for the Atlanta CDC. They wanted to conduct useful tests to thwart the effects of any future anthrax attacks. "We've put together a proposal to go into the building to do an examination which would have real-world utility," said spokesperson Kathy Skipper, who added that the AMI building would provide an ideal laboratory to observe anthrax in an office setting. "Should anything like this happen again, the tests would help us better understand how the material moves, who might be most at risk from a letter that came through the system, where the anthrax is likely to disperse, and how might it disperse," she said. Agents in portable, white, positive-pressure space suit protective gear made their way through the desolation of the sealed ghost town. White pleated fumigating tubes trailed behind them like tails, making their progress ungainly. Could they find the deadly letter and if so, would it hold the missing clue that might lead them to Amerithrax?

The movements of the intruders stirred microscopic anthrax tumbleweeds. Some spores held fast, trembling like the last leaves of fall. Pecker had been right. Nothing had changed. The breeze fluttered the crayon drawings still on Stevens's computer. Unfinished stories were strewn on desktops. The fish tanks had long gone bone dry and the fish themselves were dust. The detectives photographed and surveyed the layout of the headquarters before searching more thoroughly for evidence. A year ago they had used a random method. This time they were searching in grids.

Over the first weekend investigators concentrated on the third floor. On Labor Day, they worked to complete sampling the third floor by that night. Then it would be on to collect more evidence on the first and second floors. Also on Monday, the U.S. Justice Department sent Stephen Guillot, Hatfill's supervisor at LSU, an e-mail. It read:

Steve, This is a follow-up of the phone conversation you had with Darrell Darnell [an ODP official] earlier this afternoon. I want to reiterate that the Office of Justice Programs/Office for Domestic Preparedness directs that Louisiana State University Academy of Counter-Terrorist Education cease and desist from utilizing the subject matter and course instructor duties of Steven J. Hatfill on all Department of Justice funded programs.

On Tuesday, September 3, testing inside AMI confirmed that copier paper contaminated by the mail had spread spores to every copy machine on all three floors. The detectives were still searching the building on Tuesday while Dr. Hatfill was fired from the NCBRT's federal program at LSU to train emergency workers. That was Justice's right. Hatfill's $150,000 salary was financed with federal grants and the Justice Department maintained management oversight and control on programs they funded. The center received 93 percent of its budget from the Justice Department. Hatfill was offered no explanation by Guillot. Under the contract no justification was required.

"Justice Department officials," wrote the *Washington Post*, "effectively blackballed Hatfill by instructing LSU to prohibit him from working on the university's government-funded programs." The legality of the firing was an issue that might go to court as might every other aspect of the targeting of Dr. Hatfill.

Dr. Hatfill's spokesman Pat Clawson said the firing from LSU was an attempt to pressure Hatfill into a false confession. "We're stunned to learn of this," he said. "We're outraged. Blacklisting by the government is offensive and un-American. Obviously, Ashcroft wants to bring blacklisting back to the federal scene. Where was the due process? They fired him. No reason. No severance. No nothing. Just good-bye." It was a lot like Wen Ho Lee's firing and everyone knew how that had turned out. Hatfill said, through Clawson, "LSU did not even have the decency to phone me directly. They did not even tell my supervisor or coworkers. This could have been decided a month ago.

"Why did they wait until I moved all of my furniture and all my possessions to Baton Rouge?" On Wednesday, September 4, Stephen Guillot, the man who had hired Hatfill, was also fired by LSU. The apparent reason: Guillot didn't tell his senior bosses about the e-mail he had received. Commenting on the firing LSU chancellor Mark Emmert said, "The university is making no judgment as to Dr. Hatfill's guilt or innocence regarding the FBI investigation . . . Our ultimate concerns are the ability to fulfill its role and mission as a land-grant university."

The EPA directed two manufacturers to stop selling products that claimed to guard consumers against anthrax. Aerotech Laboratories of Arizona and American Security and Control Inc. of Virginia had been hawking their unapproved, unregistered pesticides over the Internet, the EPA said. Aerotech's product, Modec Decon Formulation, was sold as part of the company's advertised bioterrorism response kit. Aerotech claimed the pesticide would decontaminate and "mitigate chemical and biological weapons agents." American Security was enjoined to stop selling Easy Decon Spray, which the company boosted as a "personal incident anthrax and biological and chemical decontamination sprayer."

Amerithrax had drastically changed the landscape of America, whether he meant to or not. He was not insane, they knew that much. "You could not be delusional, hearing voices, and do this, absolutely not," said Candice DeLong. "Legally insane, meaning they are suffering from a severe mental illness, the most severe being schizophrenia, like Chase [the Sacramento Vampire], and that is an illness characterized by auditory hallucinations. So the voices are telling you to do things or that you are a bad person. Usually accompanied by some kind of delusion. Now a delusion is a strong belief in something that has no basis in fact and despite overwhelming evidence to the contrary. It's very difficult to convince a schizophrenic their delusion is not real, because it's real for them. Chase's delusion was that his blood was drying up and he had to replace it or he would die. And that's why he killed animals and people—to get the blood.

"Chase was caught very quickly after he finally escalated to the serious crime of murder because the thought process was disturbed, disorganized. He left a lot of evidence at both crime scenes that resulted in him being eventually identified and apprehended. When you're crazy and not thinking clearly, you leave a trail of evidence wider than the Mississippi and that is why disorganized thinkers or people who are mentally ill rarely become serial killers. It's not that they don't want to continue whatever their compulsion is but that they get stopped by the police because they are so sloppy. Oftentimes they don't realize what they're doing is criminal and therefore they don't try to cover their tracks."

Events came fast and furious now. American scientists had pledged to employ their talents in defense of the nation. First was a possible death knell for anthrax itself, the silent killer that Ernie Blanco had unwittingly carried into the AMI building.

Dr. Raymond Schuch, Dr. Daniel Nelson, and Dr. Vincent A. Fischetti at Rockefeller University in New York announced they had come up with an anthrax killer. Their new treatment would make it impossible for anthrax to mutate into a resistant form. The August issue of *Nature* headlined: VIRUS DEALS ANTHRAX A KILLER BLOW. The biologists had used three sets of animal experiments in which an amino acid called L-alanine was used as a germinating agent to activate dormant anthrax spores, so they could be detected instantly, then just as quickly be killed by the new enzyme, lysin. Lysin, a natural enzyme, is speedy and designed to pierce the anthrax cell wall from the inside, chew through the bacterium's wall, and crumble it from the outside. Lysin-based methods could also detect a sample of twenty-five hundred spores in ten minutes or as few as one hundred spores after an hour's reaction time. Not only could it detect anthrax, but it could also decontaminate infected areas. The agent, which was isolated from a virus that preys on anthrax and replicates inside the bacterium, causes "the cells literally to explode."

The CDC and the Army's biological defense lab at the Aberdeen Proving Ground in Maryland began running a series of tests using lysin against very dangerous *Bacillus anthracis* strains from Pakistan, China, Korea, and Turkey, as well as the Ames strain. Attack strains of anthrax could be made resistant to antibiotics, but not to lysin. The FDA already has given the new method "fast track" status for advanced testing to have the anthrax killer ready for large-scale stockpile supplies within three years. A virus that attacks bacteria is called a "bacteriophage" or, simply, a "phage." These bacteria-blasting phages could take on and completely destroy a whole colony of much larger bacteria. These tiny microbes (about one-fortieth the size of most bacteria cells) had once been a cure for bacterial infections but had been replaced by antibiotics, which had a broader spectrum. Now their turn had come again.

Lysin could be used like an antidote to treat people who may have been exposed to spores in an anthrax attack. If injected quickly enough, the lysin would destroy the anthrax bacteria in the bloodstream before they had multiplied and released overwhelming amounts of toxin. The government began repeating the Rockefeller experiments using the Ames strain of anthrax bacteria at the Institute. The Institute and the NIH were in the process of planning a biomedical research partnership where they would work side by side to encourage dialogue between scientists. New USAMRIID and NIAID biosafety laboratories would be built and connected on a 160-acre site on the Institute's campus.

Within six months, a small biotechnology company in Rockville, Maryland, Human Genome Sciences Inc., would announce it had created an antidote to anthrax. It would protect animals against extremely high doses of weaponized anthrax. After human testing the drug was set to enter the nation's bioterrorism arsenal in 2004. Anthony Fauci, director of the National Institute of Allergy and Infectious Diseases, called the data "impressive" and said the drug could become an important defense tool.

New documents obtained by court order suggested postal officials knew Brentwood had been contaminated after processing anthrax-contaminated letters sent to Capitol Hill, yet postal officials kept the building open for three more days. A spokesman for the conservative consumer watchdog group Judicial Watch said, "They're smoking gun documents that prove that postal officials knew that their workers' lives were at risk, yet they did nothing." But the building wasn't evacuated and postal workers were not put on antibiotics until October 21, 2001. By contrast, when the letter to Daschle was opened in the Hart Office Building, the offices were shut down immediately and staffers given medicine. Judicial Watch called for a criminal investigation, claiming the Postal Service kept Brentwood open to avoid losing half a million dollars a day.

Postal worker Leroy Richmond, a slender, older, pleasant man in a sweater, told television cameras, "It's unbelievable that an organization would put profits above human life." In defense the Postal Service said it was relying on advice from health officials who believed that there was no way enough spores could leak out of a sealed envelope to infect anyone. "Our decision," said Tom Day, "never, absolutely never, included a dollar-and-cents equation." Because of the anthrax letters, mail revenue for passenger airlines in the second quarter of 2002 was $147 million, down from $236 million for the second quarter of 2001. The Postal Service was commercial aviation's single largest customer.

Top health officials stated that their agencies could have moved more swiftly to guard the mail system. CDC workers had urged their superiors to close the local Boca Raton post office that handled the letter, but CDC officials decided not to act. Few at first believed that deadly anthrax spores could leak from sealed envelopes. No one appreciated that anthrax powder could act like an aerosol to infect bystanders.

"My immediate instinct was to close the Boca Raton post office," an expert told the press. "If we had closed the post office in Florida, it would have set a precedent to close Brentwood." Workers at Brentwood complained that not enough was done to protect them while drastic measures were taken to close offices and provide antibiotics to workers in Congress. "The risk to Brentwood facility employees by contaminated envelopes in transit was not recognized in time to prevent illness in four employees, two of whom died," Dr. Perkins, the CDC's anthrax expert, wrote in the CDC journal *Emerging Infectious Diseases*.

CDC director Dr. Julie Gerberding, a leading light in the anthrax response, said the picture was not as crystal clear at the time. "There were lots of people participating in those details," she said. "You don't close the post office without a good reason." Dr. Jim Hughes, head of the National Center for Infectious Diseases at CDC and a key participant in the decision, agreed. "There were a lot of things we thought we knew when the attack began," he said. The agency stressed that no one had ever dealt with such an attack before. Infectious disease experts were learning as they went. The decision not to close the Boca Raton post offices initially seemed vindicated because there was no cross-contamination of mail from that facility. And when anthrax cases turned up in New York, they were, as predicted, all cutaneous anthrax infections.

When the CDC suspected that the envelopes could leak an aerosol, there had been a reluctance by law enforcement agencies to make information public. They had gagged the CDC. The CDC and HHS said now they would act very differently if another attack occurred. "It turns out it was not such a big deal to close a post office," said one official. "I think we all wish we'd closed the Brentwood facility," Gerberding said. "The lessons to be learned from this are not to blame or to second-guess, but to keep all possibilities open." The CDC had learned the importance of communication. Though Brentwood remained closed, other facilities took up the slack and Washington was sending and receiving mail normally. The delivery of anthrax to the offices of Senators Daschle and Leahy in a weaponized aerosol had demonstrated how effortlessly key government buildings could be immobilized. At least now the Postal Service knew that anthrax letters could produce cross-contamination in the processing of mail in sorting centers. The CDC *Journal* has said the danger remains of another attack, as whoever sent the letters has not been found.

But Amerithrax in the end had made the mail safer. There were new machines on order or on the drawing board to detect and safeguard postal workers serving at risk for all Americans. There were irradiation machines, electron-beam purification systems, continuous dust vacuuming and air filtration with HEPA filters, and DNA-based detectors. In thirty minutes one prototype machine could identify virulent strains of anthrax by their DNA (but not yet able to continuously monitor the air). There were mass spectrometry machines that isolated submicroscopic samples and could nail anthrax's molecular profile (but they were not yet adapted for that purpose). There were "dog's nose" synthetic compounds that glowed instantly when they "smelled" distinctive particles in the air. So far, they had been used only to detect traces of TNT, but within five years could be adapted to trace anthrax. Biodetectors to detect airborne spores were inefficient or registered false positives, a problem now being addressed at Lawrence Livermore in California.

Over the past eleven months more than a billion dollars had been delivered to states to help rebuild public health services that were suffering after years of neglect. The investment has already borne fruit in states coping with West Nile Virus, a deadly mosquito-borne disease. West Nile had served as a useful test of systems set up to combat biological attack. The Postal Service was testing germ detectors at Baltimore's main postal facility on Fayette Street. Bio-detection systems for anthrax and eleven other agents, designed by Northrop Grumman Corporation, were set to be installed in fourteen more facilities. Among the anthrax-inspired inventions were the ClearView Mailbox, a transparent log cabin–shaped incubator that allowed handlers to sort mail with rubber gloves. There was the Hoax Buster, developed originally to test dairy products, that had been redesigned as a quick biotest. The Mail Defender was a desktop device that could sterilize mail without making it brittle.

But there was still great danger.

The U.S. suspected Saddam of concealing caches of bioweapons in hundreds of Iraqi desert sites. Ten thousand liters of anthrax and chemical agents were still unaccounted for by Iraq. Saddam had outfitted unmanned vehicles (UAVs) with spray tanks for anthrax. Kenneth Pollack, former director of Persian Gulf affairs at the NSC, wrote that "Saddam has taken the entire Iraqi program on the road." For the future, Saddam was apparently counting on a shadow fleet of mobile germ labs crisscrossing Iraq to dupe UN weapons inspectors. His "Winnebagos of death" looked like eighteen-wheel tractor trailer trucks or mobile homes and even ice cream trucks. Rail cars and trailers would be conveying germ agents like anthrax. The UN inspectors, though, had a new tool—ground-penetrating radar, a device dragged across the ground to detect irregularities in the earth such as hidden underground biological facilities.

Early in September 2002, the government suggested that those cleaning and searching anthrax-contaminated buildings should receive a vaccine, not just antibiotics, to protect them. This guideline had been issued specifically for anthrax cleanup crews such as the teams combing AMI. The existing rules for work in hazardous sites didn't go far enough to protect the workers. "Protective suits and antibiotics are not enough," they said. "The suits can fail and it may not be healthy to use antibiotics for the long periods of time workers can spend in a cleanup zone." So far, no cleanup workers at any of the sites of anthrax attacks had contracted the disease. Also in September, there was a minor outbreak of anthrax in South Dakota, the third that year, and it made everyone's throat catch a little. It killed a few cattle. Meanwhile, California was preparing for terror. In San Diego, the Santa Monica–based RAND Institute completed a paper on how the state could best prepare for a terrorist attack. Anthrax led the list as the biggest danger. Anthrax had always been first on the list of potential terrorist agents—if you handled one of the letters, you got skin anthrax. If you opened one, you got inhalational anthrax.

"In a worst-case scenario, a nuclear or chemical attack in San Francisco, San Diego or Los Angeles would kill as many as eighty thousand people," the RAND study said. Two hundred twenty pounds of anthrax, "if properly dispersed under optimum conditions" would saturate 180 square miles. Deaths could be in the millions. The study said California was better prepared than most states because it was used to combating natural disasters such as forest fires, mudslides, and earthquakes. A Stanford Business School report would say that the nation was still not prepared for an anthrax attack. Large amounts of antibiotics to fight anthrax were still not available. If two pounds of anthrax were dropped over New York City, estimated the report, 123,000 people would die.

FBI agents, their eyes fairly gleaming, alleged that their slow but steady investigation of an individual in the anthrax investigation was bearing fruit. They had sent investigators to South Africa where Hatfill had worked and attempted to learn whether he had taken part in the alleged anthrax poisonings there. They delved into his time in the Selous Scouts, who had been suspected of delivering anthrax to natives and their cattle. "We have a growing case of circumstantial evidence against Steven Hatfill," they said. The FBI announced it was pursuing more than a thousand leads, including one hundred overseas.

Within a few days FBI agents would root through Dr. Hatfill's Frederick apartment once more. "Why do they have to search a third time?" Pat Clawson would complain. "Isn't the FBI competent enough to do the job the first two times?"

Within three months a tip from an informant would lead Codename Amerithrax agents to a wooded area in the Catoctin Mountains. The tipster would hint that lab equipment used in the anthrax attacks might have been disposed of in a pond a few miles from the Institute and Hatfill's former residence. About a hundred federal agents conducting "forensic searches" would fine-comb a woodland clearing and a watershed area of about a dozen spring-fed ponds northwest of Frederick. The snowbound forest reposes in the hills above Fishing Creek Reservoir, the wellspring of Frederick's drinking water. Several divers would hack their way through the foot-thick ice of one pond. Below, they would discover vials wrapped in plastic and a partially submerged, clear airtight chamber with two holes in the sides. The plastic container was similar to a scientific glove box like the ones used at the Institute. Or one to make homemade PCP.

"They've been taking things out of two fire ponds and labeling everything and taking it away," a spokeswoman for the city of Frederick would say. "If they found what they're looking for, we still don't know." The next month agents would return to set up three roadblocks and close off the city-owned timberland and ponds. Speculation was that Amerithrax might have waded into the water to delicately manipulate lethal anthrax bacteria into envelopes within a partially submerged airtight chamber. This theory, called "far-fetched" by one of Dr. Hatfill's attorneys, Thomas Connolly, might explain how Amerithrax's letters had gotten wet. The fact that Dr. Hatfill had a postgraduate diploma in diving and underwater medicine from a South African naval training institute only made a few eager investigators lick their chops. However, experts doubted if spores could later be found in a natural body of water, having been long dispersed. Investigators would conduct 300 soil, water, and sediment tests anyway.

Forensic searchers would return in the summer to construct a plastic mesh fence around the perimeter of the muddy pond. A private engineering firm would feed a fire hose into the pond and, operating backhoes, a generator, and a pump, drain it. The FBI would find logs, coins, fishing lures, a street sign, a bicycle, and a handgun (which they turned over to the Frederick police), but no residual anthrax spores in the bottom mud. Agents with a sense of humor would call the exercise, "The Blair Witch Project" or "Operation Pond Scum."[12]

Dr. Timothy Holtz, a preventive medicine fellow at the New York City Health Department, was less optimistic. Speaking at an Atlanta medical meeting, he concluded his appraisal of the Amerithrax case with a slide: "We will likely never know."

ALL DAY THURSDAY, September 5, agents, exhausted now but still hopeful, combed the living tomb. They were solemn as archaeologists disinterring a Pharaoh's vault during their excavation. AMI's burial chamber was not buried in dunes, only surrounded by drifting beaches. Unlike with workmen tunneling into pyramids, there was no sound of pick and shovel, no rustle of rope tackles or shouting, singing, and clapping to work songs. In fact, there was a deliberate lack of motion on the part of the diggers. It was crucial they not stir up spores.

Instead of the heated air of a tomb, like the hottest of steam baths, the air was chilly inside. After sealing the building a year before, AMI executives had kept the air conditioner functioning full blast. This prevented humidity and heat from harming AMI's 4.5 million pages of newspaper clippings, 5 million images and slides, and 600,000 pages of bound copies. As agents wandered the dim rooms, the hollow echo of their foot-

---

[12] The diving searches would take place from December 13 to December 19, 2002, and again in January 2003. The last search would go from June 9 through June 28, 2003.

steps resounding, they wondered if those ancient papers would crumble to dust at the slightest touch. Shafts of light cut through stagnant air. Particles of dust danced there.

Because the air-conditioning system might have spirited spores to other locations, searchers from the Agency for Toxic Substances and Disease Registry, the FBI, and the CDC, using state-of-the-art technology, painstakingly remapped the tainted complex. Had there been any redistribution of anthrax spores?

The modern archeologists unearthed no libation vessels or bronze canopic jars. They saw no fine statuary, only the imagined unmoving figures of men and women who had once worked there. Instead of altars, they discovered only dust-covered desks. There were no rolled papyrus, just copying machines. It developed that only the powerful fans in two dozen high-speed copiers had been capable of dislodging, aerosolizing, and disseminating spores once they had settled. The spores had been scattered and were clinging to reams of copier paper once stored inside the "hot" mailroom.

As the searchers exited the quarantined building, they entered a shower unit. As their protective suits were hosed down, the anthrax runoff was collected in five-hundred-gallon and thousand-gallon tanks and chemically treated with chlorine before being dumped into the city sewer system.

"Things are going very well," said SAIC Pesquera. "We hope this investigation will bring to justice the person or persons responsible for this horrific act." But the FBI's fourteen-day search warrant was running out fast. There was another time limit as well. The White House wanted an answer in the Amerithrax case by the anniversary of 9-11, a symbolic deadline. A more fitting symbol would be to put the faces of Morris and Curseen, the first postal workers to die on the front lines of a new kind of war, on a stamp.

On Tuesday morning, September 10, 2002, agents finally completed their search of AMI. Exactly one year earlier, terrorists had flown jets into the Twin Towers, a Pennsylvania field, and the Pentagon. The FBI piled its considerable bounty like rubble at the foot of AMI—items for "further forensic examination." The FBI's five thousand evidence samples included air filters, culture plates, and air samplers used in their search. They packaged up two vacuum samples, six carpet samples, broom and dust mop heads, and a single wet-type mop head. Thousands of other samples would be compared to the anthrax-tainted letters.

As for the mailroom, investigators dismantled and carried out everything that had been in the mailroom—twelve shelves, thirty-three mail-cart folders, eleven mail-slot vacuum samplings, and an equal number of box tops. The FBI also transferred a dark green plastic trash bag containing 769 anthrax-tainted pieces of mail to a truck. The mail had been left in AMI's underground parking garage after the previous fall's evacuation. Agents gathered up all the letters stuffed into mail cubbyholes and snatched another forty-two letters from sorting bins. They left the heavy copiers behind. "I can confirm that we finished up today, and that we have left," Orihuela said. "We did leave the building today. I can't say anything more." She would not say if their goals had been met, that of discovering the source of the contagion—the missing letter.

"It comes down to this: the building is a public health hazard," said Gerald McKelvey, an AMI spokesman. McKelvey added that the company had offered to give the building to the federal government. AMI employees would probably never consent to return to the building. The search this time was "highly successful," said John Florence, spokesman for the Toxic Substances and Disease Registry. "This was the first time that FBI agents had worked literally side by side with public health scientists. People were determined to get results out of the time we had available."

The results would provide the FBI with valuable data to advance the ongoing Amerithrax investigation.

With the 9-11 anniversary now a reality, it was observed that panic and fear had abated and been replaced with a national anger and resolve. Empty chairs representing the 2,823 Americans lost at Ground Zero were lined up. The choking dust, unbelievably, was still there and swept over a site littered with flags and dump trucks. Even though a year had passed, Ground Zero was still buffeted by high winds which raised endless clouds of dust. The mournful benediction in New York, the empty chairs, mirrored the silent, still, and deserted AMI building in Florida.

The images were still with Americans, but it was the unforgivable cruelty of the anthrax mailings following so closely on the heels of tragedy that stayed with the detectives. As for another attack by Amerithrax, that was doubtful for several reasons. His motive had most likely been to influence a Congressional vote on a tough version of the Patriot Act that had passed on October 12, 2001. The timing and choice of targets suggested that Senators Daschle and Leahy were impediments to the bill in its most invasive form. On October 4, Leahy, who had opposed Ashcroft's nomination as Attorney General, had been attacked by several conservative talk shows as the bill's lead opposition. If Amerithrax's letters to the senators, mailed on October 8, had not gotten wet, blurring the zip code, they would have arrived in time to potentially influence the vote.

Whether Amerithrax's intention had been to alert the nation to the dangers of bioterror or not, the country was alerted. Jack the Ripper experts such as Donald Rumbelow have conjectured he was merely a social reformer. The Ripper's ghastly murders and letters to the press might have been committed to draw attention to the grinding poverty of Whitechapel's streetwalking women. Ultimately, the Amerithrax case might well be called "the Case of the Patriotic Murders."

Amerithrax might not strike again for another reason. His anthrax may have been stolen from a secret U.S. bioweapons program or appropriated from among the ten-gram shipments of anthrax sent to the Institute by Dugway to be irradiated (after the Gulf War Dugway created small quantities of freeze-dried aerosol anthrax). Amerithrax may have used up his anthrax.

The agents might not have caught Amerithrax yet, but they had gotten close. The letters had stopped. Amerithrax might have been an antisocial loner, as the profile said, a lone wolf within the United States who had no links to terrorist groups and who might have been, as the FBI speculated, "an opportunist" using 9-11 events to "vent his rage." *Newsweek* said in a cover story that the contaminated mail would be "remembered less for the pain it caused than the message it sent . . . This fall's anthrax attacks have turned a distant fear into a fact of life . . . Bioterror is no longer a hypothetical hazard but a real one."

Anger was everywhere in America, as passengers rose up and beat down skyjackers like Richard Reid the shoe-bomber, as one after another child kidnapper or killer was captured via the Amber Alert. The greatest words any manhunter had uttered were spoken—to the killer of a California child, one policeman said pointedly on television: "Don't eat. Don't sleep. We're coming for you."

Death from the tangled blood of a beast had stretched to a journalist in Florida, postal workers in Washington, and innocent women in New York and Connecticut.

Agents stood outside in the darkness of the AMI parking lot. It was nearly deserted. There was only a Boca Raton police bus, a few office trailers, and a small blue tent fluttering in the sea breeze.

They surveyed the site of the first intentional anthrax release in the United States thoughtfully. They wondered, "Where was that letter?" Inside, a breeze from somewhere fluttered the crayon drawings on Bob Stevens's computer. Untouched coffee cups and family photographs and unfinished stories remained on desks.

The clouds outside had faded and the sun began to set. Dusk was gathering, twilight settling behind the palms on the road. The huge building seemed eternal, as eternal as anthrax. The tainted envelope, possibly addressed to "J-Lo," had become a Holy Grail. Where was that letter? If the FBI had found it, they were not saying. The howling wind had ceased. The nation took a deep collective breath. It could breathe again.

Americans vowed not to live in terror. America was a country with a future.

SOURCES

Centers for Disease Control and Prevention (www.bt.cdc.gov/ Agent/ Anthrax/ Anthrax.asp). Detailed analysis and medical records of Amerithrax's victims, including X rays and examples of inhalational and cutaneous anthrax.

CDC Reports on the First Ten Bioterrorism-Related Inhalational Anthrax Cases Reported in the United States from October 4 to November 2, 2001. Research done by Centers for Disease Control and Prevention, Atlanta, Georgia, USA; Emory University School of Medicine, Atlanta, Georgia, USA; Cedars Medical Center, Miami, Florida, USA; Virtua Health, Mount Holly, New Jersey, USA; Winchester Medical Center, Winchester, Virginia, USA; Lenox Hill Hospital, New York City, New York, USA; and Palm Beach County Department of Public Health, West Palm Beach, Florida, USA.

Researchers on the CDC reports included: John A. Jernigan, David S. Stephens, David A. Ashford, Carlos Omenaca, Martin S. Topiel, Mark Galbraith, Michael Tapper, Tamara L. Fisk, Sherif Zaki, Tanja Popovic, Richard F. Meyer, Conrad P. Quinn, Scott A. Harper, Scott K. Fridkin, James J. Sejvar, Colin W. Shepard, Michelle McConnell, Jeannette Guarner, Wun-Ju Shieh, Jean M. Malecki, Julie L. Gerberding, James M. Hughes, Bradley A. Perkins, and members of the Anthrax Bioterrorism Investigation Team.

SOURCES

Sherrie Bruce, Rebecca Dixon, Anexis Lopez, Pat McConnon, Carmen Resurreccion, Kay Vydareny, the laboratories of the National Center for Infectious Diseases, the laboratories of affected states, the U.S. Department of Defense, and Epidemic Intelligence Service Officers. Dr. John Jernigan is a medical epidemiologist with the National Center for Infectious Diseases, Centers for Disease Control and Prevention, and assistant professor of medicine with Emory University School of Medicine and extensively involved in the clinical evaluation of the anthrax cases associated with this outbreak.

J. Aguilar, M. Andre, K. Baggett, B. Bell, D. Bell, M. Bowen, G. Carlone, M. Cetron, S. Chamany, B. De, C. Elie, M. Fischer, A. Hoffmaster, K. Glynn, R. Gorwitz, C. Greene, R. Hajjeh, T. Hilger, J. Kelly, R. Khabbaz, A. Khan, P. Kozarsky, M. Kuehnert, J. Lingappa, C. Marston, J. Nicholson, S. Ostroff, T. Parker, L. Petersen, R. Pinner, N. Rosenstein, A. Schuchat, V. Semenova, S. Steiner, F. Tenover, B. Tierney, T. Uyeki, S. Vong, D. Warnock, C. Spak, D. Jernigan, C. Friedman, M. Ripple, D. Patel, S. Pillai, S. Wiersma, R. Labinson, L. Kamal, E. Bresnitz, M. Layton, G. DiFerdinando, S. Kumar, P. Lurie, K. Nalluswami, L. Hathcock, L. Siegel, S. Adams, I. Walks, J. Davies-Coles, M. Richardson, K. Berry, E. Peterson, R. Stroube, H. Hochman, M. Pomeranz, A. Friedman-Kien, D. Frank, S. Bersoff-Matcha, J. Rosenthal, N. Fatteh, A. Gurtman, R. Brechner, C. Chiriboga, J. Eisold, G. Martin, K. Cahill, R. Fried, M. Grossman, and W. Borkowsky.

The FBI Amerithrax Page (www.fbi.gov/anthrax/amerithraxlinks.htm). The FBI enlists the public's help, reproducing the letters and envelopes, and detailing the opening of the Leahy letter. This is the best Bureau website yet.

The Anthrax Cases Analyzed by Ed Lake. (www.anthraxinvestigation.com). An invaluable resource and clearinghouse for every idea on the Amerithrax case.

TIGR: The Institute for Genomic Research (www.tigr.org). Important groundbreaking work which provided major clues in the Amerithrax investigation and provided a direction for the detectives.

Dr. Timothy Read, a researcher at the Institute, has worked for several years to decode the genome of the anthrax bacterium, choosing an Ames strain of anthrax that came from the British biological-warfare laboratory at Porton Down. "Comparative Genome Sequencing for Discovery of Novel Polymorphisms in *Bacillus anthracis.*" Science Reprint, Volume 296, pp. 2028-2033, June 14, 2002. Working with Dr. Read were Steven L. Salzberg, Mihai Pop, Martin Shumway, Lowell Umayam, Lingxia Jiang, Erik Holtzapple, Joseph D. Busch, Kimothy L. Smith, James M. Schupp, Daniel Solomon, Paul Keim, and Claire M. Frazer.

An astonishing two-part series on the Amerithrax case by Laurie Garrett, www.newsday.com., 7–8 October 2002.

"Brentwood." PostalWatch News Archive.

"Postal Service Ignored Contamination Rules." www.newsmax.com.

A well-done series from Phil Brennan, NewsMax.com. "FBI and Anthrax: Another TWA 800 in the Making?" "FBI Ignored Letter in Anthrax Probe," "FBI Rejects Link between Anthrax, 9-11 Terrorists." Aug. 15–17, 2002.

Brentwood United News.

"Anthrax Missing from Army Lab." Jack Dolan and Dave Altimari. *Hartford Courant.* January 20, 2002.

"Anthrax Grown Secretly at Fort Detrick." Dave Altimari and Jack Dolan. *Baltimore Sun.* June 13, 2002.

"Analysis of the Anthrax Attacks" posted on the Federation of American Scientists website, January, 2002. Barbara Hatch Rosenberg.

Audiotapes of Dr. Steven J. Hatfill's two nationally televised press conferences from Alexandria, Virginia.

Judicial Watch website.

Media Monitor, ri@aim.org. December 24, 2002.

"The Bloodhounds." AIM Report Accuracy in Media. September 27, 2002.

SELECTED READING

Alibek, Ken, with Stephen Handelman. *Biohazard: The Chilling True Story of the Largest Covert Biological Weapons Program in the World—Told from Inside by the Man Who Ran It.* New York: Random House, 1999.

Barnett, S. Anthony. *The Story of Rats.* Australia: Allen & Unwin, 2001.

Berkow, Robert, M.D., Editor-in-Chief. *Merck Manual of Medical Information, Home Edition.* New York: Pocket Books, 1997.

Bernstein, Richard. *Out of the Blue.* New York: Times Books, Henry Holt and Company, 2002.

SOURCES

Cole, Leonard A. *Clouds of Secrecy: The Army's Germ Warfare Tests over Populated Areas.* Totowa, N.J.: Rowman & Littlefield, 1988.

Cook, Robin. *Vector.* New York: Berkley Books, 2000.

Drew, Elizabeth. *Citizen McCain.* New York: Simon & Schuster, 2002.

Frist, William H. *When Every Moment Counts.* New York: Rowman & Littlefield, 2002.

Gonzalez, Juan. *Fallout: The Environmental Consequences of the World Trade Center Collapse.* New York: The New Press, 2002.

Guillemin, Jean. *Anthrax: The Investigation of a Deadly Outbreak.* Berkeley: University of California Press, 1999.

Harris, Sheldon H. *Factories of Death: Japanese Biological Warfare, 1932–1945, and the American Cover-up.* New York: Routledge, 1994.

Halberstam, David. *Firehouse.* Maine: Wheeler Publications, 2002.

Hersh, Seymour M. *Chemical and Biological Warfare: America's Hidden Arsenal.* Indianapolis: Bobbs-Merrill, 1968.

———. *Against All Enemies: Gulf War Syndrome: The War Between America's Ailing Veterans and Their Government.* New York: Ballantine, 1998.

Kaplan, David E., and Andrew Marshall. *The Cult at the End of the World.* New York: Crown Publishers, 1996.

Kessler, Ronald. *The Bureau: The Secret History of the FBI.* New York: St. Martin's Press, 2002.

Lee, Wen Ho, and Helen Zia. *My Country Versus Me.* New York: Hyperion, 2001.

Levitas, Daniel. *The Terrorist Next Door.* New York: Thomas Dunn Books, St. Martin's Press, 2002.

MacLean, Alistair. *The Satan Bug.* London: Gilach A.G., 1962.

Makris, John N. *The Silent Investigators.* New York: E. P. Dutton & Co., 1959.

Mangold, Tom, and Jeff Goldberg. *Plague Wars: The Terrifying Reality of Biological Warfare.* New York: St. Martin's Griffin, 1999.

Miller, Judith, Stephen Engelberg, and William Broad. *Germs: Biological Weapons and America's Secret War.* New York: Simon & Schuster, 2001.

Milne, Hugh. *Bhagwan: The God That Failed.* New York: St. Martin's Press, 1986.

Preston, Richard. *The Demon in the Freezer.* New York: Random House, 2002.

———. *The Hot Zone.* New York: Random House, 1994.

———. *The Cobra Event.* New York: Random House, 1997.

Siegfried, Donna Rae. *Biology for Dummies.* New York: Hungry Minds, 2001.

SOURCES

Talbott, Strobe, and Nayan Chanda, editors. *The Age of Terror*. New York: Basic Books, 2001.

Thompson, Marilyn W. *The Killer Strain*. New York: HarperCollins Publishers, 2003.

NEWSPAPERS AND PERIODICALS

Danitz, Tiffany. "Cooking Up the Plague at Home." *Insight,* January 26, 1998.

"Anthrax Hoaxes Are Sent in Mail." *Washington Post,* February 5, 1999.

"U.S. Biological Weapons Lab Locked Down, 50 Miles from Pentagon." *The Public I,* September 12, 2001.

"Bioterrorism: The Next Threat?" *Time,* September 24, 2001.

"Lantana Man Hospitalized with Anthrax." *Florida Today,* October 4, 2001.

"Scientist's Anthrax Claim Was Bogus." *Milwaukee Journal-Sentinel,* October 4, 2001.

"Senate Democrats, White House Reach a Deal on Anti-Terror Bill." *Washington Post*, October 4, 2001.

"Labs Work Overtime to Find Anthrax Source." *New Scientist,* October 5, 2001.

"Florida Cases Likely to Be First Ever Anthrax Attack." *New Scientist,* October 9, 2001.

"Brokaw's Aide Tests Positive." *St. Petersburg Times,* October 13, 2001.

"Fear Hits Newsroom in a Cloud of Powder." *New York Times,* October 14, 2001.

"Don't Blame Saddam for This One." *The Guardian,* October 19, 2001.

"Experts Doubt Anthrax a Domestic Plot." *Atlanta Journal-Constitution,* October 19, 2001.

"Secret Desert Project on Anthrax." *Scripps Howard News Service,* October 20, 2001.

"Police Say Letter to New York Post is Anthrax-Laced." *Baltimore Sun,* October 21, 2001.

"Did bin Laden Buy Bioterror? 1999 Testimony Says He Did." *San Francisco Chronicle,* October 21, 2001.

"White House Mail Machine Has Anthrax," Associated Press, October 23, 2001.

"Anthrax Threat Takes a Wider Scope, New Cases Emerge: Some Mail Halted." *Washington Post*, October 24, 2001.

SOURCES

"U.S. Says Anthrax Germ in Mail Is 'Ames Strain.' " *Washington Post,* October 26, 2001.

"List of Confirmed Anthrax Cases." *Washington Post,* November 1, 2001.

"Pre-9-11 Terrorist Mail Came from 'Indy.' " *New York Post,* November 1, 2001.

"Some Terrorism Specialists Suspect an Angry Loner with Scientific Knowledge." *Washington Post,* November 5, 2001.

"911 Call from Postal Worker." Morris's call for help appeared in the *San Francisco Chronicle,* November 8, 2001, Zachary Coile, *Chronicle* Washington Bureau, and on the Associated Press.

"Experts See F.B.I. Missteps Hampering Anthrax Inquiry." *New York Times,* November 9, 2001.

"Profile of a Killer." *Time,* November 11, 2001.

"Anthrax." *Newsweek,* November 21, 2001, pp. 31–34, Map on p. 35.

"Anthrax Type That Killed May Have Reached Iraq." *Washington Post,* November 25, 2001.

"Deadly Anthrax Strain Leaves a Muddy Trail." *Washington Post*, November 25, 2001.

"Letter Anthrax Spores Pose Many Obstacles to Analysis." *Washington Post,* November 29, 2001.

"A Solution for Anthrax Mystery." *Newsday,* November 30, 2001.

"Anthrax Inquiry Looks at U.S. Labs." *New York Times,* December 2, 2001.

"Postal Center in Connecticut Shows Traces of Anthrax." *New York Times,* December 3, 2001.

"Terror Anthrax Linked to Type Made by U.S." *New York Times,* December 3, 2001.

"Anthrax Pervades Florida Site, and Experts See Likeness to That Sent to Senators." *New York Times,* December 5, 2001.

"Anthrax Investigators Open Letter Sent to Senator Leahy." *New York Times,* December 6, 2001.

"Biologists Fight Back." *Nature,* December 10, 2001.

"Chronology of Anthrax Events." *South Florida Sun-Sentinel,* December 11, 2001.

UCLA's "Disease Detectives" site about the anthrax outbreak of 2001.

ABC, Australia. "Timeline of Atta's and Other Terrorists' Movements."

"Anthrax Probe." *Wall Street Journal,* December 11, 2001.

"Anthrax Matches Army Spores." *Baltimore Sun,* December 12, 2001.

"U.S. Recently Produced Anthrax in a Highly Lethal Powder Form." *New York Times*, December 13, 2001.

SOURCES

"FBI queries expert who sees federal lab tie to anthrax cases." *The New York Times*, December 14, 2001.

"Anthrax Matches Army Stocks." *Washington Post*, December 16, 2001.

"Anthrax Investigators Focus on Scientist." UPI, December 17, 2001.

"Anthrax Investigators Focus on Scientist." Reuters, December 19, 2001.

"Fired Scientist Not Focus of Anthrax Probe." Reuters, December 20, 2001.

"Anthrax Easy to Get Out of Lab." *Hartford Courant*, December 20, 2001.

"Authorities Identify All Victims of Flight 93." ThePittsburghChannel.com, December 20, 2001.

"FBI Investigates Possible Financial Motive in Anthrax Attacks." *Washington Post*, December 21, 2001.

"Inventor of Anthrax Process Says Spores Will Not Be 'Smoking Gun' to Identify Who Mailed Killer Letters." *Abilene Reporter-News*, December 21, 2001.

"U.S. Inquiry Tried, but Failed, to Link Iraq to Anthrax Attack." *New York Times*, December 22, 2001.

"Postal Service Is Kept Busy Tracking Down Anthrax Scares." *New York Times*, December 22, 2001.

"Army Harvested Victims' Blood to Boost Anthrax." *Baltimore Sun*, December 23, 2001.

"FBI Overlooks Foreign Sources of Anthrax." *Wall Street Journal*, December 24, 2001.

"Anthrax Probe Teaches USPS Its Machines Can Track Mail." *Linn's Stamp News*, December 24, 2001.

"2nd Letter to Land in Daschle's Office." *Washington Post*, January 4, 2002.

"Webheads Help Hunt the 'Thrax'." *New York Post*, January 13, 2002.

"F.B.I. Tests Rutgers Photocopiers for Clues to the Anthrax Mailer." *New York Times*, January 15, 2002.

"Lockheed Creates Mail Biohazard Detection System." *Reuters*, January 15, 2002.

"Anthrax Probe Centers on Labs." *Wall Street Journal*, January 18, 2002.

"Anthrax Missing from Army Lab." *Hartford Courant*, January 20, 2002.

"Army Lost Track of Anthrax Bacteria." *Washington Post*, January 21, 2002.

"FBI Says Central N.J. May Hold Key to Solving Anthrax Mystery." *Washington Post*, January 23, 2002.

"Amateur Sleuths Offer Clues to Anthrax Mailer." Scripps Howard News Service, January 23, 2002.

SOURCES

"One Anthrax Answer: Ames Strain Not from Iowa." *Washington Post*, January 29, 2002.

"FBI Sends E-Mail to 40,000 Scientists Requesting Tips." *Wall Street Journal*, January 29, 2002.

"Post Office Seeks to Ease Concerns." Associated Press, February 1, 2002.

"Anthrax Mystery Turns Scholars into Sleuths." *Hartford Courant*, February 6, 2002.

"FBI's New Approach in Search for Anthrax Mailer Focuses on Labs." *Wall Street Journal*, February 7, 2002.

"Workers Handling Government Mail Report Symptoms." *Washington Post*, February 9, 2002.

"U.S. Looks Into Health Impact of Irradiated Mail." Reuters, February 11, 2002.

"Scientist's Findings Could Aid Anthrax Inquiry." *New York Times*, February 13, 2002.

"Expert: Anthrax Scientist ID'd." *Trenton Times*, February 19, 2002.

"Anthrax Suspect 'Is US Scientist.' " *The Guardian*, February 20, 2002.

"FBI Says No Prime Anthrax Suspect." *Trenton Times*, February 20, 2002.

"Anthrax Expert Stands by her Claim." *Trenton Times*, February 21, 2002.

"FBI Scrutinizes Biodefense Labs in Anthrax Probe." *Baltimore Sun*, February 22, 2002.

"Maine Woman Acquitted in 1st Anthrax Hoax Trial." *Washington Post*, February 22, 2002.

"Suspect Worked in U.S. Lab." *Washington Times*, February 25, 2002.

"FBI Not Close to Identifying Anthrax Probe Suspect." Reuters, February 25, 2002.

"U.S. Says Short List of 'Suspects' Is Being Checked." *New York Times*, February 26, 2002.

"FBI Still Lacks Identifiable Suspect in Anthrax Probe." *Washington Post*, February 26, 2002.

"Anthrax Probe Focuses on Letter." *Washington Times*, February 26, 2002.

"Labs Are Sent Subpoenas for Samples of Anthrax." *New York Times*, February 27, 2002.

"Anthrax Tip May Yet Help." *Philadelphia Inquirer*, February 28, 2002.

"Why Is the FBI Ignoring Vital Clues in the Hunt for the Anthrax Attacker?" *New Scientist*, March 2, 2002.

"Science Could Help to Crack Anthrax Case." *Los Angeles Times*, March 3, 2002.

SOURCES

"Experience at Work in FBI Anthrax Case." *Washington Post*, March 4, 2002.

"Anthrax Story: Detrick Cleared." *Frederick News Post*, March 6, 2002.

"On the Trail of the Anthrax Killer." *Toronto Globe and Mail*, March 6, 2002.

"Report Linking Anthrax and Hijackers Is Investigated." *New York Times*, March 23, 2002.

"No New Evidence Linking Hijackers with Anthrax." Reuters, March 23, 2002.

"Hijacker's Lesion Deepens Mystery." *Baltimore Sun*, March 24, 2002.

"Britain Accused on Terror Lab Claim." *Manchester Guardian*, March 24, 2002.

"Anthrax Probe Was Complicated by Muddled Information FBI Says." *Wall Street Journal*, March 26, 2002.

"Did Junk Mail Give Woman Anthrax?" Associated Press, March 27, 2002.

"Mystery Death from Anthrax Is Analyzed." *New York Times*, March 27, 2002.

"Memo on Florida Case Roils Anthrax Probe." *Washington Post*, March 28, 2002.

"Anthrax Victim Wasn't Wearing Gloves." Associated Press, April 4, 2002.

"More Anthrax Tests Planned." *Hartford Courant*, April 5, 2002.

"Powder Used in Anthrax Attacks 'Was Not Routine.' " *Washington Post*, April 8, 2002.

" 'Thousands' Could Be Anthrax Suspects." *USA Today,* April 9, 2002.

"A Sophisticated Strain of Anthrax." *Newsweek*, April 15, 2002.

"Anthrax Patients' Ailments Linger." *Washington Post*, April 19, 2002.

"Anthrax Contaminates Army Lab; Employee Tests Positive." *New York Times*, April 20, 2002.

"Scientists Weigh In with Deductions on Anthrax Killer." *Los Angeles Times*, April 21, 2002.

"2nd Leak of Anthrax Found at Army Lab." *Washington Post*, April 24, 2002.

"Anthrax Traces Found in Post Office." Associated Press, April 26, 2002.

"Official: Atta Didn't Meet Iraqi." Associated Press, April 30, 2002.

"A Few Anthrax Spores Can Kill, Doctors Say." *Baltimore Sun*, May 1, 2002.

"FBI Agent Warned Last July That Middle Easterners Training at U.S. Flight Schools." Associated Press, May 3, 2002.

"Anthrax Sent through Mail Gained Potency by the Letter." *New York Times*, May 7, 2002.

"Postal Theory: Mail Sorter Acted as Mill for Anthrax." *New York Times*, May 9, 2002.

"Gene Research May Help Solve Anthrax Mystery." CNN.com, May 9, 2002.

"Scientists Find New Markers for Anthrax Isolates." TIGR press release, May 9, 2002.

"Anthrax Traces at Fed Could Be False Positives." Reuters, May 9, 2002.

"Anthrax Attack Bug 'Identical' to Army Strain." *New Scientist*, May 9, 2002.

"Clues to Anthrax Attacks Found." *Washington Post*, May 9, 2002.

"Anthrax Investigation Gets Boost." *Boston Globe*, May 10, 2002.

"U.S. Intercepting Messages Hinting at a New Attack." *New York Times*, May 19, 2002.

"FBI to Polygraph Workers in Md., Utah on Anthrax." *Baltimore Sun*, May 21, 2002.

"Anthrax Antidote Being Developed." Associated Press, May 31, 2002.

"The 'Lone Wolf' Theory Is Evidence of the Bureau's Ineptitude." *Wall Street Journal* editorial, June 3, 2002.

"Administration Sued in Anthrax Case." Associated Press, June 7, 2002.

"Boca Mayor: Feds Should Take Over Anthrax-Contaminated Building." *South Florida Sun-Sentinel*, June 11, 2002.

"Bush Signs Measure Boosting U.S. Bioterror Defenses." Reuters, June 12, 2002.

"Unfinished Task of Anthrax Probe." *Indianapolis Star*, June 13, 2002.

"FBI Looks into Possibility Anthrax Was Grown Secretly at Fort Detrick." *Baltimore Sun*, June 13, 2002.

"Scientists: FBI Questions Suggest Insider Grew Spores at Lab, Refined Them Elsewhere." *Hartford Courant*, June 13, 2002.

"Who Is Steven Hatfill?" *The New Prospect*, June 17, 2002.

"Genetics Not Helping Anthrax Probe." Associated Press, June 19, 2002.

"Anthrax in Mail Was Newly Made, Investigators Say." *New York Times*, June 22, 2002.

"Anthrax Spores from Hill Said to Be Made Recently." *Washington Post*, June 23, 2002.

"Anthrax Killer 'Could Grow More Bacteria.' " *The Guardian*, June 24, 2002.

"FBI Searches Home in Anthrax Probe." *Washington Post*, June 25, 2002.

"Search of Biologist Is Uneventful." *New York Times*, June 26, 2002.

"Frederick Scientist's Home Searched in Anthrax Probe." *Baltimore Sun,* June 26, 2002.

"FBI Searches Home in Anthrax Case." *Hartford Courant*, June 26, 2002.

"Scientist Theorized Anthrax Mail Attack." *Baltimore Sun*, June 27, 2002.

SOURCES

"The Case of Dr. Hatfill: Suspect or Pawn?" *Hartford Courant*, June 27, 2002.

"FBI's Anthrax Probe Focuses on Scientists." *Trenton Times*, June 28, 2002.

"No Anthrax Found in Apartment of Ex-Army Scientist Questioned in Deadly Mailings." Associated Press, July 3, 2002.

"Ex-Rhodesian under Probe for US Anthrax Attacks." *Zimbabwe Mirror*, July 9, 2002.

"Solving the Anthrax Case—with No Mistakes." *Newsweek*, July 15, 2002.

"U.S.: Al Qaeda Tried for Bio Weapons in Afghanistan." Reuters, July 17, 2002.

"Boss Says Md. Doctor Isn't Anthrax Suspect." *Baltimore Sun*, July 18, 2002.

"White House Warns on Anthrax Tests." Associated Press, July 19, 2002.

"U.S. Considers Takeover of Tainted AMI Building for Use as Anthrax Lab." *South Florida Sun-Sentinel*, July 19, 2002.

"The Noose Widens." *Time*, July 21, 2002.

"Media Manufacture Cloud of Suspicion over Hatfill." *Insight*, July 22, 2002.

"Clash of Agencies Hampered Inquiry into Anthrax Mystery." *Newsday*, July 23, 2002.

"White House: Anthrax Test Kits Not Reliable." UPI, July 23, 2002.

"FBI Searches Trash Bins near Former Army Researcher's Home." *Newsday*, August 1, 2002.

"Anthrax Investigation Leads Back to Scientist's Home." *WUSA*, August 1, 2002.

"Md. Home Searched in Probe of Anthrax." *Washington Post*, August 1, 2002.

"Apartment Searched Anew in F.B.I.'s Anthrax Inquiry." *New York Times*, August 2, 2002.

"Ex-Fort Detrick Scientist Is Put on Leave from New Job at LSU." *Baltimore Sun*, August 3, 2002.

"Germ Researcher Is Put On Leave." *Boston Globe*, August 3, 2002.

"Scientist Says FBI Asked About Setup." *Washington Times*, August 3, 2002.

"Anthrax Probe Proceeding with Increased Vigor." *USA Today*, August 8, 2002.

"Security Clearance with Faulty Resume." *Baltimore Sun*, August 8, 2002.

"Hatfill to Make Statement Sunday." Associated Press, August 9, 2002.

"Anthrax Inquiry Draws Protest from Scientist's Lawyers." *New York Times*, August 10, 2002.

"Ex-Army Scientist Denies Role in Anthrax Attacks." *Washington Post*, August 11, 2002.

"Experts: Hatfill Courting Public." Associated Press, August 11, 2002.

"Steven Hatfill's Statement." *New York Times*, August 11, 2002.

"Steven Hatfill's Statement." *Washington Post*, August 11, 2002.

"The Q&A Session with Dr. Hatfill's Lawyer Victor Glasberg." Transcript, August 11, 2002.

"Scientist Steps Up Anthrax Defense." *Washington Post*, August 11, 2002.

"US 'Anthrax Suspect' Trained at Porton Down." *London Sunday Times*, August 11, 2002.

"The Hunt for the Anthrax Killer." *Newsweek*, August 12, 2002.

"FBI Said Not Ready to Clear Hatfill." *Washington Post*, August 12, 2002.

"Anthrax Investigators Test Mailbox in Princeton Area." *Wall Street Journal*, August 12, 2002.

"Official: No Physical Evidence Links Anthrax to Hatfill." *USA Today*, August 12, 2002.

"Scientist Denies Anthrax Link." *The Guardian*, August 12, 2002.

"A 'Person of Interest.' " *Newsweek*, August 12, 2002.

"Scientist Says He's Anthrax 'Fall Guy.' " *Baltimore Sun*, August 12, 2002.

"Agency Hushed Anthrax Scandal." *Florida Today*, August 13, 2002.

"FBI Second-Guessed in Anthrax Probe." *Washington Times*, August 13, 2002.

"Anthrax Doctor Failed Lie Test." *New York Post*, August 13, 2002.

"Hatfill Novel Depicts Terror Attack." Associated Press, August 13, 2002.

"The Anthrax Files." *New York Times*, August 13, 2002.

"Anthrax Found in Mailbox." *Trenton Times*, August 13, 2002.

"Anthrax Probe Goes Door to Door." *Trenton Times*, August 14, 2002.

"Merchants near New Jersey Site Are Canvassed in Anthrax Probe." *Wall Street Journal*, August 14, 2002.

"FBI Shows Hatfill's Photo; Researcher Denies Having Been to Princeton, N.J." Associated Press, August 14, 2002.

"Anthrax Finding Prompts Questions in Princeton about Scientist." *New York Times*, August 14, 2002.

"Agents Circulate Hatfill Photo in N.J." *Baltimore Sun*, August 14, 2002.

"Anthrax Doc Denies Being at Mail Site." *New York Daily News*, August 14, 2002.

"Evidence Lacking as Probe of Scientist in Anthrax Scare Intensifies." *Washington Post*, August 15, 2002.

"FBI Agents Investigate Tainted Mailbox in N.J." *USA Today*, August 15, 2002.

"Legislator Irate over FBI's Anthrax Probe." *Express-Times,* August 15, 2002.

"Murky Past of a US Bio-Warrior." *Johannesburg Mail & Guardian,* August 16, 2002.

"Feds Hold 9/11 Hijackers' Remains." Associated Press, August 16, 2002.

"Anthrax's Killer 'Is US Defense Insider.' " BBC, August 18, 2002.

"The Hatfill Case: Essential Background." *Wall Street Journal,* August 19, 2002.

"U.S., Russia Tussle over Deadly Anthrax Sample." *USA Today,* August 19, 2002.

"Official Suspects Anthrax Is from Last Fall." *New York Times,* August 20, 2002.

"Hatfill's Work Continued after Firing." *Advocate,* August 22, 2002.

"Unconventional Detective Bears Down on a Killer." *Science,* August 22, 2002.

"Handling of Anthrax Inquiry Questioned." *Washington Post,* August 24, 2002.

"Hatfill Files Complaint on FBI Probe." Associated Press, August 25, 2002.

"FBI to Search for More Evidence at Anthrax Site in Boca." *South Florida Sun-Sentinel,* August 26, 2002.

"Anthrax Figure Steps Up Offense." *Baltimore Sun,* August 26, 2002.

"Hatfill Gives Public Statement but Refuses to Answer Questions." *Hartford Courant,* August 26, 2002.

"Anthrax Probe to Use New Methods." *Miami Herald,* August 27, 2002.

"Anthrax Mail May Still Be inside American Media Offices." *Miami Herald,* August 28, 2002.

"Hatfill to Undergo Blood Test for FBI." *Washington Times,* August 28, 2002.

"LSU Scientist Discounts Hatfill's Blood-Test Offer." *Advocate,* August 29, 2002.

"Tabloids Get Anti-Snoop Pledge." *Palm Beach Post,* August 29, 2002.

"FBI Scouts Back Issues of Tabloids in Search for Anthrax Motive." *South Florida Sun-Sentinel,* August 29, 2002.

"Former Anthrax Researcher Loses Job." Associated Press, September 3, 2002.

"U.S. Teams Scour Former AMI Building for Traces of Anthrax." *South Florida Sun-Sentinel,* September 3, 2002.

"Scientist in Anthrax Probe Fired." *Washington Post,* September 4, 2002.

"The Iraq Connection." *Wall Street Journal,* September 5, 2002.

SOURCES

"LSU: Justice Did Not Cause Hatfill Firing." *Washington Post*, September 5, 2002.

"FBI Continues Hunt for Clues in Boca Raton Anthrax Attack." *Daytona Beach News-Journal*, September 6, 2002.

"Anthrax Kills Butte County Cattle." *Rapid City Journal*, September 7, 2002.

"Anthrax Killer Outlasting the Hunters." *Hartford Courant*, September 7, 2002.

"Anthrax Investigation at AMI Still 'Day-by-Day.' " *Palm Beach Post*, September 9, 2002.

"U.S. Not Claiming Iraqi Link to Terror." *Washington Post*, September 9, 2002.

"From the Mixed-Up Files of Mr. Steven J. Hatfill." *The Weekly Standard*, September 10, 2002.

"Feds Still Stumped by Source of Anthrax in Boca." *Miami Herald*, September 10, 2002.

"FBI Concludes Search of Florida Anthrax Building." Reuters, September 10, 2002.

"FBI Finishes Searching AMI Building for Clues." *South Florida Sun-Sentinel*, September 11, 2002.

"Scientist's Apartment Searched a Third Time." *Baltimore Sun*, September 12, 2002.

"FBI Returns to Hatfill Apartment." *Washington Post*, September 12, 2002.

"Anthrax Hunters' Next Job: Checking 5,000 Samples." *Palm Beach Post*, September 12, 2002.

"FBI Finds 800 Anthrax-Tainted AMI Letters." *Palm Beach Post*, September 13, 2002.

"Anthrax at AMI Traveled via Copiers." *Palm Beach Post*, September 15, 2002.

"The Hunting of Steven J. Hatfill." *The Weekly Standard*, September 16, 2002.

"Anthrax Hits, Misses Traced in CDC Study." *Hartford Courant*, September 18, 2002.

"Dead Anthrax Spores Entered Boca Sewer." *Palm Beach Post*, September 19, 2002.

"Proof of 'Person of Interest.' " *USA Today*, September 19, 2002.

"Anthrax Probe Raises Doubts on FBI." *Boston Globe*, September 23, 2002.

"U.S. Sent Iraq Germs in Mid-'80s." *Buffalo News*, September 23, 2002.

"Other Antibiotics Work against Anthrax." UPI, September 27, 2002.

SOURCES

"St. Louis Native Labeled 'Person of Interest' in Anthrax Case Fights to Clear His Name." *St. Louis Post-Dispatch,* September 29, 2002.

"Anthrax Case Remains Frustrating." *USA Today,* September 30, 2002.

"Pat Clawson, Hatfill's PR Guru, Profiled as an 'FBI Informant.' " *St. Louis Post-Dispatch,* September 30, 2002.

Background information on anthrax. Centers for Disease Control, October 2002.

"First Case of Bioterrorism-Related Inhalational Anthrax in the United States, Palm Beach County, Florida, 2001." Centers for Disease Control, October 2002.

"For Decades, Mailing Germs Was Routine." *Philadelphia Inquirer,* October 2, 2002.

"Alibek Doubts FBI Claims on Hatfill." NewsMax.com, October 3, 2002.

"2 US Firms Banned from Selling Anti-Anthrax Sprays." Reuters, October 3, 2002.

"U.S. Officials Agonize over Anthrax Decisions." Reuters, October 4, 2002.

"1 Year Later, Yet No Anthrax Culprit Found." *South Florida Sun-Sentinel,* October 5, 2002.

"Fired Researcher in U.S. Anthrax Probe Plans to Sue." Reuters, October 6, 2002.

"The Anthrax Crisis." *Newsday,* October 8, 2002.

"Former Army Scientist Forged Ph.D. Certificate." *Baltimore Sun,* October 9, 2002.

"An Anthrax Widow May Sue U.S." *Hartford Courant,* October 9, 2002.

"Postal Security Is Hardly First Class." *Business Week Online,* October 18, 2001.

"Truckload of Anthrax-Related Waste Coming to Norfolk." *Virginian-Pilot,* October 19, 2002.

"U.S. Postal Service Removes Some Blue Letter-collections Boxes." *Washington Post,* November 11, 2002.

"Anthrax Case." December 17, 2002. Steven Mitchell, UPI.

"Anthrax Easy to Make. U.S. Scientists Concoct Similar Compound in Search for Clues." *Baltimore Sun,* April 11, 2003.

"FBI to Drain Pond for Clues in Anthrax Case." *Washington Post,* May 11, 2003.

"Pond May Hold Evidence in Anthrax Attacks. Associated Press, May 12, 2003.

"Anthrax Hunters Drain Pond." *Washington Post,* June 10, 2003.

"FBI Looks for Clues to Anthrax." Associated Press, June 10, 2003.

TELEVISION PROGRAMS

"Anthrax Suggests Government Expertise." ABC, October 16, 2001.

"911 Call from Postal Worker." Transcript released to CNN on November 7, 2001.

"Doctor May Be Missing Anthrax Link." ABC, November 12, 2001.

"Evidence Suggests Al Qaeda Pursuit of Biological, Chemical Weapons." CNN, November 14, 2001.

"U.S. Scientist Is Questioned." ABC, December 20, 2001.

"FBI: Letter in Daschle's Office a Hoax." CNN, January 3, 2002.

"FBI Giving Polygraph Tests in Anthrax Probe." CNN, April 5, 2002.

"Official: Unusual Coating in Anthrax Mailing." CNN, April 11, 2002.

"Face to Face with a Terrorist, Face to Face with Atta." ABC, June 6, 2002.

"Heat on Scientist in Anthrax Probe." CBS, August 1, 2002.

"Anthrax Probe Figure Claims Innocence, Protests Gov't 'Innuendo.' " ABC, August 11, 2002.

"Scientist Responds to Anthrax Allegations." ABC, August 11, 2002.

"Scientist Wants Leaks Investigated." CBS, August 12, 2002.

"Aaron Brown Interviews Hatfill's Spokesman Pat Clawson." CNN, August 14, 2002.

"Transcript of Dr. Steven J. Hatfill's Second Statement." CNN, August 25, 2002.

"Justice Dept. Wanted Hatfill off Its LSU Programs." CNN, September 4, 2002.

POSTAL DOCUMENTS AND PUBLICATIONS

USPS Letters to Managers, Internal Post Office Memos, National Association of Letter Carriers Union Correspondence, Employee Work Sheets and USPS Updates to Its Managers and Workers.

"How Often Do These Threats And Hoaxes Occur?" United States Postal Inspection Service Manual, October 11, 2001.

"Decision Trees, Administrative Issues and Other Guidance on Safety." *USP-NEWS Talk* for Postal Supervisors and Postmasters. Seven page document, October 18, 2001.

National Association of Letter Carriers letter to its members from Dale P. Hart, National Business Agent, San Francisco Region, October 19, 2001.

SOURCES

"A Message on Security from the Chief Postal Inspector." *Update* Postal News Letter/Pacific Area Pacific Area, October 2001.

Letter from the Office of Chief Operating Officer and Executive Vice President, USPS Patrick R. Donahoe on Procedure to Vice Presidents, Area Operations Manager, Capital Metro Operations, October 24, 2001.

Patrick R. Donahoe letter to district and senior plant managers, October 24, 2001.

"Internal Custodial Cleaning Procedures." J. Gerard Bohan, Manager, Maintenance Policies & Programs, Engineering, October 26, 2001.

"Increase Awareness of Possibility of Harmful Biological Agents at Collection and Retail Acceptance Points." USPS Latest Facts *Update*. October 29, 2001.

Testimony before the House Government Reform Committee on the Anthrax Situation, October 30, 2001.

Vince Sombrotto Testimony before the Senate Governmental Affairs Committee on the Anthrax Crisis, October 30, 2001.

"Advice to Postal Workers on How to Recognize the Signs and Signals of Stress." USPS Employee Assistance Program, October 2001

"How to Discuss Anthrax with Your Children." E.A.P. Advice to Letter Carriers, October 2001.

"Anthrax." *USPNEWS Talk*. November 1, 2001.

"Tests Show No Evidence of Anthrax at San Francisco Postal Facilities." *Localuspsnewsbreak*, November 6, 2001.

"Anthrax." *Postal Record*. November 9, 2001.

"Anthrax Editorial." National Association of Letter Carriers, December 2001.

"Anthrax." *Postal Record*, Vol. 114/No 12. National Association of Letter Carriers, December 2001.

"Carriers Face Down Fear." *Postal Record*, Vol. 114/No. 12 National Association of Letter Carriers, December 2001.

"Postal Inspectors and Anthrax." *Update. DIRECT Newsline*, February 6, 2002.

INDEX

INDEX

INDEX

INDEX

INDEX

INDEX

INDEX

INDEX

INDEX